# PRAYER, FAITH, and HEALING

## Cure Your Body, Heal Your Mind, and Restore Your Soul

By Kenneth Winston Caine and Brian Paul Kaufman

Advisor: The Reverend Siang-Yang Tan, Ph.D., professor
of psychology in the graduate school of psychology at Fuller
Theological Seminary in Pasadena, California, and senior pastor at
the First Evangelical Church in Glendale, California

Rodale Press, Inc.
Emmaus, Pennsylvania

Copyright © 1999 by Rodale Press, Inc.
Cover photograph copyright © 1999 by G. Kalt/Natural Selection
Interior illustrations copyright © 1999 by George Schill

All rights reserved. No part of this publication may be reproduced or transmitted in any form or by any means, electronic or mechanical, including photocopying, recording, or any other information storage and retrieval system, without the written permission of the publisher.

Printed in the United States of America on acid-free ∞, recycled paper ♻

Cover Photographer: G. Kalt/Natural Selection

**Library of Congress Cataloging-in-Publication Data**

Caine, K. Winston.
    Prayer, faith, and healing : cure your body, heal your mind, and
restore your soul / by Kenneth Winston Caine and Brian Paul Kaufman.
        p.    cm.
    Includes index.
    ISBN 1–57954–006–6   hardcover
    1. Prayer.   2. Spiritual healing.   I. Kaufman, Brian, 1961–   .
  II. Title.
  BL560.C26   1999
  291.3'1—dc21                              98–31577

**Distributed to the book trade by St. Martin's Press**

  4  6  8  10  9  7  5  3      hardcover

Visit us on the Web at www.rodalebooks.com or call us toll-free at (800) 848-4735

---- OUR PURPOSE ----

*"We inspire and enable people to improve
their lives and the world around them."*

# PRAYER, FAITH, and HEALING STAFF

**Senior Editor:** Kevin Ireland
**Writers:** Kenneth Winston Caine, Doug Hill, Brian Paul Kaufman, Erik Kolbell
**Associate Art Director:** Charles Beasley
**Interior Designer:** Patrick Maley
**Assistant Designer:** Susan P. Eugster
**Cover Designer:** Christopher Rhoads
**Interior Illustrator:** George Schill
**Associate Research Manager:** Jane Unger Hahn
**Book Project Researcher:** Deborah Pedron
**Editorial Researchers:** Lori Davis, Jan Eickmeier, Jennifer Fiske, Sandra Salera Lloyd, Paula Rasich, Teresa A. Yeykal
**Senior Copy Editor:** Kathy D. Everleth
**Studio Manager:** Leslie M. Keefe
**Layout Designer:** Keith Biery
**Manufacturing Coordinators:** Brenda Miller, Jodi Schaffer, Patrick T. Smith

# RODALE BOOKS

**Vice-President and Publisher:** Neil Wertheimer
**Editorial Director:** Michael Ward
**Marketing Director:** Janine Slaughter
**Product Marketing Manager:** Kristine Siessmayer
**Book Manufacturing Director:** Helen Clogston
**Manufacturing Managers:** Eileen F. Bauder, Mark Krahforst
**Research Manager:** Ann Gossy Yermish
**Copy Manager:** Lisa D. Andruscavage
**Production Manager:** Robert V. Anderson Jr.
**Office Manager:** Roberta Mulliner
**Office Staff:** Jacqueline Dornblaser, Julie Kehs, Suzanne Lynch, Mary Lou Stephen

**Photo Credits**

| | |
|---|---|
| Pages 495 and 496 (ark) | Scala/Art Resource, New York |
| Pages 496 (beads), 497, and 498 | Kurt Wilson/Rodale Images |
| Page 500 | John P. Hamel/Rodale Images |

**Prop Credits**

| | |
|---|---|
| Pages 496 (beads), 497 (Lourdes), and 498 (medal) | Courtesy of the Guild/Allentown, Pennsylvania |
| Page 500 | From the collection of C. F. Martin & Co. |

# Foreword

## —by Bernie S. Siegel, M.D.

**A**nd the prayer offered in faith will make the sick person well; the Lord will raise him up. If he has sinned, he will be forgiven.

*—James 5:15*

Though prayer and faith are generally not a part of any medical school curriculum, I have clearly seen the healing role that they have played in my life and, as a physician, in those of my patients. Over the years, I have observed people whose lives were healed and bodies cured of so-called incurable diseases by the sole therapy of leaving their troubles to God.

I don't personally prescribe prayer and faith as the sole therapy because I know how hard it is to reach such a high state of healing. For that reason, God has many agents and assistants to help the sick—from doctors to drugs to herbs and our own natural healing abilities. But my sense is that prayer and faith create group therapy with God and produce even greater benefits than traditional therapies can alone. After all, where could you get greater support, compassion, and direction than through prayer to God?

## The Power of Prayer

When you pray, find peace, and heal your life, you give a message to your body that restores it. The will to live is physiologic, and when you connect with your spiritual essence, it is felt in every aspect of your life and every cell in your body. Prayer keeps you aware of life and capable of seeing its beauty in the same way that an artist with a trained eye sees a beautiful landscape. You are aware of a different world when you pray, a world of "to-now," not today or tomorrow.

God is always listening and your prayers are heard whether you cry out from the belly of a whale, as Jonah did, or with the pain of a childless woman's heart, as Hannah did. They both received answers to their prayers, and you will, too. You are changed when you pray, and that in itself is an answer. But prayer also alters the severity of any problem you face. When you confront a monster in a dark cave, prayer shrinks him down to a size that will no longer frighten you. It makes you capable of living with and through your problems.

The answer to a prayer is not always what you want, nor will prayer remove life's difficulties. But it will help relieve your pain and help you display true compassion and love toward yourself and others. Prayer keeps you open to the possibilities and can lead you out of the darkness. Just as the noble earthworm takes in all sorts of toxins and creates compost, so you are able to create Holy Compost through your prayers and with your Creator's help.

You should also know that the answer to your prayers is not always verbal. You receive communications through many channels, including dreams and visions. Sometimes you need to be still and listen. When you do, you will see that God is like a car battery that allows you to get started. You'll also see that if you do not keep connected via your battery cables of prayer, you may never get going, or you may end up never reaching your proper goals and destination in this life. So keep praying, and don't let the cables fray or disconnect.

## The Importance of Love

If you don't have love and faith, I don't believe that you can pray. The love begins with self-love, as spiritual prophets have told us, then progresses to love and prayer for others. When you find this state of love, you will have what I call a near-life experience. That is the true spiritual experience that is never attained through spirits or drugs but only felt when near death and your Creator. I have experienced this twice. Once, as a four-year-old, when I almost choked to death on a toy I aspirated, and a few years ago, when I fell off the roof of my house. I felt God and the angels around me. And I felt saved by other forces or entities. If this seems too mystical, remember that your lives are affected by PMS: the practical, the mystical, and the spiritual.

I also realize the importance of both love and laughter when combined with prayer. They are all healers, and love for me represents the bricks that I build with, and laughter the mortar that cements them together.

# Learning to Pray

If at this point you are beginning to feel concerned because you have never prayed or don't know how to pray, I can offer simple instructions and a simple prayer that will resolve your dilemma. First, pray for the ability to pray. Second, act and behave as if you are the prayerful, spiritual person you want to become. Remember, you are changed by your thoughts and actions just as an actor's body chemistry is affected by the role he plays. Rehearse and practice and find the role models and coaches to guide you. You can always ask, what would Moses, Jesus, Mother Teresa, Martin Luther King Jr., Don Quixote, or Lassie do now? I mention the last two so you realize that prayer can be free of religious fundamentalism. Fundamentalism and laws are created by man and create problems. Oral traditions and dialogue are healthy. They take the individual into consideration as God does, whether it entails working on the Sabbath or eating on Yom Kippur.

When you find the right way to pray, you heal your life. In all spiritual writings, you'll find the theme of the "way" or "path." This book emphasizes the Christian way, but the Tao, Kabbalah, Talmud, Bible, Hindu, Muslim, and Buddhist teachings all share similar wisdom and techniques. Conversations with God are not limited by the rules of any religion. In fact, while religions may create guilt and punishment in some people's minds, God is always forgiving and responsive to your prayers and needs.

Remember, prayer and faith are not about being perfect. God is forgiving. In fact, if He had an office, one of the plaques over His desk might read: "Everything you remember I forget, and everything you forget I remember." When you know that the message is "Your sins are forgiven," the benefits of forgiveness and faith will follow. I love Gospel music, and I keep hearing the song that ends: "And though it makes Him sad to see the way we live, He'll always say, 'I'll forgive.'"

# Let This Book Guide Your Way

Now let me share with you some of my feelings about this book. As I read *Prayer, Faith, and Healing*, tears of joy came to my eyes. This is indeed a guidebook to a way of life that is filled with peace, faith, and healing resources. It frees you from desires, conflicts, and disagreements and brings a sense of rhythm into your life. Read this book and, as T. S. Eliot wrote, "the darkness will be the light and the stillness the dancing."

As you read, I hope you will pay attention to the prayers that have helped others confront physical or emotional problems. The common themes are here because they have worked for many groups.

With prayer and faith, you can build a home for all mankind. Without them, you build walls and fears that separate you from others and destroy your life. When you choose to pray and love, you are in charge of your existence. Prayer, faith, and love are the most powerful weapons you have, and you need to make them a consistent part of your life and use them wisely.

When you finish this book and start to use prayer, you will begin a new life, and forever after, your life will be a series of beginnings. When you run into a situation that you do not know how to handle, you will no longer be at a loss as to what to do. You will pray, and when you do, you will give God a home and roots with which to grow and reside on Earth and make His presence conscious.

Now read the book and begin to use its wisdom in your prayers.

*Before retiring, Bernie S. Siegel, M.D., practiced surgery in New Haven, Connecticut, where he founded Exceptional Cancer Patients (ECaP), a group for people with serious illnesses. He has written four books, including the best-selling* Love, Medicine, and Miracles. *Dr. Siegel is actively involved in humanizing medical care, and he shares his techniques through speaking engagements and workshops.*

# Contents

# Contents

---

# PART III
## PRAYER PRESCRIPTIONS

# Contents

# Contents

# *Introduction*

## The Fundamental Power of Prayer

Once upon a time, we believed in miracles—spiritual miracles. When we were ill, injured, or afflicted with any sort of curse—emotional, interpersonal, financial, legal—we made appeals to God. We turned to our spiritual guides—our holy men, our priestly purveyors of prayer therapies. We recited prayers prescribed by the church. We turned to healers, medicine men, saints, and the somehow spiritually charged symbols of faith: icons, statues, pictures, and medals. We looked for signs that prayer, faith, religion, belief, and God could heals us. And we found them. Often, they worked wondrously.

Then along came medical science—biology, pharmacology, radiology, and modern surgical practices. Suddenly, we had a pill, a treatment, or an operation for everything that could be cured—scientific miracles. And prayer and faith were shunted to the side, their incredible power forgotten. Never mind that some people got well without science and medicine. Never mind that some people got well even when the treatments and pills failed and the doctors wrote the people off. Faith was dismissed as superstition, dismissed with contempt.

Now, everyone has stopped laughing. Now, the very science that they trust is proving what we hoped, what we prayed was true all along. Somehow, for some reason, prayer, faith, and healing work.

Experiment after experiment is showing the connections, raising possibilities, and suggesting that God not only exists and answers prayers, that prayerful "intentions" not only influence physical reality but that prayer, religion, and faith are good for us—good for our health, good for our outlooks, good for our communities, good for our overall physical and mental well-being. The connections are clear. More than 200 studies prove it.

As the curtain rises on a new, post–Atomic Age millenium, we turn full-circle to "once upon a time." Prayer, faith, and spiritual miracles are once again revered. Science is exploring and harnessing their secrets. And doctors are encouraging patients (some are even joining them) to use the power of prayer and faith to assist their healing.

These days, recognized scientists like prayer research pioneer Herbert Benson, M.D., associate professor of medicine and president of the Mind/Body Medical Institute at Harvard Medical School, are teaching that prayer is an essential part of effective treatment for serious health and emotional problems, that prayer is as crucial a weapon in our total medical arsenal as antibiotics. In fact, Dr. Benson teaches, the tools of faith have been playing a role in healing all along, whether we chose to recognize them or not.

We, the people, are returning to faith also. We are experiencing an incredible spiritual awakening and a hunger greater, perhaps, than any other in history.

Evidence? We don't have to look far.

*Time, Newsweek, Life,* women's magazines, and even *Men's Health* have featured spiritual cover stories. In fact, the news magazines are putting God on the cover regularly. The bestseller list has been owned by the *Chicken Soup for the Soul* franchise, while faith has become a hit on television, where one of most popular shows features a group of "angels" who invoke God's power to help regular people deal with tough problems.

A group called Promise Keepers regularly fills football stadiums with men who sing hymns and pray to God. The Internet spawns a virtual church, with an untold number of online ministries, religious and spiritual discussion groups, and prayer gatherings going on 24 hours a day. And then there's Truckers for Christ, a group that sets up semi-trailer chapels at truck stops all across the nation. God, who *Time* magazine declared dead in 1967, may be busier than ever.

*Spirituality, faith, inspiration*—terms that in their simplest forms point to our highest values—are being actively considered almost everywhere in almost everything we do: investing, purchases, businesses, the workplace, the home, schools, and on and on.

Even churches are being transformed in this climate. Many of us still attend tiny community churches where everybody knows, works, and plays with everyone else. But this is also the day of the "mega" church, with 3,000; 5,000; even 20,000 members and "cell groups," that is, sanctioned neighborhood gatherings and study groups over-seen by the church where nearby church members meet between Sunday services. And television and radio ministries abound, with people like the Reverend Robert Schuller and Christian psychologist James Dobson drawing audiences in the millions worldwide.

As science is now starting to show and as we in our hearts know, faith can move mountains and prayer can render miracles profound and small. By integrating faith, science, prayer, psychology, Scripture, ritual, and medicine, we can lead more meaningful, vital, healthier, and more joyful lives.

# Part I

## Prayer Power

# Science Finds God

## FAITH HAS THE POWER TO HEAL

*A* traffic accident leaves Kim Shipley of Exeter, California, battered, in a coma, and close to death. As she is wheeled into surgery, her parents and friends pray in the hospital waiting room. Within minutes, Shipley's bleeding stops and her vital signs stabilize. Three months later, she is well enough to tour with her school choir.

Just four months old, Caedon Sawabi of Ware, Massachusetts, is diagnosed with a rare disorder that leaves him nearly blind in his right eye. His mother brings him to a priest, who lays hands on the child and prays. A warm, peaceful feeling flows through her. Later, an eye specialist's tests reveal that his sight has been restored.

While recovering from heart bypass surgery, church choir member James Earl Martin develops a respiratory problem so severe that he needs a machine to help him breathe. Weeks in the hospital turn into months. Yet at every Wednesday night church service, friends pray for the recovery of the Louisville, Kentucky, resident. Finally, one week, as Martin listens to a special tape that his beloved choir made for him, tears roll down his cheeks and he begins to heal. A few weeks later, he is released from the hospital. Seven months later, he's back singing in the choir.

Stories like these of miraculous healing from life-threatening problems are fascinating, but the skeptic within us wonders: Does

God really answer prayers for our health or for the health of the ones we love? Or even the stranger in the next pew?

For years, scientists and researchers have wondered, too. The answer building quietly over the past three decades is a resounding yes. Of the hundreds of studies conducted to explore the health rewards of prayer and faith, 70 to 80 percent show a benefit. That's more evidence than scientists have supporting the benefits of vitamin C as a treatment for the common cold.

In fact, studies show that religious folks who attend church regularly and practice what they believe:

- Have lower blood pressure
- Have lower cancer rates
- Are less likely to be addicted to alcohol or drugs
- Are more likely to survive major surgery
- Are less likely to experience depression or commit suicide
- Are better able to cope with chronic disease
- Live longer

Perhaps even more amazing, in certain cases, lack of religious belief has been found to be as bad for our health as smoking and drinking.

"When you sum up all of the research, you find that faith is actually a highly beneficial factor, surprisingly beneficial," says David B. Larson, M.D., president of the National Institute of Healthcare Research in Rockville, Maryland, an organization that has systematically explored and, with its fellows, published many of the studies linking faith and health.

"Like any body of research, there is some variety in the quality of the studies that are done, but there are a significant number of good studies in this area, and the evidence is growing all the time," says Dale A. Matthews, M.D., associate professor of medicine at Georgetown University School of Medicine in Washington, D.C., and author of *The Faith Factor.*

In fact, the question now isn't whether religion is good for us, it's which "faith factor" is helping people live healthier and longer. Is it prayer? Church attendance? Strong belief in God? A healthier lifestyle inspired by faith?

While all are good for us, the most up-to-date research seems to show that church attendance and how much strength and comfort you obtain from your religious beliefs pack the most health benefits, says Dr. Matthews. "I think that one can have substantial confidence that there is a genuine medical benefit in sincere religious commitment."

"The Old Testament encourages making your case based on a solid foundation," says Dr. Larson. "We have a rock on which to build when it comes to the research on religious commitment. We need follow-up studies on the value of using religion to cope: how it prevents illness, how it can improve treatment outcomes, and how it helps people with serious and chronic medical illness."

## The Test That Set the Standard

One of the earliest studies demonstrating the connection between faith and healing—and the study that galvanized the scientific discussion of the power of prayer—took place at San Francisco General Hospital between 1982 and 1983. As 393 patients entered the hospital's cardiac care unit, Randolph C. Byrd, M.D., a cardiologist there at the time and lead researcher on this study, divided them into two groups. Each patient in one group would receive intercessory prayer (offered to help others) from three to seven "born-again Christians with an active Christian life as manifested by daily devotional prayer and an active fellowship with a local church." Patients in the other group would not be prayed for.

Dr. Byrd then went a step further: He made sure that no one involved in the study knew which patients were being bathed in intercessory prayer. The only people who knew were the born-again Christians, and they conducted their prayers outside of the hospital with only the patient's first name, diagnosis, general condition, and a request to pray for their rapid recovery and freedom from complications.

After their operations, those patients who received intercessory prayer had less congestive heart failure (8 versus 20), needed less antibiotic therapy (3 versus 17), had fewer episodes of pneumonia (3 versus 13), and had fewer cardiac arrests (3 versus 14).

Additionally, when rating the patients' success in recovering from their operations, doctors observed that 163 in the prayed-for group had a good recovery, versus 147 in the other group. Two in the prayer group had an intermediate recovery versus 10 in the other group. And 27 in the prayer group did poorly while 44 of the others had a poor recovery.

The study wasn't without flaws. Dr. Byrd couldn't manage the amount of praying that the patients, their families, or others did for their recovery. Nor did the study account for such things as the fact that patients received care from many doctors, who could have pre-

## The Trouble with Humans

The biggest problem with studying the impact of prayer on real live people is just that—humans are involved. And humans have a tendency to be unpredictable and to think for themselves. For instance, the sicker people get, the more likely that they or their friends and family are to pray, notes prayer researcher Larry Dossey, M.D., author of *Healing Words*, which is used as a textbook in many medical schools, and *Prayer Is Good Medicine.* That can invalidate a study if the person praying for himself is part of a control group that is not supposed to be receiving any prayer.

Intriguingly, Dr. Dossey says, the most conclusive studies of the power of prayer do not involve people as the recipients but, rather, animals, seedlings, fungi, and blood cells.

That's because it's much easier to control the variables when dealing with simpler life forms, says Dr. Dossey. In the case of prayer experiments with animals and seedlings and so forth, we can be relatively certain that they aren't praying for themselves or each other. We can be relatively sure that they have no personal interest in the outcome of the experiment. And we can control how they are prayed for, and exactly the type of condition that is inflicted upon them.

Dr. Dossey notes that another medical doctor, Daniel J. Benor, M.D., a psychiatrist, surveyed all studies of spiritual healing that were published before 1990. Most involved nonhuman subjects. Dr. Benor located 131 such studies. In 56 of them, the possibility of

scribed different amounts of medication, tests, and procedures that could have affected the patients health. However, even with its flaws, the test results were startling enough to spawn a wealth of studies on prayer research that continues today.

"The Byrd study was groundbreaking. Not perfect, because no study ever is, but it was revolutionary," says Dr. Matthews. "It's the

chance producing the positive results reported were less than 1 in 100, says Dr. Dossey. In another 21 studies, the possibility of chance producing the positive results was between 2 and 5 in 100. That's a pretty convincing body of proof for spiritual healing. Dr. Benor defined spiritual healing as "the intentional influence of one or more people upon another living system without utilizing known physical means of intervention."

Here are details from Dr. Dossey of three fascinating studies.

- Ten people tried to retard the growth of fungus cultures simply by concentrating on them with that intent in mind, while observing them from 1½ yards. Of 194 cultures so tested, 78 percent experienced inhibited growth. In a replication of the study, people were able to inhibit the growth at distances of from 1 to 15 miles from the fungus cultures.
- Sixty people—not known "healers"—were able, through focused intent, to both stimulate and inhibit the growth rate of bacteria cultures.
- In an experiment with barley seeds, half were watered with saltwater, which is known to retard their growth. Then a spiritual healer held the saltwater for 15 minutes, and the remaining seeds were watered with the "blessed" saltwater. Those seeds germinated significantly more quickly.

one that everyone attacks or defends—the gold standard by which every other study of this kind is measured."

# Healing Crippled Hands

Inspired by Dr. Byrd's heart surgery research, Dr. Matthews launched a prayer study of his own—with a twist or two—but with equally intriguing results.

Forty people with painful rheumatoid arthritis received 12 hours of what was called intercessory prayer ministry by Christian Healing Ministries of Jacksonville, Florida, over a three-day period. The people spent 6 hours in educational lectures learning about the nature of healing and divine intervention and obstacles to healing, such as lack of forgiveness, emotional trauma, and spiritual oppression. The other 6 hours were devoted to what's called laying on of hands in soaking prayer, meaning that several intercessors placed their hands on the people and prayed for them for prolonged periods. Half of those who received intercessory prayer ministry didn't receive it right away; they served as a "waiting list" control group for the others.

Like Dr. Byrd's study, 19 of those with arthritis also received, unbeknownst to them, six months of daily intercessory prayer. The difference is that the folks who volunteered to pray for the people with arthritis were located in different cities.

The results showed that the amount of pain, impairment, and joint swelling and tenderness were all significantly decreased in those who received the 12 hours of intercessory prayer ministry, according to Dr. Matthews. However, there was no additional benefit from the distant daily prayer beyond the effects achieved by the laying on of hands.

# Faith: A Cure for the Heart

It may not be as spectacular as healed hearts or hands, but there's good evidence that frequent church attendance or viewing religion as very important can cut our risk of heart disease and stroke. How? By literally lowering blood pressure.

At least that was the conclusion of a study involving 407 men in Evans County, Georgia. On average, the men who frequently attended church had blood pressure levels that were several points lower than those who didn't. The biggest and most startling difference was that smokers who didn't find religion important had 4.3 times the risk for high blood pressure as smokers who did. Those over age 55 who didn't attend church at all were also at greater risk.

What accounts for the difference? One view is that faith helps religious people avoid anger—in particular, the hostility, or fits of rage that might send others' blood pressure and stress levels soaring.

"It looks like faith really does allow you to slow down your response and, in a way of speaking, count to ten," says Dr. Larson. "When it comes to stress, people of faith seem more willing to think about what they're doing before they act. They're less likely to rush to judgment—which may not be so good for your stress or blood pressure levels. We're talking about improved coping skills that come with the mindset of faith."

There's another bonus: Active church members lean not only on God in tough times but also on fellow members. "Let's say that I have a need tonight. If I call the people in my church and say, 'Will you do this for me?' they'll come and help," says Dr. Larson. "Most people don't have that type of resource, especially men. We don't have people willing to help us when we need the social support."

And it's not just a matter of social support. Most blood pressure studies that examine religion and blood pressure show a benefit, says Dr. Matthews. Among them, research that explored the health of members of devout religious groups like Baptist clergy, Seventh Day Adventists and Mormons—people who shun substances that have been linked to higher blood pressure such as meat, alcohol, cigarettes, and coffee. "Some will say that's just evidence that a strict diet provides health benefits," says Dr. Matthews, "to which my answer would be yes, but it's the religious commitment that encourages that lifestyle. Some wouldn't be (that way) if their religions weren't driving the lifestyles. So I would still look at this as a religious effect, even though it's an indirect one."

# The Power of "the Sunday Effect"

Would dragging ourselves out of bed on Sunday morning be any easier if we knew that regular worship wasn't just good for our hearts, souls, and minds, but for our overall health as well? Studies that involved some of the 91,900 residents surveyed in Washington

## Start Your Own Prayer Group

Want to start a prayer group in your neighborhood, with your friends at work, or in your church? The first step is to pray about it, suggests the Reverend Paul F. Everett of Pittsburgh, a Presbyterian minister at large with the Peale Center in Pawling, New York, and executive director emeritus of the Pittsburgh Experiment, a national and international ministry to the business and working communities. "Pray that you will be led to someone, or that someone will be led to you, who has a similar concern," he says. When you meet that person, the two of you should pray that others will join you, he advises. Two is enough to begin a group. He suggests these steps for developing an effective group.

**Seek prayer partners.** Place notices in the church bulletin, on community bulletin boards, in the local paper, and anywhere else where people who might be interested in the group would see it.

**Set a meeting time and place.** Will you meet in a restaurant at noon? In your home Thursday evenings? In a chapel? Will the meeting last one hour or longer?

**Make everyone feel welcome.** You want to establish a simple, non-threatening, interdenominational format that encourages members to participate and to invite friends, advises Reverend Everett. It is helpful,

County, Maryland, suggests that it probably would be. The studies found that those people who go to church once or more a week have significantly fewer deaths from coronary artery disease and other health problems like cirrhosis of the liver and emphysema. Among men between the ages of 45 and 64 who go to church less frequently than once a week, the risk for heart disease was 40 percent higher. Among women of the same age who also attend church less than once a week, the risk for heart disease was about 50 percent higher.

Investigators suspect that churchgoers develop greater self-control and probably exercise more. And that, in turn, means less of the

he says, if the founders of the group take a moment to explain the purpose of the group and its format at the outset of each meeting, introduce visitors, and explain to them that they may participate or pass as they choose. Then he recommends this format: Share, taking turns, allowing all members to tell what God has done in their lives since the last meeting. Ask each person to introduce himself and either speak or pass. Anyone may pass at any time. All the person has to do is say, "I pass." After everyone has shared, then go around again, allowing members to pray for their own and each other's needs. Again, anyone may pass, simply by saying "amen," says Reverend Everett.

Reverend Everett has helped start and has been involved in hundreds of such groups. He says that the ones that are most effective are those that concentrate on sharing and discussing experiences and praying for one another's needs, rather than trying to promote or debate theological doctrine.

"In my 30 years with these groups, none of them ever got into theology," he says. "That wasn't the purpose. Our purpose was to be with each other, to minister to each other, and to grow in our experience of God. We weren't dealing with doctrinal issues."

kind of acting-out behaviors, like drinking and smoking, that can wreak havoc with our health, says Dr. Larson. "In some ways, this research is quite important, and it came out at a time when people were thinking that 'organized religion' doesn't do any good."

## The Bible's Impact on AIDS

While treatments for AIDS have steadily improved over the years, allowing those with the virus to live significantly longer and more active lives, getting an AIDS diagnosis can still produce feelings of fear and despair. But a Yale University study found that AIDS patients who read the Bible often or regularly attended church had reduced fear of death and were better able to cope with symptoms of their condition.

Of 90 people with AIDS who were interviewed for the study, 98 percent said that they believed in a divine being called God. Sixty-nine percent of them prayed daily, 45 percent attended church weekly or monthly, and 26 percent read the Bible daily or weekly. Eighty-two percent of those with HIV-positive illness agreed that belief in God helped when thinking about death. But it was those who read their Bibles and went to church regularly who were significantly less fearful of death. Those who believed in God's forgiveness or who had more advanced disease were also more willing to talk about crucial end-of-life decisions such as whether they should be given life support. The study did not investigate whether the more devout lived longer.

Bible reading and church attendance apparently provided a degree of emotional and social support to help reduce the fears about death that the people with HIV and AIDS may have felt, says Dr. Larson. "Now that probably comes as a surprise," he says. "All these years, we've thought that religion makes us more uptight and anxious. And yet people with a severe medical illness were less afraid of death. Why? I think because the heart of the real message of the church and the Bible that they were experiencing is forgiveness through Christ."

## Faith and Immunity

Since a weakened immune system can cause so many different health problems—not just diseases associated with AIDS—a slight improvement can be a very good thing. But could improved immunity be linked to Bible reading and warming a pew on Sunday? The answer, according to one study, is yes, to a small degree. Researchers at Duke University Medical Center took blood samples from 1,718 volunteers age 65 or older to look for chemicals associated with enhanced immunity. They found that the older adults who frequently attended religious services had slightly healthier immune systems, providing some support for the theory that participation in a religion makes us healthier.

The study points out that a person's immune system may function less effectively as a person ages, contributing to a variety of infections and diseases, including AIDS, cancer, heart disease, high blood pressure, and osteoporosis.

"A lot of experts have been talking about the importance of looking at chemically measurable factors in these kinds of studies," says Dr. Larson. "This one does, and we need to do more."

## Secret Prayer Speeds Healing

Clearly, much good comes from a religious life, but our prayers also have power, scientists say, even when the people we pray for aren't aware of our prayers.

Prayer done in secret—without patients' or doctors' knowledge— remarkably sped the healing of patients' wounds in a study investigating several forms of spiritual healing. The 44 participants in this study were told that they were taking part in a test of a new medical device that measured the bioelectrical conductivity of wounds. A medical doctor took a skin biopsy from the arm of each patient to create identical full-skin-thickness surgical wounds. Then daily, for five minutes, each patient placed the wounded arm through a hole in a wall, where the wounds were supposedly measured by the new medical device.

But there was no such device. Instead, when 23 of the patients extended their arms through the hole, a spiritual-healing practitioner prayerfully, mentally communicated healing to the patient. When the other 21 patients poked their arms through the hole, no one was in the room.

None of the patients knew that any type of healing treatment was taking place. The doctor examining the patients did not know which patients were receiving spiritual healing treatments and which were not.

At specific intervals, over about three weeks, a doctor traced an outline of each wound, which technicians—also unaware of which patients were being treated—digitized for computer comparisons. This is considered an extremely accurate measure of wound healing.

On day 8, the wounds of the patients treated with spiritual healing were significantly smaller than those of the untreated group. By day 16, 13 of the 23 treated patients were completely healed—they had no wounds at all—while no one in the untreated group was healed.

This was a small, scientifically well done study that positively demonstrates the power of prayerful intent, at least on wound healing, says prayer researcher Larry Dossey, M.D., author of *Healing Words*, which is used as a textbook in many medical schools, and *Prayer Is Good Medicine.*

## Preparing for Surgery with Prayer

By the time we need an operation, especially heart surgery, we want to know that skilled hands are holding the scalpel. But two studies show that patients aren't leaving the results solely up to some guy with an advanced degree in a scrub suit.

Just one day before 100 heart patients were to go to the operating room, researchers from the U.S. Air Force Nurses Corps, the University of Alabama at Birmingham, and UAB School of Nursing posed this question: "Have you used prayer to prepare for cardiac surgery?" Ninety-six said that they had.

What's more, on a scale of 1 (not helpful at all) to 15 (extremely helpful), 94 of the faithful rated their prayers a 9 or higher, and 70 gave prayer a 15. One person who used prayer did not believe that prayer could be rated on a scale of value.

"What this shows is that before a bypass operation, nearly everyone in this group prayed," says Dr. Larson. "And about three-quarters of them say that prayer is what got them through it, not necessarily the very well trained surgeons. The doubting Thomases out there will say, 'Okay, that's nice. That's quaint. Nearly everyone going into surgery in this study prayed. So what?'"

Although the Air Force Nurse's study doesn't tell us about the outcome of the operations, a similar study population was investigated at Dartmouth Medical School, and this study answers the "so what?" questions with good news for the believers and not-so-good news for nonbelievers.

Dartmouth researchers found that among 232 people over age 55 who underwent heart surgery, those who found no strength or comfort from religion and did not participate in any group activities, such as church supper groups, a senior center, or historical society, were three to four times more likely to die after heart surgery than those who did either. In fact, none of the 37 people who considered themselves deeply religious died within six months after surgery. Even infrequent churchgoers didn't fare too badly: Only 5 percent of them passed away over the same time period.

The news wasn't as good for those who considered themselves much less religious: 21 of them passed away within six months. Four of the deaths occurred during surgery, 5 happened within 24 hours of surgery, 6 occurred in the hospital within three weeks, 5 occurred after discharge but within 3 months of surgery, and one patient who also had lung cancer died 5 months later.

The results of this study show that religion has some benefit, according to the researchers. They suggest that if further research backed up their findings, it might make sense for doctors to counsel patients on group participation and religious involvement as regularly as they advise them about cigarette smoking and high blood pressure.

"A study like this has important implications. Even if you have the best surgeons and surgery, if you're afraid, or don't have the social supports, you may be at risk," says Dr. Larson. "When confronting serious illness, you can feel like you're all alone. You need to be able to say, 'My life is in God's hands' or 'I have people praying for me.' My experience is that committed people are frequently much more at peace. And that peace can be beneficial."

## Replacing Broken Hearts with Hope

While a heart bypass or valve replacement is certainly no medical walk in the park, few operations are fraught with the same level of peril as a heart transplant. From the stress created by the delay and wait for an available organ to the continuing deterioration of the existing heart to possible rejection of the donated organ, there is much to worry about, if not pray about.

A study of 40 heart transplant recipients at the University of Pittsburgh Medical Center found that those with strong beliefs who were involved in religious activities after their transplants had better physical and emotional health and were more likely to comply with their doctors' instructions than those who weren't interested in God.

The researchers made the discovery after asking recipients about their faith and health at intervals of 2 months, 7 months, and 12 months after their operations. Those who were more likely to report better physical health by the end of 12 months were patients who felt that their beliefs exerted greater influence over their lives and who consulted God to make important decisions.

Not only that, but transplant recipients who attended religious services frequently were less worried about their health and had higher self-esteem than those who attended less often or who weren't religious.

"This is similar to what we've found in studies of patients with cancer and those undergoing dialysis," says Dr. Larson. "Faith seems to become more important when someone has severe illness. It gets them through the hard times. They not only seem to cope better but they are also more satisfied with their lives and have higher self-esteem. You don't want to get depressed when you have severe illness. You don't want patients worrying. During a transplant, the doctors have already limited your immune functioning so that you don't reject your new organ. So when you are dealing with severe illness or major surgery, you can't afford additional stress—it further weakens the immune system."

## Coping with Cancer

It's probably no surprise that committed members of religious groups who avoid meat, alcohol, smoking, and coffee have lower cancer rates than the general U.S. population. That includes breast and prostate cancer, two of the most common.

But what if we're diagnosed with cancer? What good is our faith then? A study that investigated the emotions of 147 women, ranging in age from 40 to 70, in various stages of gynecologic cancer and benign gynecologic disease found that nearly all of them drew life-sustaining hope from their faith.

When asked how religious experiences had affected the way they dealt with their illnesses, 93 percent of the women said that religion helped them sustain hope. What's more, more than half felt that they had become more religious since being diagnosed. And these were women who already knew their way around a hymnal. Eighty-five percent said that they had some connection with organized religion, and just over three-fourths indicated that religion has a serious place in their lives.

Like the Air Force Nurses Corps heart study, "This research shows that when people have severe illnesses where their lives are at risk, there's an increase in the role that religion can play," says Dr. Larson. "The implications are that (health professionals) really need to recognize the importance of the patient's religion or spirituality when dealing with such disease."

People with more advanced cancer have an even tougher challenge: sustaining faith while death closes in. Yet one study shows that among terminally ill patients, those who attended church most frequently were more satisfied with life, happier, and better able to control their pain.

"Although this particular study didn't show that survival rates improved, it did find less pain and better well-being," says Dr. Larson. "Certainly, when you have emotional problems or when you're not doing so well, you're not getting enough sleep, you're feeling down, and you're feeling alone, guess what happens? The pain feels worse than for those who feel better about life."

## Faith That Heals

Of course, folks probably shouldn't expect to see long-term health benefits by showing up at a church-sponsored potluck dinner as if it were some networking opportunity. "If you're only using your religion to obtain better health or money or status, you're actually making religion subservient to another goal, which is that of serving yourself and your own health," says Dr. Matthews. "The goal of faith is to become close to God, to seek God's face. If that is our deepest intention, there may be this wonderful by-product of an authentic searching for God: better health."

# *Why Faith Heals*

## THE 12 FAITH FACTORS

*B*elievers know it. Solid medical studies show it. But why does faith help prevent and heal health problems? A growing number of medical experts believe that they've traced the answer to a unique collection of factors that are as powerful and as vital to our emotional and physical health as certain foods, nutrients, and exercise.

In fact, research shows that no fewer than 12 aspects of faith may help deliver healing benefits—a package of all-natural health boosters that complements the medicine chest of prescription drugs, says psychiatrist and prayer researcher Dale A. Matthews, M.D., associate professor of medicine at Georgetown University School of Medicine in Washington, D.C., and author of *The Faith Factor*. Among the faith factors that Dr. Matthews and others have identified are the following:

***Social support:*** From friends bringing over meals when we've lost a loved one, to strangers who pray for us when they hear that we're in the hospital, it's hard to match the social support that church membership provides. "People who have a strong religious commitment are more connected to each other," says Dr. Matthews. "The Bible tells us to love our neighbors as ourselves. And we can't really do that if we aren't involved in other people's lives."

***Temperance.*** Needless to say, most faiths take a pretty dim view of drunkenness, sexual immorality, smoking, even overeating—all

documented risk factors for illness and disease. The Bible, for example, encourages us to treat our bodies as a "temple of the Holy
Spirit" (1 Corinthians 6:19 NKJV), even suggesting that "physical
training is of some value." (1 Timothy 4:8 NIV) "Although the main
motivation of believers should be to grow in holiness and godliness,
they often gain a secondary benefit: better health," says Dr. Matthews.

**Serenity.** Relationships falter. Jobs are lost. Health wanes. And
as the pace of life quickens, we scramble to keep up. Such events
subject us to incredible stress. Yet studies by Herbert Benson, M.D.,
associate professor and president of the Mind/Body Medical Institute
at Harvard Medical School, have found that forms of meditation,
including prayer, create something called the relaxation response,
dramatically reducing the damaging effects of stress. While Dr.
Benson believes that we can meditate on just about any single word
or phrase to reap the benefits, believers can tap God's comforting
and specific promises from the Bible. A wonderful place to start
is the book of Hebrews: "I will never leave you nor forsake you."
(Hebrews 13:5 NKJV) or the Gospel of Matthew: "Come to Me, all
you who labor and are heavy laden, and I will give you rest."
(Matthew 11:28 NKJV)

"The stress-buffering and immune-enhancing effects of meditative
prayer techniques form one of the faith factor's most powerful components," says Dr. Matthews.

**Appreciation of beauty.** A full moon on a warm, cloudless
night. Soaring snowcapped vistas. Nearly everyone revels in nature's
beauty, and the faithful are reminded to look up and enjoy the view:
"The Heavens declare the glory of God, and the firmament shows His
handiwork." (Psalm 19:1 NKJV) What's more, worship services,
though ultimately designed to give glory to God, provide a feast for
the senses. Dr. Matthews has found that profound, uplifting hymns,
stained glass, and candlelight services all serve as art therapy to help
revive our spirits.

**Worship.** Even if our church isn't an ornate cathedral, we still
benefit mightily from worship, says Everett L. Worthington, Ph.D.,
professor of psychology at Virginia Commonwealth University in
Richmond and co-author of *To Forgive Is Human*. Through song,
dance, uplifted hands, or silent prayer, worship bathes us in a variety
of healing faith factors: ritual, social support, and beauty. Also, as we

come to worship God alone, the stress of striving for things like money, sex, and power fade in importance, says Dr. Worthington.

**_Confession and starting over._** Faith can drive us to make good on our guilt. Christian faith, for example, encourages us to confess our sins—no matter how bad we think they are—to a holy and loving God who is eager to forgive. The promise is that once we confess our sins,

## Prayer Pointers

Which patients are most likely to experience that very rare "spontaneous remission" of cancer? Is it those who:

- Give up, sink into gloom, and resign themselves to doom and death?
- Insist that they will beat the disease and curse it and fight it tooth and nail?
- Embrace it as a natural event in their lives?
- Deny their disease and believe that, because they do not accept it, their mind power or some metaphysical principle will cause it to go away?

The answer is complex, says prayer researcher Larry Dossey, M.D., author of _Healing Words_, which is used as a textbook in many medical schools, and _Prayer Is Good Medicine_. We really don't know why any given case of cancer undergoes spontaneous cure, so there is no set formula for people to follow. But one effective coping strategy is to accept the disease as simply another life experience, make peace with the illness, and stay open to whatever life has to offer. With acceptance, we turn our focus to other, more positive endeavors and get on with living the most loving and helpful lives for whatever time we may have left.

Acceptance often involves a sense of spiritual connection and trust in the Divine. And spirituality almost always involves some form of prayer, which, many studies show, can also have positive effects in healing, says Dr. Dossey.

He'll forgive us (1 John 1:9 NKJV), remove them "as far as the east is from the west" (Psalm 103:12 NKJV), and restore our fellowship with Him.

It's tough to keep beating ourselves up about something if even God has forgiven us. "Confession and forgiveness allow us to learn from our mistakes and sins and move on, rather then becoming unhealthfully preoccupied with our shortcomings," says Dr. Matthews.

*The power of ritual.* Research shows that religious rituals in and of themselves have health benefits. Whether we're taking communion, saying the rosary, or repeating a familiar favorite prayer, such repetition, at minimum, provides comfort. "Ritual can give us a sense of security, assuring us that we have reached a safe harbor in a stormy world," observes Dr. Matthews.

*Hope.* For years, doctors have talked about the placebo effect—the idea that some people get better just because they believe they're taking something that will make them better. Rather than putting hope in a pill, those with deep faith believe that God has their best interests at heart regardless of their circumstances and that "all things work together for the good of those who love Him, who have been called according to his purpose." (Romans 8:28 NIV) "We evoke the power of the placebo when we connect to a transcendent realm where our present worries pale in comparison to the wonder of God's ultimate promises," explains Dr. Matthews.

*Unity.* Fast-paced life and fear of crime, among other things, have all but made the idea of community seem, well, quaint. Yet the Internet, perhaps one of the most isolating inventions of all time, is jammed with chat rooms—cyber meeting places where people of shared interests type questions and answers to one another. Why? It's an opportunity to gather and communicate. The same qualities make faith a healing activity. We long to be with people like ourselves, who like what we like. But faith provides at least one other benefit that most clubs and hobbies probably don't: We hold each other accountable. "If my faith flags momentarily, my spiritual brothers and sisters will remind me of God's promises and point me back to the tenets that we hold in common," observes Dr. Matthews.

*Meaning.* Imagine two cancer patients: One looks like he didn't move from the chair next to his bed the entire weekend. He won't talk. He doesn't want to see the chaplain. The other is in for chemotherapy but is "just as happy and positive and bright and alive as anyone you've seen in your life. I mean, her eyes are glittering. Her skin is shining. A smile busting out all over," says Dana E. King, M.D. associate professor in the department of family medicine at East Carolina University School of Medicine in Greenville, North Carolina. The difference? "She has Jesus in her heart. Her life has meaning," says Dr. King. If the severity of their illness is equal, who would you guess will live longer?

**Trust.** Find a man or woman of deep faith and you've found someone who knows how to trust. No, these aren't people who sit beside a river with an empty bucket and expect God to fill it. Rather, they're people who do what they are able with the strength and in-genuity and desire that God gave them and then trust Him for the re-sults. Such people probably don't even know the meaning of the word of anxiety and, as a result, enjoy a sense of peace that is posi-tively health-preserving, according to Dr. King.

**Love.** The awesome, healing power of love is probably best il-lustrated by what happens when we lose it, like the woman whose partner of 50 years dies. "I've seen it far too many times," says Dr. King. "She literally dies of a broken heart. No real physical causes."

Faith doesn't make us immune to the pain of such loss. But it does shield us from some of the trauma because we're reminded that God is near and His love will never fail. Such reminders might simply be a sweet assurance in our souls. But often, there are concrete ex-amples of His love, like the kind acts of someone from our church family who constantly invites us over, refusing to allow us to be alone. And then, when we are able, we reach out to others.

# Healing Faith

Yes, say the researchers, certain aspects of faith can help heal us, but there is one important point to keep in mind: It seems that to enjoy the full benefits of the 12 faith factors, we must do more than just warm a pew. We must grow in our faith. "Mother Teresa was not re-ligious because her greatest desire was to achieve better health," says Dr. Matthews. Her greatest desire was to worship and serve God. The people who seek to serve God, even though they are not looking specifically for better health, get the interesting by-product of better health." As Jesus says, "Seek first His kingdom and His righteousness, and all these things will be given to you as well." (Matthew 6:33 NIV)

# What Is Prayer?

## ACCEPTING THE GREAT MYSTERY

*P*rayer, most of us would agree, involves opening our hearts and communicating in some way with a greater presence and power. Often, we turn to prayer when seeking some change. And often, as we pray or afterward, we sense or see change taking place.

Maybe the change is simply that we are calmed or soothed while we pray. Maybe it is that we slowly or suddenly—perhaps in a dream or mid-conversation—gain a new outlook or perspective about a situation. Maybe a situation substantially changes after we pray about it. When any of those things happen, we feel that our prayers have been answered.

Prayer in its simplest form "is empathic, loving, compassionate intentionality," explains prayer researcher Larry Dossey, M.D., author of *Healing Words*, which is used as a textbook in many medical schools, and *Prayer Is Good Medicine*. Prayer is a form of alignment with God.

Prayer is focusing on an intention, focusing on a desire, or focusing on resolution of a situation. Perhaps we state it silently or aloud or simply sense it or imagine it—in faith, believing that it, or what is best, will come to pass. Prayer is seeking an answer or simply seeking to be at one with God.

"Most Americans think of prayer as talking out loud to a white

# Healing Words

## Pieces of a Greater Spirit

There are diversities of gifts, but the same Spirit.

There are differences of ministries, but the same Lord.

And there are diversities of activities, but it is the same God who works all in all.

But the manifestation of the Spirit is given to each one for the profit of all:

For to one is given the word of wisdom through the Spirit, to another the word of knowledge through the same Spirit,

To another faith by the same Spirit, to another gifts of healings by the same Spirit,

To another the working of miracles, to another prophecy, to another discerning of spirits, to another different kinds of tongues, to another the interpretation of tongues.

But one and the same Spirit works all these things, distributing to each one individually as He wills.

For as the body is one and has many members, but all the members of that one body, being many, are one body, so also is Christ.

For by one Spirit we were all baptized into one body— whether Jews or Greeks, whether slaves or free—and have all been made to drink into one Spirit.

—*1 Corinthians 12:4–13 NKJV*

male parent figure who prefers to be addressed in English," says Dr. Dossey. That definition, he says, is woefully inadequate. It does not allow for how broad and all-encompassing prayer can be, and it limits God.

In fact, as Christians believing that there is only one God, we are free to pray to any aspect or representation of the Divine that we choose. We may call it higher power. We may find God in the beauty of nature. We may simply recognize God's presence everywhere and allow that recognition to be a prayer in itself.

This teaching has been addressed for centuries by Christian mystics and by some of the great Catholic theologians. And it is biblical; the Bible teaches that God is omnipresent and almighty and holds all things together, as shown in the following verses: "For of Him, and through Him, and to Him, are all things. . . . " (Romans 11:36 KJV) "And He is before all things, and by him all things consist. (Colossians 1:17 KJV)

## Making the Quantum Leap of Faith

By what mechanisms does prayer work? We don't actually see our prayers being routed along some cosmic Internet. We don't see all the connections made. We don't see God—however we envision God—actually pushing buttons and pulling strings and rearranging scenery and manipulating events. We may choose to envision a prayerful desire or warmth actually beaming through time and space and reaching the person or thing that we hope to affect, but we don't see this with our bare eyes. We accept that it happens. We believe that it happens. This belief is called faith. "Faith is the substance of things hoped for, the evidence of things not seen." (Hebrews 11:1 KJV)

But is there some way we can explain the cause and effect of prayer that goes beyond faith? One view of one aspect of God is of a huge, all-encompassing, all-knowing mind. What if some portion of each of our smaller, separate minds were plugged in to that great Divine Intelligence, much like wires plugged in to an old-fashioned telephone switchboard? What if all of our connections to that switchboard also connect us to one another, as with the old-time party line, and any of us can just pick up and listen in any time we wish?

That's a simple image that conveys a concept of interconnectedness that cutting-edge physics and psychology are beginning to theorize, notes Dr. Dossey.

## Across the Aisles

### The Focused Power of Prayer

Prayer can heal. This is a belief that is common in religion. And nearly every world religion has prayer traditions that invoke the healing response, says Herbert Benson, M.D., associate professor of medicine and president of the Mind/Body Medical Institute at Harvard Medical School.

Dr. Benson discovered the healing effects of prayer while conducting research into the beneficial power of prayer, transcendental meditation, and other activities that heal. He refers to the healing effect as the relaxation response and the process of evoking it as focused thinking. While such terminology and rigorous laboratory experiments make this all sound cold and impersonal, "this is not reducing prayer to a scientific or mechanistic view," says Dr. Benson. "Rather, we see it as a reaffirmation of what people have been telling us for millennia: Prayer is good for you."

Two keys to producing the beneficial response, Dr. Benson discovered, are the repetition of a word, sound, prayer, thought, phrase,

Laboratory experiments suggest that such an interconnectedness does exist, reports researcher Sperry Andrews, director of the Human Connection Institute in San Francisco, which is dedicated to such study. Experiments suggest that what one of us does or thinks or desires can have some effect on any or all of the rest of us.

When we view Bible teachings in the light of modern scientific understanding, we can see how there may well be a scriptural case for interconnectedness, for the concept that God the Almighty can be in each of us and link each of us.

As Jesus says, "My prayer is not for them (the disciples) alone. I pray also for those who will believe in Me through their message, that all of them may be one, Father, just as You are in Me and I am in

or muscular activity and the ability to return to the repeated words, sounds, or such when other thoughts intrude.

Sometimes as we relax into a prayerful state, we'll find ourselves focusing on our breathing, says Dr. Benson. Or, we are trained to do that, as in the form of contemplative prayer taught by the Reverend Thomas Keating, a Trappist monk at Saint Benedict's Monastery in Snowmass, Colorado, which is based on prayer practices of the first 16 centuries of the Church. The instruction given at that time, says Dr. Benson, was to "kneel and repeat on each out-breath the word *Jesus* as you experience the feeling of love."

Reciting the Rosary and centering prayer (a form of meditative, or contemplative, prayer) are examples of repetitive prayer, Dr. Benson notes. These types of prayer tend to most quickly render physical benefits.

When Dr. Benson surveyed world religions, he found that almost all teach some form of prayer that involves focusing on the breath or on some other repetition.

You. May they also be in us so that the world may believe that You have sent Me. I have given them the glory that you gave Me, that they may be one as we are one." (John 17: 20–22 NIV)

"As it is, there are many parts, but one body. . . . If one part suffers, every part suffers with it; if one part is honored, every part rejoices with it." (1 Corinthians 12:20, 26 NIV)

Almost universally, when people think of prayer, they envision quieting or focusing the mind (and sometimes the body as well) and attempting to find a contact point with God somewhere within themselves. That contact point, or "God place," may reside in the 80 to 95 percent of our consciousness that is beyond our awareness most of the time, suggests Dr. Dossey.

# Prayer Works When You Believe

Some people pray for an empty parking space, some for remission of cancer, some for the end of a war, some for their loved one's life. Some pray to be released from life, and some may pray for all of this and much more.

What kind of prayers are most likely to be answered? No surprise here: Scientific research seems to be finding that it is the prayers we truly believe in, the ones in which we invest our deepest emotions and our strongest desires, regardless of how we choose to voice our pleas.

Scientists have conducted hundreds of experiments examining two basic forms of prayer, says Larry Dossey, M.D., author of *Healing Words*, a best-selling book that examines more than 130 studies of prayer's effectiveness and that is used as a text in many medical schools. The two types of prayer that have been most extensively studied might be called I'm the Boss and You're the Boss.

*I'm the Boss:* This is the form that researchers call directed prayer. "It is where we pray for a specific outcome," explains Dr. Dossey. We tell God (or the Divine) exactly what we want and ask that it be granted.

This is a form of prayer that Jesus taught: "Whatever you ask for in prayer, believe that you have received it, and it will be yours." (Mark 11:24 NKJV)

*You're the Boss:* This is nondirected prayer. We practice this when we do not direct God but, rather, place our concerns in His hands and ask or trust Him to do whatever is best and right in the greater overall scheme.

"Both methods work," continues Dr. Dossey. "That's the take-home lesson here. No formula was found to actually come out superior in every instance." Nondirected prayer may have a slight edge over directed prayer, but much more study is needed. "The bottom line is that people need to look into their own hearts and find out what method of prayer seems most genuine and most authentic for them. I believe that the studies show that love and compassion and deep caring are qualities that make for effective prayers. I suspect that as long as those qualities are present, everything else is probably secondary."

Along that same line, research also can tell us that, "no one has cornered the market on prayer," says Dr. Dossey. Studies show that neither the denomination to which we belong nor the type of religion that we practice has any impact on whether or not the prayer will be answered. "Prayer belongs to the entire human race."

We can worship God in prayer; we can praise God in prayer; we can say, "Thank you, thank you;" we can say, "Gimme, gimme." A prayer may be spoken, thought, felt, sung, whispered. A prayer may be wordy or wordless. A prayer can be a state of being, an attitude— perhaps one of reverence, adoration, attunement, or, as some like to say, playing on the term *atonement,* prayer may simply be a state of at-ONE-ment—just being with God.

Prayer can be joyful; prayer can be shouted; prayer can be sad; prayer can be groaned. Some people speak prayers in strange tongues. We can pray on our knees, on our bellies, in our cars, while walking, or while talking. Only we can place limits on the types of prayer available to us.

There are as many kinds of prayer as there are people. Prayer for each of us, in essence, is "my soul's adventure with God," as Crystal Cathedral founder the Reverend Dr. Robert Schuller declares in the title of his book.

## Father Knows Best

Sometimes we are puzzled when bad things happen to good people; when we do not get what we ask for in prayer; when someone we love dies or gets sicker despite our prayers for their recovery.

Religion and science, again, may converge to provide an answer. If we believe, as the Apostle Paul says: "The God who made the world and everything in it . . . gives all men life and breath and everything else" (Acts 17:24–25 NIV), then we must believe that everything is of God. If we believe that all is of God, then we should accept that God is in both sickness and health, that God creates both better and worse, and that everything that happens somehow serves God's purpose, says Dr. Dossey—that "all things work together for good to them that love God." (Romans 8:28 KJV)

We need not seek misfortune, but perhaps we should not be so hasty to judge events as good or bad, suggests Dr. Dossey. Instead, he says, let God be God. Realize that if God is an eternal, infinitely greater intelligence, He very well could have great reasons that we will never fathom for events that we consider tragic. Perhaps then the most perfect prayer that we can ask for is "the highest and best for all concerned," Dr. Dossey says, and leave it to God to decide just what that is. "For God is greater than our hearts, and He knows everything." (1 John 3:20 NIV)

## Praying Heals Us

Medical science can tell us how praying affects us physically. The news is good: Prayer has a calming, healing effect.

Two top medical scientists, Herbert Benson, M.D., associate professor of medicine and president of the Mind/Body Medical Institute at Harvard Medical School, and Harold Koenig, M.D., religion and health researcher and director of the Center for the Study of Religion, Spirituality, and Health at Duke University in Durham, North Carolina, confirm this. They report that when a patient is wired to machines that monitor brain waves, blood chemistry, heart rate, stress levels, and more and are asked to pray, phenomenal changes take place.

"Through its uplifting and calming effect, prayer may inhibit cortisol, epinephrine, and norepinephrine—stress-produced hormones that over time compromise the immune system and increase our likelihood of developing heart disease, stroke, ulcers, and many other stress-related diseases," says Dr. Koenig.

Dr. Benson says, "We see decreases in blood lactate, which is associated with a lowering of anxiety. There is decreased metabolism, decreased heart rate, decreased rate of breathing, and distinctive, slower brainwaves—profound changes in brainwaves. These changes are the opposite of those induced by stress." Eliciting those changes through prayer or other practices "has been demonstrated to be an effective therapy in a number of diseases, including hypertension, cardiac rhythm irregularities, many forms of chronic pain, insomnia, infertility, the symptoms of cancer and AIDS, premenstrual syndrome, anxiety, and mild and moderate depression," he says.

# *Unanswered Prayer*

## DOES GOD REALLY CARE?

*A* beautiful high school graduate enjoying a sunny day on the Chesapeake Bay splashes into the water and swims toward a raft. Climbing on top, Joni Eareckson Tada dives in, but badly misjudges the water's depth. Her head hits the bottom hard, and something like an electric shock surges through her body. She can't move. As she feels herself starting to drown, her sister pulls her from the bottom.

Family and friends join Tada in praying for her healing, but her arms and legs seem useless. And within a few months, Tada's teeth are black from medication, her weight has dropped from 125 to 80 pounds, and she is so deep in despair that she begs a friend to slit her wrists or help her overdose on pills. Anything to end her suffering.

Like Tada, many of us who have turned to God with specific prayers for help have come away unfulfilled. And as we wait in our emergency rooms and doctors' offices and counseling centers every hour of every day, we ask, "Why?"

Some of the greatest minds of all time have tried to tackle this question. Even the German philosopher Friedrich Nietzsche, an avowed atheist, felt compelled. His answer was, "I doubt whether such pain 'improves,'" he said, "but I do know it deepens us."

# Faith Helps Us Endure

In Christian thought, there are at least two main concepts on the problems of pain and unanswered prayer. The most commonly accepted one says that God allows sickness, possibly even sends it into our lives to mold, shape, and refine us. Like sandpaper from above, it's designed to smooth our rough spots. "God wants us to feel that our way through life is rough and perplexing so that we may learn thankfully to lean on Him," writes J. I. Packer, Ph.D., in the contemporary Christian classic *Knowing God*. Also, reasons Dr. Packer, "If God denies us something, it is only in order to make room for one or another of the things that He has in mind."

That has certainly been the case for Tada. Though she remains a quadriplegic, she has built a life of faith and inspiration. Today, millions know her for her work on behalf of the disabled, her daily radio program, her books and writing, even the pictures that she draws and paints by holding a pen or brush in her mouth.

In her writings, she states, "The purposes of God in any disability, in any suffering, are multiple." Or, as she puts it in *When God Weeps*: "God uses suffering to purge sin from our lives, strengthen our commitment to Him, force us to depend on grace, bind us together with other believers, produce discernment, foster sensitivity, discipline our minds, spend our time wisely, stretch our hope, cause us to know Christ better, make us long for the truth, lead us to the repentance of sin, teach us to give thanks in times of sorrow, increase faith, and strengthen character."

The classic biblical example is the apostle Paul. He describes praying three times for God to remove a specific health problem that he called his thorn in the flesh. Whether Paul's thorn was malaria, epilepsy, or an eye disease is unclear, but one thing is certain: God had other plans. He told Paul: "My grace is sufficient for you, for My strength is made perfect in weakness." (2 Corinthians 12:9 NKJV)

By our standards, Paul had every right to be bitter. God had answered Paul's prayers when he sought healing for others, but God denied Paul relief when he sought it for himself. Yet Paul accepted God's will and responded: "Therefore I take pleasure in infirmities, in reproaches, in needs, in persecutions, in distresses, for Christ's sake. For when I am weak, then I am strong." (2 Corinthians 12:10 NKJV)

Paul had grasped a God-size idea, says the Reverend Scotty Smith, senior pastor of Christ Community Church in Franklin, Tennessee, and co-author of *Unveiled Hope*. Paul was "far more inclined to define suffering and some of the more painful events as good things than we are," says Pastor Smith. "Much of the time, we're looking at prayer to get what we want, rather than communing with our Father who knows what we need."

In other words, we need to pray and ask for healing but recognize that we may not be happy with the reply since God knows best what we need. "I would also consider 'No' to be an answer to a prayer," says Pastor Smith. "Or 'Maybe.' Or 'Not yet.'"

As the Reverend Billy Graham writes, "God is still in control—even if you do not understand all that happens in this sin-scarred world. Like Paul, we can be 'sorrowful, yet always rejoicing.'"

## Prayers without Punch?

There is another theory on unanswered prayer that is worth considering. Some of us are so comfortable with the idea of pain and decay that we don't pray nearly long enough, hard enough, often enough, or specifically enough for healing to take place, says Francis S. MacNutt, Ph.D., author of *Healing* and *Deliverance from Evil Spirits*. Or we're praying for the wrong kind of healing. After all, how would a miraculous healing from an ulcer benefit us if the anger and bitterness and hatefulness that caused the ulcer is still tying our gut in knots?

"My own experiences have convinced me that divine healing does happen, and commonly," says Dr. MacNutt. "God does care for us—not just our souls, but all of us."

To illustrate, Dr. MacNutt says that Jesus attacked sickness as if it were evil itself, healing the deaf, the blind, the paralyzed, even raising the dead, everywhere he went. "In fact, there are many more accounts of how He healed the physically sick than how He forgave sins."

The healing tradition continued with the disciples. Like Jesus, they used ordinary commands like "Stand up!" and "Walk!" to heal the paralyzed and raise the dead, says Dr. MacNutt. "Unless we hold that healing was only meant for the early Christian community as a special grace to get the church established, the healings of the early church should somehow happen today," he says.

And in some places, according to Dr. MacNutt, they do. Missionaries in areas without access to medical care report high success rates with healing prayer. And after three decades of praying for healing, many spent with Christian Healing Ministries, which Dr. MacNutt co-founded in Jacksonville, Florida, he says that he has seen God cure suffering people with all sorts of ailments.

A former Dominican priest, he believes that too many people have bought the idea that suffering is God's will for them. No, God doesn't heal everyone who prays. "But God's normative will is that people will be healed unless there is some countervailing reason."

## Getting to Yes

Is there anything we can do to increase the odds that our healing prayers will be answered? Neither Reverend Smith nor Dr. MacNutt would even suggest that there is some magic formula that we can use to reach God. But they have observed certain things among those whose prayers for healing were answered.

*They allowed medicine to help.* Giving up medicine or doctors in an attempt to show God that we're serious about being healed is not only dumb in most cases, it's dangerous, says the Reverend Stephen Brown, professor of preaching and pastoral ministry at Reformed Theological Seminary in Orlando, Florida, host of the daily radio Bible study program *Key Life,* and author of *Approaching God.* A skilled physician or the right prescription could be the answer to our prayer, says Reverend Brown.

*They prayed, or someone prayed for them.* Does that mean we should pray 3 times a day? Or 20? "You can't put a number on it," says Reverend Brown. "The whole idea of prayer is really just g closer to God." But the more specific the prayer, the better, say

# Healing Words

## Most Richly Blessed

"I asked for strength that I might achieve; I was made weak that I might learn humbly to obey. I asked for health that I might do greater things; I was given infirmity that I might do better things. I asked for riches that I might be happy; I was given poverty that I might be wise. I asked for power that I might have the praise of men; I was given weakness that I might feel the need of God. I asked for all things that I might enjoy life; I was given life that I might enjoy all things. I got nothing that I had asked for, but everything that I had hoped for. Almost despite myself, my unspoken prayers were answered; I am, among all men, most richly blessed."

*—Prayer composed by an unknown Confederate soldier between 1861 and 1865*

MacNutt. Citing Jesus' promise in the Gospel of Mark ("And these signs will follow those who believe . . . they will lay their hands on the sick and they will recover." Mark 16:18 NKJV), he favors something that he calls soaking prayer. During such sessions, two or three people lay hands on or near the sick person's affected body part and pray specifically for his condition. "I call it God's radiation treatment," says Dr. MacNutt.

***They removed emotional obstacles to healing.*** Since research shows that emotional problems such as bitterness and the inability to forgive are often at the root of poor mental and physical health, treating the emotional problems with confession and prayer is a high priority, says Dr. MacNutt. One simple approach is to be quiet and ask Jesus to enter our most painful memories one at a time. This deep inner healing, as Dr. MacNutt calls it, can be the key to combating conditions such as heart disease, ulcers, colitis, and even cancer.

**They have faith.** "It's not mandatory," says Dr. MacNutt, "but it's an indication that we believe in God and His love for us. That's the channel for most healing to take place—a relationship where we consider God our friend. Jesus is our friend."

**They're trying to live right.** "For the same reason that you might say, 'Don't jump off that building, you'll get killed,' God says, 'Don't steal, don't bear false witness, don't covet, and don't commit adultery, because when you do that, bad emotional and physical stuff is going to happen,'" says Reverend Brown. Such self-control also helps us eliminate habits with more obvious connections to poor health, like drinking to excess, smoking, and overeating.

**They're patient.** Dr. MacNutt says that most of the healing that he has seen takes place with prayer over time. "As we get older and our health problems have been around for a while, the body doesn't respond as quickly."

**They allow other answers.** "In our church, we pray by God's spirit that the illness is either healed or rectified dramatically, and sometimes it is," says Pastor Smith. But sometimes the prayer leads to a different cure. "We have seen families emotionally healed as they have rallied around sick loved ones," says Pastor Smith. "The crisis brings the family together."

## Trust His Heart

When all around us there are answers to prayer, and ours seem like they're bouncing off the ceiling, there's an old saying we'd do well to remember: "When you can't see His hand, trust His heart."

Reverend Graham writes: "This is not an easy time for you—but you can come through this experience with a deeper sense of God's love. Christ came 'to comfort all who mourn . . . to bestow on them a crown of beauty instead of ashes, the oil of gladness instead of mourning, and a garment of praise instead of a spirit of despair.'" (Isaiah 61:2–3 NIV)

# Part II

## Paths to Prayer

# *Affirmations*

~~~

## Personify the Power
## of the Positive

*A*ffirmations are uplifting, positive, encouraging, reinforcing statements of faith that are often stated as prayers. They can be found in the Bible and are best used when we find ourselves doubting or questioning our faith, abilities, or confidence or when we wish to bolster our courage, willpower, and faith.

An affirmation can be as simple as, "I am strong and healthy." Or, "God is with me." Or it can be more complex. Psalm 23 has long been recognized as a particularly moving and beautiful affirmation, and many of the other Psalms of King David are prayerful affirmations of love, respect, joy, safety, and consolation in the Lord. Also, the Apostle's Creed, spoken in churches of many denominations and recited at each Catholic mass, can be an affirmation. It says:

I believe in God, the Father Almighty, creator of Heaven and Earth. I believe in Jesus Christ, God's only Son, our Lord, who was conceived by the Holy Spirit, born of the Virgin Mary, suffered under Pontius Pilate, was crucified, died, and was buried; He descended to the dead. On the third day He rose again; He ascended into Heaven, He is seated at the right hand of the Father, and He will come again to judge the living and the dead. I believe in the Holy Spirit, the holy catholic church, the communion of saints, the forgiveness of sins, the resurrection of the body, and the life everlasting. Amen.

Methodist and Reformed Church of America minister, the late Reverend Dr. Norman Vincent Peale, author of the multimillion-copy inspirational bestseller *The Power of Positive Thinking* and 46 other books, firmly believed in the power of affirmations. He taught that we should use positive Bible verses to bolster our confidence, and he found ready support from psychologists for his ideas of replacing destructive thinking and destructive self-talk with positive thinking and positive self-talk. A couple of his favorite verses include "I can do all things through Christ which strengtheneth me" (Philippians 4:13 KJV) and "If God be for us, who can be against us?" (Romans 8:31 KJV)

Dr. Peale also liked to advise people to spend several minutes daily sensing or imagining the presence of God and repeating to themselves, "God is with me; God is helping me; God is guiding me." He based much of his teachings on this Bible verse: ". . . as he thinketh in his heart, so is he. . . ." (Proverbs 23:7 KJV)

The concept of affirming positive faith thoughts and Scripture is found all across the Christian spectrum.

In effect, adopting positive affirmations as a spiritual exercise carries out Paul's instruction: ". . . be filled with the Spirit; Speaking to yourselves in Psalms and hymns and spiritual songs, singing and making melody in your heart to the Lord; Giving thanks always for all things unto God and the Father in the name of our Lord Jesus Christ. . . ." (Ephesians 5:18–20 KJV)

How do we best phrase and use affirmations? First of all, "affirmations need to be set in the context of the 'chief' affirmation, 'Thy will be done,'" says William Backus, Ph.D., a Christian-licensed psychologist in Roseville, Minnesota, founder and director of the Center for Christian Psychological Services in St. Paul, and author of *Telling Yourself the Truth* and *The Healing Power of a Healthy Mind*. This means that not everything we ask for will be granted because it doesn't all fit within God's plan. Beyond that, our affirmations should reflect God's teachings in the Bible, says Dr. Backus. For example, if we feel nervous about something, instead of saying, "I'm a nervous wreck; I'm going to make an idiot of myself," we should say, "Thank you, Lord, for your peace, because your Word says: 'Peace I leave with you, my peace I give to you.'" (John 14:27 NIV)

Also, we should understand that while some prayers of affirmation seem to get answered immediately, others take time. We need to be patient, diligent, and hopeful in our affirming. Dr. Backus suggests repeating prayer affirmations until we believe that we have God's answer. One theologian likens it to planting a seed and watering it. Repetition is watering the seed. We shouldn't expect a full-grown plant the next day. We should go on with life, knowing and trusting that God is working on our needs.

# Prayer
## of Agreement

## MULTIPLYING
## THE POWER OF PRAYER

*T*hink of running after a flock of gulls on the seashore. The Bible says that one person can chase 1,000, but two people can put 10,000 to flight. (Deuteronomy 32:30 KJV)

This is the concept behind the prayer of agreement, which Jesus taught in the Gospel of Matthew: "Again, truly I tell you, if two of you agree on Earth about anything you ask, it will be done for you by my Father in Heaven." (Matthew 18:19 NRSV)

A prayer of agreement is particularly helpful when we are discouraged, worrying about something, or doubting. A prayer partner lifts up our spirits when we are down. We are able to lean on the partner's faith to build our own.

The partner doesn't need to be nearby when we pray, says the Reverend Mac Hammond of Living Word Christian Center in Minneapolis. "You don't have to be in the same room with someone. You don't even need to be in the same city or country, for that matter."

Key elements to note in exercising the prayer of agreement are:

- We may pray about anything; no aspect of our lives is off limits to God.
- We are to ask for that which we wish to come to pass.
- Only two people need to be in agreement, but you can have more.

Pastor Hammond points out that the other biblical rules about prayer also apply. For instance, we can't expect God to approve lustful or selfish desires, even if we are able to find someone to agree with us about them.

# *Pray without Ceasing*

---

## THE DANCE OF LIFE
## BECOMES A PRAYER

*P*ray without ceasing," commanded the Apostle Paul, when writing to the church at Thessalonica. (1 Thessalonians 5:17 KJV)

"Always pray and (do) not give up," Jesus taught the disciples. (Luke 18:1 NIV)

It sounds impossible at first take, the idea that we could "always pray" or "pray without ceasing." When would we eat? Sleep? Breathe?

But that's the point, say many spiritual teachers. Prayer takes many forms. We are not praying only when we close our eyes and recite a wish list of items. Caring, loving, and living life are forms of prayer and worship. And, yes, eating, sleeping, breathing, and everything else that we do can be done as a prayer, can be consecrated to God.

Consider this from an ancient prayer book of the Russian Orthodox church: "Prayer is not a part of our life; it is our life. Our every thought, word, deed—indeed, every breath—ought to be a part of the soul's constant conversation with the ever-present God, 'in Whom we live, and move, and have our being.'"

If we offer our every thought and action to God, if we acknowledge God in all that we encounter, then we do pray without ceasing.

If we seek to do our best and seek to please God at all times or are open to his nudgings of the spirit and revelations in our lives and are waiting expectantly for them, then we are in an unending communion with God. How can we do this? As thirteenth-century monk Meister Eckhart put it, "One must learn an inner solitude, where or with whomsoever he may be. He must learn to penetrate things and find God there, to get a strong impression of God firmly fixed on his mind."

When should we invoke this form of prayer? Well, always, of course.

The concept of praying without ceasing is at the core of teachings about mindfulness and watchfulness and, in some denominations, "praying in the spirit" (see Prayer in the Spirit on page 118). The core of those teachings is that as we attempt to remain in the present, in the moment, and with God in integrity and at peace, we are living life most effectively and are, in fact, making life a prayer.

# Praying Nonstop in Words

Another concept involves purposeful verbal prayer while awake, a process that will put you in a state of being with the Lord, says the Reverend Paul F. Everett of Pittsburgh, a Presbyterian minister at large with the Peale Center in Pawling, New York, and executive director emeritus of the Pittsburgh Experiment, a national and international ministry to the business and working communities.

We can maintain a constant dialogue with God, talking to Him as though He is an ever-present friend. Isn't He? It's the ongoing work of the spirit, says Reverend Everett. Even though we're constantly involved with the world—talking on the phone, going to meetings, driving to the store—we can be thinking of and praying for our loved ones at the same time. This is a result of God and His Spirit in us moving us and directing the prayers in the depths of our hearts.

Nineteenth-century lawyer-turned-preacher Edward M. Bounds points out that even the prayers of biblical saints probably involved many more words than are recorded in the Scriptures and, in many cases, probably involved more than words. He expounds upon this in his classic work *Power through Prayer.*

It is true that Bible prayers in word and print are short, but the praying men of the Bible were with God through many a sweet and holy wrestling hour. They won by few words but long waiting. The prayers Moses records may be short, but Moses prayed to God with fastings and mighty cryings forty days and nights.

The statement of Elijah's praying may be condensed to a few brief paragraphs, but doubtless Elijah . . . spent many hours of fiery struggle and lofty intercourse with God. . . . The verbal brief of Paul's prayers is short, but Paul 'prayed night and day exceedingly.' Christ Jesus prayed many an all-night ere his work was done; and his all-night and long-sustained devotions gave to his work its finish and perfection, and to his character the fullness and glory of its divinity.

# Daily Prayer

## NINE WAYS TO STAY IN TOUCH

Imagine the tender shoot of an apple tree carefully tucked into the ground. That little plant is ready to grow. It wants to grow. Every fiber is focused on becoming a towering tree.

But what will happen if that shoot isn't watered regularly? The same thing that will happen to us spiritually if we don't pray regularly.

Jesus put it this way: "As the branch cannot bear fruit of itself, unless it abides in the vine, neither can you, unless you abide in Me." (John 15:4 NKJV)

Yes, regular prayer is important. Daily prayer is important. In the Reverend Billy Graham's book *Billy Graham, the Inspirational Writings*, he even suggests setting aside several times a day to pray so that "your unconscious life will be saturated with prayer between the prayer periods. . . . It is not enough for you to get out of bed in the morning and just bow your knee and repeat a few sentences." Instead, he advises, we should establish specific prayer periods during the day and use them to talk alone with God. "There should be stated periods where you slip apart with God," he advises.

How can we find the time and a method to make our daily prayer meaningful? Here are a few ideas from the Reverend Stephen Brown, professor of preaching and pastoral ministry at Reformed Theological

Seminary in Orlando, Florida, host of the daily radio Bible study program *Key Life*, and author of *Approaching God*.

**Use a daily devotional.** Whether we draw the words from the Oswald Chambers intellectually challenging classic, *My Utmost for His Highest*, or the practical *Daily Bread*, or a variety of Internet offerings, a daily devotional uniquely helps us focus our spiritual lives and prayers with a new thought to ponder each day.

**Stick with the Word.** Students of Scripture often go straight to a passage from the Bible as the starting point for their daily prayers and then allow the Spirit of God to bring to light how it applies to their lives. A typical session might include reading a chapter each from the Proverbs and Psalms and one from a favorite book of the Bible, followed by a time for prayer.

**Keep a journal.** Some of us can pray without ceasing and without our minds wandering. The rest of us can keep a prayer journal. This is often no more than a spiral-bound notebook in which we write our prayers daily to God. If we keep it faithfully, though, it is a wonderful window to our souls at that particular time and place, and it gives us a way like no other to chart how God has answered our prayers.

**Pray in the morning.** At the start of the day, your mind isn't distracted by the projects, the facts, the figures, or the emotions that will occupy it later. So you can bring more concentration to your prayers. Reverend Brown arises each morning at 4:00 A.M. to talk to God about his life and the folks on his prayer list—at last count, "a couple hundred."

"That sounds pretty awesome, but it's not. I just picture the person and lift him before Christ for a few seconds," he says. He also spends some of his prayer time saying nothing at all—"just simply in the presence of someone who accepts me unconditionally."

**Tap a liturgy.** Some people use liturgies (a body of denomination- or church-approved prayers and rites) as a devotional. They feel that this spiritually jump-starts their daily praying. We can find one in most Catholic, Methodist, Lutheran, and Episcopal prayer books. Reverend Brown's prayer time wouldn't be complete without repeating the liturgy of the Church of Scotland.

**Make it a family affair.** Getting everyone around the dinner table at the same time is a minor miracle itself, but when we do, it's a great opportunity to say some daily prayers together. To start, we might only be able to offer a brief word of thanks for the food before the kids start to squirm, says Brian Dodd, Ph.D., professor of philosophy at Asbury Seminary in Wilmore, Kentucky, and author of *Praying Jesus' Way*. But as the kids get used to praying, too, we can gradually lengthen our prayers to include what's happening in our homes and in our lives.

# Healing Words

## Just for To-day

Lord, for to-morrow and its needs,
I do not pray;
Keep me, my God, from stain of sin
Just for to-day.
Let me both diligently work,
And duly pray.
Let me be kind in word and deed,
Just for to-day.
Let me be slow to do my will,
Prompt to obey;
Help me to sacrifice myself
Just for to-day.
And if to-day my tide of life
Should ebb away,
Give me thy Sacraments divine,
Sweet Lord to-day.
So for to-morrow and its needs
I do not pray,
But keep me, guide me, love me, Lord,
Just for to-day.

—*Morning prayer from* St. Augustine's Prayer Book

**Pray at work.** Of course, we're not talking about reciting Scripture at the next department meeting. We're talking about making God an integral part of our work lives. Go straight to Him when crises come up, says Dr. Dodd. Thank Him when things go better than expected. Ask for wisdom as we manage or interact, and so forth. After all, ultimately, He is our boss.

**Pray at night.** Talking to God in the quiet of the evening gives us a chance to patiently reflect on the events of our day, says Dr. Dodd. *Saint Augustine's Prayer Book*, a devotional for members of the Episcopal Church, however, gives this advice for P.M. worshippers: "If possible, get your evening prayers said in the early evening. Don't wait until bedtime. That would mean giving the last, tired minutes of the day to God."

**Read the work of the saints.** From the *Confessions of St. Augustine* to James Gilchrist Lawson's *Deeper Experiences of Famous Christians*, inspiring biographies of the faithful provide much to consider and make the matter of daily prayer more rewarding.

"One of the genuinely rewarding experiences in reading the devotional masters for ourselves is discovering how readily and how naturally they flow from precise description into the most passionate prayer and then on into narrative again without the slightest artificiality," writes Richard J. Foster, author of *Prayer*. "I believe they did this because they experienced work and prayer as a seamless robe."

# Prayer for Enemies

## FORGIVE AND LET GO

It's in the Lord's Prayer. It's in the Sermon on the Mount.

We must love our enemies. We must pray for those who have hurt us. We must forgive those about whom we are embittered.

Why? Jesus said so. Why else? Here's a "selfish" reason. It's for our own good. We must be willing to love unconditionally, which is what forgiveness is, if we want to experience the blessings of God's love, says Vernon M. Sylvest, M.D., a physician with a prayer-based holistic medical practice in Richmond, Virginia, and author of *The Formula: Who Gets Sick, Who Gets Well*. If we want God to answer our prayers, then we must forgive those we feel have harmed us and we must ask God to bless them. It's the rule.

The Gospel of Saint Mark quotes Jesus on this: "And whenever you stand praying, if you have anything against anyone, forgive him, that your Father in Heaven may also forgive you your trespasses. But if you do not forgive, neither will your Father in Heaven forgive your trespasses." (Mark 11:25–26 NKJV)

Before we can expect our prayers to be answered, we need to

develop and maintain forgiving hearts, letting go of grudges, bitterness, hatred, or a desire for revenge and retaliation, says the Reverend Siang-Yang Tan, Ph.D., professor of psychology in the graduate school of psychology at Fuller Theological Seminary in Pasadena, California, and senior pastor of First Evangelical Church in Glendale, California. What we hold against someone else will hurt us, hinder us, and stymie our prayer efforts.

Here's another good reason to forgive: If we are unwilling to let go of our anger toward another or ourselves, it becomes our block to God's love; thus we do not witness prayers answered, says Dr. Sylvest.

This sentiment is echoed by Catholic Scripture scholar Marilyn Gustin in her treatise, "What the Bible Says about Forgiveness." She writes: "The capacity to love and receive love and the capacity to forgive and receive forgiveness are intimately bound to each other. Who could say which comes first in all the complexities of a human life. It is vital to see that both capacities move circularly."

So pray for forgiveness. Ask God to forgive us for any ill or vengeful thoughts, and ask God to help us learn to forgive others, recommends Dr. Sylvest.

This is not some new or controversial faith teaching. Some ancient wisdom on this comes from the monks of the first few centuries known as the Desert Fathers. For instance, Abbot Zeno said, "If a man wants God to hear his prayer quickly, then before he prays for anything else, even his own soul, when he stands and stretches out his hands toward God, he must pray with all his heart for his enemies. Through this action God will hear everything that he asks."

When should we forgive those who have hurt us? When should we pray for our enemies? Jesus is pretty clear on this. He says that we should do it any time we pray.

## How to Forgive

It's not enough just to say, "I forgive you," says Dr. Sylvest.

It is important to understand what forgiveness is and what it is not, he says. Forgiveness is not saying, "Although you are a miserable person who does terrible things, I forgive you because I am spiritually mature and evolved" or "I'm a terrible, miserable person, too, who also does miserable things, so of course I forgive you." And forgiveness doesn't have "ifs" or "buts" attached, such as, "I'll forgive you if you change" or "I'll forgive, but I'll never forget." Forgiveness, he says, like the love that makes it possible, is unconditional.

True forgiveness is willingness to let go of judgments and see the situation differently. It has to do with experiencing love and joy instead of fear and hate, says Dr. Sylvest.

How do we do this? We need to surrender old perceptions and open ourselves to new ones that reflect the love of God—releasing fear, guilt, unresolved grief, and anger and letting it be replaced by love and joy.

We can't change our feelings, but God can, says Dr. Sylvest. We should acknowledge in prayer that we are angry at a person or that we feel guilty, but that we are willing to not have those feelings. We need to acknowledge that we're willing to see the situation differently and feel love for that person and ourselves. Then we need to open our minds and allow God to work on us; allow God to show us how to love that person; allow God to create a new perspective. He always will if we ask.

We may choke on those words and have to say them over and over in prayer after prayer until we really feel them. But that is our job, says Dr. Sylvest. We should pray it through until it happens, he advises.

Another thing to remember: The concept "I will forgive, but I will not forget" is not forgiveness at all, says Dr. Sylvest. "Real forgiveness is to forgive and forget," he says.

And forgetting without forgiveness does not work either, says Dr. Sylvest. "When we repress negative memories and feelings, they may have to be remembered so that we can know how to reach forgiveness. The order of things is to forgive and then forget.

If we master this, it will have profound effects on us, even improve our health. Research has shown that there are definite biological links between hostility and anger and the increased risk of certain diseases like coronary heart disease, says Redford B. Williams, M.D., professor of psychiatry and director of the Behavioral Medicine Research Center at Duke University Medical Center in Durham, North Carolina, in his book *The Trusting Heart.*

Dr. Williams also states that other positive emotions like trust, forgiveness, and love seem to enhance physical health.

Yes, forgiving is powerful, says Dr. Sylvest, powerful enough to affect all aspects of our lives.

# Prayer and Fasting

## HUNGERING FOR POWER

*J*esus, we know, fasted for 40 days and 40 nights while waging a mighty battle of wills with the Devil. But Jesus doesn't really teach much about fasting.

One of the statements attributed to Him about the value of fasting has Jesus explaining to the disciples why they were unable to cast out a demon without His help. "This kind," says Jesus, "can come forth by nothing, but by prayer and fasting." (Mark 9:29 KJV)

Jesus placed a strong emphasis on fasting by fasting for 40 days before He began His earthly ministry. Fasting has always played a major part in religious life. It was, and is, significant in Jewish tradition and is often a rite of penance. Fasting was practiced in the early Christian church and still has many advocates today. It can be a transforming, empowering spiritual experience, says Dr. Bill Bright, founder and president of the evangelistic ministry Campus Crusade for Christ based in Orlando, Florida, holder of six honorary doctorates, and author of *The Coming Revival: America's Call to Fast, Pray, and Seek God's Face.*

When should we use fasting? It is particularly effective when combined with prayer during times of emergency or special crisis, advises nineteenth-century evangelist R. A. Torrey in his book *How to Pray*. Devoting our attention to God and withdrawing from eating can supercharge and intensify our prayer lives, according to Torrey.

Also, fasting is a way to "truly humble yourself in the sight of God," says Dr. Bright.

## How to Do It

The first step when considering a fast is to consult with a doctor. We may have physical problems that would make it dangerous or unwise for us to alter our normal eating patterns. Ask the doctor to perform a basic blood test to check for kidney and liver health prior to a fast, says Joel Fuhrman, M.D., director of the Amwell Health Center in Belle Mead, New Jersey, and author of *Fasting—And Eating—for Health*. He recommends that anyone who is pregnant, nursing, or taking medication avoid fasting.

Once we're cleared to fast, we might want to get a vegetable juicer to conduct the type of fast that Dr. Bright considers most healthful. He stresses that we should use fresh juices or, if we must buy off-the-shelf, we should avoid any that are not 100 percent juice or that have additives, like sugar.

Drinking fresh vegetable and fruit juices during a fast can give us the energy that we'll need to continue working if we must work during a fast, says Dr. Fuhrman.

The idea of a juice fast is acceptable biblically, says Dr. Bright, because, besides water fasts, the Bible talks of partial fasts, such as that mentioned in Daniel 10:3, where Daniel abstained from choice foods, meat, and wine.

We can also try a water-only fast, says Dr. Fuhrman, so long as it is done only under careful medical supervision with a physician who is knowledgeable about fasting. He recommends that we conserve our energy and avoid work of any kind when doing this kind of fast.

How long should fasting last? Fasts have been known to range from 1 to 40 days. But fasting is about a heartfelt need or longing, not a length of time, says Dr. Bright. It is up to us, following the lead of the Holy Spirit, to determine the length of our fasts. Before beginning any fast, Dr. Bright reiterates that it is essential we have our doctor's approval.

Here are some other tips.

- First-timers should start slowly and gently and work up to longer fasts. Fast for one meal daily, one day weekly, or one week monthly to develop "spiritual muscles," says Dr. Bright.
- Always drink one to three quarts of water a day, says Dr. Fuhrman.
- Have fruit juices in the mornings, vegetable juices in the afternoons and evenings, and water all around the clock, suggests Dr. Bright.
- When approaching a fast that will last several days or longer, cut back on the size of meals for a few days before beginning the fast, says Dr. Fuhrman.
- Two to three days prior to the fast, Dr. Fuhrman recommends that we prepare our digestive systems for the slow-down by eating only cooked green vegetables and fruit.
- Cut back physical activity during the fast—a nice walk each day is okay on juice fasts if it's approved by a doctor, he says. Expect to feel weaker than normal. Rest more.
- Spend as much time praying, worshipping, meditating, and reading the Bible as possible during the fast. Lighten work schedules if possible to allow this, recommends Dr. Bright.
- Avoid telling strangers or casual acquaintances that we are fasting, he says. It just subjects us to lots of questions that we may not want to answer. Do seek the support of understanding spiritual acquaintances, friends, and family members and ask them to pray for us. If work associates notice that we are skipping meals, we can just say that we have other plans for lunch.
- Especially during times when we feel vulnerable, weak, or irritable, it is important to read the Bible and pray. This is also important at other times, such as during normal mealtimes or if we awaken at night.

- Re-enter the world of eating slowly and gently, starting with steamed and boiled vegetables and salads. Dr. Fuhrman recommends breaking the fast by eating a piece of fruit every two hours for the first day. On the second day after the fast, eat salad and fruit, he says. He also recommends avoiding salty or spicy foods and alcohol for the first week or two after the fast because they can cause indigestion.

Material from Dr. Bright and others about how to conduct a prayerful fast is available at nominal cost from New Life Publications, Campus Crusade for Christ, 100 Sunport Lane, Department 3400, Orlando, FL 32809.

# Fervent Prayer

## CRIES OF THE HEART,
## SONGS OF THE SOUL

The effective, fervent prayer of a righteous man avails much."
(James 5:16 NKJV)

While many modern Bible translations omit the word *fervent*,
which occurs in the King James Version of the Bible, this line from
the Apostle James has been the heart of many a sermon and Bible
teaching.

Such teachings are powerful, inspiring, and relevant to our prayer
lives. Nineteenth century lawyer-turned-preacher Edward M. Bounds
passionately taught about effectual, fervent prayer in at least two
books now considered Christian classics: *Purpose in Prayer* and *The
Necessity of Prayer*.

"Few, short, feeble prayers" always indicate a feeble spiritual
condition, Reverend Bounds says pointedly in *Purpose in Prayer*.
Those who desire results "ought to pray much and apply themselves
to it with energy and perseverance. Eminent Christians have been
eminent in prayer. The deep things of God are learned nowhere else.
Great things for God are done by great prayers. He who prays much,
studies much, loves much, works much, does much for God and
humanity."

Scientific experiments with prayer show that Reverend Bounds may have been on to something. They suggest that emotions such as love and compassion and genuineness in prayer are vitally important factors that help prayers get answered, says prayer researcher Larry Dossey, M.D., author of *Healing Words*, which is used as a textbook in many medical schools, and *Prayer Is Good Medicine*. "But there is no clear-cut evidence that the longer or more often you pray the greater the results. A short, heartfelt prayer may avail more than a lengthy prayer that is not as genuine."

So how do we pray the "great prayers," as Reverend Bounds calls them? Here are his clear, concise instructions from *Purpose in Prayer*.

**Pray with urgency.** "We must be thoroughly in earnest, deeply concerned about the things for which we ask, for Jesus Christ made it very plain that the secret of prayer and its success lie in its urgency. We must press our prayers upon God."

**Pray boldly and with total commitment.** "Inflamed desires, impassioned, unwearied insistence delight Heaven. . . . Heaven is too busy to listen to half-hearted prayers . . . Our whole being must be in our praying."

**Pray and pray again.** "We are to press the matter, not with vain repetitions, but with urgent repetitions. We repeat, not to count the times, but to gain the prayer. We cannot quit praying, because heart and soul are in it. We pray 'with all perseverance.' We hang to our prayers because by them we live. We press our pleas because we must have them or die."

**Touch the Father's heart.** "The Heavens must feel the force of our crying, and must be brought into oppressed sympathy for our bitter and needy state. A need that oppresses us, and has no relief but in our crying to God, must voice our praying. . . . Prayer is the helpless and needy child crying to the compassion of the Father's heart and the bounty and power of a Father's hand. The answer is as sure to come as the Father's heart can be touched and the Father's hand moved."

# Prayer for Healing

## "BY HIS STRIPES"

Teachings on divine healing are many and diverse, with entire ministries devoted to it.

Some believe that we can invoke divine healing by uttering a simple plea to God for His will to be done. Others say that it takes laying on hands in prayer, or condemning Satan as the author of illness, or commanding death to Satan's evil spirits and demons and disease, or demanding our God-given rights as Christians to perfect health. Yet other ministries teach some combination of these.

How can we summon the power of healing prayer? Here are some ways taught by ministries that most strongly advocate divine healing.

### Incorporate Jesus' Power

Jesus healed people a number of ways. Among them, He used words to cast out evil spirits and demons. He touched people to remove their illness or malady. And he commanded healing. "Be healed!" He said. And people were.

He also gave others the ability to heal. Jesus transferred to all believers the power to "in My name . . . cast out devils . . . (and) lay hands on the sick, and they shall recover." (Mark 16:15–18 KJV)

Anyone with strong enough faith can, as the Spirit wills, do those things, preaches the Pentecostal word-faith movement, which places tremendous emphasis on divine healing and claims 430 million believers worldwide. One of the movement's leading teachers is charismatic faith minister the Reverend Norvel Hayes, director of New Life Bible College in Cleveland, Tennessee.

We need not accept disease and illness in our lives, teaches Reverend Hayes. Based on the Bible, we can claim for ourselves and for others that we have a divine right to wellness—that through Jesus' suffering, we were healed. And if we *were* healed, then we *are* healed, points out Reverend Hayes. If the Bible says it, then we can pray it and claim it.

Here are three Bible verses frequently cited by Christian faith-healing advocates. Reading and meditating on these verses can be comforting during periods of illness, whether our faith is Pentecostal in orientation or not, whether we accept the full thrust of the faith-movement teachings or not.

Surely He has borne our griefs
    And carried our sorrows;
    Yet we esteemed Him stricken,
    Smitten by God, and afflicted.
But He was wounded for our transgressions,
    He was bruised for our iniquities;
    The chastisement for our peace was upon Him,
    And by His stripes we are healed.

    —*Isaiah 53:4–5 NKJV*

And He cast out the spirits with a word, and healed all who were sick, that it might be fulfilled which was spoken by Isaiah the prophet, saying:

"He Himself took our infirmities
And bore our sicknesses."

*—Matthew 8:17 NKJV*

Who Himself bore our sins in His own body on the tree,
that we, having died to sins, might live for
righteousness—by whose stripes you were healed.

*—1 Peter 2:24 NKJV*

*Stripes* is translated in most newer versions of the Bible as *wounds*, and refers to marks on Jesus' body from being whipped before His crucifixion. In more modern English, the verse is, "By His wounds you have been healed." (1 Peter 2:24 NIV)

## Five Miraculous Methods

The Bible and modern-day spiritual advisors say that we can and should use prayer and faith for healing. Here's what they suggest.

1. Express faith. Sometimes, simply faith in God is enough. If we have strong enough faith, we should express it—in prayer and perhaps to others.

In the Bible, two blind men were healed in this way. They called out to Jesus, "Son of David, have mercy on us!" Jesus asked them, "Do you believe that I am able to do this?" They said, "'Yes, Lord.' Then He touched their eyes, saying, 'According to your faith let it be to you.' And their eyes were opened." (Matthew 9:27–31 NKJV)

The Bible also tells of a woman who had suffered continuous bleeding (some say a menstrual flow) for 12 years and had spent all her money on worthless cures from the physicians of the day. She had heard of Jesus' healing power and as He walked through town, thronged by people, she sought to get close to Him. She said, "If only I may touch His garments, I shall be made well." She got close enough behind Him to touch the hem of His clothes.

"Immediately the fountain of her blood was dried up, and she felt in her body that she was healed of the affliction. And Jesus, immediately knowing in Himself that power had gone out of Him, turned around in the crowd and said, 'Who touched My clothes?'

". . . the woman, fearing and trembling, knowing what had happened to her, came and fell down before Him and told Him the whole truth. And He said to her, 'Daughter, your faith has made you well. Go in peace. . . .'" (Mark 5:25–33 NKJV)

2. Call for elders. If our own faith is wavering, we can call on those who are spiritual powerhouses, or more learned in the faith, and their prayers can heal us. "Is anyone among you sick? Let him call for the elders of the church, and let them pray over him, anointing him with oil in the name of the Lord. And the prayer of faith will save the sick, and the Lord will raise him up. And if he has committed sins, he will be forgiven." (James 5:13–15 NKJV)

Our faith can be stimulated when olive oil or other oil is applied in the sign of the cross onto our foreheads while the person applying it repeats, "In the name of the Father, and the Son, and the Holy Spirit." Doing this in accordance with Scripture deepens our intimacy with God and helps brings about His purpose. Certainly, there are times in our lives when our faith could use the boost that comes from having others pray and minister to, for, and with us, says the Reverend Paul F. Everett of Pittsburgh, a Presbyterian minister at large with the Peale Center in Pawling, New York, and executive director emeritus of the Pittsburgh Experiment, a national and international ministry to the business and working communities.

3. Confess to one another. The verse mentioned above, in James 5, goes on to say, "If he (the sick person) has committed sins, he will be forgiven. Confess your trespasses to one another, and pray for one another, that you may be healed." (James 5:15–16 NKJV) That doesn't mean that we need to run out and tell all our friends and neighbors about our latest indiscretions. That means that if we have unconfessed sin in our lives, we should confess it to the elders whom we have asked to pray for our healing.

4. Ask for helping hands. Request that a believer lay hands on us and pray for our recovery in Jesus' name. In Mark 16:18, Jesus says that those who believe in Him can lay their hands on the sick, in His name, and the sick will get well. Proponents of this practice say that the Spirit of God dwells in every believer, and it is the power of that Spirit that goes out through the believer's hands.

5. Call the doctor. God also uses doctors and medicine to heal. Even major faith-healing advocates will agree. A well-known pastor in this movement has said: "Don't die of something treatable just because it seems like it would be a failure of faith to see a doctor. Pray and call God to lead you to the right doctor and right treatment for your rapid recovery."

## Simple Prayers

Father Victor Hoagland, a Passionist priest from Union City, New Jersey, says that prayers for healing do not have to be complicated to be heard. He says, "At times, a prayer during illness may be only a brief word or cry because our minds can imagine nothing more. Yet God can hear even a simple cry."

He has edited a book of some simple, effective prayers called *Companion in Illness*. Here are a few of the suggested short prayers that we might pray when ill.

Lord, I believe in you.
Lord, I hope in you.

Lord, I love you.
Lord, hear me.
Lord, increase my faith.

Lord Jesus Christ,
Son of the living God,
have mercy on me.

For related information, see Science Finds God (page 3), Laying On of Hands (page 77), and Prayer in the Name of Jesus (page 91).

# *Intercessory Prayer*

## How to Pray for Others

*W*hen Yolanda Jones' arthritis flares, she is often in such pain that it wakes her out of a sound sleep. Instead of taking a prescription drug, the Uhrichsville, Ohio, resident picks up one of the many prayer requests sent to her by friends and talks to God about them. Before long, Jones' pain is gone and she falls asleep. But a week or two later, invariably, there's a letter in the mailbox thanking her for her help in getting another prayer answered.

If Jones had a motto, it might be this: "Far be it from me that I should sin against the Lord in ceasing to pray for you." (1 Samuel 12:23 NKJV)

Praying for others—this is what intercessory prayer is all about. And it has been practiced since earliest times. Look to the Bible and you'll find Moses raising his hands over Joshua and the children of Israel as they battled the Amalekites (Exodus 17:8–13) and Christ carrying our prayers before God from His place in Heaven. (Romans 8:34)

But intercessory prayer is not just a phenomenon of biblical times. You'll find it practiced everywhere from the 50,000-member mega-churches in South Korea to tiny clapboard buildings in the American heartland. In fact, theologians suggest that the greatest intercessory prayer movement in the history of the church is taking place now.

While much of the focus of these prayers is fanning the flames of spiritual revival, there also is renewed interest in praying for the healing and well-being of others. And at least some of that interest is thought to stem from an increasing number of medical studies that seem to show a link between prayer, faith, and healing. Among the most fascinating: One study showed that heart patients who received intercessory prayer from people they didn't even know had a more favorable outcome, had fewer complications, and needed less medication than those who didn't receive intercessory prayer.

The key thing to remember when we pray for others is that the results aren't up to us; they're up to God. Yet Jesus himself suggests that we shouldn't take no for an answer. He describes a poor widow who repeatedly takes her ill treatment to a judge, who can't help but give in after all her complaining. (Luke 18:1–8)

If we wish to practice intercessory prayer, here are some other things to keep in mind.

**Make a list.** It's a good idea to record the names of the people we pray for so that we don't leave anyone out. Some people have multiple lists so that each day, they're praying for someone else outside of their immediate families.

**Keep a holy family album.** A holy family album is a visual reminder of the people we have in our hearts. Richard J. Foster, author of *Prayer*, writes, "I once visited a very holy lady who was confined to a bed. She showed me her 'family album' of some 200 photographs of missionaries and others she was concerned to hold before the throne of Heaven. I was a teenager at the time, but even at that young age I knew that the place where I stood beside that bed was holy ground."

**Wait for further guidance.** After we've covered our friends, neighbors, leaders of church and state, and anything else that lays heavy on our hearts, we may feel like we're prayed-out. That's okay.

Some intercessors then wait silently for further guidance on who to pray for. And if no guidance seems to come, that's fine. We can't pray for everything, so we shouldn't try.

**Keep a journal.** Sometimes when praying for someone, an insight into a problem or dilemma will be revealed. Keeping paper and pen handy will ensure that we don't forget the answer.

**Go to the person for whom we're praying.** How better to find out exactly how we should pray for someone than asking him? "Remember, prayer is a way of loving others, and so courtesy, grace, and respect are always in order," Foster points out.

**Get our church into the act.** If the church doesn't have an active intercessory prayer group, we can talk to our pastors, reverends, or priests about starting one.

# Listening to the Holy Spirit

## KNOWING GOD'S WILL

In Bible days, according to the stories passed down, God spoke to men in ways that He seemingly never does now.

His voice thundered from the sky. His words roared from a burning bush. He emblazoned commandments on stone tablets. He sent angels, with wings aflutter, to deliver messages. He shook the desert, twisted oaks, hurled fire and, in other dramatic ways, made His will known.

Now He seems more likely to use the "still small voice" referred to in 1 Kings 19:12 (KJV). God also uses some of the other more subtle methods of communication that He employed in Bible days. He communicates to us in dreams, visions, omens, feelings, happenings, seeming coincidences, and through other people. Sometimes we just intuitively know, deep inside, that we are being led to do something, or that something is so, contrary to appearances. We just know in our spirits. God can use anything in His creation to reveal truth to us.

Jesus promises us this "knowing." He says, ". . . the Counselor, the Holy Spirit, whom the Father will send in My name, will teach you all things. . . ." (John 14:26 NIV)

Jesus also says, ". . . when He, the Spirit of truth, comes, He will guide you into all truth." (John 16:13 NIV)

# Try a Prayer Experiment

How can we learn to recognize these revelations? How can we develop our sensitivity and pay more attention to the leadings of the Holy Spirit? How can we learn to better know God's will?

We can learn much, says the Reverend Paul F. Everett of Pittsburgh, a Presbyterian minister at large with the Peale Center in Pawling, New York, from trying our own rendition of the Pittsburgh Experiment, a test of faith that was first tried in Pittsburgh in the 1950s and since has been taught worldwide.

The Pittsburgh Experiment was the brainchild of the Reverend Sam Shoemaker. Reverend Shoemaker had moved from New York City to Pittsburgh and was rector of Pittsburgh's prestigious Calvary Episcopal Church in the middle 1950s.

He was disappointed that the most successful and influential male members of his congregation were to be found not in church on Sunday mornings but on the golf course. So Reverend Shoemaker, always an innovator, set up spiritual meetings for businessmen at the golf course country club.

Some of the men, Reverend Shoemaker found, were spiritually and theologically confused. Others were ambivalent about the church, thinking that it was only for women. Still others were approaching agnosticism. As tough-minded businessmen, however, they all thought that it was impossible to be Christians in business and survive, reports Reverend Everett, who for almost 30 years was executive director of the ministry that evolved from these early meetings. So Reverend Shoemaker proposed a challenge—an experiment.

Each man, he said, was to pray a simple prayer daily for 30 days: "God, if You are real, reveal Yourself to me."

They were to pray the prayer in the morning upon arising and again any time they thought of it during the day. And they were to pray for each others' success with the experiment. "I promise you," said Shoemaker, "there will be some illumination on your request within 30 days."

The men met again in 30 days. "They went around the room and reported their experiences. Every one of those men had come in touch with the living God in that 30-day period in their own unique way," says Reverend Everett. "Of course," he says, "that had an incendiary effect," and these prestigious men dedicated themselves to the Lord, to each other, and to the city of Pittsburgh. They formed the Pittsburgh Experiment, which is known in other parts of the world.

The 30-day prayer experiment can be applied any time direction is needed, says Reverend Everett. We should find a partner, he says, and agree to pray every day and as often as we think about it for illumination—God's will—about one particular thing: a broken relationship, a job search, or whatever. And then do our part. Gather information about the subject of our prayers and keep our eyes open for possible answers and leadings in our everyday lives.

A key to the experiment's success, says Reverend Everett, is to let go of expectations of how God will answer the prayer or what the answer will be. Be open to the answer that comes. It helps to have a partner in the project because we can advise and encourage each other and discuss whatever leadings we perceive.

# Feel the Spirit

Here are some more ways to learn God's will.

**Prayerfully read Scripture.** Expect that, while reading, an answer or an understanding will come through the verses themselves, advises Christian psychiatrist and theologian Paul Meier, M.D., cofounder of New Life Clinics, the world's largest provider of Christian-based counseling in the United States.

**Meditate and write.** Reverend Shoemaker taught that after praying for God's will, we should allow a period of quiet time and write down all of our thoughts, then analyze which might be from God based on whether or not they are in alignment with scriptural teachings. A prayer partner or group is important to help give confirmation. Those from God should be acted upon, according to Reverend Shoemaker.

**Pray till the answer comes.** In his classic, *Purpose in Prayer*, nineteenth-century lawyer-turned-preacher Edward M. Bounds writes, "'I tell the Lord my troubles and difficulties, and wait for Him to give me the answers to them,' says one man of God. 'And it is wonderful how a matter that looked very dark will in prayer become clear as crystal by the help of God's Spirit. I think Christians fail so often to get answers to their prayers because they do not wait long enough on God. They just drop down and say a few words, and then jump up and forget it and expect God to answer them. Such praying always reminds me of the small boy ringing his neighbour's doorbell, and then running away as fast as he can go.'"

**Picture Jesus.** What would He do in this situation? That can shed a whole new light on a dilemma.

**Develop a contemplative soul.** That is what is required to comprehend the mysteries of Scripture and God, says second-century theologian Saint Clement of Alexandria in *The Stromata*. The more we turn to the Spirit and expect the Spirit to lead us, the more readily we find direction in the process and the more we become spiritual beings rather than worldly beings. As Saint Clement put it: "For he who is still blind and dumb, not having understanding, or the undazzled and keen vision of the contemplative soul, which the Saviour confers . . . must stand outside of the divine choir. For we compare spiritual things with spiritual."

# Prayer of Joy and Rejoicing

## STOMP, CLAP, SING!

People shout in joy, sing, clang, and bang percussion instruments and otherwise praise God throughout the Old and New Testaments. Here's a loud example.

"David and all the house of Israel were dancing before the Lord with all their might, with song and lyres and harps and tambourines and castanets and cymbals." (2 Samuel 6:5 NRSV)

Also, the Apostles were not necessarily perfectly proper and refined and quiet in their worship practices. ". . . they worshiped Him, and returned to Jerusalem with great joy, and were continually in the temple praising and blessing God." (Luke 24:52–53 NKJV) When Paul and Silas were imprisoned, they sang and praised God—even at midnight—and were so noisy that all the other prisoners heard them. (Acts 16:25)

In current-day praise rallies and services, believers gather, sing songs, wave their arms in the air (holding up "holy hands"), pray out loud murmuring, shouting, and whispering, intoning "thank you," "praise the Lord," "hallelujah!" "mighty is the Name," or whatever other words inspire them. This practice is most common in the charismatic faith movement but is spreading to other churches. The joy and spontaneity is infectious and uplifting to the soul.

Praying in joy and rejoicing in the Lord need not be done only in a group atmosphere. We can celebrate the love of God and receive his gifts when we are alone. Vernon M. Sylvest, M.D., a physician with a prayer-based holistic medical practice in Richmond, Virginia, and author of *The Formula: Who Gets Sick, Who Gets Well*, says that when we speak our private prayers out loud, we know that we are putting more energy into them and are thus open to receiving more. Putting body language into prayer may also be helpful. Before we can fully experience the joy of God, it may be necessary to cry out our pain in prayer so that it can be healed. Dr. Sylvest says that this not only brings joy to our minds but to our bodies as well, with great health benefits.

"Celebration saves us from taking ourselves too seriously," says the Reverend Rowland Croucher, doctor of ministry, an evangelist in Healthmont, Victoria, Australia, and director of John Mark Ministries in Melbourne. "It adds a note of gaiety, festivity, and hilarity to our lives."

# When?

Prayers of praise and joy are particularly effective when expressed during periods of great difficulty and trial. Joyful worship can bring wondrous breakthroughs and revelation, say some teachers.

Remember how, even at midnight, locked in prison and with their feet in stocks, Paul and Silas sang praises to God and the prisoners heard them?

God heard, too.

"And suddenly there was a great earthquake, so that the foundations of the prison were shaken: and immediately all the doors were opened, and every one's bands were loosed." (Acts 16:26 KJV) This exhibition of prayer power so frightened the magistrates that they set Paul and Silas free.

When troubled, when our faith is tested, we should "count it all joy," says the Apostle James, for it is simply an opportunity to prove our faith and prove that it works. (James 1:2 KJV) And as author, evangelist, and teacher Jerry Savelle of Crowley, Texas, says in the title of his book, "If Satan can't steal your joy, he can't keep your goods."

Prayers of joy and adoration also can be expressed any time as a beautiful form of private and public worship.

If this is a new prayer experience, a nice way to start, according to Christian spiritual leaders, might be to focus on the sentiments of the following verses and join the author in celebration.

Give thanks to the Lord, call on His name;
   make known among the nations what He has done.
Sing to Him, sing praise to Him;
   tell of all His wonderful acts.
Glory in His holy name;
   let the hearts of those who seek the Lord rejoice.
Look to the Lord and His strength;
   seek His face always.
Remember the wonders He has done,
   His miracles, and the judgments He pronounced.

   *—I Chronicles 16:8–12 NIV*

Let the Heavens rejoice, let the Earth be glad;
   let them say among the nations, "The Lord reigns!"

   *—I Chronicles 16:31 NIV*

# Laying On of Hands

## THE ULTIMATE HANDS-ON TREATMENT

*T*hese days, the phrase *laying on of hands* may bring to mind images of televangelists healing someone instantly with a tap on the forehead. But healing with hands is a practice described throughout the Bible.

Biblical figures laid on hands to bestow blessings, to commission someone for ministry, and to heal, as Jesus did in raising a girl from the dead (Mark 5:23), and as Paul did in curing a man who was suffering from dysentery and fever. (Acts 28:8)

In more traditional churches today, it's common to see the pastor and elders lay hands on missionaries and pray for them before they go out into the field, or dab oil on someone who is troubled and pray for him. More than a few churches even have services specifically dedicated to praying for healing.

What's it like to experience laying on of hands? Well, obviously, it's meaningful for the one who is ill. For one thing, everyone can benefit from some form of compassionate, nonsexual touching. And when we're experiencing pain or suffering emotional problems, that need increases. Combine that with the power released through prayer, and you have a healing agent that some say is second to none.

But the experience also affects the people praying. They often feel "something like a flow of energy, the flow of God's healing power coming through," says Francis S. MacNutt, Ph.D., author of *Healing* and *Deliverance from Evil Spirits* and co-founder of Christian Healing Ministries in Jacksonville, Florida.

Richard J. Foster, author of *Prayer*, writes that he also "sometimes detects a gentle flow of energy" when laying on hands.

## The Key Steps in Healing

How to practice the laying on of hands? Here's some advice.

**Ask permission first.** No matter how pure our motives, it's not appropriate just to lay our hands on people and start praying anymore than it would be to hug someone whom we just met, says Dr. MacNutt.

**Cop a (good) attitude.** Both the person who is sick and the healer need to open their minds to healing and free themselves of negative feelings, Foster says, "I have found that if I resist or refuse to be an open conduit for God's power to come into a person, the flow of energy will stop. Also, a spirit of hate or resentment arrests the flow immediately."

In fact, Norma Dearing, director of prayer ministry at Christian Healing Ministries, says that the ability of the sick person to open up the heart and confess known sin actually may be an important key to the healing itself. While conditions like heart disease, arthritis, ulcers, and others obviously have physical causes, they can also be rooted in emotional issues such as bitterness and unforgiveness, she says.

**Pray in twos.** If we're going to be praying for someone else, we should try to make sure that we're joined by a prayer partner.

**Be simple but specific.** If someone is suffering from back pain, for example, lay hands on the spot and pray something like this, says Dearing: "Lord, we ask that you draw this pain out. Pour your healing power into (the person's) back so that it feels better." Or, if someone broke an arm: "Lord, let the cast do what it's supposed to do. Let them not be in any pain. We ask that they have peace and comfort and that the bone will be repaired and corrected through your healing power."

**Visualize.** Dearing says that while she prays, she alternately visualizes the face of Jesus and the problem improving in some way, such as a tumor shrinking or bones mending. She also listens to see if Jesus is going to tell her something about the person or the health problem.

**Check your progress—and praise.** After praying silently and out loud for a few minutes, we should check with the person for whom we're praying to see if the pain has decreased or if the problem has improved. If we can't see a result, that's okay; keep praying. If the person feels better, thank God. If not, stop and pray again when we have time.

Dearing also advises that we start small when we attempt to heal. She has laid hands on and prayed for literally thousands of people, but she got her start with her crippled dog. While reading about laying on hands, she decided to pray for her dog, who was suffering from an arthritis-like condition that made him unable use his back legs. Slowly, her dog improved—and her faith grew.

"It didn't happen immediately, and I had to do it regularly, but I could see improvement every time I did it," she says. "And that gave me more strength and courage and energy to try to pray for my children, girlfriends, and my parents. That built my faith to move on and keep praying."

# *Mindfulness and Meditation*

## PRACTICE THE PRESENCE

*M*indfulness, meditation, and centering or contemplative prayer were considered by the early Christian church fathers as the ultimate, deepest, and most intimate forms of prayer fellowship with God. Catholic catechism still teaches that contemplative prayer is the most intense prayer communication and recommends that we practice it regularly. Interestingly, variations of these three types of prayer have long been taught by most other world religions as well.

Mindfulness, meditation, and contemplative prayer share much in common. In fact, in that order, one can be a preparation for the next.

## Mindfulness

Mindfulness is a prayerful state that we are urged to practice at all times, but particularly, any time that we wish to sense the presence of God. Essentially, that is what mindfulness is all about. It is about fixing our attention in the present, which is where God lives.

One step in doing this, as seventeenth-century French Carmelite Friar Brother Lawrence taught, is to maintain a "loving gaze that finds

God everywhere." We do this when we recognize God as the breath of life and the holy glue that holds everything together. When we realize that we are in Him and He in us. When we look for his presence in everyone.

What does it mean to sense the presence of God? According to sixteenth-century doctor of the church Saint Francis de Sales, "The presence of God' means (recognizing that) . . . God is everywhere, in all places, in all things, in all people. Wherever birds fly, they encounter the air; so wherever we go or wherever we are, we find God present."

More than that, we must enter the moment. We must take our thoughts off what has happened and what might happen and focus on what is happening right now. According to Saint Francis de Sales, "We know the theology that God is here, right now. . . . Remember that He not only is in this place with you, but in a very true way He is in your heart, in the very center of your spirit. Saint Paul reminds us that 'we live and move and have our very being' in God. (Acts 17:28) You must excite in your heart a very real reverence for the God who is present to and in you."

Psychologists teach that mindfulness is a healthy state. We tend to worry about what has happened in the past that we cannot change and what might happen in the future, which is not here. Generally, we have little to worry about if we move our attention toward what we can responsibly and positively best do with God's help right now, says Christian psychiatrist and theologian Paul Meier, M.D., cofounder of New Life Clinics, the largest provider of Christian-based counseling in the United States and author of more than 60 best-selling Christian self-help books. That is, being mindful.

Jesus says, ". . . do not worry about tomorrow, for tomorrow will worry about itself." (Matthew 6:34 NIV) That is the teaching of mindfulness. How do we do this? According to Dr. Meier, we can try the following:

- Monitor our thoughts regularly—perhaps every time we hear the floor creak, or the wind murmur in the tree outside our window.
- Any time we find that our minds have wandered from the present and are focusing negatively or fearfully on the past or future, gently draw our attention back to the present.

- Recognize and be grateful that we are with God, now; God is with us, now; and that in this moment, we can actively sense and serve God.

We can do this even when we are busy, says Saint Francis de Sales. "Retire at various times into the solitude of your own heart, even while outwardly engaged in discussions or transactions with others, and talk to God." One way to do this, taught by the Quakers, is to recognize the spirit of Christ, "the true light, which enlightens everyone . . . " (John 1:9 NRSV) in those with whom we are speaking. Another is to offer silent thanks. Another is to pay attention to the Spirit's inner leadings—our intuitive impressions—as we continue our outward conversation.

Creating a state of mindfulness is a prelude to both meditation and contemplative prayer.

# Meditation

The Christian version of meditation differs from that of Eastern religions. In eastern meditation, we sit quietly at one with God, sensing and soaking up the peace, joy, and fullness of divine presence. Christian meditation is discursive; that is, it is more active in the sense of making use of imagination, memory, reflection, and multiplying acts of the will, says the Reverend Thomas Keating, a Trappist monk at Saint Benedict's Monastery in Snowmass, Colorado. It moves from one reflection to another with a view of stirring up the will to encourage acts of prayer such as praise, adoration, and thanksgiving. It is a more active, more directed, more expectant form of prayer.

Meditation, explains the Catholic catechism, is a quest, a reflection on Jesus' life and teachings, through which we can achieve a union with Christ and from which new understanding and relevancy emerge.

The first couple of steps, though, are rather universal. As Saint Francis de Sales taught, "Two points are always used to prepare oneself for the meditation: Place yourself in the presence of God, and ask for His help in praying." To practice Christian meditation, we need to mentally separate ourselves from the world and spend our time only in the presence of God.

We are to focus on a spiritual concept, question, teaching, Bible verse, or phrase from a verse and simply let it loll around in our minds and reveal itself to us as it will. Meditation is particularly useful when we seek enlightenment or guidance or direction from the Spirit on a specific matter, says Dr. Meier.

Dr. Meier suggests that we read the Bible until a verse or phrase strikes us as particularly significant to us. Then, in the quiet, we should close our eyes and ask God to reveal to us what we need to know about this phrase or verse and its relevance to our lives and just sit and let the process happen.

Meditation is not an analytical exercise, points out the Reverend Rowland Croucher, doctor of ministry, an evangelist in Healthmont, Victoria, Australia, and director of John Mark Ministries in Melbourne. "Meditation is devotional; study is analytical. Meditation will relish a word; study will explicate it," he says.

"By turning your eyes on God in meditation, your whole soul will be filled with God," said Saint Francis de Sales.

# Contemplative Prayer

Contemplative prayer is a development of discursive meditation. It was an honored form of prayer for clergy and laity alike during the first 16 centuries of the church, but it was virtually lost during the Reformation and has only been recovered and restored to its eminence in the twentieth century.

This prayer is an intentional quiet state in which we become aware of God with and within us. The purpose is simply to be still and be with God, to sense and develop the holy, healing presence of the Divine in and around us, and to grow from the experience.

The Catholic catechism says that when we practice this prayer, the "Father strengthens our inner being with power through His Spirit . . . 'I look at Him and He looks at me.' . . . His gaze illumines the eyes of our heart and teaches us to see everything in the light of His truth and His compassion for all men."

Sixteenth-century nun Saint Teresa of Avila called this type of prayer recollection. It helps us to remember, she says, "how important it is to have understood this truth—that the Lord is within us and that we should be there with Him. . . . It is called recollection because the soul collects together all the faculties and enters within itself to be with its God."

Fifteenth-century priest Thomas Kempis, in *The Imitation of Christ*, writes: "Turn, then, to God . . . devote yourself to those (things) that are within, and you will see the Kingdom of God come unto you, that Kingdom which is peace and joy in the Holy Spirit."

How do we do this? Father Keating, who has been teaching contemplative prayer since the 1970s, suggests trying this method.

1. Choose a sacred word, such as *Abba* or *love*. Gently repeat this word silently, symbolizing the intent to commune with God within.

2. Sit comfortably, eyes closed, quiet the mind, and "introduce the sacred word inwardly and as gently as laying a feather on a piece of cotton," advises Father Keating.

3. When we find our attention drifting from our sacred word, gently guide it back. "During the course of our prayer, the sacred word may become vague or even disappear," says Father Keating, and that is perfectly normal.

4. At the end of the prayer session, sit in silence for a few minutes, allowing yourself to slowly emerge from the experience into your customary thinking pattern.

Father Keating recommends two periods of centering prayer daily. He suggests that they be at least 20 minutes long each.

What can we expect during the prayer period? Normal memories; wanderings of the imagination; "thoughts that give rise to attractions or aversions; insights and psychological breakthroughs; self reflections such as 'How am I doing?' or 'This peace is just great!'; and thoughts that arise from the unloading of the unconscious," such as insights into past behaviors and events, says Father Keating.

According to Herbert Benson, M.D., associate professor of medicine and president of the Mind/Body Medical Institute at Harvard Medical School, daily meditative prayer has been shown by medical scientists to substantially reduce physical and mental stress and, consequently, render many health benefits.

Father Kempis seemed to know this back in the 1400s. He writes that the man who practices contemplative prayer "quickly recollects himself because he has never wasted his attention" on external distractions. "No outside work, no business that cannot wait stands in his way. He adjusts himself to things as they happen."

# How Jesus Prayed

## THE MASTER AS OUR ROLE MODEL

*J*ust one thing.

The disciples asked Jesus to teach them just one thing. "They wanted Him to teach them to pray," observes Harry Emerson Fosdick, founding minister of New York City's Riverside Church, in *The Manhood of the Master*.

And so Jesus taught the disciples the Lord's Prayer—as good a guide as it gets for praying. But that isn't all we need to know about Jesus' advice on prayer, any more than the shore is all we need to know about the ocean. When He prayed, where He prayed, why He prayed, what He said about prayer—all these help us understand prayer's importance.

And to be more like Him, we must pray the same way—not read about prayer or talk about it, or even write about it. But pray.

How?

"I think that for most of us, prayer seems like a mystery, this weighty thing. And I think that Jesus simplifies it, demystifies it," says Brian J. Dodd, Ph.D., professor of philosophy at Asbury Seminary and director of the Share Jesus Ministry, both in Wilmore, Kentucky, and author of *Praying Jesus' Way*. "We just need to pay attention." With Dr. Dodd and other experts as our guides, let's look at a brief guide to Jesus' praying.

**He often prayed alone.** Sometimes it must just have been to get away from the crowds. "So He Himself often withdrew into the wilderness and prayed" (Luke 5:16 NKJV), and always before a big event—like when He chose the disciples. But over and over again, Jesus prayed alone, often on a mountaintop. What's the message in that for us, besides the fact that He may have enjoyed the scenery?

The Reverend Charles Spurgeon, a nineteenth-century English pastor nicknamed the Prince of Preachers, put it this way: "If you would draw near to God in an extraordinary manner, you must take care to be entirely undisturbed. I know not why it is, but whenever one desires to approach very near to God, there is sure to be a knock at the door, or some matter of urgent business, or some difficult circumstance to tempt us from our knees."

**He prayed with others.** Whether praying at His own baptism or taking Peter, James, and John to pray on a mountain, Jesus' intercessions weren't strictly private affairs by any means. "Relationship with God is personal but not private, and Jesus balanced the personal and the community aspects of prayer," says Dr. Dodd. "This should counteract a me-and-Jesus-only approach to God. Jesus balances the 'me' and the 'us' of praying."

**He prayed for others.** His praying for the disciples, and Peter in particular, at the end of his earthly ministry makes it clear that Jesus prayed for those He loved. "Simon, Simon! Indeed, Satan has asked for you, that he may sift you as wheat. But I have prayed for you, that your faith should not fail; and when you have returned to Me, strengthen your brethren." (Luke 22:31 NKJV)

**He prayed before meals.** The Bible doesn't record the specific words that Jesus prayed before eating, only that He did, as evidenced in this reference: "And He took bread, gave thanks and broke it, and gave it to them, saying, 'This is My body which is given for you; do this in remembrance of Me.'" (Luke 22:19 NKJV)

"The fact that giving thanks is mentioned does suggest that it is important for us—it was an integral part of Jewish culture at the time," says Dr. Dodd.

***Sometimes He prayed all night.*** And this extraordinary devotion sets an example for all of us, writes Spurgeon. "I do not think that we are bound to pray long as a general rule. I am afraid, however . . . most Christians are short enough, if not far too short, in private worship."

***He gave God thanks and glory when He prayed.*** "I thank You, Father, Lord of Heaven and Earth, that You have hidden these things from the wise and prudent and have revealed them to babes. . . ." (Matthew 11:25 NKJV)

***He prayed for God's will.*** Before his arrest, Jesus prayed: "Father, if it is Your will, take this cup away from Me; nevertheless not My will but Yours, be done." (Luke 22:42 NKJV)

***He humbled Himself before God when He prayed.*** In the book of Matthew, Jesus "(falls) on His face, saying, 'O My Father, if it is possible, let this cup pass from Me. . . .'" (Matthew 26:39 NKJV)

***He prayed for Himself.*** "Father, the hour has come. Glorify Your Son, that Your Son also may glorify You, as You have given Him authority over all flesh, that He should give eternal life to as many as You have given Him." (John 17:1–2 NKJV)

***He prayed until the end.*** Jesus' last words before his resurrection were, "Father, into Your hands I commit My spirit." (Luke 23:46 NKJV)

***He prays for us today.*** Calling to God on our own "would be like ants speaking to humans," says Richard J. Foster, author of *Prayer.* "We need an interpreter, an intermediary, a go-between. This is what Jesus Christ does for us in his role as eternal intercessor."

"There is one mediator between God and men, the man Christ Jesus." (1 Timothy 2:5 RSV) "He opens the door and grants us access to the heavenlies, says Foster. "Even more, He straightens out and cleanses our feeble, misguided intercessions and makes them acceptable before a holy God. . . . His prayers sustain our desires to pray, urging us on and giving us hope of being heard. The sight of Jesus in His heavenly intercession gives us strength to pray in His name."

# Jesus' Prayer Instructions for Us

Jesus doesn't just serve as a role model for our prayer. He also gives us specific instructions on how to pray and what to pray for.

**He told us to pray daily.** When Jesus gave the disciples the Lord's Prayer, tucked inside was a reminder to do it daily. And not just to ask God to meet our physical needs. Among other things, He wanted us to confess our sins to Him so that we could keep our relationship close. He wanted us to constantly forgive others so that bitterness and unforgivingness wouldn't take root. And He wanted us to be on our guard against temptation and Satan.

**He told us to pray that others would know Him.** At times, Jesus was so burdened about the human suffering around Him that He sounded like a farmer short of field hands while ripe fruit hangs on the trees. "Pray the Lord of the harvest to send out laborers into His harvest." (Matthew 9:38 NKJV) In their commentary on this passage, the editors of the Life Application Bible (New King James Version) point out: "Often when we pray for something, God answers our prayers by using us. Be prepared for God to use you to show another person the way to Him."

**He told us to pray for our enemies.** It's one of the most challenging things that Jesus says about prayer. Yet it can make the difference between living a life of love or a tortured existence. In his book, Foster reveals one such prayer, found at the Ravensbruck Nazi concentration camp near the body of a dead child.

O Lord, remember not only the men and women of good will, but also those of ill will. But do not only remember the suffering they have inflicted on us; remember the fruits we bought, thanks to this suffering: our comradeship, our loyalty, our humility, the courage, the generosity, the greatness of heart which has grown out of all this. And when they come to judgment, let all the fruits that we have borne be their forgiveness.

**He told us to pray in His name.** Rather than just tacking on "in Jesus' name" at the end of our heavenly wish list, Jesus says that we can pray boldly when we are asking for His will to be done in our lives. "I say to you, whatever you ask the Father in My name

He will give you. Until now you have asked nothing in My name. Ask, and you will receive, that your joy may be full." (John 16:23 NKJV) Foster says: "To pray in the name of Jesus means to pray in full assurance of the great work Christ accomplished—in His life, by His death, through His resurrection, and by means of His continuing reign at the right hand of God the Father and praying in accord with the way and nature of Christ. It means that we are making the kinds of intercessions He would make if He were with us in the flesh."

**He encouraged us to pray with others.** "Again I say to you that if two of you agree on Earth concerning anything that they ask, it will be done for them by My Father in Heaven. For where two or three are gathered together in My name, I am there in the midst of them." (Matthew 18:19 NKJV)

**He told us to have faith when we pray.** It's not a blank check, but if our lives are in harmony with God's will and we pray with faith, Jesus suggests that amazing things can happen, according to the editors of the Life Application Bible. "So Jesus answered and said to them, "Assuredly, I say to you, if you have faith and do not doubt, you will not only do what was done to the fig tree, but also if you say to this mountain, 'Be removed and be cast into the sea' it will be done. And whatever things you ask in prayer, believing, you will receive." (Matthew 21:21 NKJV)

**He told us to pray persistently.** Jesus' parable about the persistent widow before a crooked judge reminds us that "we should pray and not give up," says Pastor David Roper, co-founder with his wife, Carolyn, of Idaho Mountain Ministries in Boise and author of *A Man to Match the Mountain* and *Psalm 23: The Song of a Passionate Heart.* "The judge flatly refused (to listen to her) at first. There was nothing in it for him. But the widow would not be put off. She kept persisting until the exasperated magistrate finally gave in."

**He told us to pray to overcome temptation.** We can't eliminate temptation entirely, but we can pray that we don't succumb to it. "Then He came to the disciples and found them sleeping, and said to Peter, 'What! Could you not watch with Me one hour? Watch and pray, lest you enter into temptation. The spirit indeed is willing, but the flesh is weak." (Matthew 26:40 NKJV)

**He told us to pray in secret.** No grandstanding for us, Jesus says. "And when you pray, you shall not be like the hypocrites. For they love to pray standing in the synagogues and on the corners of the streets, that they may be seen by men. Assuredly, I say to you, they have their reward. But you, when you pray, go into your room, and when you have shut your door, pray to your Father who is in the secret place; and your Father who sees in secret will reward you openly." (Matthew 6:5–6 NKJV)

***He told us to keep it simple.*** Lots of fancy words don't matter. "And when you pray, do not use vain repetitions as the heathen do. For they think that they will he heard for their many words. . . . your Father knows the things you have need of before you ask Him." (Matthew 6:7–8 NKJV)

***He told us to be humble.*** Jesus didn't seem to be too thrilled with people who thought that they were better than others—especially when they prayed, as we learn from this parable: "Two men went up to the temple to pray, one a Pharisee and the other a tax collector. The Pharisee stood and prayed thus with himself, 'God, I thank You that I am not like other men—extortioners, unjust, adulterers, or even as this tax collector. I fast twice a week; I give tithes of all that I possess.' And the tax collector, standing afar off, would not so much as raise his eyes to Heaven, but beat his breast saying, 'God be merciful to me a sinner!' I tell you, this man went down to his house justified rather than the other, for everyone who exalts himself will be humbled, and he who humbles himself will be exalted." (Luke 18:10–14 NKJV)

# Prayer in the Name of Jesus

## SOMETHING ABOUT THAT NAME

*C*atholics begin and end each prayer by making the sign of the cross and saying, "In the name of the Father, and of the Son, and of the Holy Spirit."

There is good reason for this. It covers all the bases. And it follows the instructions of Jesus.

Jesus says, "Very truly, I tell you, the one who believes in Me will also do the works that I do and, in fact, will do greater works than these, because I am going to the Father. I will do whatever you ask in My name, so that the Father may be glorified in the Son. If in My name you ask Me for anything, I will do it." (John 14:12–14 NRSV)

The book of Acts has examples of the disciples using Jesus' name to heal the sick. Peter is quoted as saying to a man who had been bedridden for eight years: "'Aeneas, Jesus the Christ heals you. Arise and make your bed.' Then he arose immediately." (Acts 9:34 NKJV)

Peter and John (in Acts 3:2–6 KJV), pass a crippled beggar. Peter said to him, "Silver and gold have I none; but such as I have give I thee: In the name of Jesus Christ of Nazareth rise up and walk." (Acts 3:6 KJV)

And he did.

The man ". . . went with them into the temple courts, walking and jumping, and praising God." (Acts 3:8 NIV)

Onlookers were amazed. So Peter implored of them, "Why do you stare at us as if by our own power or godliness we had made this man walk? By faith in the name of Jesus, this man whom you see and know was made strong. It is Jesus' name and the faith that comes through Him that has given this complete healing to him, as you can all see." (Acts 3:12, 16 NIV)

# In Jesus' Name

Jesus gave us the authority to use His name to ask for something. "In Jesus' name" means that we come to God in prayer solely on the merits of Jesus and His death and resurrection for our salvation and not on our own merits, says the Reverend Siang-Yang Tan, Ph.D., professor of psychology in the graduate school of psychology at Fuller Theological Seminary in Pasadena, California, and senior pastor of First Evangelical Church in Glendale, California.

We all have the authority to use Jesus' name for specific purposes outlined by Jesus in the book of Mark.

When Jesus commissioned the Apostles to go and preach the Gospel to all the world, He said, "And these signs will follow those who believe: In My name they will cast out demons; they will speak with new tongues; they will take up serpents; and if they drink anything deadly, it will by no means hurt them; they will lay hands on the sick, and they will recover." (Mark 16:17–18 NKJV)

The New Testament tells us of many blessings that we are entitled to "in Him," "in Christ," "in whom." Grab a concordance—an alphabetical listing of the key words in the Bible—and locate and mark all these blessings or list them on a sheet of paper and refer to them regularly. It is an empowering exercise that reveals just how mighty and privileged we are in His name. By one estimate, there are roughly 140 such verses.

When should we use Jesus' name in prayer? We can use it any time we wish to ask for something. We can use His name any time we wish to exercise our rights as believers, says Dr. Tan.

When else? Always. "And whatever you do in word or deed, do all in the name of the Lord Jesus, giving thanks to God the Father through Him." (Colossians 3:17 NKJV) Do everything, every day, in the name of, and for the glory of, Jesus.

# Prayer for Our Country and Our Leaders

## EXTRA HELP FOR THE PEOPLE'S PILOTS

It was the bitter winter of 1777 in Valley Forge, Pennsylvania, and the ragtag soldiers of the Revolutionary army—many without clothes, blankets, or shoes—were dying at rate of 12 a day.

In the midst of all this misery, historians say that a man named Isaac Potts wandered near the soldiers' encampment and heard someone in the distance, speaking in earnest. Approaching cautiously, he found the Commander in Chief himself, George Washington, kneeling in prayer. Motionless with surprise, Potts watched quietly until "the general, having ended his devotions, arose, and, with a countenance of angel serenity, retired to headquarters."

Amazed, Potts returned home and greeted his wife with a shout: "Sarah, my dear! Sarah! All's well! All's well! George Washington will yet prevail!"

Why are you so excited? she asked. He replied, "Thee knows that I always thought the sword and the Gospel utterly inconsistent; and that no man could be a soldier and a Christian at the same time. But George Washington has this day convinced me of my mistake."

Like General Washington, many of us earnestly pray when our country is in war or crisis. But what of the rest of the time? How many of us ask God daily to protect and heal our country? Or pray for the people who are our elected leaders?

For Christians, praying for our leaders is really an obligation, as the Apostle Paul explains to Timothy: "Therefore I exhort first of all that supplications, prayers, intercessions, *and* giving of thanks be made for all men, for kings and all who are in authority, that we may lead a quiet peaceable life, in all godliness and reverence." (1 Timothy 2:1–2 NKJV)

If we want to start following Paul's advice, there is ample opportunity. Here are some suggestions.

**Join the crowd.** There are a series of national prayer events that can help us focus our prayers for our country and leaders. Perhaps the biggest of these is the National Day of Prayer. Designated by Congress in 1952 and observed on the first Thursday in May, the National Day of Prayer has grown to include millions of people. Each year in parks, on capital and courthouse steps, in hospitals, and in churches, participants gather to pray for our leaders and for God's help against such national problems as crime, drug use, child abuse, and divorce.

There is also a youth-oriented prayer observance that's called See You at the Poles. Each September, students gather around flag poles at schools throughout the country, and adults meet at city halls, court houses, and workplaces to offer prayers for our leaders as well as our country. Young people in every U.S. state and at least 20 other countries on five continents gather in a spirit of unity to pray on the same day, making it a national and international day of student prayer.

**Add them to our list.** Another approach is to include key state, local, and national leaders on the list of people for whom we pray daily and use news reports to guide the content of the prayers that we offer for them, says the Reverend David Wigley, pastor of the First Congregational Church in Kennebunkport, Maine.

**Pick someone special.** The National Day of Prayer Task Force suggests that we adopt a single state, local, or national leader to pray for each day, and then send the leaders notes of encouragement throughout the year reminding them that we're praying for them.

**Make it specific.** Says Reverend Wigley, "I often pray that our leaders be endowed with wisdom and are obedient to God so that through their leadership, there might be peace at home and around the world. I also pray that they might govern justly and work for healing among the nations."

Leadership like that takes vision—lots of it.

"There's a verse of Scripture that says 'without vision, my people will perish,'" says Reverend Wigley. "Leaders need to have that kind of wisdom and courage, which sees beyond immediate concerns to the whole family of God. And if they don't have that kind of vision, we need to pray that they get it. God is the only source for that."

According to the National Day of Prayer Task Force, President Abraham Lincoln said as much: "I have been driven many times to my knees by the overwhelming conviction that I had nowhere else to go. My own wisdom, and that of all about me, seemed insufficient for that day."

For more information on the National Day of Prayer and related resources, write the National Day of Prayer Task Force, P.O. Box 15616, Colorado Springs, CO 80935–5616. If you would like materials to organize a See You at the Poles activity, write to the National Network of Youth Ministries South Region, P.O. Box 60134, Fort Worth, TX 76115.

# Prayer
# with Others

## "Wherever Two
## or Three Gather . . ."

How may we pray with others? Let us count the ways.

*In agreement.* We may find someone or several people to join us in a prayer of agreement.

*In unison.* We can gather in chorale or liturgical, responsive prayer.

*In joyful praise.* At a praise and worship rally or service, we can turn to prayer.

*When separated.* The distance does not matter. We can ask a relative or one friend or several to pray for and with us about something, even at a particular time each day.

*With a computer.* On the Internet, there are prayer pages and prayer chains where anyone may post prayers or prayer needs.

*In an audience.* We can pray with head bowed, sitting or standing in silence while a leader prays aloud.

*Aloud in a group.* This is a common Pentecostal form of praying in which all individuals pray their own individual prayers at once.

***In silence.*** While sitting or standing, we can be one with a group engaged in worshipful silence.

***With a rosary.*** Yes, even the rosary may be done as a shared activity, if we and our friends take turns leading the prayers and responding.

The Apostle Paul exhorted the early church to make time for assembling together to "encourage one another and build each other up . . ." (1 Thessalonians 5:11 NIV) and to "spur one another on toward love and good deeds." (Hebrews 10:24 NIV)

The mutual encouragement and support is one of the great advantages of praying with others, says the Reverend Paul F. Everett of Pittsburgh, a Presbyterian minister at large with the Peale Center in Pawling, New York, and executive director emeritus of the Pittsburgh Experiment, a national and international ministry to the business and working communities.

When should we do it? When we need support from others; when we need sympathy, empathy, or condolence; when we need to share intimate needs; or when we need to confess weaknesses or unburden our hearts and minds, says Reverend Everett.

Some say that praying with others intensifies the effect of the prayer. Reverend Everett says that shared prayer stirs and builds our faith. Jesus puts it simply: "For where two or three are gathered together in my name, there I am in the midst of them." (Matthew 18:20 KJV)

# Nurture a Shared Prayer Life

How can we increase the amount of time that we pray with others?

- Attend a regularly held prayer breakfast or prayer group.
- Let it be known among friends and acquaintances that we are always available for prayer.
- Participate in a prayer chain on the Internet.
- Attend praise rallies and services.

Praying with others imparts a richness to prayer life that it otherwise would lack. As Paul says, "When you come together, everyone has a hymn, or a word of instruction, a revelation, a tongue or an interpretation. All of these must be done for the strengthening of the church. . . . you can all prophesy in turn so that everyone may be instructed and encouraged." (1 Corinthians 14:26, 31 NIV)

Numerous studies have found that there are health benefits gained from the sense of community that religious activities such as group prayer foster in those who regularly do them, points out religion and health researcher and physician Harold G. Koenig, M.D., director of the Center for the Study of Religion, Spirituality, and Health at Duke University Medical Center in Durham, North Carolina.

For more information, see Prayer of Agreement (page 44).

# Prayer of Petition

## ASK AND YE SHALL RECEIVE

*N*o prayer is more common than the prayer of petition, says the Reverend Rowland Croucher, doctor of ministry, an evangelist in Healthmont, Victoria, Australia, and director of John Mark Ministries in Melbourne. It's our way of asking God for something—an action, a possession, a state of being. "Dear Lord, please make this _____ (fill in the blank) happen." "Dear Lord, please give me this _____ (fill in the blank)." These are examples of prayers of petition.

Asking is the most common type of prayer, and asking prayers are referred to 30 times in the New Testament, according Dr. Croucher. Of course, it's okay to ask God for things. We should not view God only as a Mr. Fix-It, however, and seek Him only when we have a need, he says. That would not be a mature relationship. As with any father, He wants His children to enjoy his company and presence every day, not just Christmas morning.

## How to Get Results

When should we use prayers of petition? When we have a legitimate need. But how do we know if we are asking according to His will? By following a few simple guidelines.

**Check the motive:** "You ask and do not receive, because you ask amiss, that you may spend *it* on your pleasures," explains Jesus' brother, James, a leader of the Jerusalem church, in his letter to Christian Jews residing outside Palestine. (James 4:3 NKJV) His message, simply, is this: When approaching God, don't be selfish, and don't focus solely on your own pleasures, as a hedonist would.

"A selfish purpose in prayer robs prayer of power," writes nineteenth-century evangelist R. A. Torrey in his book *How to Pray*. Torrey, a graduate of Yale Divinity School and the first superintendent of the Moody Bible Institute, also writes: "Very many prayers are selfish. . . . These may be prayers for things for which it is perfectly proper to ask, for things which it is the will of God to give. But the motive of the prayer is entirely wrong . . . The true purpose of prayer is that God may be glorified in the answer. If we ask any petition merely to receive something to use for our pleasure or gratification, we 'ask amiss' and should not expect to receive what we ask."

**Ask in Jesus' name.** Jesus told us to. Torrey and others teach that this doesn't just mean to add the phrase "in Jesus' name" to the prayer but to ask on the grounds of the merit of Christ and his atoning work on the cross.

**Find supporting Scripture.** "If, when I pray, I can find some definite promise in God's Word and lay that promise before God, I know that He hears me. . . . that I have the petition that I have asked of Him," writes Torrey.

It is said by some Bible teachers that God made 7,000 promises in the Bible. The Apostle John put it this way: "This is the confidence we have in approaching God: that if we ask anything according to His will, He hears us. And if we know that He hears us—whatever we ask—we know that we have what we asked of Him." (1 John 5:14–15 NIV)

Consider these words of J. Kennedy MacLean, quoted by nineteenth-century lawyer-turned-preacher Edward M. Bounds in *Purpose in Prayer*.

> I do not mean that every prayer we offer is answered exactly as we desire it to be. Were this the

case, it would mean that we would be dictating to God, and prayer would degenerate into a mere system of begging. Just as an earthly father knows what is best for his children's welfare, so does God take into consideration the particular needs of His human family, and meets them out of His wonderful storehouse. If our petitions are in accordance with His will, and if we seek His glory in the asking, the answers will come in ways that will astonish us and fill our hearts with songs of thanksgiving. God is a rich and bountiful Father, and He does not forget His children, nor withhold from them anything which it would be to their advantage to receive.

# Prayer of Praise and Worship

## SHOWING GRATITUDE TO GOD

*I*t's not hard to praise God when the sky is blue and the grass is green and all is right in the world.

But let the first raindrop fall, or let the leaves turn brown, and we're more likely to shake our fists at Heaven than give God praise.

Yet the *Eerdmans Bible Dictionary* says that "praise is regarded by the Bible as the response due to God from all creation because of his majesty and saving actions . . . (and) the dominant characteristic of true piety." In fact, glorifying God is such an ingrained and important part of the Christian faith that in the Psalms alone, the word *praise* is used 132 times out of 150 chapters—almost enough for one in every Psalm.

The irony is that once we do give glory and honor to God through prayer or song, our minds are lifted off our pain and heartaches, and often, they seem tiny in comparison, says Brian J. Dodd, Ph.D., professor of philosophy at Asbury Seminary and director of the Share Jesus Ministry, both in Wilmore, Kentucky, and author of *Praying Jesus' Way*.

As the Reverend Charles Spurgeon, nineteenth-century English pastor, observes about the worship of King David: "It is almost always the case that David by the fire of prayer warms himself into praise. . . ." David "begins low, with many a broken note of complaining, but he mounts and glows, and, like the lark, sings as he ascends."

It seems that David was on to something. One of the best ways to begin to develop a feeling of praise and worship toward God is by starting small. "We learn about the goodness of God not by contemplating the goodness of God but by watching a butterfly," says Richard J. Foster, author of *Prayer*. Regularly watching birds, ducks, and squirrels and the leaves on trees blowing in the wind—"tiny pleasures"—draws us beyond them to "the Giver of pleasures. As this happens, thanksgiving and praise will flow naturally in their proper time," he says.

It also helps if we can develop an attitude of gratitude about the good things in our lives. What are the things that we truly love about our lives? Our spouses? Our backyard gardens? The time that we spend each summer at our cabins? "Try to live one day in utter thanksgiving. Balance every compliment with ten gratitudes. Every criticism with ten compliments," Foster suggests.

Here's how to put praise and worship into our prayer lives.

**Do like David.** The Psalms are probably the best examples of how prayer can help us release praise and worship, even that which is trapped within our mourning. Consider Psalm 51, written after Nathan the prophet confronted David about his affair with Bathsheba. As Reverend Spurgeon points out, in a matter of a few lines, David moves from "Have mercy upon me, O God" (Psalm 51:1 NKJV) and "Create in me a clean heart, O God" (Psalm 51:10 NKJV) to "O Lord, open my lips, and my mouth shall show forth Your praise." (Psalm 51:15 NKJV)

**Work in a worship song.** Is it any wonder that most church services begin with songs of praise and worship? Nothing fires our praying time quite like song, says Foster. But even if we don't have a hymn book handy, we can always turn to the Psalms. Many of them are meant to be sung as well as read and are so noted in most Bibles.

And we're in good company when we sing the Psalms; Jesus did the same with his disciples, says Dr. Dodd.

**Get into the A.C.T.S.** One of the early church fathers, a second-century teacher from northern Egypt named Origen, is said to have studied the Lord's Prayer and identified four areas that it covers: praise, thanksgiving, confession, and petition. Today, this is known as the A.C.T.S. prayer model, for adoration, confession, thanksgiving, and supplication. The idea is that by spending our prayer time first adoring God, then confessing, then giving Him thanks, and, finally, humbly making our requests, we'll naturally incorporate praise (thanksgiving) and worship (adoration) into our prayer time.

**Pray Jesus' way.** Given as a guide for praying by Jesus Himself, the Lord's Prayer devotes 2 lines ("Our Father in Heaven, hallowed be Your name," and "For Yours is the kingdom and the power and the glory forever") to deliver praise and worship. Whether we repeat the Lord's Prayer from memory or use it as a model to address our specific needs, praying this way will put praise on our lips, says Dr. Dodd.

# *Private Prayer*

## Just between Us and God

*M*any people worship God for an hour each week, perhaps from 11:00 A.M. to noon on Sunday. And they get a little antsy if the service runs past noon because that means that people from the other churches will beat them to the restaurants.

Nothing is wrong with worshipping God in church, but God does expect more than that. He expects us to worship all week long. Jesus says, ". . . seek first the Kingdom of God." (Matthew 6:33 NKJV) He puts that ahead of worrying about life's basics, like food and clothing: ". . . seek first the Kingdom of God," Jesus says, ". . . and . . . these things shall be added to you." (Matthew 6:33 NKJV).

God doesn't want us to make a big public to-do of being oh-so-holy; He wants intimate relationships with us. The only reward for people who make a show of being super-religious is the audience and attention that they attract, says Jesus: ". . . they love to pray standing in the synagogues and on the corners of the streets, that they may be seen by men. Assuredly, I say to you, they have their reward." (Matthew 6:5 NKJV)

If we expect a rich communion with God and expect our prayers to be heard and answered, we must develop close, personal, and private relationships with Him, Jesus says. He says that if we make a practice of praying in private and in secret, God will reward us openly.

## Take God Everywhere

The King James Version of the Bible quotes Jesus as telling us to go into the "closet," close the door, and pray in secret. (Matthew 6:6 KJV) But Jesus does not mean that we are to serve God only in secret, says the Reverend Edward M. Bounds, nineteenth-century lawyer-turned-preacher.

In his book *Purpose in Prayer*, Reverend Bounds writes: "We must do God's will in our lives if we would have God's ear in the closet. We must listen to God's voice in public if we would have God listen to our voice in private. God must have our hearts out of the closet, if we would have God's presence in the closet. If we would have God in the closet, God must have us out of the closet. There is no way of praying to God, but by living to God. The closet is not a confessional, simply, but the hour of holy communion and high and sweet intercourse and of intense intercession."

No, Jesus didn't mean that we should pray only in private. "Public prayer together in church and in the home are also crucial for strengthening church and family life," says the Reverend Siang-Yang Tan, Ph.D, professor of psychology in the graduate school of psychology at Fuller Theological Seminary in Pasadena, California, and senior pastor of First Evangelical Church in Glendale, California.

## When, Why, and How Long?

Daily, regularly, we should pray privately to God—and not just when we are in crisis or have pressing needs, most Christian faith leaders agree. When should we worship with God privately? Anytime, day or night.

We can set a regular time and place, but we should be prepared to meet God in private anywhere, anytime, stresses the Reverend Norvel Hayes, charismatic faith minister and director of New Life Bible College in Cleveland, Tennessee. Don't let a schedule create pressure and resentment. Make worship and prayer a way of living, he advises. How long should we spend in private prayer? Since God doesn't wear a watch, any length of time that feels comfortable is all right, says Reverend Hayes.

We can approach God in private prayer when we are confused, troubled, or hurting, especially if pursuing the problem with others might only add to the difficulty. Vernon M. Sylvest, M.D., a physician with a prayer-based holistic medical practice in Richmond, Virginia, and author of *The Formula: Who Gets Sick, Who Gets Well*, suggests to his patients that every day they allot three formal prayer periods of five minutes each as a "minimal dose."

"This not only heals, it also maintains and prevents," Dr. Sylvest notes. If we're willing to be shown another perspective and we want to be free of stress emotions such as fear, guilt, grief, and anger, these emotions will be lifted from us, so that we may receive what God has for us. As stated in Jeremiah, God will reveal ". . . great and mighty things, which you do not know." (Jeremiah 33:3 NKJV)

## How to Talk to God

Any form of prayer that we choose is okay. The Reverend Rowland Croucher, doctor of ministry, an evangelist in Healthmont, Victoria, Australia, and director of John Mark Ministries in Melbourne, recommends a prayer of praise and worship. Meditation is a form of private prayer, as can be mindfulness, visualization, and silent prayer.

Some people find it helpful to have a consecrated area in their homes for private prayer, perhaps a prayer corner. They may dedicate a tabletop or wall space in their homes where they place religious mementos such as Scriptures, candles, crosses, or pictures. Wherever our secret place, Jesus says, the Father will meet us there.

A 1908 prayer book quotes St. Alphonsus as saying that we can privately pray "in every place, at home or elsewhere, even in walking and at our work. How many are there who, not having any better opportunity, raise their hearts to God and apply their minds to mental prayer, without leaving their occupations, their work, or who meditate even while traveling. He who seeks God will find Him, everywhere and at all times."

# Prayer of Release

## LEARNING TO PUT OUR
## PROBLEMS ASIDE

*M*emories. They're not just the topic for a Barbra Streisand song. Memories, whether positive or negative, have the power to affect our lives, and our health, in significant and long-lasting ways. In fact, researchers have found that festering anger and hostility are linked to heart disease. Where do those ill feelings reside? In our memories of painful and tragic incidents.

Fortunately, we have a way out of this emotional abyss. It's called the prayer of release, a potent weapon that allows us to hand our concerns over to God, removing their burden and destructive power from us once and for all.

Norma Dearing, director of prayer ministry for Christian Healing Ministries in Jacksonville, Florida, says that prayers of release have incredible power to heal. "When people are able to release the resentment and bitterness in their hearts, their physical problems often improve significantly," she says.

But this type of prayer isn't reserved solely for those who have long harbored ill feelings toward someone. We also can use it to shed ourselves of mistakes, problems, or difficulties.

How does this prayer of release work? Here's one method that Dearing offers.

• While sitting, standing, or kneeling in a comfortable position, cup your hands in front of you. (If you'd feel comfortable sharing intimate details of your life with a close friend or pastor, you can ask them to join you.)

• Say out loud the things that someone has done to trouble or upset you. These may be memories that have hurt or disappointed you. Don't justify or make excuses for the person's behavior. Instead of saying, "Dad was an alcoholic, so he couldn't spend time with me," say, "Dad was an alcoholic. He missed some important times in my life, like my graduation." (While you're trying to remember, your prayer partner can silently ask God to help you bring to mind the most damaging behaviors and incidents.)

• Visualize placing each memory or incident into your cupped hands.

• When you have difficulty remembering any more, remain silent for a few minutes, allowing time for any other associated memories to come to mind. When you feel ready, imagine handing the pile to God, who then takes them from you. Meanwhile, the prayer partner can say: "Lord, we ask you to take this pain and hurt and sorrow. Lift it from my friend's heart and spirit as you take the burden of these memories and pain." If you don't have a prayer partner, you can pray this prayer yourself.

• Repeat the entire procedure from the perspective of the person who has hurt you, this time remembering ways that you troubled or let the person down. For example: "I never went on to college. I know my father wanted me to, and it hurt him." Repeat the prayer of release.

• While symbolically lifting the other person up to the Lord, tell Jesus what the desire of your heart is for the person—what you really would like to see the Lord do in this person's life.

• Cupping your hands again, make an imaginary pile of the desires of your heart for yourself, particularly as it relates to your relationship with this person. Then state any other heart's desires for your life or relationships. Be specific. Now give all of these prayers to Jesus.

"After you've prayed this prayer, you've touched the burden, seen it, spoken it, and heard it," says Dearing.

"There's something life-changing about getting these burdens out of your body, out of your heart, and out in front of you and releasing them to God," she says.

# Prayer
## with Saints

### DRAWING ON OUR HEAVENLY PARTNERS

Do we have a prayer partner, someone we can share our personal problems with and ask to intercede for us? That's the idea behind the Catholic practice of praying with the saints. When Christians die, the theory goes, they enter the presence of the Lord and are before Him in Heaven, worshipping and praising, but also praying for the rest of us still here on Earth.

The *Catholic Prayer Book* puts it this way: "The Church militant on Earth is linked through Christ's resurrection with the Church triumphant in Heaven. We ask their help in our earthly pilgrimage so that we, too, one day, may share their glory and destiny. We pray especially for the intercession of the saints and angels whose patron name was given us in baptism."

In other words, in times of crisis or concern, Catholics pray first to God and Jesus and then with the Saints, enlisting their prayers to God in the heavenly realm, says Father Kurt Stasiak, a Benedictine priest and associate professor of sacramental and liturgical theology at St. Meinrad School of Theology in St. Meinrad, Indiana.

# The Motherly Intercessor

As the mother of Jesus and, literally, the first person to believe in Him, Mary plays a special role to Catholics the world over. Catholics pray with her, not to worship her above God or Jesus but because she has taken her place in Heaven with the rest of the saints, rooting for us and praying for our healing and salvation.

"Mary is the ultimate first-class saint," says Father Kurt Stasiak, a Benedictine priest and associate professor of sacramental and liturgical theology at St. Meinrad School of Theology in St. Meinrad, Indiana. "Saying that Mary could heal would put her on an equal footing with Christ, which the church does not do, but in terms of protection, in terms of help, in terms of support, in terms of inspiration, she lived a life that was worthy of our study."

Mary is said to have appeared in Lourdes, France, in 1858, where she healed a 14-year-old schoolgirl with asthma. Subsequently, a chapel was built at Lourdes to dispense healing water. Citings of Mary and healings have also been reported in Guadalupe, Mexico, and Fátima, Portugal, among other places.

Here's a prayer with Mary called "Our Lady of Lourdes."

**Ever immaculate Virgin, Mother of mercy, health of the sick, refuge of sinners, comfort of the afflicted, you know my needs, my troubles, my sufferings; cast on me a look of pity. By appearing in the grotto of Lourdes, you were pleased to make it a privileged sanctuary, from which you dispense your favours, and already many sufferers have obtained the cure of their infirmities, both spiritual and physical. I come, therefore, with the most unbounded confidence to implore your maternal intercession. Obtain most loving mother, my requests, through Jesus Christ your Son our Lord.**

"We pray to God, and then we might stand at a shrine and remember how a saint lived his life and what God's grace can do," says Father Stasiak. "And in a spirit of companionship with them and a spirit of community or solidarity with them, we join our prayers with theirs and ask them to join our prayers with us. We have gone through the same things. Every pain or trouble is a cousin to every other pain or trouble. But above all, we share faith in God and what God can do for us."

# Praying for Special Needs

While Catholics are urged to ask their patron saints to pray with them, they can also ask for the intercession of those saints who had the same occupation, interests, careers, or challenges. Here are some examples.

cancer patients . . . . . . . . . Saint Peregrine

the bodily ill . . . . . . . . . . . Our Lady of Lourdes

the deaf . . . . . . . . . . . . . Blessed Don Luigi Orione

the dying . . . . . . . . . . . . Saint Joseph

those with eye diseases . . . . Saint Lucy

those with headaches . . . . . Saint Teresa Avila and
Saint Rita of Cascia

invalids . . . . . . . . . . . . . . Saint Roch

the mentally ill . . . . . . . . . Saint Dymphna

the despairing . . . . . . . . . . Saint Jude Thaddeus

those with throat ailments . . Saint Blase

Here is a prayer to Saint Jude the Apostle from *The Manual of Prayers.*

Saint Jude, glorious Apostle, faithful servant and friend of Jesus: The name of the traitor has caused you to be forgotten by many, but the true Church invokes you universally as the Patron of things despaired of. Pray for me, that finally I may receive the consolations and the succor of Heaven in all my necessities, tribulations, sufferings, particularly, (*here, make your request*), and that I may bless God with the Elect throughout eternity. Amen.

If we aren't comfortable asking saints to pray with us, we can always pray the prayers of the saints, says Father Stasiak, like this one, "Evening Prayer of Saint Augustine."

Watch, Lord, with those who wake or weep tonight. Give the angels and saints charge over those who sleep. O Lord Jesus Christ, tend Your sick ones, rest Your weary ones, bless Your dying ones, soothe the suffering ones, pity all the afflicted ones, shield the joyful ones, and all for Your love's sake. Amen.

# Silent Prayer

## SHHH . . . GOD'S TALKING

The Sacred Silence. Catholic monks teach it. Quakers know all about it. The Bible blesses it. Nearly every world religious tradition respects it. It is in the silence, some say, that we are most likely to hear God talking. It is in the silence that we connect most powerfully with the nudgings of the Holy Spirit. "Be still and know that I am God," instructs the Lord. (Psalm 46:10 KJV)

Knowing God in the silence, or practicing the presence, as seventeenth-century French Carmelite Friar Brother Lawrence put it, can take many forms. A powerful form is to quiet the mind, turn to the Spirit of God within, and wait for God to provide inspiration, revelation, a new perception, a sense of comfort, or otherwise make His presence known. But there is more to silent prayer than the process of waiting on God. And simply speaking a prayer in our minds, but not aloud, is another form of silent prayer.

When should we use silent prayer? Whenever we are seeking an answer, when we are confused, when we are seeking direction or inspiration, or when we just wish to experience the peace of God. How? Here's one way, according to Christian psychiatrist and theologian Paul Meier, M.D., co-founder of New Life Clinics, the largest provider of Christian-based counseling in the United States, and author of more than 60 best-selling Christian self-help books. If we're seeking an answer or solution, we can take the problem or question to God, then "listen quietly for his answer to come to us in our stillness," he advises.

When else can we use silent prayer? When prayer aloud is inappropriate or inopportune, such as when eating in a restaurant with boisterous friends who do not say grace. We can silently offer gratitude to God before or anytime during our meals. We can pray with our eyes open or closed.

We can offer silent prayer or silently call upon God anytime when facing a frightening, intimidating, or otherwise difficult situation in an environment where religious behavior would not be appreciated or understood. We can offer silent prayer anytime we like without seeming pious or overly religious, says Dr. Meier. No one needs to know. Silent prayer is between us and God.

Quakers teach that silent prayer need not be a solo activity—that there is much power in gathering with others in the silence and waiting for the Spirit to move us. Often, in a Quaker worship service, after about 20 minutes of silence, people will stand and share short observations, experiences, or hymns that they feel the Holy Spirit (Inner Light, in Quaker parlance) has brought to their attention. After someone shares, the gathering returns to silence for a while so that all can let the Spirit reveal what the message holds for them.

## Entering the Silence

How can we learn to practice a contemplative or revelatory form of silent prayer, either as a solo activity or with others? If we are new to the silence, we need to be aware that even a minute of silence can seem like an eternity, says the Reverend William Wilson, a Trappist monk at the New Melleray Abbey in Peosta, Iowa. So we should start gently and extend the silent periods as we grow comfortable with them.

The first step is to quiet the mind, says Dr. Meier. This does not mean blanking the mind or emptying the mind. Rather, it involves focusing on some aspect of God's beauty and creation; a pleasing, holy, inspiring, or calming thought; or a short repetitive prayer or a prayer word.

We'll find that in the quiet, "there is a stillness; and it is a stillness that speaks," as Catholic Cardinal John Henry Newman of Oxford,

England, taught in his Easter Sunday sermon in 1839. He continued, "We know how strange the feeling is of perfect silence after continued sound. Such is our blessedness now."

The quieting focus also can be the Bible. We can take a question to the Holy Spirit and then read the Bible—any section that we are drawn to—expecting God to lead us to a verse that suggests a new perspective or answer, recommends Dr. Meier.

Catholics teach a ritualized version of this called *Lectio Divina* (Latin for "divine reading"). This involves Scripture reading, meditation, prayer, and contemplation. The initial instruction is to read Scripture slowly, not thinking about meaning at all but maintaining a prayerful and expectant state.

The *Lectio Divina* experience of enlightenment does not occur always when we undertake this prayer, says Father Wilson. If it does, a particular sentence or verse will seem to light up before our eyes or in some other way stand out from the page and impress itself upon us. When that happens, we are to read that verse over and over, memorize it, repeat it in our hearts, and meditate on it until the Holy Spirit has completely revealed the meaning that it holds for us.

For more information, see Mindfulness and Meditation (page 80).

# Prayer in the Spirit

## THE GREAT INTERCESSOR

What is praying in the Spirit?

To nearly all divisions of Christianity, praying in the Spirit means deep, inner prayer directed by the Holy Spirit. To the Pentecostals (charismatics), it also means praying in unknown tongues—using words that are not in an actual human language but instead are part of a special language that is considered a gift from the Holy Spirit. (Acts 2:4) But both those who practice speaking in tongues and those who don't do so believe that in this type of prayer, the Spirit intercedes for us in accordance with God's will, even when we do not know what God's will is. (Romans 8:26–27)

And both share the stance of the Reverend Thomas Keating, a Trappist monk at Saint Benedict's Monastery in Snowmass, Colorado, that in the presence and power of the Holy Spirit, "Christ lives in each of us as the Enlightened One, present everywhere and at all times, empowering us to experience and manifest the fruits of the Spirit, both in prayer and action."

When should we pray in the Spirit? Both camps teach that when we are confused or facing situations that we do not know how to handle or approach, we should ask the Holy Spirit to pray for us. "For we do not know what we should pray for as we ought, but the Spirit Himself makes intercession for us with groanings which cannot be uttered. Now He who searches the hearts knows what the mind of the Spirit is, because he makes intercession for the saints according to the will of God." (Romans 8:26–27 NKJV)

The Life Application Bible tells us that even when we aren't sure what words we should use in prayer, the Holy Spirit knows and prays with us and for us, and intercedes on our behalf according to the will of God. So when we are unsure of God's will or of what to pray, we can ask, "Holy Spirit, please intercede on my behalf in this matter, according to God's will," and rest assured that the Spirit will intercede.

# Trust in Prayer

---

## LEARNING TO LEAN

A young mother was struggling with the idea of trusting God to do what was best for her. So her friend posed this question: "Suppose your little Charley should come running to you tomorrow and say, 'Mother, I have made up my mind . . . I am always going to obey you, and I want you to do just whatever you think best with me. I will trust your love.' How would you feel toward him?" asked the friend. "Would you say to yourself, 'Now I shall have a chance to make Charley miserable. I will take away all his pleasures and fill his life with every hard and disagreeable thing that I can find.'"

"Oh no!" exclaimed the indignant mother. "I would hug him to my heart and cover him with kisses and would hasten to fill his life with all that was sweetest and best."

"And that is just how God will treat you if you place your trust in Him," the friend said.

As this story from *The Christian's Secret of a Happy Life* by Hannah Whitall Smith shows, we have every reason to believe that God will care for us and guide us.

Yet when the road is rough or the night is long, we all wonder: Can we really trust God? Is He truly faithful?

## Building a Sense of Trust

How do we prove ourselves faithful? Or trustworthy? By what we've done in the past. Our track records. God's track record, Christians believe, is recorded in the Bible. And as we examine the lives of the people found in the pages of Scripture, we don't see an absence of pain, heartache, or calamity. But we do see peace in the midst of pain, as in the case of Job: "Though He slay me, yet will I trust Him. . . ." (Job 13:15 NKJV)

Or courage in the midst of battle, as was David's experience. "Some trust in chariots, and some in horses; But we will remember the name of the Lord our God." (Psalm 20:7 NKJV) Or in Jesus' case, a desire to comfort others just a few days before his brutal death on a cross. "Let not your heart be troubled; you believe in God, believe also in Me." (John 14:1 NKJV)

"Romans 15:4 basically says that everything written about Job, David, or other Biblical characters was written to teach us," says Steven

## An Ultimate Prayer of Trust

Awaiting his hanging in a Nazi prison for plotting to overthrow Adolf Hitler, Dietrich Bonhoeffer wrote this prayer.

> O God, early in the morning I cry to You. Help me to pray and to concentrate my thoughts on You: I cannot do this alone. In me there is darkness, but with You there is light. I am lonely, but You do not leave me. I am feeble in heart, but with You there is help. I am restless, but with You there is peace. In me there is bitterness, but with You there is patience. I do not understand Your ways, but You know the way for me . . . Restore me to liberty, and enable me so to live now that I may answer before You and before me. Lord, whatever this day may bring, Your name be praised.

Estes, senior pastor of Community Evangelical Free Church in Elverson, Pennsylvania, and co-author of *When God Weeps*. "Even the Israelites going through the Red Sea and the desert—these occurred as examples to instruct us."

These examples also help us learn how to trust. The problem is, some of us are trusting that God will answer our prayers like some kind of celestial Santa, granting our every whim.

Obviously, we haven't read the Bible. For example, John 16:23–24 says that when we pray, we need to ask for God's will—not our own—to be done. And it may very well be that God is protecting us by not granting our desires.

"Sometimes God knows that we are praying for 'serpents' and does not give us what we ask for, even if we persist in our prayers," write the editors of the New King James Version of the Bible. "As we learn to know God better as a loving Father, we learn to ask for what is good for us, and then he grants it . . . God is not selfish, begrudging, or stingy, and we don't have to beg or grovel as we come with our requests. He is a loving Father who understands, cares, and comforts. If humans can be kind, imagine how kind God, the Creator of kindness, can be."

A word on the real meaning of kindness: While we may think "ease," "comfort" and "pleasure," God is more interested in making us the kind of people he wants us to be. As Charles Stanley, pastor of First Baptist Church in Atlanta and author of *How to Listen to God* and *The Reason for My Hope*, says, "God always calls us to live in the now, to face the present honestly and fully, to do what we can do immediately, and to trust the future to God. Hope does not lie solely in anticipating that God will give us a wonderful future and resolve all things to our good. Rather, hope lies in knowing that God is with us in the here and now, and He will impart His love and grace to us to enable us to go from minute to minute, hour to hour, day to day."

What will help us trust God more? One way is to write down our prayers, hour by hour, day by day, and then look at God's track record of answering them in our lives, suggests Pastor Estes.

King Solomon, reputed to be the wisest man who ever lived, said it like this: "Trust in the Lord with all your heart, and lean not on your own understanding; in all your ways acknowledge Him, and He shall direct your paths." (Proverbs 3:5–6 NKJV)

# *Visualization*

## MAKE A MENTAL MOVIE

*P*sychologist and best-selling author Wayne Dyer, Ph.D., published a popular book with the intriguing title, *You'll See It When You Believe It.*

Seeing it and believing it is what visualization is all about. It is a practice taught, with variations, by numerous denominations, not to mention professionals in the medical and mental health fields.

Visualization essentially means applying our God-given gift of imagination to our faith. We can use it to enhance our feelings of faith, to help some event, such as healing, come to pass, and even to strengthen our relationships. Or we can use it to discover ways to work through difficulties, to lift us above a morass of problems so we can look down and see the possibilities of a solution.

Faith-building visualization can be as simple as holding a consoling or moving image in mind while praying and meditating and waiting on the Spirit. Some people vividly picture Bible scenes. Some picture Christ on the cross, or Christ smiling, or Mother Mary, or a beautiful nature scene. Any image that represents holiness and helps us feel prayerful or worshipful is useful.

Saint Francis de Sales urged us "to imagine that Christ in His sacred humanity is gazing at us from Heaven, on all humanity, on Christians who are His special children, but especially on us when we are in prayer."

Teachers of visualization suggest that the practice makes our prayer lives more real to us and can help strengthen our faith. Some ministries teach that if we visualize our prayers as being answered, it enhances our results.

# Believe That We Receive

The Word of Faith sector of Christianity, one Pentecostal (charismatic) branch, offers a teaching on visualization, based on Mark 11:23–24. It suggests that we should hold the vision of that for which we are praying in our minds and hearts as though it is real until it actually comes to pass in the worldly realm. If Jesus promised that we could do certain things, such as lay hands on the sick to bring them healing, some charismatics say, then we have the right to do these things. And we have the right to claim that the healing is accomplished in Jesus' name and to rest assured that it is being done. To say, "maybe it will happen in a few days" would be expressing doubt, wavering in faith.

Doubt, say proponents of this theology, nullifies prayers. They say, quoting the Bible, we must ". . . ask in faith, with no doubting, for he who doubts is like a wave of the sea driven and tossed by the wind. For let not that man suppose that he will receive anything from the Lord; he is a double-minded man, unstable in all his ways." (James 1:6–8 NKJV)

This teaching is considered controversial by some people. It is based on several Bible verses, such as this example of Jesus' teaching: ". . . whatever things you ask when you pray, believe that you receive them, and you will have them." (Mark 11:24 NKJV)

Other verses cited as support for this teaching include: ". . . do not look at the things which are seen, but at the things which are not seen. . . ." (2 Corinthians 4:18 NKJV); "For we walk by faith, not by sight." (2 Corinthians 5:7 NKJV); and "Faith is the substance of things hoped for, the evidence of things not seen." (Hebrews 11:1 NKJV)

"Believe that you have received" does not mean we deny that circumstances are the way they are, explains Frederick K. C. Price, Ph.D., in his book *How Faith Works*. Instead, says Dr. Price, who is pastor of the more than 18,000-member Crenshaw Christian Center in Los Angeles, it means that we ignore the way they are and look through "the eye of faith." That is, we believe, act, think, and talk as though our prayers have been answered.

## Prayer Removes Growths

Full-gospel faith minister Norvel Hayes of Cleveland, Tennessee, insists, as do many Pentecostal (charismatic) teachers in the Word of Faith sector of Christianity, that if we truly believe what we are praying about, it will come to pass. He tells about his daughter who had 42 "boils, knots, and ugly warts" on her hands and body. They had been surgically removed once and then had grown back. So, as Reverend Hayes recounts in *Divine Healing*, he turned to God for help.

He cursed the warts and thanked God in Jesus's name for removing them. Every time he thought of it, he thanked God for removing those warts. He says that within a couple of weeks, he had thanked God thousands of times. "Thank you, Lord , for removing all the knots and warts from my daughter's body, in Jesus' name."

His daughter was beginning to get annoyed. "But look at me!" she said, holding out her hands. "The knots are still there."

"No," said Reverend Hayes, "I don't see anything except new hands. I'm looking through the eyes of faith."

After a month of praying, the warts, which had plagued his daughter for years, suddenly began vanishing, one by one, never to return, writes Reverend Hayes.

## Prayerize, Picturize, Actualize

The late Reverend Dr. Norman Vincent Peale, author of *The Power of Positive Thinking*, taught that we could invigorate our lives through prayerful visualizing. He recommended a formula for vibrant prayer: prayerize, picturize, actualize. Here's how it works.

***Prayerize.*** Hold a conversation with God throughout the day. Talk as with a friend. Discuss any matters that need resolution. Fill daily life with prayer.

***Picturize.*** Give the problem to God and visualize it as successfully solved. Hold that picture of success in mind day in and day out.

In the meantime, do all that is for possible diligent, intelligent, resourceful beings to achieve success in the matter.

***Actualize.*** When we invoke God's power and give ourselves fully to our basic wishes, what we have prayed about and pictured comes to pass, sometimes in the strangest ways.

There is much strength in visualization, Dr. Peale taught. Psychologists know, he said, that people who picture themselves as failures tend to fail, and people who picture themselves as successful tend to succeed. Why not employ God's help in the process?

# Visualize Love and Forgiveness

We know that we are to forgive and love one another, as Jesus commands. There are times, though, when we just aren't sure how to do it. Those are times when we can use visualization, says Vernon M. Sylvest, M.D., a physician with a prayer-based holistic medical practice in Richmond, Virginia, and author of *The Formula: Who Gets Sick, Who Gets Well.* Here's how Dr. Sylvest suggests using visualization to help communicate forgiveness and love.

1. Look at the person and mentally acknowledge the intent to love him and see him as innocent. Ask the Holy Spirit to envelop us in love to bring love and peace to the person.

2. Affirm, mentally, a statement like "I trust and love my brother with whom I am one."

3. Focus on the emotion of love.

4. Visualize love—perhaps as a light—emanating from our hearts and reaching out and enveloping the person.

"Sometimes I visualize the person as a small child in need of love. And I mentally visualize myself holding them in my arms as you might imagine God holding his Son," says Dr. Sylvest.

Practicing this can create immediate and amazing changes in how people respond to us, explains Dr. Sylvest. "It's a vertical connection between me and God, combined with the horizontal connection between me and the individual, and they really feel it."

# Prayer for God's Will

## LEARNING TO LISTEN

Should I take this job?"

"Is this the person I should marry?"

"What is God's will for my life?"

What *is* God's will? This is one of the most common questions we ask, and it's often one of the hardest to answer.

Some of us longingly wish for the direction that God provided in the Old Testament, where He guided the Israelites out of Egypt with a cloud to follow by day and a pillar of fire by night. "Even if we don't have wonders from Heaven and someone named Moses to help us get around, God hasn't abandoned us in our decision making," says the Reverend Steven Estes, senior pastor of Community Evangelical Free Church in Elverson, Pennsylvania, and co-author of *When God Weeps*. "In fact, when we apply the following principles, one after another, we find something remarkable: God does us the honor of requiring us to think things out, while simultaneously making available His own infinite wisdom."

**Learn from the past.** The Bible itself provides specific stories and examples that make clear some of God's guidelines for our lives. For example, we see that He demands that we avoid sexual immorality, that we love our neighbors, that we follow the Ten Commandments—in other words, be holy: ". . . present your bodies a living sacrifice, holy, acceptable to God, which is your reasonable service. And do not be conformed to this world, but be transformed by the renewing of your mind. . . ." (Romans 12:1–2 NKJV)

Theologians call this God's preceptive will, and it's not optional for Christians, says Pastor Estes. "When the Bible mentions God's will, it's speaking of precepts—commands—that God has laid down."

So if what we want to do conflicts with something in Scripture, we're certainly on the wrong track.

**Meditate on the Word.** Sometimes the key to God's will lies buried in the Bible—in places where it takes some mental mining to dig it out. That means we need to ponder it, study it, and really pour over it, says Pastor Estes. "It's easy to let our eyes skim really fast over passages," he says. What we should be doing is contemplating it the way David did. Throughout the Psalms, he says, "I meditate on your words." True meditating as David meant it "is a declining art, because it takes time and reflection and study," says Pastor Estes.

How is this done? Well, if we're trying to figure out whether we should marry that special someone, we could study all the verses that deal with marriage—and those describing marriages that have gone awry—to get a sense of God's will. Or if we're considering starting a business or changing careers, we could look at those that deal with work and the special gifts or talents that God has given each of us. And so forth.

**Listen to the Holy Spirit.** Sent to live inside Christians, the Holy Spirit is said to lead and enlighten us, principally by reminding us when we're messing up and helping us understand how Scripture applies to our specific situations.

But what form does that directing take? It's often described as a "still small voice" (1 Kings 19:12 NKJV) that we learn to recognize over time. Jesus puts it this way: "My sheep hear My voice, and I know them, and they follow me." (John 10:27 NKJV)

The Reverend David Wigley, pastor of the First Congregational Church in Kennebunkport, Maine, says that when he's trying to discern God's will on a matter that he has little time to ponder, he simply prays: "Guide me Dear God, and by your Holy Spirit, give me the wisdom I need for what I should do or say."

"If we strive to be open to the guidance of the Holy Spirit and just offer that brief kind of prayer, then the Holy Spirit comes, and the guidance is there. And it's always beyond my own personal wisdom," says Reverend Wigley.

That guidance will never violate teaching found in the Bible. It may very well come from it. "I heard someone say long ago that if we are ignorant of God's Word, we will also be ignorant of God's will, and that is true," observes the Reverend Billy Graham in *Billy Graham: The Inspirational Writings*. "At the same time, when we are open to His will, we find He also will direct us through circumstances and through the inner promptings of the Holy Spirit. But that directing is never in conflict with the written Word of God."

**Pay attention to events around us.** Although often overlooked in our decision making, everyday events can speak volumes about our situations, says Pastor Estes. For example, we consider hiring a talented job candidate to quickly fill a spot on an important team project, all the while ignoring clues that the person is moody and temperamental and doesn't get along well with others. Do we really need writing in the sky to figure out that this isn't going to work?

Jean Pierre de Caussade, a priest who lived between 1675 and 1751, put it this way: "You speak to us in particular through particular events, as they occur moment by moment. But instead of hearing Your voice, instead of respecting events as signals of Your loving guidance, people see nothing else but blind chance and human decision . . . Teach me dear Lord, to read clearly this book of life."

Charles Stanley, pastor of First Baptist Church in Atlanta and author of *How to Listen to God* and *The Reason for My Hope*, agrees. "Thus, in everything God allows in our lives, we must always look for His fingerprint. We must listen for the voice of God in every sound."

**Get some wise counsel.** Whether it's a pastor, Christian counselor, a trusted friend, or, better yet, all three, the Bible advises over and over again that when we're trying to discover God's will, we need to get input from others whose opinions we trust and respect. "Where there is no counsel, the people fall; But in the multitude of counselors there is safety." (Proverbs 11:14 NKJV)

## Prayer for Guidance

Lord, grant that I may always allow myself to be guided by you, always follow your plans, and perfectly accomplish your holy will. Grant that in all things, great and small, today and all the days of my life, I may do whatever you may require of me. Help me to respond to the slightest prompting of your grace, so that I may be your trustworthy instrument, for your honor. May your will be done in time and eternity—by me, in me, and through me. Amen.

—*Saint Teresa of Avila*

**Spend some time alone.** The night before He made one of the biggest decisions of His ministry—choosing the disciples—Jesus spent the entire night on a mountain praying. Now there's no guarantee that the correct answer is going to pop out of the silence. But once we have studied what the Scripture has to say about a situation and listened for the Holy Spirit's guidance, spending time alone allows us time for prayer without distraction. We don't need to fly to a deserted island; any quiet place will do. And if we're distracted as we pray, we can read a Psalm or simply praise God for a time until we refocus, suggests Pastor Stanley.

## Let God Point Out a Path

Once our study, our meditation, and our other work is complete, we can ask God's help in reaching a decision. Pastor Estes uses this prayer.

Lord, You haven't promised to whisper guidance in my ear. But You do promise to give me wisdom for these

decisions I have to make, these shots that I have to call.
Please keep Your promise by steering my thinking in the
right direction. And let Your will be done.

If we feel restless or have a hard time sleeping after we make our
decisions, it may be the Holy Spirit's way of letting us know that
we've come to the wrong conclusion about God's will for us. "On the
other hand, a deep sense of peace will often confirm if our decisions
are the right ones, especially if it's a tough decision," suggests Pastor
Estes.

What happens if we go ahead and do what we think we were
supposed to do and things still get fouled up? "If it isn't precisely
what He desires for you to do, He'll open another door for you and
move you into the precise position," says Pastor Stanley.

# The Lord's Prayer

## THE ORIGINAL HOW-TO INTERCESSION

f we could pick the expert of our dreams for some one-on-one instruction on how to create a really impressive dessert, would we choose Julia Child? How about Martha Stewart to help redecorate the old homestead? To have a deep and meaningful prayer life, look no further than Jesus and the Lord's Prayer. Perhaps the most quoted words in the Christian tradition, the Lord's Prayer is the one Jesus recommended when the disciples asked him how to pray.

Forget the fact that we all have the tendency to say these sacred words with as much depth and feeling as we might use to read the back of a cereal box. If we can get past reciting it mindlessly, the Lord's Prayer has the power to change our lives and the lives of others.

"When we survey the four Gospels, it becomes apparent that the Lord's Prayer compacts Jesus' teaching about prayer and his personal example of praying," says Brian J. Dodd, Ph.D., professor of philosophy at Asbury Seminary and director of the Share Jesus Ministry, both in Wilmore, Kentucky, and author of *Praying Jesus' Way*. "When we emulate Jesus' example and obey his inspired teaching, we release incredible spiritual power and vitality in our own praying. Praying Jesus' way is the only way to pray."

"To me, there's a difference between saying the Lord's Prayer and praying the Lord's Prayer," says the Reverend Steve Harper, Ph.D., vice president and dean of Asbury Theological Seminary in Orlando, Florida. "Both are valid, in my judgment, but I feel like I'm praying the Lord's Prayer when I let the words come alive."

## Where It All Began

Two passages of Scripture, Matthew 6 and Luke 11, contain accounts of Jesus sharing the Lord's Prayer with his disciples for the first time. But it is Luke's version that suggests the disciples raised the question in the first place. "Now it came to pass, as He was praying in a certain place, when He ceased, that one of his disciples said to Him, 'Lord, teach us to pray, as John also taught his disciples.' (Luke 11:1 NKJV) So He said to them, 'When you pray, say:'

Our Father in Heaven,
Hallowed be Your name.
Your Kingdom come.
Your will be done
On Earth as it is in Heaven.
Give us day by day our daily bread.
And forgive us our sins,
For we also forgive everyone who is indebted to us.
And do not lead us into temptation,
But deliver us from the evil one.

    *—Luke 11:2–4 NKJV*

The version in Matthew adds:

For Yours is the kingdom and the power and the glory forever. Amen.

    *—Matthew 6:13 NKJV*

What was it about Jesus that led the disciples to ask him how to pray, anyway? Probably the power of his prayer life, says Dr. Harper.

"You only ask for something when you don't think you have it. If they had been satisfied by their prayer lives or thought that theirs was as good as His, they wouldn't have had reason to ask. But I think they saw something in His praying. It might have been the tone of His voice or the words that He used. Maybe even the look in His eyes," he says.

Not only that, but sharing a prayer was one of Jesus' duties as a rabbi. "In the giving of the prayer, a rabbi established a kind of communal relationship, not in competition and exclusiveness, but a sense of identity with the people who followed him," says Dr. Harper.

In fact, in some ways, the Lord's Prayer is like a Jewish prayer of the period called the Eighteen Benedictions, says Dr. Dodd. Among the similarities: Both were used as an outline for praying, and the wording was flexible. The semblance ends when it comes to familiarity, however: No other prayer has come close to gaining the same acceptance or recognition. "It's the best known Christian prayer of all time," he says.

But of all Christian denominations, few incorporate the Lord's Prayer into their worship as frequently as Catholics. "How important is it to us? It's everything," says the Reverend John Buckel, Ph.D., a Roman Catholic priest of the Archdiocese of Indianapolis, associate professor of Scripture at St. Meinrad School of Theology in St. Meinrad, Indiana, and author of *Free to Love*. Priests, nuns, and other religious leaders, he says, pray the Lord's Prayer at least three times a day during the Liturgy of the Hours (a prayer time for priests and nuns and other Catholic religious leaders held morning, noon, and night). "We also pray it every Mass, and I think that many Catholics pray the Lord's Prayer before they go to bed."

## Giving Life to Familiar Words

Does the sheer repetition ever take away from its meaning? "Absolutely not. Certain words don't become tiresome; they become more important, just like the words *I love you*. You might hear that every day of your life and it never gets old," says Reverend Buckel.

Many Protestants and Catholics have a slightly different view of how to pray the Lord's Prayer. "When we pray the Lord's Prayer word for word, we need to note that this is the beginning place of Jesus' instruction on prayer. This is not all that Jesus taught about prayer, nor did He suggest that we should limit our prayers to a recitation of the Lord's Prayer. Rather, as a good teacher, Jesus provided a solid beginning place for learning to pray Jesus' way," says Dr. Dodd.

At the same time, we should also resist the temptation to focus so much on what we're getting out of the Lord's Prayer and instead think about what we might give to God as an act of worship and communication, says Reverend Buckel. "In fact, when prayer becomes boring and we don't always get that zing, that's when our prayer lives can really deepen, because then we pray not for just what we get out of it but also for the love of God alone.

"Think of a married couple. As the years go by, the thrill is not there. That's the time when they can deepen their love. You remain married and keep on doing things for the benefit of the other and not just for what you get out of it. Prayer is basically communication," says Reverend Buckel. You might not always feel like praying, but that's when praying is particularly important. Because your faith tells you that it's important. "And God gets something out of it, too." Worship.

## Digging Deeper into the Words

An exploration of the Lord's Prayer shows that the deeper we dig, the more we find to nourish our souls. Take the first line: 'Our Father in Heaven' as an example. Jesus seems to be saying that we can have a level of intimacy with God as close, if not closer, than with our earthly fathers. But it's a slightly more respectful tone than the heavenly "daddy" references made popular in the 1960s—"an interpretation not supported by the original texts," says Dr. Dodd.

"The image of a father in the ancient world usually carried connotations of obedience, provision, and mercy," Dr. Dodd says. "Jesus teaches us to approach God as one who loves us dearly and cares deeply about our concerns and our lives—but reverently. Because God knows us intimately, and because we have been adopted as beloved children, we are encouraged to pour out our hearts to our heavenly Father."

Also striking is the word that begins the Lord's Prayer: *Our.* "If we pay attention, it helps us understand that we never really pray alone," says Dr. Harper. "We always pray in community, even if we are by ourselves." And our prayer is added to the thousands or millions of others that people around the world are offering at that same moment, he says.

The next line, "Hallowed be Your name," immediately underscores the power and majesty of God. "Some people casually refer to God as 'the man upstairs' or 'my co-pilot.' Nobody is going to be chastised for having a folksy view of God," says Dr. Harper. "But the Jewish tradition and understanding was that if you touch the Ark of the Covenant (a sacred wooden chest that the Hebrews believed represented the presence of God), you die. This is the God, the Holy One of all creation. So even though Jesus wants to highlight the intimacy by using 'Father,' He does not want us to lose sight in our praying of who this Father is. This is the same God who said, 'Let there be light' (Genesis 1:3), and there was light."

Although we may not have considered it, 'praying for God's name to be honored, for His kingdom to come, for God's will to be done, is deep intercessory prayer," says Dr. Dodd. "There's an evangelistic nature to it, too: that his name will come to be honored, versus dishonored by those who name it and don't mean it, those who don't respect the honor of God's name because they don't know it, have another God, or worship something else."

While "Give us day by day our daily bread" is a part of the Lord's Prayer that makes us think of food, clothing, and immediate needs, it can be a special source of comfort for those of us who are so ill that we can barely make it through the day, says Dr. Dodd. "Asking for our daily bread and seeing God's provision takes on new meaning when each meal could literally be our last. By focusing narrowly on the needs of the day, with God's help we can make it through."

Forgiveness is another area that the Lord's Prayer reminds us is simply out of reach without God. ("And forgive us our sins, for we also forgive everyone who is indebted to us.") "We must do what we call horizontal forgiveness—between us and others—to receive vertical forgiveness—between us and God. He makes it very clear: If you don't forgive, you won't be forgiven," says Dr. Dodd.

Even in a day when the Devil is more often seen as a bad joke than the destroyer of lives and souls, praying "deliver us from the evil one" can have meaning. Make no mistake, the Bible says: "your adversary the Devil walks about like a roaring lion, seeking whom he may devour." (1 Peter 5:8 NKJV) Namely, us.

"Ten years ago or more I might have said, 'I don't have the need to pray for that because Jesus has already delivered us, right? And he died once for all.' Well, the evil one is chained up, but he's still barking and biting," says Dr. Dodd. "My experience in front-line evangelism has taught me that the more you are out on the front line of what God is doing, the more likely you are to be attacked by the evil one."

## Ways to Use Prayer

That we pray the Lord's Prayer sincerely, of course, is more important than how. Still, there are several ways that may make our time more meaningful—to Him and to us.

**Pray it with your kids.** The cadence and brevity of the Lord's Prayer makes it easy for kids to learn, even if they don't get it exactly right at first. "When my daughter was three, we lived in England and we were going to a British Methodist Church, so she heard and prayed the Lord's Prayer every week," says Dr. Dodd. "Of course, it was her version: 'my Kingdom come, my will be done . . .' And when she was three, we thought she really meant that."

Today, Dr. Dodd and his kids pray spontaneously most of the time, but they still offer the Lord's Prayer once or twice a week before bed. "It's probably my high time in prayer. Hearing them pray just seems to help me believe it afresh, and it sparks a new sense of appreciation in me." His kids are comfortable enough now to pray it verbatim or as an outline where they can add other prayer needs, says Dr. Dodd.

"The first time we ever prayed for others with our children, they were watching children's BBC television in the afternoon. That program gave basically the same news and images from Bosnia that the adults got, but the language was toned down. So when we prayed, 'Thy Kingdom come,' to hear my little daughter pray for the people of Bosnia with passion and tears in her eyes, I thought, 'Wow, why do we keep our kids from hearing the real news? They get it, as outrageous as it is.' And it was a life-changing thing for me."

**Pray it with a new believer.** If an adult has never prayed before, the Lord's Prayer is one of the best places to start, says Dr. Harper. "I'd meet with new believers once a week and have them commit the prayer to memory. We then might start using it together at the end of our times and then talk about the prayer once we had it down. Something like: 'Now that you know how to say it, let's think about what we're saying. What does it really mean?' It's a simple, powerful, time-honored way. It's what the disciples said: 'Lord, teach us to pray. . . .'" (Luke 11:1 NKJV)

**Pray it in church.** Who among us hasn't plodded through the Lord's Prayer in church? To make the event more meaningful to you and your congregation, why not ask your pastor, reverend, or priest if the group can pause and pray spontaneously between lines.

"When we do it in our church," says Dr. Harper, "we just say, 'We're going to bow our heads and close our eyes and walk through the Lord's Prayer together. When you hear the words *Our Father*, what does that make you want to pray about?' And then there's silence. And then somebody will say: 'Dear God, I just want to thank You that You are with me all the time. I thank that You love me as Your daughter' or 'as Your son.' And so on."

Reverend Buckel agrees that this is meaningful, saying that spontaneous prayer is "something that is encouraged in Catholic tradition—very much so."

**Pray it solo.** Ultimately, if we're going to be people of prayer, we have to pray the Lord's Prayer ourselves, says Dr. Harper. "Someone once defined meditation as thinking in the presence of God. It's a great, simple definition. And so that's the way that I use the Lord's Prayer. 'Forgive me my trespasses, as we forgive those who trespass against us.' Stopping right there and saying, 'Lord, is there anybody in the world right now in my life who is rubbing me the wrong way and may not even know it, and I just need to be more forgiving toward them?' The Lord's Prayer kicks the ball into play, and my mind and heart begin to ponder and walk around it."

**Pray it in times of crisis.** Sometimes we're so numb that the words don't come, and we just want to be held by our heavenly Father. That may be the best time of all for the Lord's Prayer. "I can't tell you how many times I have been with people when a loved one lies dying and we pray the Lord's Prayer," says Reverend Buckel. "In times of tragedy, it's such a familiar and beautiful prayer that people just naturally turn to it. The key thing is that you pray. I think that whether it's the Lord's Prayer or any prayer, the fact that you want to offer a prayer to God means everything."

# Part III

To Heal Yourself:
Focus on Forgiving
Focus on Acceptance
Focus on the Wonderful

# Prayer Prescriptions

# *Abuse*

## How to Stop Being a Victim

$\mathcal{S}$he was a successful, driven businesswoman. But she also had a terrible secret—one that damaged her relationships and even made her angry at God.

When she was a child, she had been raped by her grandfather while her parents were in the next room.

"To me, there were two kinds of abuse going on in this situation: the grandfather's sexual abuse and the parents' neglect by failing to protect her," says Charles Zeiders, doctor of psychology, a Christian psychologist and clinical coordinator of Christian Counseling Associates with offices in West Chester and Havertown, Pennsylvania, and a consultant to the neuro-behavioral unit at Riddle Hospital in Springfield, Pennsylvania. "She felt used and abandoned."

After several sessions, Dr. Zeiders, who treated the woman, recommended that they pray for her inner healing, a specific prayer where she would ask Jesus to enter into her memory of the incident. The woman agreed. And then, as they prayed, something amazing happened: The woman "experienced Jesus coming in and slipping His hand between her and her grandfather and pushing him off her," says Dr. Zeiders.

"And then, with His right hand, Jesus scooped her up, wrapped part of His clothing around her to clothe her nakedness, and tenderly cradled her," says Dr. Zeiders. After decades of pain and shame, the woman suddenly felt that "God was a protecting God and that she was worth protecting and worth being kept safe."

## Defining Abuse

Unfortunately, this concept of having value and significance is tough for most abuse victims to grasp. Whether they've been sexually, physically, or verbally abused, many have such poor self-esteem that they feel like they deserve to be treated poorly.

Nothing could be further from the truth, says Dr. Zeiders. "We are all made in the image of God. So if someone is being abused, the very first thing I'm going to think is that someone who is made in the image of God is being sinned against, and that's never okay."

But just what constitutes abuse? Daryle R. Woodward, a licensed counselor, founder, and clinical director of Colorado MOVES (Men Overcoming Violence Effectively Services) in Denver, one of the largest state-certified domestic violence treatment programs, suggests that abuse is "any treatment that negatively impacts the self-worth of another person." And that includes verbal assaults.

"They don't have to be obscenities. Even calling someone dumb, stupid, or an idiot or saying, 'I don't know why I stay married to you' can really impact someone," says Woodward. "A lot of people think that constantly hearing things like that is worse than getting slugged."

And it may be more common that we think; roughly one in four families regularly suffers from incidents of abuse.

## A Violent Struggle for Control

Charming one moment but scared, angry, violent, and sometimes downright dangerous the next—that's the world of an abuser. But what could possibly turn Mr. or Ms. Wonderful into a nasty brute? Often, the root is a fear of abandonment, says Joan Winfrey, Ph.D., professor of counseling at Denver Seminary and contributor to *Women, Abuse, and the Bible*. Abusers are scared, dependent people who cling so tightly to their relationships that they often squeeze the life out of them, she says.

As a result, a common trigger among abusive men is the feeling that they're losing power or control. Take a classic issue that causes conflict, such as child-rearing. If a couple can't agree how to discipline their child, an abusive husband won't try to negotiate or compromise. Rather, he'll assert his authority by yelling at his wife, says Dr. Winfrey. If that doesn't work, he'll use threatening gestures, call his wife names, or throw something. Failing that, he may hit her or sexually abuse her—or someone else.

As it turns out, roughly 60 percent of the men who batter their spouses will also sexually assault them. "These are angry men who feel like victims, and this is their way of gaining power, by humiliating other people," says Dr. Winfrey. "After all, sexual abuse isn't about sex; it's about power and control."

There are fewer reports of physical attacks by wives against their husbands, but verbal assaults might even be more common and include attempts to belittle their husbands in the eyes of their children. Another, more subtle way that a woman can heap abuse on her spouse is by spending so much money that it threatens the family budget.

After a sexual, physical, or verbal attack takes place, abusers often feel bad for their actions and will try to show that they're sorry—something that Woodward describes as a hearts-and-flowers routine. "He says all the words that she's been wanting to hear, and he gets really nice. All is forgotten, supposedly," says Woodward. "But the couple hasn't resolved the real issue, which is his choice to be violent, so it's just a matter of time before the tension and stress build again."

Some female victims of abuse respond by changing their behavior, hoping that the problem will just go away. "The abused wife says to herself, 'If I'm good enough or do the things that he wants me to and I don't upset him, he won't hurt me,'" says Woodward.

The problem is that the victimized spouse will never be "good enough" since that's not the true source of the difficulty. Often, the abusers "are men and women who were abused as children, and they may never have known another kind of relationship," says Dr. Winfrey.

Christian women are particularly prone to a nonconfrontational approach since some have the mistaken idea that they are supposed to endure hardship like a good soldier in their marriages. "There has been teaching from the pulpit in the past that if you will just get your own spiritual life in order and pray for your husband, God will change

# Portrait of an Abuser

Here are some of the characteristics of an abusive person, according to Daryle R. Woodward, a licensed counselor, founder, and clinical director of Colorado MOVES (Men Overcoming Violence Effectively Services) in Denver, one of the largest state-certified domestic violence treatment programs.

- Observed family violence themselves and were likely to have been abused by either or both parents
- May exhibit chemical dependency, such as alcoholism or drug use
- May have been cruel to animals and family pets
- Intolerant of and hostile toward life in general
- Cynical, judgmental, and unable to trust
- Emotionally isolated but volatile
- Rationalizes, minimizes, and denies abuse; either can't or won't empathize with the victim's pain; shows little or no remorse
- Poor relationship boundaries, such as talking at an intimate level on the first meeting or falling in love with new acquaintances
- Unable to apologize; attempts to gloss over abuse with affection and gifts
- Poor coping skills and unable to resolve conflict constructively
- Lacks social skills; has low self-esteem and self-worth and blames others for their problems
- Moves fast in relationships and pushes for quick commitment
- Gets defensive when angered
- Uses guilt to control others and may threaten suicide or homicide if spouse attempts to leave the relationship
- Uses power and control to gain advantage in relationships
- Is both manipulative and charming

him," says Dr. Winfrey. "But he probably isn't going to change without some consequences." Besides, she says, "never does God say that He expects the wife to suffer at the hands of her husband."

# Ending the Cycle

All this may seem like a pretty bleak picture. But there's a much more hopeful scenario found in the Bible for abuse victims—in people from Joseph and David to Jesus. Each was wrongly accused and abused but ultimately, restored. Or, in the case of Christ, glorified.

Like the woman abused by her grandfather, such healing is available to us if we respond to the problem with common sense, prayer, and faith. Here's how.

**Leave home.** Having an argument is one thing. They happen all the time even in the best homes. But when there's even the suggestion that women and children are in physical danger, they should leave the house to stay with a relative or a friend or at a shelter for at least a brief cooling-off period, says Woodward. Danger signs include threats against children, use of objects or weapons or threatened use of them, and threats of suicide, such as, "I'll kill myself and it will be your fault."

"Threatening suicide is a way to use power and control over another person and hold them hostage," says Woodward. "The only way that women can protect themselves is by leaving because there is no guarantee that they wouldn't get hurt." They should leave, then alert authorities that their spouse has threatened suicide so that someone can check on him. Then, if the harassment continues, reporting the violence and getting a restraining order are probably the next steps.

**Set some boundaries.** It takes courage, but setting boundaries will in some cases stop abuse before it spirals out of control. "One of our slogans is 'refuse abuse,'" says Woodward. "We have to refuse to do it, and we have to refuse to accept it."

"When someone is beating us up verbally, we should say, 'That is unacceptable to me. I deserve to be treated with dignity and respect. And I refuse to accept that kind of language from you. If you want to be in a relationship with me, that is totally unacceptable.' It's not shaming them," says Woodward, "but it's saying that this is unacceptable behavior." It's also a biblically sound concept. "If your brother sins against you, go and show him his fault. . . ." (Matthew 18:15 NIV)

**Tell church leadership.** Since one of the main functions of the church is to discipline members, making a pastor or an elder aware of the situation could help address the problem.

Today, a pastor might demand that an abuser undergo treatment or face punishment from the church. "There's been a tendency to say, 'Oh, no, this can't be happening to one of our members,' but that's changing," says Woodward. "The church could be a powerful instrument to hold abusers responsible and provide safety for victims and children, but church leaders need to be trained."

**Insist on change.** Since most states now have mandatory arrest laws for domestic violence, spending the night or a few days in jail can make most abusers feel sad. But that's not enough, says Woodward. "Anyone would feel bad when he was arrested, but I think that true repentance is sorrow for our actions, willingness to change, and, in fact, making those changes."

Possible changes include giving up drinking alcohol and refraining from reading pornography. Alcoholism has been found to increase the risk for abuse because it lowers inhibitions and impairs judgment, while pornography is thought to devalue people in the eyes of the abuser, says Dr. Winfrey.

Also, a Christian man who is fixated on ruling his home with an iron fist should adopt the attitude of servant leadership that is described in the Bible, where husbands are directed: ". . . love your wives, just as Christ loved the church . . ." (Ephesians 5:25 NIV) and told that they should ". . . love their wives as their own bodies." (Ephesians 5:28 NIV)

**Get them to a group.** At first glance, marital counseling seems like the answer to the problem of abuse between a husband and wife. It's not. "It works against the victim. If she discloses things about him, he'll use them against her later," says Dr. Winfrey. Not only that, most abusers are so manipulative that they can sometimes outsmart counselors.

Instead, Dr. Winfrey says that the preferred treatment is group therapy, "where he will be with other men who will hold him accountable." If there's no group therapy program in a nearby church, call an area domestic violence program and ask.

**Don't rush a reunion.** "Certainly, the Lord can work very quickly in changing someone, but I would be very leery of fast improvements," says Woodward. The abuser may just be disguising his feelings so that he can rejoin the family.

"There's a lot that abusers can gain by getting back. They're lonely and often paying additional living expenses." Rather than rushing back, however, it's probably best to first meet only when another person is present and then evaluate whether or not it's a good idea to resume the relationship, says Woodward. Research shows that it can take abusers between one and five years to change their ways.

**Forgive.** The Bible commands us to forgive—in other words, hate the sin and love the sinner, reminds Dr. Zeiders. "One woman I worked with desired for the man who abused her to die, so we worked on forgiving him and not requiring that a terrible thing happen to him. Eventually, she prayed, 'God, I am willing to have your Spirit of love come into this wounded place in my heart and be healed of this oppressive hatred that is messing up my body.' That prayer was like removing a barrier that stood between her and the healing power of the Spirit," he says. "When the barrier of unforgivingness was removed, the Holy Spirit rushed in and took away the burden of the hate and the hurt connected with that, and restored her."

**Pray for inner healing.** As with the woman mentioned earlier in the chapter who was molested by her grandfather, Dr. Zeiders and other counselors say that they've seen extraordinary improvement among those abuse victims who have prayed for inner healing. "Jesus is a healer and He will heal the body, but He will also heal the mind— the memories," says Dr. Zeiders.

**Consider counseling.** Whether it's guiding us through a prayer for inner healing, helping us establish healthy relationship boundaries, or changing wrong conclusions about ourselves, abuse victims generally benefit from at least a few sessions with a counselor or pastor, says Dr. Zeiders.

**Think twice about reconciliation.** Although through Christ's strength we can forgive, sometimes it's simply too dangerous to try to reconcile. "If the abuser is truly remorseful and willing to make amends, then we certainly encourage reconciliation," says Woodward. But, she adds, if our spouse is violent toward us, we have every right to break the marriage covenant and leave the abusive spouse.

# *Addictions*

—✦—

## THE PILGRIM'S ROAD TO RECOVERY

With a heart attack and a nasty recurring case of bronchitis to show for 50 years of smoking, Marge Waterbury knew that she had to quit her two-pack-a-day habit. The question was how. The best that she'd ever done over the years was stop for a few days—and then she'd started right back up again.

So she turned to God, and sometimes through tears, the Rochester Hills, Michigan, resident prayed: "I don't have the strength to do this on my own, Lord. I need Your help."

Then one morning, after eight months of fervent prayer, her craving, amazingly, was gone. Her prayer had been answered. "When I realized what had happened, I just started thanking God," says Waterbury, who has now gone for more than seven years without cigarettes.

With God's help, Waterbury kicked her habit. But there are millions more who are still struggling to overcome addictions. Consider these statistics: More than 40 percent of the U.S. adult population has been exposed to alcoholism in their families. Nearly 30 percent of Americans age 12 or older are smokers. Nearly 600,000 are heroin addicts. Whether it's tobacco, alcohol, gambling, marijuana, or even things like chocolate and soap operas, we're one addicted culture.

# The ABCs of Addiction

How do we become addicted to something in the first place? More often than not, it starts as an attempt to "self-medicate" a severe emotional problem or trauma with alcohol, drugs, or other substances, says David Stoop, Ph.D., an addictions counselor in Newport Beach, California, executive editor of *The Life Recovery Bible*, and author of *Forgiving Our Parents, Forgiving Ourselves*. For example, a child who feels unloved or unwanted might begin to smoke marijuana as a way of rebelling against his family or to get attention. Or if the child grows up watching Mom swill martinis after fighting with Dad, he may learn from her that drinking is the best way to cope. And of course, some start on the road to substance abuse after the death of a spouse or a divorce. "Instead of dealing with the reality of relationships, we learn to numb ourselves with some kind of chemical," says Dr. Stoop.

There are other factors as well. Those with a deep-seated fear of rejection have been known to turn to sexual addiction to fill their emotional voids, while people who abuse food may overeat in a desperate attempt to control at least part of their lives, says Dr. Stoop.

But while any number of emotional problems can put us on the road to addiction, emotions are only half of the story. The other is how substances such as tobacco, alcohol, or even chocolate chemically help us soothe our sorrows. As it turns out, powerful chemicals within these and other abused items find their way to receptors in our brains, often generating a feeling of euphoria that will indeed temporarily relieve stress and generally make us feel better.

In fact, some drugs create such good feelings and cravings that even the most disciplined among us would have trouble resisting if we were exposed to them. "If someone shoots you up with heroin, there is a 99 percent probability that you will become addicted to it," says Dr. Stoop. "The same thing with crack cocaine." Often, the first time someone smokes the stuff, he says, he's hooked. It's that powerful.

What's the key to knowing if we're truly addicted to something? If our desire for it becomes unmanageable. If we say, "I want to stop a certain activity or using a substance but I haven't been able to," we're addicted, says Mark Laaser, Ph.D., author of *Faithful and True*.

As time goes on and our addictions grow stronger, we develop another problem: Our bodies develop a tolerance toward what we're abusing, which means that we need more and more to make us feel "good," says Dr. Stoop.

It isn't long before our lives begin to reflect the consequences of such behavior. Depending on what we're abusing, we gain weight, lose our jobs, steal from our friends, wreck our cars or marriages, or worse. But true addicts are so enslaved physically and psychologically that they often just keep using, says Dr. Laaser. "We're talking about all kinds of social, legal, financial, and physical ramifications. Some sex addicts, for example, have been arrested and literally risk their lives having intercourse with people who have multiple sexually transmitted diseases, but they just won't stop."

"Whatever controls them is what they worship. The drug addict, the sex addict, the food addict, nothing matters but the fulfillment of the addiction. They will do anything they have to in order to maintain it," says Dr. Stoop.

# Finding the Way Back

"There's a saying that goes something like this: 'If you always do what you did, you always get what you got,'" says Charles Zeiders, doctor of psychology, a Christian psychologist and clinical coordinator of Christian Counseling Associates with offices in West Chester and Havertown, Pennsylvania, and a consultant to the neuro-behavioral unit at Riddle Hospital in Springfield, Pennsylvania. "If you keep hanging out in the bar, you're going to see yourself as kind of a pathetic addicted person who just hangs out in the bar all the time."

Instead, try these suggestions for breaking the stranglehold of addiction.

**See a doctor.** One of the most dangerous times for people addicted to alcohol or drugs is just after they have stopped abusing substances, says Dr. Stoop. "The process of detoxification is so hard on the body that it's a good idea to go to a detoxification center or have the assistance of an M.D.," he says. "They have medications not just to make the withdrawal easier but also to alleviate some of the physical danger."

**Hand it over to God.** Until they hit the wall, addicts say, "I can control this. I can manage this." But the clear message of Scripture is that "our lives are a mess and we can't manage them. The only one who can manage them is God, and we have to turn the control of our lives over to Him. That's the basic message of salvation. That's the message of Gospel. And it's the message of recovery as well," says Dr. Stoop.

**Change the scenery.** One of the subtle factors that can help keep us trapped in addiction is the twisted social acceptance of addicted friends. This can take the place of the real love and caring that we really need. "If you get a group of people together who haven't come to grips with their problems, anything goes. It's a pity party with drugs or alcohol," says Dr. Stoop. The solution is to seek out people who really care about our welfare.

**Make amends.** Take out a pencil and a piece of paper and write down the names of all the people who have been wronged and hurt by our addictive behavior. Then make atonement. That means that if you borrowed money, you need to pay it back. If you caused some damage to someone's personal property, you need to pay for it. And if you insulted someone, you need to apologize. "This is where people get stuck," says Dr. Stoop. But we have to redeem ourselves, as painful as it might be. "If this is overlooked, it can short-circuit the whole recovery process."

**Develop humility.** Making amends goes a long way in helping us develop humility. "Not shame, but humility," says Dr. Stoop. "And that means God is the one who is powerful here. I'm powerless. And I need to do what He tells me to do on an ongoing basis."

**Tell others.** "The people I see who have really licked this are those who are still in the process, still sharing the message, still helping those who are struggling," says Dr. Stoop "They never get to a place where they say, 'I have arrived; I don't need this anymore.' They may not need it anymore, but they say, 'I'm going to stay here because it continues to help me.'"

**Pray for healing.** Although Marge Waterbury doesn't have any documentation that God removed her desire for cigarettes, she's convinced that He did. And some experts say that her miracle isn't uncommon. One study that looked at 20 northern California Alcoholics Anonymous (AA) groups, for example, found that prayer helped drive out the use of alcohol. Those AA members who practiced the eleventh step in AA's 12-step program—seeking "through prayer and meditation to improve our conscious contact with God . . . praying only for knowledge of His will for us and the power to carry that out"—reported being sober longer and felt like they had more purpose in life.

"I have talked to several people who were in the advanced stages of alcohol addiction who sought out Christian prayer for being delivered from alcohol. And I am convinced from my interviews with these people that the phenomenon does occur," says Dr. Zeiders.

**Have a vision.** "Many people who are addicted have trouble understanding that God has a special calling for them, or they don't know how to pursue it," says Dr. Zeiders. "So if we give them a vision of who they really are and the things that they can do if they enter into their calling, they're going to be more likely to disengage from the activity that keeps them from it."

**Get plugged in.** A solid church, a strong 12-step program, or even going to a counselor all offer positive, chemical-free alternatives to the addictive life. "If you get people connected with a really healthy, vital church community, where they are understanding themselves as children of God rather than guys at a bar, where they are participating in things like outreach or volunteer services, where they are having a meaningful impact on society and they are playing a direct role—all of these things are tangible, practical ways to incarnate the vision and work against the addiction," says Dr. Zeiders.

**Discover true love.** Since addicts fundamentally don't believe that they're loved, many are freed when they discover that God loves and cares about them. "Providing those insights, helping the person own it and grasp it intellectually and feel it within his spirit, is going to be part of the healing," says Dr. Zeiders.

# Alzheimer's Disease

## SURVIVING A LOVED ONE'S ILLNESS

It was one of those mornings for Sharon Fish. She was trying to get her 78-year-old mother out of bed, but Pearle, typical of many people with late-stage Alzheimer's disease, didn't want to cooperate. When Fish finally managed to get her mother out of the bed, Pearle decided to sit on the floor. To make matters worse, she began striking Fish's legs with her cane.

Although her mother didn't hit her hard, Fish lost her patience. She grabbed the cane and banged it on the floor, causing it to snap in two. Immediately, Fish was horrified and ashamed of what she had done. Putting her arms around her mother, who was now laughing beside her on the floor, Fish laughed until she cried, wondering all the time if her anger and frustration would ever cause her to treat her mother like the cane.

Later, while Fish was reading her Bible, she turned to Isaiah and found a passage that she had never seen before. It said: "A bruised reed He will not break, and a smoldering wick He will not snuff out." (Isaiah 42:3 NIV) "That really spoke to me about my frustration," says Fish, "but also about God's gentleness with us."

After reading the verse, Fish says that she knew she needed to strive even harder to reach that delicate balance between firmness and gentleness with her ailing, recalcitrant mom.

## The Child Becomes the Parent

Such frustration is common among Alzheimer's caregivers. In fact, more than 80 percent report that they frequently experience high levels of stress. What's more, nearly half of all caregivers say that they experience depression, according to the Alzheimer's Association, a national information and support group based in Chicago. In another study, 20 percent said that their caregiving tasks were so frustrating and difficult that they were afraid they might hurt their parents.

No wonder: While those who have the disease gradually experience memory loss and a worsening ability to think, understand, or make decisions, they also commonly exhibit agitation, aggression, and depression and are likely to wander as the disease progresses. Giving care under these circumstances can become more a battle than a balm.

Fish, an R.N. and a Ph.D. candidate in Rochester, New York, and author of *Alzheimer's: Caring for Your Loved One, Caring for Yourself* says that the emotional stress of caring for her mother for the last 10 years of her life was far more difficult than any of the physical work required. "The role change that took place was particularly difficult," she says. "I can remember the time when she first called me 'Mom.' And then I became 'Grandma' as her dementia became worse. She actually saw me as a different person, not as her daughter anymore. I became the parent. That created a profound sadness in me. It was very difficult."

## Caring for Lillie

The Reverend Herman Riffel has had a similar experience. Although he still writes and occasionally conducts religious seminars, the Villanova, Pennsylvania, resident's biggest job now is helping care for Lillie, his beloved wife of 55 years. She has not formally been diagnosed with Alzheimer's, but she has many of the symptoms, such as severe memory loss and confusion.

Instead of childlike aggression and agitated behavior, Lillie insists on staying active. But that often means that she sets the dining room table with the wrong items. Or, she keeps the house so tidy that things that should be out are no longer where they're supposed to be, and she can't remember where she put them. "She loves to do these things and tries to be helpful, but it's frustrating sometimes—no question about it," says Reverend Riffel.

So far, Reverend Riffel's deep faith and the support of his daughter have helped him avoid the symptoms of caregiver stress. These include anger, social withdrawal, anxiety, depression, exhaustion, sleeplessness, irritability, lack of concentration, and health problems.

"We don't want to get into a situation where we're gritting our teeth about this," says Reverend Riffel. "For me, it's a matter of loving and recognizing that my wife is a wonderful person who has been very helpful to me. Now she has a disability. I need to show her my love and God's love."

Here are some other suggestions to keep our stress levels under control.

**Find faith.** In one study conducted by researchers at Indiana University School of Nursing, Alzheimer caregivers who said that their spiritual needs were being met and who attended worship services regularly reported greater levels of well-being and less stress than those whose spiritual needs were not addressed.

Fish, too, learned firsthand how big a difference faith can make. After her mother was diagnosed with Alzheimer's, she found herself angry at God, and the further she drifted from Him, the more miserable and angry she became. "It took a while, but thankfully, that wasn't a permanent condition for me," she says. "Eventually, I found a church that accepted my Mom and really reached out to me. When I moved back into a church family, I re-experienced the love of God in a very special way. He was my strength in all of this."

**Encourage family to pitch in.** Not all of us are suited to or are good at primary Alzheimer's care. But from financial assistance to carpentry, there's plenty to do, and it can make a big difference if all family members, including those out of town, help out, says Fish.

If we're reluctant to assist ourselves, says Reverend Riffel, we might consider these strong words: "If anyone does not provide for his relatives, and especially for his immediate family, he has denied the faith and is worse than an unbeliever." (1 Timothy 5:8 NIV)

## Helping Them Stay Connected

At least one study shows that nursing-home residents who are religious have higher levels of self-esteem and less depression than those who aren't. So if our loved ones liked to worship before becoming ill, it's probably a good idea to help them continue.

Here are some ways to help keep their faith intact.

**Search for a good church.** It took some searching, but Sharon Fish, R.N., a Ph.D. candidate in Rochester, New York, and author of *Alzheimer's: Caring for Your Loved One, Caring for Yourself*, found a church that met in a home that accepted her and her ailing mother with open arms.

"I remember the first Sunday I went in," says Fish. "They had a real ministry to the elderly from a nearby nursing home, so there were wheelchairs and oxygen tanks and people in recliners everywhere. I thought, 'This is the place to be.' Mom was very comfortable there. They used to carry her in and gently set her down in her favorite chair."

**Ask the church to help.** Many churches create small groups to help newly divorced people or substance abusers get together to dis-

**Lean on good friends.** Fish says that she wouldn't suggest we ask friends to provide extended care for a loved one with Alzheimer's. But friends can help in other ways. "I wasn't shy about letting them pick up groceries or run an errand," she says. And if we're the friends of someone who is caring for an Alzheimer's patient, we should understand that this is the best time to pitch in: ". . . better a neighbor nearby than a brother far away." (Proverbs 27:10 NIV)

**Be patient.** When his tolerance with his wife begins to wane, Reverend Riffel reminds himself about God's love for us. "He's very patient, very loving, and accepting of us in the midst of all of our foolish mistakes and all of our stubbornness," he says. "It's kind of hard to be tough on someone else when we recognize how much we ourselves fail."

cuss their problems. Why not suggest that our church start a similar outreach group for Alzheimer's caregivers? "It would be neat if more churches took on this kind of responsibility," says Wilford Wooten, a licensed marriage, family, and child counselor, a licensed clinical social worker, and director of the counseling department for Focus on the Family in Colorado Springs, Colorado. "You know the biblical mandates for churches to help the destitute? Well, I think that this falls into that category. Unfortunately, a lot of people are too embarrassed to ask for help."

**Help them worship at home.** Although some Alzheimer's patients are too ill to worship in churches, with a little help, they can take advantage of inspirational programming offered on television and radio. "Turn on the TV on Sunday morning and you can get several hours of music and sermons, even if you don't get one of the cable channels devoted to worship," says Wooten. Most communities have at least one radio station on the dial devoted to inspirational programming 24 hours a day.

**Pray for solutions to specific problems.** When Lillie wants to get up and get dressed in the middle of the night, Reverend Riffel says he has discovered that she's following the directions of voices inside her head. Instead of trying to convince her to go back to sleep, Reverend Riffel says that he prays with her that God will silence those voices, and it has been his experience that God does.

**Have fun together.** It takes work, but we can find simple things that we can do with our loved one that bring joy and, as a result, make the journey a little easier. "As Mom's dementia progressed, her table manners regressed. But that didn't mean we had to stay home. I found a restaurant where I would take Mom routinely for pancakes because she loved them," says Fish. "We had our own little booth and since we went at two or three in the afternoon, we had the place pretty much to ourselves."

**Gain strength from the Psalms.** "David struggled a lot with his emotions, but was very honest about those emotions in the Psalms," says Fish. Reading them, she says, "helped me identify my own emotions and be more honest about them with God. Through them and other passages in the Bible, I learned that He can take my ranting and raving and give me hope."

**Talk it through.** Another huge potential source of stress is the strain that caring for a parent who has Alzheimer's disease can place on a marriage. "There have to be discussions about what we're going to do about Mom or Dad," says Wilford Wooten, a licensed marriage, family, and child counselor, a licensed clinical social worker, and director of the counseling department for Focus on the Family in Colorado Springs, Colorado. He says that we need to ask, "'Does she have the funds to place her somewhere? Can she live closer and be in her own apartment?' Whatever the situation, we have to talk."

**Know where to go for help.** Whether it's a community health nursing department or a local office on aging, we probably have caregiving resources literally in our own backyards, says Fish. "Sometimes, even local nursing homes have support groups not only for those people with loved ones who stay at the nursing home but also for people in the community." Check the phone book for more information or write to the Alzheimer's Association, National Headquarters, 919 North Michigan Avenue, Suite 1000, Chicago, IL 60611-1676.

**Remember to take care of ourselves** "Eating right, exercising, and getting plenty of sleep helped me have the physical and emotional resources to assist my mom. I was much more patient when I was able to get out and have a life of my own rather than just staying in the house all day long," says Fish. "That can produce a lot of anxiety. Being able to maintain a life and relationships out of the home is very important."

**Roll with the changes.** Sometimes, the decline is gradual; other times, it's fast and steep. But until more effective medical treatment is available, decline is inevitable for people who have this disease. Fish says she found that the key was being prepared mentally and emotionally. In some cases, for example, a person could go from a moderate memory loss to asking the same questions over and over in just a few months.

"It can be very trying and frustrating for the person who might have to answer the same question 15 times in an hour," says Fish. "But we have to realize that this is part of the disease process. Some of these are phases that they pass through; they won't necessarily become fixated on them forever."

**Get real.** We want to do all that we can, and we should. But as sad as it seems, we may not be able to care for our loved ones in our homes for the duration of the disease. To determine when we need to let them go, Fish suggests that we ask ourselves two questions: Is the loved one safe at home? And is caring for the person harming our health? "When an older person is caring for a loved one, the person without Alzheimer's may give out quicker than the person with it. We need to be realistic about our limits and listen to others who may be more aware of our limits."

**Remind them of our love.** "I would tell Mom a lot that I loved her," says Fish. "And often, I would be sitting doing something and out of the blue this little voice would say, 'I love you.' Until I came back to the Lord and began to see things from His perspective, I thought that this was a burden. But after that, I felt like it was a privilege, even though there were many difficult times."

# *Anger*

## HOW TO TAME THE BEAST

*E*veryone knows that good people aren't supposed to get angry, right? Just stuff the emotions and keep our lips zipped. But look to the Bible.

There are 455 references to anger in the Old Testament, and of those, 375 refer to God's anger. "Anger is clearly not a sin," says the Reverend Gary J. Oliver, Ph.D., executive director of the Center for Marriage and Family Studies at John Brown University in Siloam Springs, Arkansas, and co-author of *When Anger Hits Home*. "If it is, then God is in serious trouble."

In fact, the Bible records several incidents where Jesus himself was angry. "Probably the best known episode is when he overturned tables and drove the money changers out of the temple with a whip," says William Backus, Ph.D., a Christian-licensed psychologist in Roseville, Minnesota, founder and director of the Center for Christian Psychological Services in St. Paul, and author of *Telling Yourself the Truth* and *The Healing Power of a Healthy Mind*.

Yes, we are allowed, even expected, to get angry sometimes. Righteous indignation, among other things, eventually helped free the slaves, defeat Hitler, and further the civil rights movement. It's how we handle our anger—or don't—that gets us into physical and emotional trouble. "Moral outrage can be a powerful, positive force, but it has to be controlled," says Pastor David Roper, co-founder with his wife, Carolyn, of Idaho Mountain Ministries in Boise and author of *A Man to Match the Mountain* and *Psalm 23: The Song of a Passionate Heart.*

So what's the difference between healthy and destructive anger? The simple answer is that anytime we think about harming someone else—with our tongues or otherwise—we've probably crossed the line, says Pastor Roper.

## The Dark Side of Anger

Though we think of anger as by far the most powerful emotion, it's actually a secondary emotion. "Underneath anger is either fear, hurt, or frustration," says Dr. Oliver. "We need to understand what our anger is really about, or we won't be expressing the core emotion."

We also need to understand how damaging anger can be and how it can take years off our lives. Anger has been linked to a laundry list of health problems, from depression, high blood pressure, heart disease, arthritis, and stress to drug and alcohol abuse and obesity.

Not only that, but women who suppress anger have been found to have higher breast cancer rates and unhappier marriages and are two times more likely to die prematurely than those who directly expressed their anger. Angry guys don't get off any easier: They're twice as likely to die from cardiovascular disease.

That's not the only way that anger kills. After all, most murders aren't "premeditated acts of violence, but crimes of passion committed in moments of uncontrolled frenzy," says Pastor Roper. "Although we probably move in incremental, escalating steps, when anger intensifies, it can become uncontrolled rage." Clearly, not the reaction prescribed in the Bible. "My dear brothers, take note of this: Everyone should be quick to listen, slow to speak and slow to become angry, for man's anger does not bring about the righteous life that God desires." (James 1:19 NIV)

## Quenching the Fury

There's plenty of sound advice on how to better handle anger and, as a result, live the mandate of Ephesians: "In your anger do not sin." (Ephesians 4:26 NIV) Here's how it's done.

**Express and explain it.** Since stuffed anger is bound to ignite someday like dry timber, it's probably best to express it early, preferably with some kind of "I" statement. So, instead of the typical accusatory approach ("You're making me angry!"), we should "own" our reaction to events. "I sometimes say to my wife, 'You know, this conversation is bugging me. I'm feeling angry now. Let's take a break,'" says Pastor Roper.

But don't stop there, cautions Dr. Oliver. We then need to identify for the other person the emotion underneath the anger. "If I say, 'What you did really hurt me or really frustrated me,' you can do something

## Our Arrows in the Battle

When it comes to anger, the Reverend Steve Harper, Ph.D., has a way of putting the problem—in all its blazing glory—into perspective: "It's better to put out a fire when it's in the wastebasket than when it's racing up the wall." For that very reason, Dr. Harper, vice president and dean of Asbury Theological Seminary in Orlando, Florida, advocates what are called arrow prayers. Also known as flash prayers, a term thought to have originated with turn-of-the-century missionary and literacy advocate Frank Laubach, arrow prayers are brief intercessions that can be offered lightning-fast in any situation, says Dr. Harper. And they're potential life- or reputation-savers when tempers and emotions flare.

"Suppose you spotted a mother in a supermarket parking lot reacting angrily to her child. You would simply pray, 'Mother, Jesus' to link the mother to Jesus," Dr. Harper says. Or, just pray, "Jesus." Some even believe that repeating parts of verses like "Create in me a clean heart" and "Have mercy upon me, O God"—both portions of Psalm 51—are valid arrow prayers. The *Catholic Prayer Book* calls them aspirations— short prayers such as "Make haste, O God, to deliver me; make haste to help me, O Lord" (Psalm 70) and "From all sin deliver us, Lord."

But wouldn't God prefer to hear something more profound?

about that. Otherwise, just expressing your anger is no more effective than rearranging the deck chairs on the Titanic," he says.

**Go to God.** If we can't quite identify the true source of our anger, the Bible promises that God will help if we will only pray. "We're asking God to show us any hidden anger or resentment that's in our hearts based on the authority of John 16:13: 'He will guide you into all truth,'" says Dr. Backus.

Obviously, the need for prayer is more urgent if the discussion has degenerated into arguing or fighting. "If I were in a situation like that, I'd say something like, 'My sense is that I'm either not doing a

Maybe, if you believe that you need to impress some intergalactic potentate. Jesus and the God of the Bible seem to go out of their way to encourage brief prayer. "The Gospels are loaded with examples of short prayers: 'Lord, save me' being one of them," says the Reverend Brian J. Dodd, Ph.D., professor of philosophy at Asbury Seminary and director of the Share Jesus Ministry, both in Wilmore, Kentucky, and author of *Praying Jesus' Way*. "Jesus, in Matthew 6, says to make your prayers less wordy. The reverent, one-word prayer 'Jesus' would probably take the prize for best fulfilling Jesus' teaching, focusing worship and prayer on the Savior of the world."

Adds Dr. Harper, "The fact is that God hears the intentions of our hearts whenever we pray. The number of words isn't important. Paul, in Romans chapter 8, talks about the Spirit interceding for us with sighs and groans too deep for words. Sometimes those wordless prayers come out of the very core of our being. The great Methodist preacher Charles Wesley wrote a hymn with the phrase, 'If to the right or left I stray, that moment Lord reprove.' He wanted almost an instant spiritual sensibility so that things didn't linger or build up. I think that's what arrow prayers or flash prayers are about. They are to deal with real-life situations at the earliest possible moment."

good job of communicating right now or you're not hearing, and so we're only going to shed a lot more heat than light. Let's stop and pray together,'" says Dr. Oliver. "And then I would say, 'Lord, the desire of my heart right now with so-and-so is not to blame or trash or dump on him, and so I would pray that you would help me communicate more clearly.' If the other person is unwilling to pray, pray something similar silently," says Dr. Oliver.

**Take a time-out.** If our hearts aren't in it, sometimes even prayer can't immediately diffuse angry situations. That's probably the right time to take a time-out. "Depending on the circumstance, a time-out might be short enough to simply say the alphabet backwards or long enough to take a walk or even work in the yard—anything that gives me enough time to permit my emotions to stabilize," says Dr. Oliver. Just don't forget to re-engage eventually. "You don't want to leave the other person hanging," he says. One guideline for the length of the time-out: It takes, on average, 20 minutes for the stress hormones released during an angry outburst to work their way through our systems, he says.

**Seek to understand.** One of the first things that we forget when we're angry is that we're dealing with another person who may not agree with us but deserves our understanding. "Our old dog barks and bites and is a ferocious terror to strangers, but I understand her," says Pastor Roper. "She was abused by a man when she was a pup before we got her and reacts adversely to men. It's important to recognize the latent forces that lie within us and other people's anger. It helps us to be more understanding and patient with them."

**Forgive.** We all know that it's the best way to end just about any problem, including anger. And it's healthy, too. Studies show that anger has been implicated in a variety of health problems, including depression and high blood pressure). But how do we do it? Not by serving as doormats. "I think that forgiveness actually means 'I am not going to hold this against you,'" says Dr. Backus. "It doesn't mean that I'm not angry. It doesn't mean that I don't want you to do something differently in the future or make proper reparation. The core idea is, 'I'm choosing to make what you've done a nonfactor in our relationship. I won't treat you badly for what you've done.'"

**Write a letter.** Pouring our feelings out onto paper is a good way to release them without harming ourselves or anyone else. When we're done writing, often the best thing to do is simply throw the letter away, says Dr. Oliver.

What if the person with whom we're angry is unavailable—or gone for good—like an abusive ex-spouse or a deceased parent? We can still forgive. We can go to a quiet place with an empty chair across from us and then talk as if the person were sitting there. We can explain why we're angry. When we've poured out our hearts, we can choose to forgive, says Dr. Oliver.

**Do it now.** A verse from the Bible reads: "Do not let the sun go down while you are still angry, and do not give the Devil a foothold. (Ephesians 4:26 NIV) "The idea is that walking in anger, nursing it, hanging on to it, and enjoying the fantasies of getting even are harmful," says Dr. Backus. "The best alternative is to resolve it."

**Fess up.** We may have our anger under control, but we need to remember that careless words or actions can raise the ire of others. "When someone gets mad at us, the natural inclination is to strike back or be defensive. 'I was late because . . . I did this because . . . what I did wasn't really bad. . . . ' And that only increases the rift between you and the other person," says Dr. Backus. "If we say, 'You're right; you have a point; I can see where you're coming from; I can see why that hurt; I never wanted to do anything to hurt you,' you will win them over. The best way to handle criticism is to agree with it."

**Change that self-talk.** When helping a patient deal with anger, Dr. Backus says that he frequently discovers that they are subjecting themselves to something he calls "catastrophic self-talk," in other words, thinking the worst.

So how should we react? "Instead of dwelling on how mad you are about losing your wallet and how it's driving you crazy, tell yourself the truth. Something like, 'It's no big deal about my wallet. I can do something about this. I can place it in the same place every day so I'll know where to find it,'" he says. And best of all, it's biblical advice. The Bible doesn't say, "focus on your anger." It doesn't say, "beat yourself up" or "drive yourself crazy." It says to focus on whatever is true, noble, right, pure, admirable, excellent, or praiseworthy. (Philippians 4:8)

**Avoid extremes.** Some folks make even more trouble for themselves by throwing around words like *always, never,* and *every* when they're angry or in an argument. Some classic examples: "Why do you always do that?" or "You never listen to me!"

Not only are such generalizations rarely true but they're also infuriating to hear, says Dr. Oliver. "And what are the three core emotions of anger? Fear, hurt, and frustration. If I communicate in ways that frustrate you, then you will probably respond in frustration or anger as well. The result is misunderstanding and hurt feelings. In one interaction, we can find ourselves about a mile off course."

**Carry a STOP! card.** We carry cards that make us feel like big shots—credit cards and business cards, to name a few. So why not carry one that will keep us from getting into big trouble? Called the STOP! card, its purpose is to help put the brakes on emotional situations that are careening out of control.

To make a STOP! card, simply write "STOP!" in big red letters on one side of a three- by five-inch index card. Then, says Dr. Oliver, write a Bible verse on the other side, such as: "For the weapons of our warfare are not carnal but mighty in God for pulling down strongholds, casting down arguments and every high thing that exalts itself against the knowledge of God, bringing every thought into captivity to the obedience of Christ." (2 Corinthians 10:4–5 NKJV)

Then, when we feel anger building, we can pull the STOP! card out of our wallets or day planners, says Dr. Oliver, and say to ourselves, "STOP! I'm taking this emotion, this thought, captive to the obedience of Christ." Remember: This isn't something to wave in another person's face. This is for us.

**Lower those expectations.** In some cases, it's entirely possible that we're more likely to be elected President than ever see our spouses, friends, or co-workers change their ways. Instead of staying angry all the time, we should state our cases, lower our expectations, and hope for the best. To put it bluntly, the other person's problem doesn't have to be—nor should it be—the focus of our existence. And when we let that problem go, it can have a positive effect on both of us.

In one such situation, a pastor's wife saw her husband change dramatically after she simply stopped nagging him about not spending time with his family. Instead of drifting further away—as she originally feared—he came running back, and their marriage is better than ever, says Dr. Backus.

**Find a healthy outlet.** Anger can be the fuel for social change, if we allow it. Mothers Against Drunk Driving, for example, was founded by women who had family killed by drunk drivers. Channeling our anger into Christian service may very well make the world a better place instead of making us bitter, says Pastor Roper.

**Go the other way—for now.** What if we've repeatedly made an honest effort to resolve a problem and the other person is still angry at us? If the story about Paul and Barnabas—two solid believers—in Acts 15 is any indication, it may take some time and maturity before we're able to work together again. They had to split up for a time after a disagreement. "But later they got back together, and that's good advice for us. Eventually, there should be some mutual forgiveness," says Dr. Backus.

# *Anxiety*

━━━✦━━━

## WHEN WORRY AND FEAR GO AWRY

*G*ood, healthy fear as well as common sense is what keeps us from stepping up to a podium to address thousands without some sort of preparation. But if we refuse even to be a part of the crowd because we're afraid that people are going to stare at us, it's likely that we have a form of anxiety or a phobia.

The last thing that we should feel is alone. More than 23 million Americans experience some form of anxiety, making it the most common mental illness in the country. From chronic worrying, called generalized anxiety disorder by experts, to panic attacks, most seem to have the same root cause: unrealistic, overwhelming fears that can not only paralyze the mind but also cause serious physical problems, says William Backus, Ph.D., a Christian-licensed psychologist in Roseville, Minnesota, founder and director of the Center for Christian Psychological Services in St. Paul, and author of *Telling Yourself the Truth* and *The Healing Power of a Healthy Mind.*

Of course, in biblical times, medical diagnosis for emotional problems hadn't the reached the high art that it is today. But surprisingly, Scripture is replete with stories that urge us to take the consequences of anxiety and worry seriously—from Caleb's spy mission to Israel to Jesus' Sermon on the Mount.

# The Good Side of Worry

For all the trouble that it can cause, a certain amount of worry or anxiety is actually healthy. Concern over what the boss will say if we're repeatedly late to work literally helps us get up and out of the bed in the morning lest we lose our jobs. Fear of being flattened by oncoming traffic reminds us to look both ways before crossing the street.

A bit of anxiety over how we'll fare against the competition stimulates our adrenal glands, improving blood flow, concentration, and other aspects that are key to enhanced performance, according to the Reverend Gary J. Oliver, Ph.D., executive director of the Center for Marriage and Family Studies at John Brown University in Siloam Springs, Arkansas, and co-author of *When Anger Hits Home*.

When anxiety goes bad, it gets ugly fast. The sudden feelings of terror associated with panic attacks often trigger chest pains, heart palpitations, shortness of breath, dizziness, abdominal discomfort, and even fear of death. Those who have obsessive-compulsive disorders, also considered forms of anxiety, often find themselves performing bizarre rituals, like cleaning part of the house or washing their hands dozens or even hundreds of times a day. Post-traumatic stress disorder, a form of anxiety caused by traumatic events such as rape, exposure to war, abuse, or other forms of violence, can result in nightmares, flashbacks, numb emotions, depression, and feelings of anger, irritability, and distraction.

For some people with anxiety, the relief provided by drug therapy would be considered a true example of divine healing, and a health practitioner can determine who would benefit from this treatment if any of the symptoms mentioned above are present. Early religious believers, although certainly not immune from anxiety and worry, didn't have that luxury. But whether facing hostile Romans, hungry lions, or fiery furnaces, they often used faith, prayer, and wisdom from Scripture to overcome.

# Putting the Problem to Rest

"A key to overcoming worry is to choose to make the God-given emotion of anxiety work for you rather than against you," says Dr. Oliver. "Before Christ was able to heal the paralyzed man at the pool

# Healing Words

## Saying Adieu to Anxiety

Several Bible verses remind us that no matter how anxiety-producing the situation, the Holy Spirit, Jesus, and God the Father are there also. "With these verses, we can imagine God leading us every step of the way," says William Backus, Ph.D., a Christian-licensed psychologist in Roseville, Minnesota, founder and director of the Center for Christian Psychological Services in St. Paul, and author of *Telling Yourself the Truth* and *The Healing Power of a Healthy Mind.*

> Teaching them to observe all things whatsoever I have commanded you: and, lo, I am with you always, even unto the end of the world. Amen.
>
> —*Matthew 28:20 KJV*

> So do not fear, for I am with you; do not be dismayed, for I am your God. I will strengthen you and help you; I will uphold you with my righteous right hand.
>
> —*Isaiah 41:10 NIV*

of Bethesda, He asked him: 'Do you want to be made whole?' That's the same question that He asks each of us today." Here's what you can do to beat anxiety from a Christian perspective.

**Do one day at a time.** It goes without saying that Jesus covered some pretty important topics during the Sermon on the Mount, not the least of which were murder, divorce, the poor, and prayer. Is it just a coincidence that He devoted as much time or more to worry and anxiety, or is He trying to tell us something? "Therefore do not worry about tomorrow, for tomorrow will worry about its own things.

Ye are of God, little children, and have overcome them: because greater is He that is in you, than he that is in the world.

—*1 John 4:4 KJV*

But they that wait upon the Lord shall renew their strength; they shall mount up with wings as eagles; they shall run, and not be weary; and they shall walk, and not faint.

—*Isaiah 40:31 KJV*

There is no fear in love; but perfect love casteth out fear: because fear hath torment. He that feareth is not made perfect in love.

—*1 John 4:18 KJV*

Create in me a clean heart, O God; and renew a right spirit within me.

—*Psalm 51:10 KJV*

Sufficient for the day is its own trouble," Jesus concludes. (Matthew 6:34 NKJV)

"I find it interesting that 'one day at a time' has become the motto of many recovery programs," says Dr. Oliver. "Remember that worry usually involves reaching into and borrowing potential problems from tomorrow. One friend told me, 'Yesterday is a canceled check, tomorrow is a promissory note. Today is cash. Spend it wisely.' That's sound biblical advice."

**Axe avoidance behavior.** Those who experience anxiety often

*(continued on page 174)*

# The Soothing Psalm

When we're feeling anxious or depressed, we can turn to God, the Bible, family, friends, or our pastors for comfort and guidance. But where does a pastor turn?

In the case of Pastor David Roper, co-founder of Idaho Mountain Ministries, a group that he and his wife, Carolyn, launched to help minister to the needs of pastors in Boise, Idaho, it was Psalm 23. During a stretch of melancholy that lasted more than two years, Pastor Roper meditated and compiled a journal on every aspect of that chapter—so much so that by the time the gloom lifted, he had the origins of a book, *Psalm 23: The Song of a Passionate Heart*.

"I've found that fear and anxiety come from feelings of inadequacy and impotency," says Pastor Roper. "We're usually facing some kind of situation that we can't control: deteriorating marriages, disintegrating health, financial difficulties. These are the factors that break us down and bring us to the end of ourselves. And that's where Psalm 23 comes in."

> The Lord is my shepherd, I shall not be in want.
> He makes me lie down in green pastures, he leads me beside
>     quiet waters,
> He restores my soul. He guides me in paths of righteousness
>     for His name's sake.
> Even though I walk through the valley of the shadow of
>     death, I will fear no evil, for You are with me; Your rod
>     and Your staff, they comfort me.
> You prepare a table before me in the presence of my
>     enemies. You anoint my head with oil; my cup overflows.
> Surely goodness and love will follow me all the days of my
>     life, and I will dwell in the house of the Lord forever.

—*Psalm 23:1–6 NIV*

While pondering the text, Pastor Roper was convinced that the author, King David, was someone from whom we all can learn. "Even though he failed a lot, he was a man after God's own heart. God saw something to which he could respond. This was a man who hungered and thirsted for righteousness more than anything else in the world. And God satisfied him."

The third verse of the Psalm, which includes "He restores my soul," is a powerful enough promise. Yet Pastor Roper says that understanding the Hebrew term for "restore" makes it more profound. "I understand the word to mean that He actually turns us around. That when we are wayward, he follows us into our guilt and shame. He comes and gets us and turns us around as a good shepherd does," he says.

And we don't have to wait until the end of our lives to reap the benefits found in the fourth verse, according to Pastor Roper. ("Even though I walk through the valley of the shadow of death, I will fear no evil, for You are with me; Your rod and Your staff, they comfort me." NIV) "It refers to end of life, but it also refers to those dark periods through which we pass." Even the rod and staff are relevant. "I came across a reference in Jewish literature that implied that David kept the implements that he used when he was a shepherd boy—his rod and staff—in his tent and later in his house, even when he became king, and would often contemplate the meaning of those," says Pastor Roper.

Perhaps most important, the Hebrew word for "love" as it is found in the sixth verse of the passage reveals a much deeper form of emotion than what passes for the word today, says Pastor Roper. This is translated as love, mercy, or kindness in some versions of the Bible, "but more recently, scholars have discovered that that word is used in other near-eastern texts as a commitment," he says. "More than just 'I love you' but 'I am committed to this thing for life.' It's a vow of loyalty."

Pastor Roper is convinced that such insight into God's love and, as a result, comfort, could have only come after great trial, hardship and, yes, anxiety. "This is the wisdom of a man much closer to the end of his life than the beginning," he says.

# Answered Prayers

## Turning to the Lord

"I had a psychology student who claimed to be an atheist, but he was riddled with anxiety," says William Backus, Ph.D., a Christian-licensed psychologist in Roseville, Minnesota, founder and director of the Center for Christian Psychological Services in St. Paul, and author of *Telling Yourself the Truth* and *The Healing Power of a Healthy Mind*. "So I suggested that he might turn to the Lord. And he said, 'How could I do that? There isn't any God.'

"I said, okay, why don't you try this? The next time you're at home and you're paralyzed with fear, get down on your hands and knees and say, 'Lord, if You are there, manifest Yourself to me and I will believe in you and walk in your truth forever.'

"The next week, he came back and said, 'I did it.'" The man prayed the simple prayer that Dr. Backus suggested, and not only was he relieved of his anxiety but he also became a Christian. Years later, he was a man of deep faith."

try to avoid whatever it is they think is the source of their problems. Unfortunately, this approach can make the problems worse, so much so that psychologists have given it a name: avoidance behavior.

"Suppose I'm a kid who doesn't want to go to school because all the kids are picking on me. And I tell my mom and she says 'Aw honey, you stay home today.' Guess what happens to the knot that I had in my stomach? It goes away. That's the reward," says Dr. Backus. "But that kind of avoidance in the long run will cause anxiety to get worse. The anxiety response is strengthened by avoidance behavior."

**Face the fear.** Ending avoidance behavior is a big step toward recovery. Challenging anxieties or worries to see if they are realistic is another. "One of the best ways to abandon the merry-go-round of worry is to simply jump off and do something," says Dr. Oliver. Been anxious about making that important phone call for weeks or months? Start dialing—it's probably nowhere near as bad as you think, he says.

Lest we forget, this advice also has some scriptural basis: ". . . ask, and it will be given to you; seek and you will find; knock, and it will be opened to you." (Luke 11:9 NKJV)

**Study the Psalms.** Soldiers have carried copies into battle; business leaders and secretaries keep framed passages on their desks. For more than 4,000 years, the Psalms have helped provide an unparalleled sense of peace in times of anxiety and fear. "Just thumb through them. One of my favorites is 'What time I am afraid, I will call upon the name of the Lord.' (Psalm 56:3) Or the twenty-third Psalm: 'The Lord is my shepherd; I shall not want. He maketh me to lie down in green pastures: he leadeth me beside the still waters. He restoreth my soul . . . '" says Dr. Backus. "Now I know this isn't magic, and it doesn't immediately banish every wisp of fear, but it sure makes it possible to tolerate it—to know that you have the greatest power in the universe available to you during this difficulty."

**Pray for peace of mind.** Prayer has a way of "clarifying our worries," says Dr. Oliver. "God can help us weed out the outrageous and irrational fears from the legitimate and rational concerns. He can help us identify the real issues." Best of all, prayer works. In one study, 20 out of 22 people who practiced prayer or meditation to reduce moderate to severe anxiety showed marked improvement after three months.

**Re-examine motivations.** Since one cause of anxiety is a fear of not being liked, our problems can be rooted in an unhealthy compulsion to gain the approval of others. "Jesus never said to work overtime to get people to love us. He said to love Him, trust Him, have faith in Him, and love your neighbor as yourself," says Dr. Backus. "That's where our focus should be."

**Pop in some praise.** Listening to Christian praise music that reminds us of God's grace, goodness, power, and majesty is perfect for those moments when we're feeling anxious and fearful, says Dr. Oliver.

**Watch your mouth.** While we're getting our thoughts right, it's also a good idea to control our speech, whether we are talking to ourselves or others. "An anxious heart weighs a man down, but a kind word cheers him up." (Proverbs 12:25 NIV)

**Desensitize yourself.** Although people with phobias rarely seek counseling, a treatment called systematic desensitization has a significant cure rate, says Dr. Backus.

Simply stated, systematic desensitization is nothing more than facing the fear bit by bit over time until the phobia is gone, Dr. Backus says. For example, take someone with claustrophobia—fear of confined spaces. During a typical desensitization, we would imagine going to the dentist and being enclosed in an eight- by eight-foot office, probably not too confining for even someone with claustrophobia. Next, we would imagine a tighter space until we were comfortable with that. "Probably the worst thing for someone like this to imagine would be this: 'You're in a small, dark closet and the door is locked. You can't get out. There is no one in the house. And you are surrounded on all sides by walls. You can hardly move.'" he says. "And when you're comfortable with the smallest space, that would probably be your last session."

**Explore implosion therapy.** Another form of treatment for phobias and other forms of anxiety is called implosion therapy. The idea behind it is facing serious fears directly until they subside.

In one such example, Dr. Backus says that he helped a salesman overcome a paralyzing fear of heights by taking him to a restaurant on the top floor of a building, finding a table next to a window, and looking down. "The guy fell apart. His teeth chattered, his body shook, and he wanted to leave. I said, 'If you go down, we're through; there's no more treatment,'" says Dr. Backus. "He hung in there, and over the course of about a half-hour, all his terrible anxiety began to subside. By the time we left, he was reasonably okay. Every treatment session, we found another high building to go to. But the result was that he became completely free, and he started taking planes all over the place just for the fun of it." (Be sure to consult a trained professional before starting therapy like this.)

We may not have the chance to soar quite as high as the flying salesman now does, but when we allow our faith to help beat anxiety, it can certainly feel that way.

# Arguing

## HOW TO FIGHT FAIR

Whether we come from the Lucy Ricardo School of Communications—hands waving, volume on full—or a have a more Mother Teresa–like demeanor, we're all bound to find ourselves involved in an occasional argument.

As things become heated, the voice of reason in our heads that says, "DON'T SAY THAT!" can get overwhelmed by a raging emotion that says "DO!" If we're not careful, what starts as a rational discussion can degenerate into verbal abuse and name-calling. "It's okay for people to express their views," says the Reverend Terry Wise, Ph.D., director of the Trinity Center for Conflict Management at Trinity Theological Seminary in Newburgh, Indiana, and author of *Conflict Scenarios.* "What's not okay is the destructive way that we share them sometimes. There's room to disagree and do it in a manner that glorifies God."

It's hard to imagine people accepting our remarks when we're snarling, yapping, or being sarcastic. Such sniping and griping doesn't just sound pathetic: Research shows that frequent, nasty arguing permanently damages our relationships. In fact, some marital counselors say that they can predict with 90 percent accuracy whether a marriage will survive based on the couple's conflict resolution skills. Those who learn to fight fair—because *every* marriage has conflict—seem to stay together longer. Those who don't, often end up in divorce court.

# Curbing Conflicts

If we want to improve our relationships and shine the next time an argument threatens, here's what to do.

**Pick your battles.** It would have saved Goliath from one heck of a headache. And, truth be told, this ancient piece of advice would probably have saved most of us from a few as well. But it still bears repeating: Even before a conflict erupts, we need to decide if the issue is really worth the time, energy, and stress on our relationships. If not, we need to move on, says Dr. Wise.

And if we choose to press the issue, we also need to know when it's wise to back off. "If you're really upset and I can hear it in your tone of voice and see it in your facial expression, I will suggest that we postpone our discussion until you're calm enough to listen," says Cheryl Cutrona, executive director of the Good Shepherd Neighborhood Mediation Program in Philadelphia.

**Play a role.** We don't have to rehearse what we're going to say as if we're quoting Shakespeare. But when we're not seeing eye-to-eye with someone and it's causing controversy, it helps to visualize the conflict from the other person's perspective. "One way is to look at the conflict as if you're watching a play," says Cutrona. "Stage the conflict in your mind and cast yourself as the other person. Script each character's response to various words, phrases and strategies. Choose what you predict will work best before you actually approach the other person."

**Hold a family powwow.** When the bickering involves a spouse or child, there's no reason we can't iron things out at a family summit. No need for red carpets or fancy speeches, though; just calm, honest sharing. "Sit around the kitchen table and talk about how each person was affected by the situation. Listen for feelings. Then brainstorm ways to handle similar situations differently in the future," says Cutrona.

**Relish variety.** Each of us has different personalities, communication styles, even mannerisms—some more annoying than others. If we begin to see this as a strength, that others' abilities actually complement our weaknesses, we're bound to have fewer feuds. "Diversity is not something that divides or threatens us but should unite us to do the work that each of us is called to do," says Dr. Wise.

# Did You Hear What I Said?

It's not enough just to keep quiet while someone else is talking, especially if the next thing out of our mouths invalidates everything they just said, says the Reverend Terry Wise, Ph.D., director of the Trinity Center for Conflict Management at Trinity Theological Seminary in Newburgh, Indiana, and author of *Conflict Scenarios*. (Example: You're a liar and your mother dresses you funny!)

Instead, we need to practice something that communication experts call active listening. During active listening, we pay strict attention to what others are saying so that we're able to paraphrase what they just said. For example: "So I hear you saying that you'd prefer that I ask you before inviting my mother to stay with us for the weekend?"

This helps establish what the real issue is, and if our paraphrase doesn't capture it, the other person knows immediately and can correct it. And then, "the person feels like he has been heard," says Dr. Wise. "Good listening is keeping our ears open and promoting dialogue. It doesn't shut it down; it invites people to speak."

And it's not just a newfangled communication technique. As it says in Proverbs 18:13 (NIV): "He who answers before listening— that is his folly and his shame."

**Give thanks.** The next time we're tempted to yell at someone for not seeing things our way or for pointing out one of our shortcomings, we might want to thank them for sharing a perspective that we have yet to consider, says Dr. Wise. The Bible puts it this way: "Let the righteous strike me; it shall be a kindness. And let him rebuke me; It shall be as excellent oil; Let my head not refuse it." (Psalm 141:5 NKJV) For those among us who feel that they have the right to rebuke, watch out: We should be more concerned about keeping reign on our tongues than sharing our opinions.

**Look in the mirror.** Before we blast others for their various insufficiencies and flaws, it's always a good idea to take a long, hard look at our own. "I like what Jesus says about this: 'Do not judge, or you too will be judged' (John 7:1 NIV) and ' . . . why do you look at the speck in your brother's eye, but do not consider the plank in your own eye?' (Matthew 7:3 NKJV) Rarely do we find this kind of self-examination prior to verbal outbursts," says Dr. Wise. But if we did, we'd definitely have fewer of them.

# When the Words Are Flying

Some people are just spoiling for a fight, no matter how hard we try to avoid it. (And, truth be told, sometimes we're the ones who are inciting the fight.) Here's what to do when the venom starts to fly.

**Dump the "yous."** Nothing accelerates verbal conflict quicker than accusing statements like "You make me so mad!" or "You're the problem!" And if we really want double trouble, we can throw in some generalities like 'You always mess up the kitchen!' Or 'You never pick up your socks!'

"'You' messages are the verbal equivalent of pointing your finger at somebody," says Dr. Wise. Generalities are even worse, since no one ever does anything all of the time, regardless of how terrible we might think they are. When tempted to generalize, we'd do well to remember the first part of Ephesians 4:15: ". . . speaking the truth in love . . ."

**Trade "yous" for a vowel.** Using "I" statements allows us to speak nonconfrontationally and straight from the heart—and for those reasons, are difficult to challenge. For example: "I really get frustrated when I come home and discover that someone has left clothes all over the bedroom floor."

"When we teach this technique, a lot of people say, 'Look, if I have a problem and want to express it, I'm not going to pussyfoot around with these little 'I' messages. It isn't real,'" says Cutrona. "But we also talk about consequences and what happens if we don't express ourselves the right way. The other person gets defensive and before you know it, the conflict just escalates."

**Avoid personal attacks.** We all know that name-calling is a no-no during an argument, but don't forget that the other person's parents, spouse, and kids shouldn't be used for verbal target practice either. Sinking to that level can damage the very foundation of the relationship, says Dr. Wise. We can and should ask for forgiveness after saying something hateful, but all wounds take time to heal and often leave scars. But why get in that deep in the first place? Remember: "A soft answer turns away wrath, but a harsh word stirs up anger. The tongue of the wise uses knowledge rightly, but the mouth of fools pours forth foolishness." (Proverbs 15:1 NKJV)

# Finding Solutions

Once we've learned to keep the emotional level low, we can try these tips to find solutions for our problems.

**Stick to the issue.** We get nasty. We get personal. We dredge up things that have been bugging us for weeks or even decades. But such behavior is more likely to get us into shouting matches than resolve the problem. "It's our natural tendency. Somebody brings up something that we don't want to talk about, so we say, 'Hey, what about when you did this?'" says Anne Bachle Fifer, an attorney, Christian mediator, and conflict resolution consultant based in Grand Rapids, Michigan. It may be that the issue needs to be addressed at some point. But if a conflict is raging, don't push it now. "This probably isn't the time to bring out the list that you have been keeping since Thanksgiving 1952 of all the things that he has done wrong in the past. Stick to the one that you really think needs to be addressed."

**Set some ground rules.** If both people agree to talk it out, setting ground rules for the discussion will help keep peace, says Cutrona. "For example, I might know you well enough to say, 'When you're angry, you yell and scream. I, on the other hand, become intimidated when someone yells at me. So for me to be able to negotiate equally with you, I'm going to need you to use a lower tone of voice.' And if you agree, then I might say, 'Is there anything that you would like me to do to make you more comfortable in this situation?'"

**Shoot for win-win.** Suppose we "win" the argument, grinding the other person and their logic into a fine powder. What's the likelihood that our relationship is going to improve? Instead, consider "win-win."

"That's what we should be aiming for," says Cutrona, "when both people are satisfied by the outcome." How does win-win work? Simple: You get to pick the restaurant and I get to pick the movie. If we're just going to the movies? You pick it this time and I'll pick it next time.

**Switch songs.** One sure sign that the discussion is going nowhere fast is when we're repeating ourselves over and over again. "It's one of my rules as a mediator: When you hear yourself saying the same things or you can sense that you're covering the same ground, then it's time to stop and see if you can get to a different plane or see if you can discuss it at a different time," says Fifer.

In other words, instead of going around and around, try to attack the problem from a different angle or offer a solution.

**See a mediator.** Unless we're unusually cantankerous, about once in a lifetime, we'll run into an argument that we can't resolve. While some people might be tempted to wash their hands of the whole affair, the Bible is clear: We're to seek reconciliation. "Leave your gift there in front of the altar. First go and be reconciled to your brother; then come and offer your gift." (Matthew 5:24 NIV) How? With the help of a third party, like a pastor, elder, Christian counselor, or trained mediator. "Unfortunately, it may not be enough to just pray through it," says Dr. Wise. "The Lord has given Christian mediators the training and experience to help both parties come to a mutually satisfying solution that is both good for the relationship and glorifies the Lord as well."

For information on controlling anger, see Anger (page 160). For more information on Christian mediation, see Enemies (page 265).

# Attitude

## It's All a Matter of Choice

*S*tuff happens. Things go wrong. Life isn't always easy or exciting. We don't always get what we want. We make mistakes. And we aren't always happy.

That's okay.

Life is a series of experiences, tests, and learning opportunities. Our part in the scheme is not to be perfect, says theologian and Christian psychiatrist Paul Meier, M.D., co-founder of New Life Clinics, the largest provider of Christian-based counseling in the United States, and author of more than 60 best-selling Christian self-help books. Our job is to remain resilient and maintain hope, despite whatever adversities we face, he says.

That is a healing attitude, says prayer teacher Vernon M. Sylvest, M.D., a physician with a prayer-based holistic medical practice in Richmond, Virginia, and the author of *The Formula: Who Gets Sick, Who Gets Well*, a book about faith and healing. Our job is to respond to life's challenges in ways that honor the sacred nature of existence.

We do get to make that choice, says Dr. Meier. The process ultimately boils down to attitude, and we do have control over our attitudes.

At any particular moment, we have the ability to choose how we will respond in any situation, to paraphrase the late Victor Frankl, renowned psychologist.

# Answered Prayers

## Faith Hastened My Healing

"In 1970, at age 48, I was told that I needed a colon resection to correct diverticulitis. My father had died three months previously, and my mother, age 80, lived alone 250 miles from me. The surgeon was concerned about the surgery primarily because of my size: five feet three inches and 90 pounds.

"The night before surgery, before I fell asleep, a strong sense of calm and well-being came over me. I thought, 'God will not let anything happen to me because my mother needs me. She has had enough pain.'

"After the surgery, when I was discharged, the surgeon said that he was amazed at my quick recovery. He felt that my positive attitude contributed to my healing. I attribute it to faith."

—*Helen G. Jones, Kennett Square, Pennsylvania*

God wants us to respond to situations morally, lovingly, and constructively. We are human, though, and we won't always be able to accomplish that. That's why Jesus met the cross, says the Reverend Paul F. Everett of Pittsburgh, a Presbyterian minister at large with the Peale Center in Pawling, New York, and executive director emeritus of the Pittsburgh Experiment, a national and international ministry to the business and working communities. Jesus died so that we might be forgiven our shortcomings, he says.

## Give Peace a Chance

So often we focus so much on what is wrong that we don't give ourselves a chance to celebrate that which is right, says lecturer and ordained Episcopalian priest Harold Ivan Smith, doctor of ministry, who leads grief gatherings at St. Luke's Medical Center in Kansas

City, Missouri, and is the author of many Christian self-help books. Focusing on that which is unsatisfactory is irritating and discouraging. Focusing on that which is right is soothing and encouraging, and it encourages that which is right in us and others.

Here are some ways to maintain a constructive focus.

**Forgive mistakes.** We're humans. We make errors. We shouldn't dwell on them, and we shouldn't inflict self-punishment. God knows our shortcomings and loves us anyway. We should act the same way, says Dr. Meier.

This is particularly important if we tend to be perfectionists, says Michele Novotni, Ph.D., psychologist and assistant professor of counseling at Eastern College, a Christian college of arts and sciences in St. Davids, Pennsylvania. The more we try to attain the ever-unattainable standard of perfection in everything, the more it eludes us and the more we feel defeated, inferior, worthless, and guilty. That's not an attitude to cultivate.

**Wave off jerks.** Yes, there are jerks in this world. Some are even in our churches, acknowledges Dr. Meier, who has written a book called *Don't Let the Jerks Get the Best of You.* Generally, he says, three out of four people we encounter are jerks who will somehow disturb us, through their judgment, rejection, or abuse of some fashion. We need to accept that and not let it bother us too much.

Dr. Smith points out that frequently, our efforts at loving, kindness, and fairness will be challenged by unloving, unkind, and unfair behavior, but that doesn't mean that we should quit loving or helping. It just means that for us to find satisfaction, happiness, and good emotional health, we do need to recognize and accept that this is the way this world really is.

**Avoid gossip and rumors.** Participating in either can bring us down emotionally and create feelings of fear, doubt, mistrust, and anger—all for no real reason. Contemplate life with accurate information, not with information based on secondhand speculation, slurs, and twisted tales, says Dr. Smith.

**Believe the promises.** Buy an inexpensive Bible and a highlighting pen, then mark up all the inspiring, hopeful, and faith-building verses and read through them during dark and doubtful times, suggests Dr. Smith. Copy some of the verses onto index cards

# Faithbuilders

## Hum the High Notes

Success is not an accident. We create it out of our expectations, actions, and words, says the Reverend John Osteen, doctor of divinity, pastor of the 20,000-member Lakewood Church in Houston and author of numerous books and booklets on adopting a successful attitude spiritually. It is God's will for us, he says.

As Jesus says, ". . . I am come that they might have life, and that they might have it more abundantly." (John 10:10 KJV) To live life fully, or to have it "more abundantly" as some Bible versions translate Jesus' words, we need to believe that it is what we deserve, says Dr. Osteen. We need to stand on the Bible's promises and walk by faith, not by sight." (2 Corinthians 5:7 KJV)

How do we do that? Get in the habit of expressing spiritually positive desires to ourselves and to others, Dr. Osteen advises in his booklet *What to Do When Nothing Seems to Work*. Additionally, the Bible tells us that "Death and life are in the power of the tongue. . . ." (Proverbs 18:21 KJV)

When things aren't going right, usually "it is because you are not saying what God says about the situation," continues Dr. Osteen. "Instead, you are speculating, surmising, reasoning, and looking at cir-

and post them in conspicuous places where they're visible during the day or carry some with you, he suggests.

Memorize the verses in which God makes promises to walk with us through our difficulties, guide us, never leave us or forsake us, give us peace, and so on. Living these promises and discovering that the Lord is faithful in keeping his promises will deepen our convictions of and trust in his faithfulness, says Reverend Everett.

The Bible holds about 8,810 such promises, according to British

cumstances instead of God's Word." He teaches that we should talk about what God is doing for us and what God promises to do for us, and put our negative thoughts aside.

Yes, contrary thoughts may come to mind, but "as long as you refuse to say those thoughts, they will die. Once you speak them, you give them life. Replace negative thoughts with God's thoughts—the Bible. Say what God says about your situation," writes Dr. Osteen.

As the late Reverend Dr. Norman Vincent Peale, Methodist and Reformed Church of America minister and author of the multi-million-copy inspirational bestseller *The Power of Positive Thinking* said, "You can make your life what you want it to be through belief in God and in yourself."

Besides focusing on the positive and speaking the positive, we need to rub shoulders with the positive, says Dr. Osteen. We need to associate with positive, spiritual people. Besides watching what words leave our mouths, we need to watch what words enter our ears, he writes.

As Jesus says, "Be careful what you are hearing. The measure of thought and study you give to the truth you hear will be the measure of virtue and knowledge that comes back to you. . . ." (Mark 4:24 AMP)

Bible teacher and author Herbert Lockyer in his book *All the Promises of the Bible.*

In addition, we can compile a list of some encouraging experiences, simple and great successes that we have had, and some of the positive things that the Bible says we are entitled to or positive attitudes that the Bible says we should take, advises Dr. Meier. Then, when a less-than-helpful thought enters our minds, we can counter it with a positive one from the list. If we counter negatives with true and inspirational positives, he advises, we'll cultivate winning attitudes.

## Take In the Big Picture

Up close, everything seems larger, so standing toe-to-toe with frustrations, pressures, and problems can make them seem overwhelmingly big. We begin to really feel sorry for ourselves. That is not a holy view, says Dr. Meier. Successful people do not spend a lot of time feeling sorry for themselves.

When we find that we're feeling overwhelmed by situations, we can do a couple of things to immediately change our perspective, says Dr. Meier.

**Take the long view.** How much will anything that we're tempted to fret over today matter 100 years from now, or even 1, 2, 5, or 10 years from now? Keeping our lives in perspective helps us avoid reacting based on how something appears through the magnifying lens of the moment, says Dr. Meier.

**Think of others first.** "Don't be selfish . . . Be humble, thinking of others as better than yourself. Don't just think about your own affairs, but be interested in others, too, and in what they are doing." (Philippians 2:3–4 TLB)

What better time to do this but when we seemingly can't see beyond our own troubles?

# *Children*

———✦———

## GUIDING THEM TOWARD ADULTHOOD

*I*n a family, the primary job of children is to prepare to leave, and the primary job of parents is to equip them to do so.

From the first gulp of air to the first gulp of food, from the first classroom to the first apartment, childhood is about departure. And the road that leads our children toward independent lives is one that is marked by joy and anger, by sharing and secrets, and by emotional changes and growth that alter our relationships fundamentally.

"The parent-child relationship is profoundly spiritual if for no other reason than that it must constantly deal with the reality of love and loss for both parties," says the Reverend John Boyle, Ph.D., founder of the pastoral counseling center at Chicago's Fourth Presbyterian Church. "We may love our kids, and they us, but we lose them to adulthood, the world, and the inevitability of independence. Parenthood is a full-time job and one that changes as our children grow."

How can we maintain loving, supportive, nurturing relationships during this temporary time together? How can we help our children develop the religious character to make the right choices as they grow?

# Helping Children Reach Independence

The first step in letting children grow is letting them go. We must accept that our children will have goals and ambitions that don't always match ours, and we must give them the freedom to seek their own paths, says the Reverend Mahan Siler, master of divinity, former pastor of Pullen Memorial Baptist Church in Raleigh, North Carolina. "There's a tremendous danger in investing in our kids the obligation to satisfy our unmet needs and unfinished dreams, to become what we wanted but failed to become, to make the money or earn the degree or star in the big game," Reverend Siler says. "We need to allow them to become their own independent beings, even if that means questioning some of the values or ideals that we've tried to instill in them. Better that they try to be children of God than 'chips off the ole block.'"

And if their searching leads to difficult relationships and rebellion at home, we should remember that these, too, will likely pass. "The rebellious years, usually the adolescent years, represent turbulent times in the lives of our children. They are feeling a tremendous urge to separate from their families, if only symbolically," says Iris Yob, doctor of education and author of *Keys to Teaching Children about God.* "They're trying to discover their own identities, which may also include their own faiths—a relationship with God on their own terms. We need to keep in mind that this is a transition time in their lives, not a permanent state of existence."

Letting children rebel, letting them venture out in order to define themselves is a tremendous act of faith on the part of the parent, notes Dr. Boyle. "The father of the prodigal son (Luke 15:11–32) let that boy go irrespective of what he may have been feeling internally. All he had to lean on was faith in God to protect his boy and faith in himself as a parent who tried to instill in his son the knowledge that he would always be loved and could always come home. His effectiveness as a loving father should not be dismissed by his son's willingness to rebel but vindicated by his willingness to return."

So how does a family survive the rough spots, the inevitable times when parents and children are crossing swords rather than paths?

**Find comfort in others.** Often when our kids are in rebellion, our greatest anxiety comes from feeling as though we're alone in the

## Faithbuilders

### From the Mouths of Babes

"It was a Fourth of July celebration and I was at a fireworks display with some colleagues of mine and their young daughter," says Iris Yob, doctor of education and author of *Keys to Teaching Children about God.* "When the first of the great explosions lit up the sky and we all oohed and aahed, the little girl asked no one in particular, 'Do you think that was high enough to touch God?' What ensued was a lively exploration of how God could be up above, looking over us and also down below, sitting in our midst, right there with us. The child was both the teacher and the student. She enriched us all, but only because we respected the wisdom of her question."

struggle, says Reverend Siler. If we find ourselves questioning, we should search out other parents who are going or have gone through much the same thing, he says. Not only can they relieve the guilt we feel when we assume that our kids are the only ones prone to rebellion, but their collective wisdom can help us learn how to deal with some of our kids' rebellious ways. Our pastors can help us find other parents we can speak to, and perhaps even bring us together to share our common concerns.

**Allow children their doubts.** If our children rebel against their faith and we try to repress it, there is a good chance that the rebellion will deepen, if only as a matter of principle, says Dr. Yob. "It ceases to be an exploration of alternative values and becomes instead a tug-of-war between our desire to impose obedience and their demand to assert independence.

"The first order of business is to give children the space they need to question the assumptions that we've taught. I remember a young girl who, when being put to bed by her grandmother, was asked, 'What do you want to say to Jesus tonight?' She answered, 'I don't want to say anything. I don't believe in Jesus anymore!' The

# Prayer Pointers

## Worshipping with a Young Child

Here are tips to consider when you want to help your young child feel comfortable in worship, according to Lois Brokering, contributing writer for *The Lutheran* magazine.

**Play church at home.** Set up stuffed animals and dolls and encourage your child to be the pastor. Practice "church behavior" such as listening or looking quietly at books.

**Pack a church bag.** Bring along colored pencils and paper, soft toys, and picture books, preferably of Bible stories. Add something new once in a while for a surprise. Use these materials only at church so that there is some novelty for your child. Don't include noisy toys or markers.

**Get ready for church on Saturday night.** Do this so that Sunday morning can be as leisurely as possible. Keep a positive outlook; young children who can't understand the words at church go on how it feels.

**Visit the restroom.** And make the trip before church.

**Sit near the front.** Children can see what's going on better, and that helps focus their attention.

**Sit near other parents.** They're less likely to shoot you a disapproving look if your child is overactive.

**Engage the child.** Talk quietly to the child about what's happening during worship. Even a one-year-old can enjoy sitting during moments of silent reflection, watching a baptism, and listening to the music.

grandmother, instead of resisting the girl's anger, responded by saying, 'All right, you just lie quietly while I pray,' and then proceeded to offer a prayer that acknowledged how angry and dismayed we can become at God when things upset us and God seems so far away. It was a brilliant way to affirm the girl's search for answers while at the same time allowing for God's presence to be acknowledged."

**Picture God as a parent.** Because the biblical God is so often presented with metaphors (judge, bridegroom, tender of the vineyard), we can try envisioning Him as a parent who shares many of the same frustrations and anxieties about our kids that we do, says Dr. Yob. When we pray to the parent God, we can ask to feel His empathy for us, His love for our children, and His guidance through the stormy seas that all families must ultimately weather.

# Helping Children Build Faith

Our children's faith development parallels their physical development. It matures and reshapes itself as our children acquire deeper understanding of their places in the world. "Children are always inquisitive," says Dr. Yob. "It's just that over the years, the nature of their inquiry changes and becomes more complex, and we as parents must be adaptable to these changes." Dr. Yob offers these specific suggestions to help equip our children with the tools of prayer and spiritual curiosity.

**Model prayerful behavior.** Children will be more apt to establish a prayer life if they are used to seeing us pray.

**Avoid rules.** When children begin to pray, we only get in the way of their spontaneity if we give them a lot of instructions. Instead, we should encourage them to experience the freedom of simply talking to God in language that makes them comfortable.

**Give them choices.** Young children can be given choices about how they pray: "Do you want to pray out loud or quietly? Together with me or by yourself? What sort of things do you want to talk to God about? What are you angry or happy or sad about?" Older children can be granted more leeway in their spiritual lives: "When you come to church, would you like to sit with us or with your friends? Would you rather attend Sunday school or the worship service?"

**Respect their questions.** Children's curiosity often opens up great treasure chests of questions, which should be applauded and explored. "I remember a mother and her daughter walking by a nativity scene one Christmas season," recalls Dr. Yob. "The child asked her mother if the baby in the cradle was a boy baby or a girl baby.

# Answered Prayers

## Prayer Restored My Son's Health

"Our oldest child, Greg, had a brush with death in 1988. He came down with flulike symptoms, and the doctor at the hospital told us that he was in septic shock. The first few hours were very critical, and the doctor was preparing us for the worst. As my husband and I and Greg's wife huddled and cried, my husband cried out, 'He's going to die.' I said, 'No, he's not going to die.' When I said that, I felt like something made me say it. I didn't just say it to be the strong one.

"As the days passed and friends and family gathered, many prayers were said. People whom I didn't even know were praying. But one person in particular, my sister, JoAnn, has the strongest faith of anyone I know. At one point, Greg's toes had turned black and the doctors said that they might have to amputate. My sister concentrated her prayer on Greg's toes, and the pink came back. Greg spent 13 days in intensive care and 7 days on the regular floor. But he is the picture of health today, and I thank God every day."

—*Peggy Dunn, Barberton, Ohio*

When the mother answered, 'It's a boy; Jesus came to Earth as a boy,' the dismayed daughter quickly responded with, 'Well that's no good, we need a girl in there, too!' It launched a delightfully rich discussion between them about the male and female qualities of God."

Our journey as parents may be trying. It may test our resolve and our patience. But we can take comfort in knowing that we're not traveling alone. "For me, it all comes down to Philippians 2:1," says Dr. Boyle. "We are literally *encouraged* in Christ. Christ instills in us the courage to be parents by assuring us that God is the partner in our labors, and we encourage our children to believe that with God's help and our love, they are better able to find their rightful places in the world."

# *Courage*

———✦———

## DRAWING STRENGTH FROM GOD

*T*he morning when an escaped convict put a handgun in her husband's side and forced his way into their home, Louise DeGrafinried was in the kitchen cooking breakfast.

Lots of cooks would have dropped their spatulas in fear. Not DeGrafinried. A 70-year-old grandmother and a faithful member of the Mount Sinai Missionary Baptist Church in Mason, Tennessee, she laid down the law with the bad guy. "I'm a Christian lady and I don't want any violence in my house, so put that gun down," DeGrafinried said. "Now, do you want something to eat?"

The convict complied and sat down for breakfast, and Louise went to work, calmly whipping up another portion of eggs, sausage, bacon, and toast. When she set a plate before him, he got an even clearer sense of who he was dealing with. DeGrafinried wouldn't let him eat without first saying grace, and then went on to explain how a life without Jesus was no life at all.

Eventually, the police arrived and surrounded the house, and DeGrafinried had some words for them as well. "I'll walk him out of here myself," she said. And that she did, standing by until he was safely ensconced in the back of a patrol car.

"He was ready to give up," says DeGrafinried now. Maybe so. But where did she get the courage to stick around and find out? Or to stand up to a gun-toting outlaw? "I wasn't praying all the time, because I was talking to him, but I knew the Lord was surely protecting me."

## Confident, Courageous Living

When we think of courage, the focus is often on people who spontaneously do brave things—war heroes, for example, or lifeguards, police, or fire-rescue personnel who are paid to put their lives in jeopardy. But perhaps just as inspiring are the everyday folks who face an extreme challenge in their lives and, with God's help, overcome it. Especially when that challenge is before them every day.

"I often think that the most courageous people I see are single moms and single dads," says Ray Pritchard, doctor of ministry, senior pastor of Calvary Memorial Church in Oak Park, Illinois, and author of *The ABC's of Wisdom* and *What a Christian Believes*. "They get up early every morning, get themselves and the kids ready, and drop them off at school or day care. Then they go to work, come home and fix supper, spend time with their children, do a million other things, and finally crawl into bed late at night, dead tired. Then they get up the next morning and do it all over again. To me, that takes just as much courage as any soldier on any battlefield in the world," says Dr. Pritchard.

But whether it's soldiers or single moms, the cornerstone of courage is the same: training—and lots of it. Soldiers undergo basic training, getting in shape, learning to fire and clean weapons, developing teamwork, and building the skills that will help them stand up to adversity under fire.

For single moms and, really, all the rest of us, life is our boot camp. And if we begin to view day-to-day events as mini training sessions, we can build our courage to face hardships, great or small, says Dr. Pritchard.

Admittedly, it's not always an easy thing to do. "We often want to turn away from the difficulties and adversities that we face in life, and yet clinging to God even in the face of adversity is the thing that makes us become people of courage, people of spiritual faith who can't be shaken," says Ruthanne Garlock, a former missionary and co-author of *A Woman's Guide to Getting through Tough Times in Life* and *Prayers Women Pray*.

But when we do respond to such tasks with courage and faith, amazing things happen. "It's like a stone being thrown into a pond,"

## A Prayer to Fight Fear

God of confidence,
I'm afraid today.
It's not an energizing fear
moving me toward action.
It's a demoralizing fear,
paralyzing me,
making me weak, listless and useless.
I need Your love that casts out fear.
I long for the power of Your presence
to release the fear that binds me.
Thank You for the gift of Your confidence.
I receive it;
I rest in it; and
I release my fear
to You.
Thank You for
being my Confidence . . .
Thank You most of all
for loving me.

—*Norm Nelson, from* Thank You Most of All for Loving Me

says Dr. Pritchard. "Our courage and faith ripple out from that moment, that place of difficulty, and it just goes and goes."

Here are some ways that we can build our courage, step-by-step.

**Prepare.** For challenges big and small, doing some advance work is the best way to nurture courage. So if we're trying to develop the nerve to confront a difficult situation, like dealing with an alcoholic and abusive spouse, it can help to learn how to set proper emotional boundaries, the verbal techniques that can literally shut down abusers. Or, if we're normally afraid of talking in front of groups and we have to make a presentation, we simply need to study and practice the material until we know it as well as our own names, says Dr. Pritchard. (For more information on boundary setting, see Abuse on page 141.)

**Find a mentor.** Just as a skilled instructor can teach us a musical instrument or a foreign language, we can learn to act more confidently and courageously by watching people who live this way day-by-day. And the closer we get to them, the better, says the Reverend Neva Coyle, a conference speaker based in Ahnwahnee, California, and author of *A Woman of Strength* and *Loved on a Grander Scale.* Look for people who have been where you are now, who have grown through their experiences, and who have the skills to pass on to you what they have learned. "When I see someone exhibiting a virtue such as godly courage, then I get close to that person," she says.

**Fast and pray.** We're not talking about 40 days in the desert, but countless fearful and weak people develop courage and confidence in God through fasting and prayer. "The book of Esther is an example of recognizing the need to fast, to call out to God before we try to come up with our human solutions to whatever difficulties we're dealing with," says Garlock. "As scary it as might have been, Esther got her answer, obeyed, and did specifically what God revealed to her, and He delivered her and her people."

**Tap courage from above.** A man fends off the attack of a rabid animal. A child risks his life pushing a classmate out of the way of a speeding bus. People act courageously when challenged in all types of circumstances. But over time, human courage will let us down. "You get to the point where you say, 'I just can't keep doing this; I can't go on,'" says Garlock. "And that's when we have to recognize that God is bigger than our problems and receive our courage from Him." The only way to do that is by crying out to Him. One verse says it all: "But blessed is the man who trusts in the Lord, whose confidence is in Him." (Jeremiah 17:7 NIV)

**Attend church.** What takes more courage than facing the Grim Reaper? In a small study of terminally ill patients at a large Veterans Administration hospital in Long Beach, California, those who attended church more frequently and felt that religion was important reported having more courage and less fear of death than those who weren't interested in faith. One reviewer of the study said that these patients exhibited improved coping skills that not only led to a better quality of life than the less religious but also might lower their health-care costs. Plus, a good church can go a long way in helping provide encouraging friendships, says Dr. Pritchard.

**Look for a purpose.** If we knew that our one courageous act would have eternal significance, would we rise to the occasion? A single act can and does have significance, and that knowledge should be enough to embolden our efforts, says Dr. Pritchard. "Whether we see it or feel it or understand it, God puts us in situations or allows us to be there for a purpose," he says.

**Take the next step.** The Bible is loaded with characters who didn't believe that they had the talent, brains, or ambition to get the job done the way God wanted. But when they responded with courage and faith and moved when He said it was time, seas parted, giants fell, and walls tumbled. "Simply taking the next step in front of us and trusting God with the results—that is when the exciting stuff starts to happen," says Dr. Pritchard.

**Hang in there.** Once we take those courageous first steps, rest assured that we'll be met with stiff or even harsh opposition. But this, of course, is no time to fold, says Dr. Pritchard. After all, ". . . the Lord, He is the One who goes before you. He will be with you, He will not leave you nor forsake you; do not fear nor be dismayed." (Deuteronomy 31:8 NKJV)

"I have learned not to ask God to relieve me from something one minute sooner than it has served His purpose for developing His character within me," says Reverend Coyle. "That's a tough thing to pray, but we need to be prepared to be changed by what happens."

# Death of a Loved One

## Beyond the Pain, There Is Hope

Think of how the Earth revolves around the sun. If the sun were to suddenly disappear from the sky, the gravitational pull on the Earth would be drastically altered, and the planet would be knocked completely off course. The climate and every aspect of life on Earth would be skewed, in flux, and in question.

When a loved one dies, it's as though we're the Earth and the sun has disappeared, suggests the Reverend Mel Lawrenz, Ph.D., senior associate pastor at Elmbrook Church and director of the Elmbrook Christian Study Center, both in Brookfield, Wisconsin, and co-author of six books, including *Life after Grief* and *Overcoming Grief and Trauma*. We may feel completely lost or completely bewildered, he says. We may find ourselves thrown off course. We may find our lives in crisis. We need to expect this and accept this. "A person might sit at the breakfast table realizing, 'I have never made the coffee in this house, ever. I don't even know how to do that. My spouse used to have a cup of coffee here for me.' And that one little thing can become the crisis of the moment," he says.

Dr. Lawrenz and other spiritual counselors note that not only may we find our lives in crisis but we may also find ourselves in a crisis of faith.

# Keep the Faith

When we lose a person who has been an anchor in our lives, we naturally question God. We may ask, "Why?" We may cry, "How could you?" We may express anger at a God who would let this happen.

We may feel guilty about being angry with God. But we should let out that anger, says psychologist Michele Novotni, Ph.D., assistant professor of counseling at Eastern College, a Christian college of arts and sciences in St. Davids, Pennsylvania.

It is important to let God know how we feel, says Dr. Novotni. "People oftentimes feel that it is unreligious to say that they're mad with God. Yet, if you're going to have a relationship with someone, sometimes you are mad. It's often as you move through that anger that you're able to get to a deeper place. Whereas, if you deny any feelings of anger, it becomes very difficult to get to a deeper relationship."

Don't suppress the anger. Don't give up on God. And don't give up the faith, says grief educator John W. James, co-founder of the Grief Recovery Institute in Beverly Hills, California, and co-author of *The Grief Recovery Handbook.* The faith crisis that follows the death of a close loved one causes many people to drop out of church and to abandon lifelong belief systems.

Often, when we're tempted to abandon our faith after the death of a loved one, it is not because God changes or the tenants of the faith change. It is because we have not been given helpful counsel from those to whom we turn in the church; we have suffered from poor teaching; we have been criticized for questioning God; or we have been "Bible-whacked," as Dr. Novotni puts it.

Bible-whacked?

Far too often, people who don't know how to help us, who don't know what to say or do, just slap a lofty platitude or Bible verse on us as though that is the ultimate, end-all answer, as though that will solve our grief, says Dr. Novotni. Far too often, they act as though we are wrong to question God, that we are pitifully lacking in faith if we do. Wrong. The Bible is full of examples of people questioning God, point out theologians. Even Jesus cried out in the garden of Gethsemane, "My God, my God, why has thou forsaken me?"

"Oftentimes, grievers turn to the church for emotional support," says James. "What they get back is intellectual truth. They say, 'Gee, I still miss my mother,' which is an emotional comment, and they get back, 'Oh, she is in a better place,' which is an intellectual comment."

Denying our true feelings doesn't help. It just buries the grief or anger deeper so that it can boil in the belly of the volcano.

# Take the Pain to God

When we're in the throes of loss, we need to seek sympathetic people and turn to God and talk to God. We need to tell Him how we feel and ask Him what we are to do next and how we are to get from here to there. We need to express anger and disappointment. The very process of expressing disappointment is an expression of faith. We don't get mad at someone we don't believe exists, says Dr. Lawrenz.

Remember, says Dr. Novotni, God never promised us that life would be easy or that it wouldn't hurt at times. He just promised to be with us through it all. As the Psalmist sang:

God is our refuge and strength,
 an ever-present help in trouble.
Therefore we will not fear, though the Earth give way
 and the mountains fall into the heart of the sea,
Though its waters roar and foam
 and the mountains quake with their surging.

—*Psalm 46:1–3 NIV*

Here are some other things that will help us in the early days following a loss.

**Find an on-call friend.** We need someone sympathetic who says that it's okay if we call them anytime, even at 3:00 A.M., if we're feeling desperate. We shouldn't abuse the privilege but make use of it if we really need to, says the Reverend James E. Miller, doctor of ministry, United Methodist minister of Willowgreen Productions in Fort Wayne, Indiana, a center that helps those experiencing grief and loss, and author of numerous books and videotapes used in hospices, hospitals, funeral homes, and counseling services.

**Avoid toxic people.** It just plain hurts to be around some people. They don't let us grieve. They lecture, denigrate, chide, or otherwise upset us, either intentionally or unintentionally. It's okay to avoid such people for awhile if it makes us feel better, says Dr. Miller.

Some people will think that it is their duty to jolt us out of our grief, says Dr. Lawrenz. We will want to avoid them in particular.

**Track thoughts.** We need to record what we learn. As we go through a profound loss experience, we can learn many lessons and gain many insights. We can write these down in a notebook or journal, day by day, then reflect on them occasionally, says Dr. Miller.

## How Much Will It Hurt?

For some people, there is no greater hurt than losing a spouse—their friend, lover, and confidante. But this is not always so. The impact of the loss and the extent of the hurt depend on the nature of the relationship. Lecturer and ordained Episcopalian priest Harold Ivan Smith, doctor of ministry, who leads grief gatherings at St. Luke's Medical Center in Kansas City, Missouri, and is the author of many Christian self-help books, explains that we might think that if we lost a spouse of 50 years, the gravity of the grief would be much greater than if we lost a spouse after 2 years.

"If it was an awful marriage, a constantly awful marriage that went on for 50 years, the surviving partner may actually feel a great sense of relief," points out Dr. Smith. Along with that, they may feel a great sense of guilt "because they know that they are expected to be feeling sorrow and loss, but they do not feel that." We need to know that it is acceptable for us to feel what we feel, and we need not harbor guilt about it, advises Dr. Smith.

# How to Pray

We have a natural tendency to turn to God when we suffer a great loss, such as when a dearly loved one dies, says the Reverend Mel Lawrenz, Ph.D., senior associate pastor at Elmbrook Church and director of the Elmbrook Christian Study Center, both in Brookfield, Wisconsin, and co-author of six books, including *Life after Grief* and *Overcoming Grief and Trauma.*

We may turn to God in anger. We may do so in confusion. We may do so in utter desperation. We may do so because we know that God is always there, no matter how uncertain everything else seems. In any case, we turn to God seeking comfort and reassurance.

We may wonder how best to approach God at such a time. Dr. Lawrenz offers these suggestions.

**Seek out the faithful.** We need to spend time with people whose faith is strong and whose faith we respect and feel comfortable with.

**Seek inspirational reading material.** For additional help, Harold Ivan Smith, doctor of ministry, lecturer and ordained Episcopalian priest who leads grief gatherings at St. Luke's Medical Center in Kansas City, Missouri, and is the author of many Christian self-help books, recommends the Willowgreen Life Transition books, which advise how we can cope with problems such as illness, grief, or death.

Then there is the loss of a son or daughter of any age, an especially difficult loss "because it goes so against the grain. Your child is supposed to bury you, not you bury your child," says Dr. Smith. "And for the families that I've worked with, that's the one that seems to be the most difficult to get a handle on.

Such deaths shake our faith to the core, says Dr. Smith. Losing a child is even more difficult, he says, "when it's a violent death, or it's a death that has some degree of choice—a suicide, or someone was

Dr. Lawrenz suggests that we read the Psalms. "Just open up the book of Psalms and poke around in it. Read them aloud." We'll find that many of the Psalms are conversations with God recalling the times when He has been there for people. Others ask questions like, "What do I do now?" The Psalms tend to deal pretty directly with the issues that we deal with at a time like this. "The Lord is near to the brokenhearted, and saves the crushed in spirit." (Psalm 34:18 RSV)

**Speak our minds.** "The most important thing that people should say to God is whatever it is they want to say—whatever question they have or whatever request they have," advises Dr. Lawrenz.

"A prayer is an unscripted talk with God. It's unscripted in that a person can say anything to Him at any time. So if it's questions, it's questions: 'God, what do I do next?' 'God, where are you?' Or statements: 'God, help me.' 'God, help my kids in this situation.' 'God, help me get through this day.' 'God, help me get out of bed.'"

Whatever we want to ask or say is all right. We can talk openly and freely with God.

For related comforting Scripture, see "Across the Aisles" (page 370).

drinking or taking drugs or getting involved in a prank and as a result, died."

# Face the Pain

The current thinking is that we are not supposed to run from our pain or hide from it. In fact, we are to dive in and experience it and all the issues that it brings up so that we grieve fully and work our way through the hard questions that arise. Losing a loved one is supposed to hurt. There are ways to deal with that hurt effectively that do help it heal. Here are a few.

**Write a letter to the deceased.** We can say things that we wish we could say if they were here. Maybe they are here in some way, says Dr. Miller. We can keep what we write in a journal or on the computer, or write it down and throw it away or burn each piece. After a while, the urge to write to the loved one will fade, but while it's there, we should do it. It's a great release, he says.

**Talk to the deceased one.** We can do this out loud, under our breath, or in our minds whenever the urge strikes. It is probably best, though, if we are alone when we do this. Some people sense the presence of their loved one, says Dr. Miller. Often, he says, it "is a feeling that the one who has died is somehow nearby, if not physically, then emotionally or spiritually. These are usually comforting and confirming experiences."

**Create a memorial at home.** An area with a framed photo or two and other memorabilia can help us remember and honor our loved one.

**Make time to be alone.** That is, unless we're by ourselves most of the time. It's important to spend time in reassessing and considering our thoughts. It's part of the healing process. However, we should not isolate ourselves completely, says Dr. Miller. We should not totally withdraw from our friends and families and associates. We do need to talk with others and get out into the real world sometimes.

**Go ahead and cry.** It's natural. Jesus wept when he was told that his friend Lazarus had passed on.

**Give thanks.** Find something every day to be thankful for and spend some time appreciating it.

## How Long Will It Take?

A question that we frequently ask God when enduring the pain of a loss is, "How long will this go on?" The truth is, grief counselors say, we never get over it completely. The loss, the pain, and the transformation that they bring about in our lives are with us forever. We will never be the same, says Dr. Novotni. But we will also not feel the pain as intensely as time passes and healing takes place.

The key to getting over the death of a loved one is this: Don't try to get over it, say the experts.

What?

The thinking at one time was that we should try to erase the person from our minds and deconstruct the relationship, says Dr. Smith. But, he points out, "it takes as much investment to deconstruct the relationship as it took to construct it across the years. There's a whole school of thought that's called continuing bond. This is a theory and belief of many specialists in grief communities that those bonds do not need to be severed. They do not need to be amputated," he says.

"There need to be ways of honoring that person in your life. Whether that's leaving the pictures up, remembering their birthday, observing your anniversary and those red-letter days on your calendar, you honor the memory," says Dr. Smith.

This is easier, Dr. Smith notes, "for those who believe in eternal life. They can view this time as a mere interlude without the loved one and look forward to a rejoining in eternity. That's the faith context for many people." It is less painful to gaze upon the picture of a loved one we eagerly anticipate seeing again than one we believe is gone forever.

Fine. We're keeping the memory alive. But how long will we be in agony? How long will we cry uncontrollably at unexpected moments? "The rule of thumb is that there is no rule of thumb," says Dr. Lawrenz.

"It will take as long as it is supposed to take," says Dr. Miller.

"It's remarkable," says Dr. Lawrenz, "a week after someone loses their spouse, people are starting to ask, 'Well are things getting back to normal for you now?' The fact of the matter is, no, that is not at all going to be the case. Things are not going to be getting back to normal." Things may never get back to normal.

"It's not at all abnormal for someone to still be grieving the loss of a spouse a year or two later," says Dr. Lawrenz. "It's a lifelong thing for many, and that is normal." Parents who have lost children probably will still find tears coming to their eyes 10 years later, he says. How prepared we are for a loss can have some effect on how long we will grieve. He offers two scenarios as examples: losing a father suddenly who was a best buddy or losing a father who lived into his nineties and spent his last few years in deteriorating health in a nursing home. We're better prepared for the latter and less likely to grieve as long.

# How to Survive Red-Letter Days

Simply anticipating the first Christmas without a recently deceased spouse, parent, child, brother, sister, or best friend can be frightening and painful.

Christmas is one of the "red-letter days"—warm celebratory occasions that we generally spend pleasantly with our loved ones, days that we highlight on the calendar, such as birthdays, anniversaries, and holidays.

These days recall and re-jar our grief and loneliness. It is as if the world has gone on without us, says author, lecturer, and ordained Episcopalian priest Harold Ivan Smith, doctor of ministry, who leads grief gatherings at St. Luke's Medical Center in Kansas City, Missouri. "Mother's Day, Father's Day, Christmas, Valentine's Day for the husband whose wife is gone, for the wife whose husband is gone and won't be bringing her flowers or candy or taking her out someplace romantic and special to celebrate their love—another wave of grief comes in. She feels out of synch with where the rest of the world is on February 14th," he says.

Here's how can we best handle our red-letter days.

**Acknowledge them.** Plan for them, says Dr. Smith. Anticipate them. Recognize that, yes, this day was very special to us and our loved one in the past. Plan time to grieve that day. Perhaps visit the grave.

**Honor the memory.** "Make time that day to offer gratitude for the life of the loved one," advises Dr. Smith. Focus on how much our lives were enriched because we had the privilege of knowing them. Make the red-letter days days of thanksgiving.

**Realize that they may be painful.** But don't forgo the joy and enjoyment that these days can bring, says the Reverend James E. Miller, doctor of ministry, United Methodist minister of Willowgreen

Productions in Fort Wayne, Indiana, a center that helps those experiencing grief and loss, and author of numerous books and videotapes used in hospices, hospitals, funeral homes, and counseling services. Often, people report that the day was not nearly as horrendous as they had expected.

**Help others.** If our friends are enduring their own red-letter days, we can help them by remembering them and remembering and honoring their departed loved ones, say pastoral grief counselors.

Of course, it takes courage to do this, notes the Reverend Mel Lawrenz, Ph.D., senior associate pastor at Elmbrook Church and director of the Elmbrook Christian Study Center, both in Brookfield, Wisconsin, and co-author of six books, including *Life after Grief* and *Overcoming Grief and Trauma*. "On the anniversary of the wife's death, say to the husband, 'I was thinking about your wife just the other day,'" he suggests. "Most people would be very afraid to say that because they don't want to make people think about or remember their loss. But, almost universally, for the grieving person this validates the living memory of the person they have lost. It is an honorable thing and it may bring tears to their eyes. But the person who is not threatened by their grief and is willing to stand with them and talk with them to the degree that they want to talk is a rare person, one who understands."

Yes, says Dr. Smith, "it is important for other people to recognize those dates. I send notes or cards to the families of friends that have died. For instance, I sent a Mother's Day card to someone who was experiencing her first Mother's Day without her mother. I added a note saying, 'I realize this is a very important day for you.'"

# Living with the Memory

How do we create that continuing bond that the experts say we need? How do we do it in a way that is not morbid and that won't drag us deep into depression? Here are some healthy ways that counselors say we can keep a loved one's memory alive in our hearts and heal the hurt from their passing.

**Carry a memento.** Choosing something that fits in a pocket or purse and recalls the person who died creates links to them in a special way. "Whenever you want, reach for or gaze upon this object and remember what it signifies," says Dr. Miller.

**Walk in their shoes.** If it feels comforting, spend time in the deceased person's room, chair, or bed, suggests Dr. Miller.

**Be prepared.** Expect memories of earlier losses to flood forth. Particularly, those that we have not completely processed and those that we have not completely grieved, says James. This is an opportunity to work through them as well, he says, a time to seek completion and closure.

**Accept change.** We shouldn't enshrine their existence. Yes, we can create memorials, but we shouldn't go to the extreme and refuse to change anything about our homes and routines or try to keep everything precisely as it was when the loved one was alive, says Dr. Miller.

When the time is right, we can give away some of the things that will never be used again or rearrange the furniture so that it works well for us and anyone else sharing our home now. At some point, we will want to make some changes in our environment to make it clear that a profound change has taken place in our lives, says Dr. Miller. As it says in Isaiah 43:19, "Behold, I am doing a new thing!"

**Carry on the work.** Give to the deceased person's favorite charities and causes in the person's name and honor. Help sustain good things that were important to that person. Realize, says Dr. Smith, that "charitable organizations are wounded when a giver dies. The money stops." But we can help and deal with our grief at the same time by "embracing causes, organizations, or charities that were very much a part of our loved ones' lives. That's a wonderful way to memorialize them," he says.

For more help, see Emotional Pain (page 259), Grief (page 290), Heartache (page 311), and Loss (page 365).

# *Defeat*

## LOSING DOESN'T MEAN GIVING UP

*H*ow's this for a résumé?

1832: Loses job.
    Loses race for state legislature.
1833: Business fails.
1834: Wins election to state legislature.
1835: Girlfriend dies.
1838: Loses race for speaker of the state legislature.
    Loses election for party nomination for U.S. Congress.
1846: Wins seat in Congress.
1848: Loses Congressional seat.
1849: Loses bid for land officer position.
1854: Loses race for U.S. Senate.
1856: Loses bid for U.S. vice presidential nomination.
1858: Again loses race for U.S. Senate.
1860: Elected president of the United States.

This encapsulates the anything-but-charmed or meteoric rise of Abraham Lincoln, the man whom many consider to be one of the greatest-ever U.S. presidents.

Clearly, Abraham Lincoln knew defeat. He knew what it meant to be beaten. Yet he also knew what it meant to try again or to start over.

We have to realize, as did Lincoln, that getting beaten is just one of those things that happens in life. It's not the end of our lives.

The key is to keep things in perspective, says theologian and Christian psychiatrist Paul Meier, M.D., co-founder of New Life Clinics, the largest provider of Christian-based counseling in the United States and author of more than 60 best-selling Christian self-help books. He suggests that we consider an eternal perspective. "The eternal perspective is realizing that we're going to live billions and trillions and zillions of years," says Dr. Meier. We are more than bodies, in the spiritual view; we are eternal beings, eternal souls.

"So when things go wrong," says Dr. Meier, "I ask myself the question: A hundred years from now, what difference will it make? When I'm up in Heaven with my friends a hundred years from now looking back on that day—if I can remember that day—or somebody reminds me of what happened that day, what's my perspective going to be then?"

The long view is always less frightening, more enlightening, and, ultimately, clearer, than a close-up examination of a problem through a magnifying glass. Most of the time, little good is accomplished by magnifying our problems.

This is not to say that we shouldn't dissect problems or shouldn't learn from them, says Dr. Meier. This is not to say that we won't grieve. But grief and hopelessness are not synonymous. Problems may torment us, circumstances may haunt us, death may pluck away those closest to our hearts, but we must not give up hope. That, he says, is what is meant in the Bible, where it says that we should not "grieve as others do who have no hope." (1 Thessalonians 4:13 NRSV)

Moses believed that God takes the long view. He said, in a prayer, "For a thousand years in Thy sight are like yesterday when it is past, or as a watch in the night." (Psalm 90:4 RSV)

We overcome defeat by seeing what a tiny blip it really is in the long view. "Having that kind of attitude really helps keep circumstances from overwhelming us when things go wrong in life," says Dr. Meier.

## How to Weather the Worst

Maybe our business has collapsed. Maybe a fire has consumed our home, destroying our clothes, our furniture, and our possessions.

## Faithbuilders

### Let God Be Our Guide

God is able to make a way out of no way and transform dark yesterdays into bright tomorrows. This is our hope for becoming better men and women. This is our mandate for seeking to make a better world.

—*Dr. Martin Luther King Jr.*

Lord, be Thou within me, to strengthen me;
without me, to keep me;
above me, to protect me;
beneath me, to uphold me;
before me, to direct me;
behind me, to keep me from straying;
round about me, to defend me.

—*Lancelot Andrewes, Bishop of Winchester (1555–1626)*

Maybe we allowed the fire insurance to lapse. Regardless, we've lost family memorabilia that can never be replaced.

Maybe we've waged a neighborhood battle to keep a shopping center at bay but lost, and now the bulldozers are rumbling and changing the landscape.

Maybe we've thrown our hearts and souls and substantial savings into an election campaign and lost, and now, everywhere we go we feel humiliated because people recognize that we're the also-ran.

Maybe our child's invincible soccer team makes it to the finals in the state championships and gets totally, humiliatingly mopped off the field.

We're talking real defeat here. When we literally must give up something, let go of something, in order to move on. How do we do that with grace?

It's really a matter of choice, says the Reverend James E. Miller, doctor of ministry, United Methodist minister of Willowgreen Productions in Fort Wayne, Indiana, a center that helps those experiencing grief and loss, and author of numerous books and videotapes used in hospices, hospitals, funeral homes, and counseling services. Four simple, fundamental choices make all the difference in the world in how we overcome and heal from defeat, says Dr. Miller. They don't take money or require any special equipment. They are simply positive mindsets that we can choose to hold on to. What are they?

**Accept the pain.** "Accept it and find ways to express it," says Dr. Miller. Accepting it and expressing it is healing. Sure it hurts. Feel it. Let it out. "Release the pain through expression, and it will release you," he says.

**Look for the helpful lesson.** "Remain open to the possibility that this seeming disaster can teach us something of worth, even if we have no idea what that might be," says Dr. Miller.

After King David's son deposed him and he and his entourage were being pelted with dirt and rocks as they fled, King David held on to hope. "It may be," he said, "that the Lord will see my distress and repay me with good for the cursing I am receiving today." (2 Samuel 16:12 NIV)

**Endure.** Do not hide or shirk. Endure what must be endured. "Adopt the belief that we grow stronger at our broken parts," says Dr. Miller.

**Reach out.** Invite others to stand with us through the ordeal, advises Dr. Miller. Going it alone, as we sometimes are tempted to do, nearly always carries with it a heaviness and sadness. Sharing our defeat with others can be comforting and uniting and bring together a caring community of support that will exist long after the current ordeal is forgotten.

For more advice on expressing pain healthfully, see Anger (page 160), Grief (page 290), and Loss (page 365).

# Depression

———✦———

## BATTLE WITH THE
## BLACK BEAST

*A* parent dies. A spouse leaves. A child is lost.

We are devastated, sad, morose, frantic—but are we depressed? We may think so. We may say so. But doctors, psychologists, counselors, and therapists might not classify it that way. They say that we are *supposed* to be disturbed when bad things happen. But feeling normal sadness and hopelessness is not the same as clinical depression. Depression is more than deep disappointment.

Depression is crippling despondency with a combination of symptoms that may include lethargy, listlessness, physical pain, hopelessness, loss of appetite, and others.

Depression may also include morbid thoughts or, in critical (emergency) cases, suicidal thinking, talk, threats, or attempts. In fact, depression is the number one cause of suicide, says Christian psychiatrist and theologian Paul Meier, M.D., co-founder of New Life Clinics, the largest provider of Christian-based counseling in the United States, and author of more than 60 best-selling Christian self-help books.

Depression is a black cloud that doesn't blow away, dissipate, or lift as it should. When depression hits, our brain chemistry goes awry—

the chemicals that regulate our senses of well-being, joy, pleasure, our sex drive, and our ability to concentrate vary and wane, says Dr. Meier.

Depression may develop following an emotional trauma. Or it may develop because something else causes our feel-good brain chemicals to be depleted. Here are some things that drain them.

- Stress and anxiety
- Poor eating habits or poor nutritional choices
- Lack of sleep
- Lack of exercise
- Side effects from prescription and/or over-the-counter medications
- Feeling unloved
- Feeling helpless, lost, or worthless.
- Feeling guilty over unconfessed wrongdoing
- In a small percentage of cases, a physical defect depletes the pleasure-producing brain chemicals or otherwise interferes with their operation

Regardless of the trigger, in all cases, once depression sets in and our brain chemistry changes, we can end up plunging into the black abyss.

Untreated, depression can ruin lives, limit lives, and take lives. Yes, depression is a physical condition and a curse. But it is not a sin. There is no Eleventh Commandment saying "Thou shall not be depressed," says lecturer and ordained Episcopalian priest Harold Ivan Smith, doctor of ministry, who leads grief gatherings at St. Luke's Medical Center in Kansas City, Missouri, and is the author of *Life-Changing Answers to Depression.*

Jesus, Elijah, Job, Jeremiah, and other saints appear to have been depressed, according to today's standards, sometimes to the point of being suicidal, says Dr. Smith. Elijah, trembling in fear, "sat down under a juniper tree; and he requested for himself that he might die." Jesus, in the Garden of Gethsemane, said to his disciples, "my soul is deeply grieved to the point of death."

We need not let depression nor guilt about it crucify us. We can climb out of it, one positive, constructive, certain step at a time. And we can take steps to domesticate and defang depression so that the beast's bite will never again be quite so ferocious.

# Turn Gloom to Zoom

Fortunately, many types of help are available for those with depression. Some is self-help. Some is professional help. All is of God, says Dr. Smith. God may bring us books, cassettes, groups, friends, helpers, counselors, doctors, or medications.

But if we're in deep despair, feeling hopeless, the immediate thing that we should do is get to a professional therapist, says Dr. Meier.

"Run to counseling," urges psychologist Michele Novotni, Ph.D., assistant professor of counseling at Eastern College, a Christian college of arts and sciences in St. Davids, Pennsylvania. A good therapist can quickly assess the depth of our depression and can help us immediately begin to break the downward spiral. A good counselor will not start preaching to us, accusing us of having hidden sin in our lives, or otherwise make us feel guilty or shameful.

A good counselor may refer us to someone who will prescribe antidepressant medication. Medication can make all the difference in the world. Antidepressant medications are not "happy pills," explains Dr. Novotni. They simply help coax wayward, depressed brain chemistry back to relative normality. Those who use antidepressant medication still feel sadness when confronted with sad events. But with the proper medication (often, it takes quite a bit of experimentation to find the right medication since reactions are quite individualized), people are much less likely to sink into a deep, life-threatening despondency that seems impossible to overcome or interferes with our ability to function effectively.

Medication and other positive measures can give us the boost that we need so we can find our balance, says Dr. Novotni. Then, when we're in a stronger and clearer frame of mind, we can tackle the tough issues that may be at the root of our depression. That is when we are better able to examine our pain, deep-rooted guilt or secrets, or repressed inappropriate behaviors. "Jesus often healed first, and then had people restored to service to God. But He didn't tell them, get right with God and then I'll heal you," she says.

Why take medicine? Dr. Meier describes one patient who came to him after spending eight years with severe depression that Christian counseling couldn't help. "We dug and we probed. We looked for root problems because most people have them. He really didn't have any. He was a real, fine committed Christian. He was doing everything that he ought to be doing. But when I studied his pattern, his depression was regular and it was biological. I put him on the right medication, and he went home feeling just great. He said, 'I can't believe that I feel good after eight years.

## Signs and Symptoms

Depression comes in various shapes and sizes, but the two most common are major depression—the most crippling form of the condition—and chronic mild depression.

Below are the symptoms, as defined by the American Psychiatric Association, that therapists, psychologists, and psychiatrists assess to diagnose these types of depression. If you fall into either category, it is recommended that you discuss your situation with a mental health professional such as a psychiatrist, psychologist, or therapist. The professional will be able to advise you on appropriate treatment, says psychologist Michele Novotni, Ph.D, assistant professor of counseling at Eastern College, a Christian college of arts and sciences in St. Davids, Pennsylvania.

*Indications of major depression:* Either of the first two symptoms below, plus four or more of the other symptoms that last for at least two consecutive weeks.

1. A depressed mood, daily, for most of the day; that is, feeling sad or empty or being tearful; in children and teens, constant grumpiness is considered a depressed mood
2. A substantial loss of interest or pleasure in most activities most of the day, most days
3. A 5 percent or greater weight change in a month (without conscious dieting) or a noted increase or decrease in appetite most days

Is this going to last?' I said, 'Yes. Just take the medicine the rest of your life.'"

Some people need medication only for a single brief period, or several brief periods, to recover or maintain equilibrium. Give medication a fair chance, doctors say. Many drugs take up to eight weeks to fully kick in. Be patient.

4. Excessive sleepiness or inability to sleep most nights (or days)
5. Physical agitation, restlessness, or sluggishness most days
6. Lack of energy or feeling fatigued most days
7. A deep sense of worthlessness or of extreme or inappropriate guilt most days
8. Impaired concentration or indecisiveness most days
9. Recurring thoughts about death, thoughts about suicide without any specific plan, suicide planning, or a suicide attempt

*Indications of chronic mild depression (dysthymic disorder):* The first symptom below plus two or more of the other symptoms.

1. A chronic depressed mood more days than not or not being symptom-free for at least two months at a time over the course of two years or more (this is a depression that usually is not disabling, but there is a sense of "just going through the motions" most of the time)
2. Decreased or increased appetite
3. Sleeplessness or increased sleeping
4. Decreased energy or fatigue
5. Dampened self-esteem
6. Poor concentration or difficulty when faced with decision making
7. A sense of hopelessness

Even if we aren't scraping bottom or even if we are against taking medication, a therapist can help speed our recovery, says Dr. Novotni.

A counselor can listen to us describe our lives and often identify distorted thinking patterns that we can correct to ease our depressive episodes or reduce the frequency of them, says Dr. Novotni. To find a good counselor, she says, we could:

- Ask friends for referrals.
- Interview potential therapists over the phone or in person before making a decision.
- Look for a comfortable, positive rapport.
- Ask: Is this therapist listening? Is the therapist empathic, understanding and relating to my important values? Is this therapist inspiring and encouraging?
- Realize that we may need to visit several therapists until we find the right chemistry and really hit it off.

Getting treatment can be a matter of life or death, success or failure, a future filled with bright, promising days or with melancholy and struggle. Get help. Don't shy away from therapy, urges Dr. Meier.

# Climb toward the Light

Defeating depression and reigniting life can be an exciting prospect and project. It does require a vigilant and ongoing effort for many of us. And it does require that we start somewhere. If we haven't already, why not start here, now?

We can do a lot ourselves and/or with the help of a counselor. Here are some exercises that can help us both get better now and stave off future depression.

**Monitor thinking.** Dr. Meier recommends that we identify and alter critical, angry, resentful, painful, self-effacing, and gloomy thoughts. All of these are negative and fuel depression, particularly angry thoughts. If we change our thinking, we will see our moods begin to lift.

We talk to ourselves mentally at a rate 5 to 10 times the speed that we talk with our mouths, says Dr. Meier. We talk inwardly with

# Answered Prayers

## Prayer Lifted the Depression

"The Lord gave me the most wonderful husband that a girl could ever ask for, and a year later I became the mother of a beautiful and happy son. I recognized God's touch in everything—the little everyday blessings like a hug, a kiss, an 'I love you,' a flower, a sunset, and so much more.

"Then, when my son was four years old, I came down with severe depression. I did not know what was happening to me. I had always been so happy, loving, and caring and had enjoyed life so much. Now, here I was crying all the time, not wanting to get up in the mornings, not wanting to shower, not wanting to wash my hair, not wanting to do any of the daily activities that I usually would do.

"I was hospitalized so many times, trying vitamin therapy, different doctors, different medications, shock treatments. The doctors finally concluded that I had a chemical imbalance.

"This is where prayer, faith, and healing came in. So many family members and friends prayed for me, and I read all kinds of Christian books tying to find help. I prayed that God would deliver me from this. My favorite Bible verse was, "I can do all things through Christ which strengthens me." (Philippians 4:13) He did.

"I know without a doubt that if I had not turned to my dear Lord and Savior, and without the prayers of family and friends, I would not have made it. I have been well for about 14 years now, and what a blessing. I truly give all the glory to God for where I am today."

—*Janice Dick, St. Peters, Missouri*

images, concepts, and ideas. We need to try to catch the negatives in our minds and refocus them on positives.

How should we think? Dr. Meier cites this passage: ". . . whatever things are true, whatever things *are* noble, whatever things *are* just, whatever things *are* pure, whatever things are lovely, whatever things *are* of good report, if there is any virtue and if *there is* anything praiseworthy—meditate on these things." (Philippians 4:8 NKJV)

**Confront anger.** We need to make sure that we're in touch with our anger and are handling it biblically. Obey Ephesians, Dr. Meier says. "Be angry and do not sin: do not let the sun go down on your wrath. . . ." (Ephesians 4:26–27 NKJV)

"If you hang on to your anger, Ephesians 4:27 says, you give Satan a foothold in your life," says Dr. Meier. "Leviticus 19:17–19 says that if you're angry at your neighbor, tell him how you feel. But don't get vengeance on him. Just tell him that you're angry." Vengeance belongs to God, as it says in Romans 12:19, notes Dr. Meier. "We need to turn all vengeance over to God. Basically, we need to be aware of our anger. We need to verbalize it. The anger can be at God. It can be at others. It can be at ourselves. We need to take our anger to God. We need to trust Him to take care of it."

**Release resentment.** Let it go. Easier said than done? Yes, but harboring resentment is self-punishment, self-emasculation. We replay over and over a hurt that we felt was inflicted on us by someone else and make ourselves feel awful again and again, says Dr. Smith. We can't change the past, but we can change how we choose to perceive it now. Forgive, as Jesus instructs. Release the matter to God. Ask for a healing change of perspective.

Just think of the title of the best-selling book by stress therapist Richard Carlson, Ph.D.: "Don't sweat the small stuff; and it's all small stuff."

**Cry for help.** When darkness descends, call friends and loved ones and ask for help with basic needs like food, shelter, cleaning—because all of these can be nearly impossible to cope with in the midst of major depression, says Dr. Novotni. And having friends and people we love around helps brighten our moods.

**Seek social solace.** Numerous medical and sociological studies show that regular, positive social interaction—the greater number of different types of contacts, the better—tends to enhance our overall well-being and limit depressive episodes in our lives, says heart specialist and best-selling author Dean Ornish, M.D., president and director of the Preventive Medicine Research Institute in Sausalito, California, and clinical professor of medicine at the University of California at San Francisco, who has conducted such studies. Some studies indicate that we get a healthy emotional boost from our spiritual communities; that is, from interacting with groups of people and individuals whom we feel comfortable with and enjoy being around and who inspire and encourage us and share our values, says Dr. Ornish.

Going to church seems to help, says Dale A. Matthews, M.D., associate professor of medicine at Georgetown University School of Medicine in Washington, D.C., and author of *The Faith Factor*, who has published studies of the effects of religiosity on well-being and depression. The research demonstrates that the benefits from simple church attendance go beyond social support. Attending church regularly seems to help people develop better coping skills and greater self-control.

**Kick depression cognitively.** Cognitive therapy, pioneered by Aaron T. Beck, M.D., in the 1950s, has been proven to help in curing and coping with depression and is widely used, says Dr. Novotni.

Dr. Beck identified specific distorted thinking patterns in which we all engage at times that confound and confuse things. An example is a tendency that we sometimes have to contrast ourselves with people who are more successful and, in the process, condemn ourselves as failures. Rather, we could recognize how well we've done compared with people who have accomplished less. Another distorted thinking pattern is to blow a little thing all out of proportion and let it ruin our whole morning, afternoon, day, or week.

Cognitive therapy teaches us to recognize and constructively counter many common distorted-thought spirals. Therapists can help us with this. And, says Dr. Novotni, "Many of my clients have found that books that teach this are really helpful, such as *The Ten Dumbest Mistakes Smart People Make and How to Avoid Them* by Arthur Freeman and Rose DeWolf."

**Reduce stress.** Learn calming methods of breathing, praying, and meditating, advises Dr. Meier. For more information on these techniques, see Mindfulness and Meditation (page 80), Prayer of Release (page 109), and Visualization (page 123).

# *Disaster*

~~✦~~

## AN EVENT THAT MAKES
## US QUESTION GOD

*I*n the spring of 1974, a tornado ripped through the town of Louisville, Kentucky, with such quick and devastating force that it ripped the facades off rows of beautiful homes, leaving the structures standing but with damaged, littered, disheveled interiors exposed for all the world to see.

The image of those homes still remains for the Reverend John Boyle, Ph.D., founder of the pastoral counseling center at Chicago's Fourth Presbyterian Church, who witnessed the Kentucky tornado while a faculty member at Southern Baptist Theological Seminary in Louisville. For him, it has come to symbolize one of the things that happens to all of us when disaster hits. "Our facades, our assumptions and appearances, and our long-held beliefs are removed, and we're left to deal with one another in disheveled, not always pretty, states of raw emotion," he says. "What's inside of us is laid bare."

## Can Faith Survive?

Be it by the happenstance of nature, the calculation of a crazed gunman, or any of a hundred other scenarios, disaster does this to us: It bares our fears, uproots our beliefs in the orderliness of life, makes us question our sense of safety, and, as Charles Gerkin, doctor of divinity, points out in *Crisis Experience in Modern Life*, severely challenges our long-held faith in an all-loving, all-powerful God.

In the face of such turmoil, can our faith still be of any use to us? That depends on our attitudes toward God.

It can be difficult to accept disasters if we think of God as a benevolent fairy godfather who is supposed to lead us through life unscathed, steering us clear of any and all calamities. If that's our view, then "that's a theology that life will take from us " says Kathleen Greider, Ph.D., associate professor of pastoral care and counseling at Claremont School of Theology in California. "Once we've experienced untold, unjustified, inexplicable disaster, we simply can no longer hold fast to a belief in a God whose will it is to shield the faithful from such things."

Or, as Dr. Boyle says, "We learn what Job learned, that God does not simply reward the saint and punish the sinner. Life is a good deal more random than that."

We can, however, believe in a biblical God who remained steadfast to the Hebrews through their 40 years of wandering and deprivation in the wilderness: "Happy are you, O Israel! Who is like you, a people saved by the Lord?" (Deuteronomy 33:29 NRSV) To Jesus in His moment of death: "Father, into Your hands I commend My Spirit." (Luke 23:46 NRSV). And from an imprisoned Paul to the faithful in the city of Colossae: "May you be made strong with all the strength that comes from His glorious power . . . giving thanks to the Father, who has enabled you to share in the inheritance of the saints in the light." (Colossians 1:11–12 NRSV) As Dr. Gerkin, professor emeritus at Candler School of Theology of Emory University in Atlanta, says, "God's partnership with the descendants of Israel has always included suffering and tragedy as well as hope and the assurance of his presence."

To many, the incarnation of God as Jesus shows his willingness to share our lot. It is God demonstrating that His love of us does not preclude disasters but instead impels Him to suffer them with us. Jesus crucified is the ultimate enactment of divine love, that is, the guarantee that God's love is such that even in the face of disaster, it does not desert us but, in Paul's words, "remains obedient."

"Nowhere in the Bible does it say that God wills suffering," says Dr. Boyle. "Nor does it say that God insulates the faithful from it.

# Prayer Pointers

## The Story Behind the 23rd Psalm

Most of us are familiar with the 23rd Psalm, but what many of us don't realize are the circumstances that led King David to write it. The Reverend Gregory Sutterlin, pastor of Ascension Lutheran Church of Franklin Square in New York City, suggests that we consider the following the next time we read it.

David wrote the Psalm in response to a disaster involving his beloved son, Absalom. Wanting to take over his father's kingdom, Absalom had gathered an army and prepared to attack the king's forces. When David learned of this, he knew that victory meant saving his empire but quite possibly losing Absalom, so he ordered his forces to spare the boy's life. When his generals later reported to him the good news that his kingdom was saved, they also had the unenviable task of telling him that Absalom had died in a freak accident when his charging horse carried him into a low-limbed tree that broke the son's neck.

Psalm 23 is the result of a man coming to grips with the pain of a family divided against itself, a king measuring the burdens of faithfulness to a sometimes unfathomable God, and a father experiencing the inestimable grief that comes when a child has beaten him to the grave.

What it does testify to is the fact that God participates in it with us. Faith in God does not mean a life without pain; it means a life without ultimate and total abandonment."

## Coping with Disaster

A popular poster in offices, classrooms, and church bulletin boards reads: "Be prepared; it wasn't raining when Noah built the ark." While no one goes looking for a calamity, let alone anticipates one, it's worth being prepared for the reactions that disaster can bring. Here is some advice that counselors offer.

**Don't assume you know the limits of your pain.** "There are surprises, hidden faults, and subtle problems that come to the surface when disaster strikes," says the Reverend Ron Mahn, licensed professional counselor, licensed marriage and family therapist, and a pastoral counselor with the Center for Counseling and Care of Oklahoma in Oklahoma City, who helped counsel families after the 1995 bombing of the Federal Building in Oklahoma City that left 169 dead. "After the bombing, some families really came together and others really came apart. What we discovered is that by and large, the families that couldn't hold up had deep-seated problems that they had been keeping from view. If disaster besets any family where there's even a suggestion of instability, they would do well to commit themselves to seeking outside help, either with their pastors or with professional therapists."

**Anticipate the guilt of unexpected blessings.** There's often an enormous sense of guilt that settles into the lives of survivors. We may feel guilt-ridden because we survived and another did not. Or we may feel a sense of guilt simply because something good inadvertently came to us as a result of a disaster.

For example, says Reverend Mahn, "The church that I belong to was severely damaged in the Oklahoma City blast. As a result, we were awarded funds and completed a $6 million renovation that we never would have been able to afford otherwise. This is a blessing for us, but as parishioners, we feel so very torn when we recall what it was that made this possible. And as the city rebuilds, there are stories like this all over town."

Dr. Greider says that while such guilt feelings are inevitable, we can cope with them by meditating on the Easter story, in which life emerges from death. "It is the essence of redemption that we weave something positive out of the threads of disaster—that death is not final, but that it yields to life," she says.

**Don't minimize the importance of material things.** When others die in a disaster that may have inflicted only a loss of property on us, we want to embrace our blessings and dismiss our losses. But we ought to remember that physical things can carry great sentimental attachment. "When the tornado hit Louisville in 1974," Dr. Boyle recalls, "people grieved the loss of the lone family photograph, the great-grandmother's quilt, or the parents' wedding license—irreplaceable things that were links to other times and to people they loved who are long since gone." When we feel pain over the loss of such things, we need to allow ourselves to experience it rather than trying to dismiss is as frivolous or self-absorbing. How can we express the pain? Dr. Boyle suggests that we talk with friends and family who understand how much meaning those objects held for us.

# Healing after Tragedy Strikes

Just as there are things that we can do to prepare for disaster, there are steps that we can take to heal ourselves and our communities after disaster strikes.

**Get angry with God.** If you want to that is. Don't worry, He can take it. "I recall visiting with two of my parishioners, a married couple," says the Reverend Mahan Siler, master of divinity, former pastor of Pullen Memorial Baptist Church in Raleigh, North Carolina. "They had suffered the loss of two of their young children, at different times and under different circumstances. It was a horrible blow, and at one point, the wife said to me, 'I'm so angry at God that I can't even pray and tell Him how angry I am!' To which I answered, 'You've been praying already. This is what your anger is.' I referred her to the Psalms, and how so many of them, such as Psalm 10 ("Why, O Lord, do You stand far off? Why do You hide Yourself in times of trouble?" Psalm 10:1 NIV) are prayers of anger. That they are part of our Scripture assures us that this is a valued form of prayer." In addition to reading appropriate Psalms, we can harness our anger at God by actually writing our own psalm, says Reverend Siler.

**Help one another.** To live in the image of God, as the Bible recommends in Genesis, means to help one another in a loving, healing manner. "In the face of disaster," says Dr. Boyle, "church members can do God's work by simply being there for one another and by being able to share with one another their rage, their fears, their puzzlement, and their support. In the case of a disaster that is visited on a whole community, pastors and lay leaders can gather groups together and facilitate conversation. If it's the kind of calamity that befalls one family, others can go to them quietly, privately, with a dish of food and simply listen without comment to what the person wants to say."

# Faithbuilders

## The Paradox of God and Evil

There may be no way that we can rationalize the paradox of a loving God with the suffering that occurs around us. But speaking from personal experience, the Reverend David Kelsey, Ph.D., professor of theology at Yale Divinity School, says that that paradox can lead us to a mission. During a few years in the mid 1970s, Reverend Kelsey suffered a series of profound personal setbacks and losses as he and his family dealt with serious illnesses. This is what he gleaned from them: "I know that a loving God exists because I have experienced that love. And I know that evil exists, because I have experienced that evil. I cannot explain this seeming contradiction, but I can say this: The reality of the first compels us to minister to the reality of the second. I believe that this is the essence of what it means to live a Christian life."

**Create a memorial.** While we must get on with our lives after a disaster, it's important to realize that the memory of what happened will continue for future generations. To help them cope, we might want to create some kind of memorial, says Reverend Mahn, "a fund, a statue, a park, or whatever is a useful way of securing the event in the community's shared history." However, he also suggests that we consider our choices carefully so that the memorial will have meaning for people 50 to 100 years from now who will have no firsthand knowledge of the event. If our community wants to memorialize an event, he suggests that we visit other cities and towns for ideas.

When disaster strikes, it will disrupt our lives, not just for this day or this month, but forever, says Dr. Boyle. And, he says, we must remember that recovery from disaster is not restoration of the way life was before the disaster hit. Rather, it is a new start in many ways. It requires a new appreciation for the arbitrariness of disaster, a new understanding of the fragility of the world, and a new interpretation of both God's place in it and ours.

# Discipline
# and Self-Control

## THE POWER IN THE HEART AND MIND

*E*very two years, we marvel at Olympic athletes who have dedicated themselves to greatness in their chosen sports. In the quest for Olympic gold, for example, a track star could log more than 5,000 miles in training just to run a single 100-meter event that will be over in less than 11 seconds.

But does the track star's 5,000 miles of disciplined training start with her first step? Not really, says the Reverend R. Kent Hughes, doctor of ministry, senior pastor at the College Church in Wheaton, Illinois, and author of *Disciplines of a Godly Man* and *Liberating Ministry from the Success Syndrome*. It begins when she thinks about running and considers the physical and financial costs of her effort, how great the wind feels in her face, and what it's going to be like to win.

In other words, it starts in her mind and her heart, the same places where we begin our efforts to develop a sense of discipline and self-control over the challenges in our lives.

The same techniques that help the athlete triumph on the track can help us reach our goals in discipline and self-control, whether we're trying to tame our tongues, keep neater houses, bypass the all-you-can eat buffets, or master a hundred other troublesome issues in our lives, says the Reverend Richard L. Ganz, master of divinity, Ph.D., pastor of the Ottawa Reformed Presbyterian Church, president of Ottawa Theological Hall in Ontario, Canada, and author of *The Secret of Self Control.*

Unfortunately, many people believe that learning discipline is impossibly boring—about as much fun as Marine Corps boot camp. But it doesn't have to be that way, contends Donald S. Whitney in his book *Spiritual Disciplines for the Christian Life.* Sure, there's work involved. But we soon discover that, like the track star, developing control over the important parts of our lives gives us the freedom to achieve our highest goals and aspirations. And what could be a greater source of joy? "Jesus was the most disciplined man who ever lived, yet the most joyful and passionately alive. He is our example of discipline," writes Whitney.

# Developing Mental Discipline

Some people think of their brains as a sort of black hole where thoughts over which they have no control just suddenly come and go. They're not. Our thinking is actually the sum of all the information that we take in. What we watch. And read. And hear. And see. Everything from those annoying television theme songs and billboards that we pass on the highways to the conversations around the coffee machines at work. And whether we realize it or not, it's all potential subject matter for what's called our thought life—that seemingly secret realm where we ponder, mull, consider, entertain, and fantasize, says Dr. Ganz.

But what we think about doesn't just stay inside our minds. It's the inspiration for our actions. We literally become what we think about and value. The Bible puts it this way: "For as he thinks within himself, so he is." (Proverbs 23:7 NIV)

To control our behavior, then, we need to get a handle on our thinking first. Easier said than done? Maybe not. Over and over again the Bible says that those who follow Jesus are empowered to gain control of their thought lives. This doesn't mean that tempting, slothful, or gluttonous thoughts will simply stop coming one day. It means that if we control the input of inappropriate material and replace our bad thoughts with those described in Philippians 4:8 (NIV) as true, noble, right, pure, lovely, admirable, excellent, or praiseworthy, we'll be better able to keep ourselves under control.

Here are some simple suggestions for keeping our thought lives in check.

**Create a think list—and use it.** Since our thought lives are key to winning the battle for self-control and discipline, every thought that is greedy, gluttonous, or otherwise unrestrained needs to be shut off when it comes to mind and replaced with something that is truly worthy of our consideration. One of the best ways to discipline our minds is by developing a think list of good thoughts that we can refer to when something inappropriate creeps up on us, Dr. Ganz says.

We might fill our think lists with Scripture verses, for example, but Dr. Ganz says that he also likes to focus his thoughts on family or friends who need a hand, and then devote mental energy to figuring how he can help them.

**Turn off the TV—at least once in a while.** The average American spends about six hours a day watching TV. "But if we say no to TV, then we can say yes to undistracted conversation, yes to reading, yes to exercise, yes to cleaning the house, yes to washing the car—all sorts of things," says Dr. Hughes.

Not only that, but we may also be preserving our mental discipline, says Dr. Hughes. "It's my belief that the way TV is produced today feeds and engenders the inability to concentrate by delivering a constant barrage of images." People who watch a lot of TV, he reasons, find it difficult to listen to intelligent discourse such as arguments, speeches, or even sermons because those activities lack the visual stimulation of TV.

**Clean out the in box.** Let's face it, it's hard to maintain, let alone develop, discipline and self-control when we're watching or reading things that don't support those virtues, says Dr. Hughes. Does that mean that we should cancel our subscriptions to *Casino Gambling Today*? Probably.

"Psalm 1 speaks to this idea," says Dr. Hughes. "It says, 'Blessed is the man who does not walk in the counsel of the wicked . . . But his delight is in the law of the Lord, and on His law he meditates day and night. He is like a tree planted by streams of water, which yields its fruit in season and whose leaf does not wither. Whatever he does prospers.'" (Psalm 1:1–3 NIV)

# Taking Action

Once we have our thinking right, we have the ability to change our actions, and that includes building practices and habits into our lives that strengthen discipline and self-control, like these:

**Find a coach.** Aaron had Moses. The disciples had Jesus. Timothy had Paul. And if we need to develop discipline, or any other positive attribute, one of the best ways is by finding a mentor, says Dr. Hughes. "Seek out someone you perceive to be a disciplined person and watch them in action. Ask for advice on how they control their desires. Have them hold you accountable for what you say you're going to do. That's going to help a lot."

**Start small and stay at it.** Trying to change our entire lives in one day is impossible, but we can start on the path toward self-control by taking small steps, like returning phone calls when we say we will, arriving on time for appointments, or getting into a regular pattern of cleaning up around the house and office. Starting with small tasks like these, says Dr. Hughes, makes it easier to succeed, and each success helps us build the resolve and discipline to stick with our goals. That will help when we take on larger challenges.

**Dump petty sins.** Stealing pens and paper clips seems like a minor offense compared with cheating on our expense reports or embezzling from the company. But giving up petty sins can strengthen our self-control and discipline exponentially, says Dr. Ganz. That's because restraining ourselves in these small ways teaches us the skills that we need to use in other situations, like cutting down on credit-card use.

**Make a covenant.** To maintain financial discipline, we follow budgets. To enforce agreements, we sign contracts. So why not write a covenant to God to ensure that we stay disciplined in challenging areas of our lives? For example, we might write a covenant that we will stop listening to hurtful gossip about the

# Introduction to the Classics

What's the best inspiration for a life of discipline and self-control? The classic works in the world around us, says the Reverend R. Kent Hughes, doctor of ministry, senior pastor at the College Church in Wheaton, Illinois, and author of *Disciplines of a Godly Man* and *Liberating Ministry from the Success Syndrome*.

"If we feed our minds on good books, good music, excellent thoughts, excellent pursuits, and hobbies, then we become much of what we feed ourselves on," he says.

Here are some Christian classics that he recommends to build a disciplined life.

> *The Practice of the Presence of God* by Brother Lawrence
> *Pursuit of God* and *The Knowledge of the Holy* by A.W. Tozer
> *Knowing God* by J. I. Packer
> *Mere Christianity* by C. S. Lewis
> *Basic Christianity* by John R. Stott
> *The Cost of Discipleship* by Dietrich Bonhoeffer

people we know—or contributing to it. Renewed every year and checked regularly, covenants can help us during those moments of frustration when we're tempted to forget everything we believe, says Ganz.

"I think that when we write things out and read them to ourselves and solemnly commit to keep them, by God's grace we can reflect upon them, and it helps us remember what God really wants us to be," says Pastor Ganz.

# Discouragement

## FAITH AND HOPE
## ARE THE BEST DEFENSE

Consider the case of Thomas Edison.

He publicly announced in 1878, boldly and unequivocally, that he was going to invent an electric incandescent bulb that would light homes worldwide. He solicited funding from New York's financial elite. Many invested, joining him in forming the Edison Electric Light Company (later known as General Electric).

A key to creating this incandescent bulb, Edison determined, was finding the right filament fiber, one that wouldn't burn too quickly. He was sure that he'd find it soon. He tested fiber after fiber. He failed to find a fiber that would work. He failed more than 6,000 times.

Think he was a little discouraged? Humiliated?

Apparently not our Thomas Alva Edison. Sometime after the 6,000th fiber, he discovered that carbonized filaments from cotton thread worked well.

Within the span of 13 months, Edison actually built 1,199 light bulbs that did not work. Then he invented the one that did. The one that lights the world today. What kind of mindset does it take to fail 6,000 times, or 1,199 times, or a combined total of 7,199 times and still keep at it?

It's a genius mindset, a saintly mindset that we all should cultivate, says Christian psychiatrist and theologian Paul Meier, M.D., co-founder of New Life Clinics, the largest provider of Christian-based counseling in the United States, and author of more than 60 best-selling Christian self-help books.

## Keep On Keeping On

The Bible teaches us to keep hope alive, says Dr. Meier. We are to be diligent; we are to learn from our mistakes; as it says in 2 Timothy 2:15, we are to be workmen that need not be ashamed.

But wait. What about when we're certain that we've hit the wall, come to the end of the line, feel let down, feel that someone—or God, for that matter—has failed us?

Obviously, we feel disappointment. Obviously, we feel discouragement. And that's fine, says Dr. Meier. But it's not acceptable for us to let it cripple us. Instead, we need to follow the example of Thomas Edison and endure. Ideally, we run the race to win the prize, as Apostle Paul instructs. That's what faith is all about. It's about holding on in the face of disappointment and discouragement: ". . . faith is the substance of things hoped for, the evidence of things not seen." (Hebrews 11:1 KJV)

Sure, we will be disappointed in life. We will feel the disappointment. And it will hurt. We just can't surrender to it, says the Reverend Mel Lawrenz, Ph.D., senior associate pastor at Elmbrook Church and director of the Elmbrook Christian Study Center, both in Brookfield, Wisconsin, and co-author of six books, including *Life after Grief* and *Overcoming Grief and Trauma*.

## God Promises a Brighter Tomorrow

Apostle Paul, in his letter to the Romans, said that if we believe in God and the promises that God has made to take care of us, then we can ". . . rejoice in our sufferings, knowing that suffering produces endurance, and endurance produces character, and character produces hope, and hope does not disappoint us. . . ." (Romans 5:3–5 RSV)

So we may not exactly feel like rejoicing. But certainly, we can build our character by keeping a constructive attitude. Here are some great ways to do that.

# Faithbuilders

## The Danger in Demanding Perfection

"It's important that we look at people with compassion, that we accept that people are not perfect," says psychologist Michele Novotni, Ph.D., assistant professor of counseling at Eastern College, a Christian college of arts and sciences in St. Davids, Pennsylvania. "My son was angry when he was younger. I forget what I was reprimanding him for, but at one point he said, 'You should have had Jesus for a son, because He was perfect. He would have made you happy.'

"That really took me aback because our faith teaches that there has only been one perfect human," she says. "And all the rest of us are going to fall short quite regularly. So I think that we have to realize that our job is not to judge. Many of us enter into relationships or situations with almost superhuman expectations. That has us judging, trying to make sure that people are matching up. I think that if we enter things with more of a heart of compassion and understanding, with a healthy dose of forgiveness, we'd find ourselves experiencing a lot less disappointment."

**Think prayerfully and carefully.** Being in a state of discouragement clouds our outlook and hampers our ability to make good choices, says Dr. Lawrenz. Making poor choices only leads to greater discouragement and despair. Spend time in spiritual reflection, seeking positive choices that will lead to positive outcomes.

**Look for the lesson.** If we look, we'll find a lesson in everything that happens to us. Sometimes it is not evident immediately, but it's there. We need to be patient and look for it while holding hope. That's faith.

"When I get up in the morning," says Dr. Meier, "I ask God, 'If I have a flat tire or whatever else it is that may go wrong today, help me to learn from it. Help me to grow from it. Help me realize that everything that happens is good. Everything works together for good.' I wake up expecting not to have everything go perfectly. Then, when it doesn't, I'm not disappointed. So when something goes wrong, I just say, 'What can I learn from this experience?'"

# Healing Words
## The Blessings of the Lord

And all these blessings shall come upon you and overtake you, because you obey the voice of the Lord your God:

Blessed shall you be in the city, and blessed shall you be in the country.

Blessed shall be the fruit of your body, the produce of your ground and the increase of your herds, the increase of your cattle and the offspring of your flocks.

Blessed shall be your basket and your kneading bowl.

Blessed shall you be when you come in, and blessed shall you be when you go out.

The Lord will cause your enemies who rise against you to be defeated before your face; they shall come out against you one way and flee before you seven ways.

The Lord will command the blessing on you in your store-houses and in all to which you set your hand, and He will bless you in the land which the Lord your God is giving you.

The Lord will establish you as a holy people to Himself, just as He has sworn to you, if you keep the commandments of the Lord your God and walk in His ways.

**Be patient.** Press on during times of discouragement, recommends the Reverend Paul F. Everett of Pittsburgh, a Presbyterian minister at large with the Peale Center in Pawling, New York, and executive director emeritus of the Pittsburgh Experiment, a national

> Then all peoples of the Earth shall see that you are called by the name of the Lord, and they shall be afraid of you.
>
> And the Lord will grant you plenty of goods, in the fruit of your body, in the increase of your livestock, and in the produce of your ground, in the land of which the Lord swore to your fathers to give you.
>
> The Lord will open to you His good treasure, the Heavens, to give the rain to your land in its season, and to bless all the work of your hand. You shall lend to many nations, but you shall not borrow.
>
> And the Lord will make you the head and not the tail . . .
>
> *—Deuteronomy 28:2–13 NKJV*

> Give, and it will be given to you; good measure, pressed down, shaken together, running over, will be put into your lap. For the measure you give will be the measure you get back.
>
> *—Luke 6:38 RSV*

and international ministry to the business and working communities. Believe that good will come, that the lesson will become evident, and that the solutions will appear in their time. Don't rush or force them to happen. "Because what will emerge will emerge," Reverend Everett says. And there is no way I am going to know what it will look like ahead of time."

Yes, sometimes the lessons are hard. Sometimes we aren't patient enough. Sometimes we won't just sit still and endure and let God work. We keep pricking open our cocoons to see how things are coming along, says Reverend Everett, and, as a result, all we end up with is cocoon mush. Yet, if we wait patiently, when the time is just right, a glorious butterfly will burst forth.

**Seek encouragement.** Turn to inspirational writings, people, and Bible verses. It is hard to remain discouraged when we surround ourselves with hope. Visit, call, and talk with positive, proactive, affirming, upbeat people, recommends psychologist Michele Novotni, Ph.D., assistant professor of counseling at Eastern College, a Christian college of arts and sciences in St. Davids, Pennsylvania. "Encouragement," she says, "basically means 'offering courage' or 'supplying energy to others to help them go on.'" When we need it, we should seek it. When others need it, we should give it.

"Encouragement can help build self-confidence and stimulate courage, which is the will to act even when you're scared or discouraged, when you feel like you can't go on," says Dr. Novotni. It is something that we all need at times. And it is something that we all need to share at times. The world is not divided into two classes of people: helpers and people who need help. All of us are actually both at differing times. By recognizing this, we build understanding and empathy and are better able to cope with our own dark times and better able to help others with theirs. And that's living our faith, she says.

# Helping Someone Who is Discouraged

Remember what it feels like to be discouraged, says Dr. Novotni. Then we'll begin to understand what our friends, loved ones, or acquaintances are going through. Here's how she says we can help them.

**Treat them as equals.** "When someone is discouraged, they don't need all these people who want to tell them exactly what it is they should do. That up-down relationship feels very uncomfortable to most people. That almost makes them dig deeper into the hole. It's as though everybody else knows how to do this. The truth is, each of us is going to go through times where we struggle," Dr. Novotni points out.

**Listen to them.** Let them express what they are feeling. Don't try to fix the problem.

**Locate the problem.** "It usually falls in a particular area of life: friendships, work, making a contribution to life, achieving intimacy, having loving relationships, money, self-acceptance, or problems in the spiritual dimension," says Dr. Novotni.

By encouraging a person to identify the problem area causing the discouragement, we help them keep it in perspective. It's one problem, not their whole life.

**Offer encouragement.** Be positive, upbeat, helpful, inspiring. Offer hope. Show respect and admiration. "This should be a goal of every church. It could be an intentional activity. Help people within the church to be more helpful and more encouraging of one another," she says. There would be less of a need for professional counselors if people would really encourage one another."

# Divorce

## After the Havoc Comes Redemption

Her finances in ruin, her husband embroiled in an affair, Victoria Sorensen cried herself to sleep in her cramped New York City apartment. Her wish at that time: only to die. "All I saw was a tangled mess," she says.

Then, after chance encounters with a woman who talked about the love of Jesus, Sorensen traded depression for faith. She banished her suicidal thoughts, allowed the divorce to become final, and spent the next few years growing in her faith as a single adult—without a man.

Until one night, at a Bible study, she met Peter. They were just friends at first and were even dating other people at the time. But slowly, Sorensen realized that she had found the man with whom she wanted to spend the rest of her life.

Now married with two beautiful girls and an active role with Peter in a variety of Christian ministries, Sorensen can see the good that came from her divorce. "I look back on this and all I can say is praise the Lord. God had to strip me of everything that I had—my family, friends, money, religion. I was literally so hopeless. But He was at work weaving a wonderful tapestry. And I didn't even know it."

While it's true that most health professionals rank divorce among life's most traumatic and stressful events, the irony is that many who cling to their faith during divorce find that their faith deepens. Or, as in Sorensen's case, they find genuine faith for the first time.

"Only God can take the worst thing that we've been through and use it for good," says Tom Whiteman, Ph.D., director of Fresh Start seminars, author of *Fresh Start,* and co-author of *The Fresh Start Divorce Recovery Workbook.* "The corporate mentality is, hide your weaknesses and accentuate your strengths. But in God's economy, he takes weakness and says, 'I will make you strong.'"

Dr. Whiteman didn't always feel that way. A Bible college graduate and youth pastor, he was devastated when his wife told him one tearful evening that she didn't love him and probably never did. After she walked out, Dr. Whiteman lost his job, felt ostracized by his church, and sank into a depression that lasted nearly two years.

"Although I had been working in ministry and read all these books on helping people, when that happened to me, I found that I had no answers and no hope. I really felt like God could never use me again, that my life was over," says Dr. Whiteman.

In fact, his divorce eventually led him to consider becoming a school guidance counselor, a career move that led to both a master's degree and a Ph.D. in psychology. He never did work with kids, but today, he is a licensed psychologist and president of Life Counseling Services in Paoli, Pennsylvania, and conducts church-sponsored recovery groups around the country. Many groups study the books that he has written about divorce.

As strange as it may sound, the end of Sorensen's and Dr. Whiteman's marriages were actually new beginnings, time for fresh starts and closer examinations of what went wrong in the first place. The goal: that it might never happen again. "We either get better and learn from our mistakes, or we get bitter," says Dr. Whiteman.

## Researching Reasons

The reasons cited for divorce are legion and vary from relationship to relationship, everything from alcoholism and unfaithfulness to unrealistic expectations about marriage to falling out of love. But research suggests that miscommunication and, more specifically, poor conflict-resolution skills are probably at the root of most failed marriages. Whether characterized by sniping and griping that slowly

# Divorced . . .with Children

While couples without kids can split up and never see each other again, if we've had children we face the lifelong challenges of visitation and child exchanges. One way to make this a lot easier is to apply this simple rule: Don't try to instruct the former spouse in child rearing.

"If the kids have been up until midnight watching R-rated movies, you have the right to say, 'I don't appreciate that.' But deal with it as an individual issue, rather than saying something like, 'You've always been that way and you were that way when we were married,'" says Tom Whiteman, Ph.D. president of Life Counseling Services in Paoli, Pennsylvania, director of Fresh Start seminars, author of *Fresh Start*, and co-author of *The Fresh Start Divorce Recovery Workbook*.

Instead of bringing up the past, address the issue at hand and, as the Bible says, "Speak the truth in love." Say things such as, "I don't appreciate the way that you handled this, but you're still their father and I'm going to encourage them to respect you and have a relationship with you."

"I always say that you should encourage the relationship unless it's really abusive," says Dr. Whiteman. "If they're giving your kids marijuana cigarettes, then you need to consult an attorney. But you have no control over that other house, so stop trying to browbeat this person into the parent that you want him to be."

erode respect or explosive episodes that cripple intimacy, these are the acts that can inflict the deepest, hardest-to-heal wounds.

"Very vicious, very painful cycles get started when a partner says something and the other person gets hurt. And when they're hurt, they often respond by some sort of automatic counterattack," says William Richardson, Ph.D., clinical director and professor in the department of marriage and family therapy at Reformed Theological Seminary in Jackson, Mississippi. "When this reactive, offensive-defensive communication spins out of control for years, the relationship becomes such a painful place to be that the partners naturally withdraw from each other."

For some, the loneliness and pain caused by such estrangement is the gateway to an affair. Others simply walk away. And though they may look back from time to time, they simply never come back. The Bible, of course, has plenty to say about proper communication. "If anyone considers himself religious and yet does not keep a tight rein on his tongue, he deceives himself and his religion is worthless." (James 1:26 NIV)

# The Bible and Divorce

It's understandable how angry communication can tear once-romantic lovers apart. But is it reason enough to end a marriage for good? A closer look at Scripture suggests probably not. "Scripture is for fidelity and forgiving and staying together. God hates divorce. He hates divorce because he loves people and it causes them such pain—them and their children," says Dr. Richardson.

Christian counselors generally agree that there are three circumstances under which the Bible allows divorce: adultery, abandonment, and abuse. Jesus himself addresses the issue of adultery: "It has been said, 'Anyone who divorces his wife must give her a certificate of divorce.' But I tell you that anyone who divorces his wife, except for marital unfaithfulness, causes her to become an adulteress, and anyone who marries the divorced woman commits adultery." (Matthew 5:31–32 NIV)

Based on that teaching, we might assume that there's no other reason granted for divorce. Yet the Apostle Paul includes abandonment in his first letter to the Corinthians. "To the rest I say this (I, not the Lord): If any brother has a wife who is not a believer and she is willing to live with him, he must not divorce her. . . . But if the unbeliever leaves, let him do so. A believing man or woman is not bound in such circumstances." (1 Corinthians 7:12, 15 NIV)

Finding a scriptural basis in the case of abuse, and even a definition of abuse in marriage, is a little more challenging since no specific biblical reference exists. "What most conservative scholars do with the abuse issue is say that it is such a violation, it's such a

neglecting, harmful act, it's like a forsaking of the marriage, like abandonment," says Dr. Richardson.

Still, many abuse cases require an almost Solomon-like wisdom
to sort out. "For instance, when the wife says that she's being abused
and she tries to work on that relationship with her pastor or in Christian counseling and the abuse continues, that's going to be a
problem," says Dr. Richardson. In that situation, she would be ad-
vised to move away from the relationship. On the other hand, if the
woman or man says that they cannot endure the abuse and flee for
a while, and then both agree to work with a counselor, "you're probably going to have a more positive outcome," says Dr. Richardson.

A quick note to those who have divorced for other reasons: There
may be such a thing as the unforgivable sin, but divorce probably
isn't it, says Dr. Whiteman. If we have questions about the legitimacy
of the reason for our breakups, we should talk to a Christian counselor or pastor.

## The Long Road to Recovery

Whether we're the ones who leave or the ones who are left, separation and divorce cause emotional damage so severe that it can take
two to five years to truly recover. It takes so long because we have
to fully grieve the loss of the relationship before we can heal. And,
just like the emotions experienced during the death of a loved one,
this grieving process has five distinct stages: denial, anger, bargaining,
depression, and acceptance.

These stages don't occur in the same order for everyone, explains
Dr. Whiteman, but they must occur before healing is complete. "We
think this is going to hurt for a couple of weeks and then we're going
to get over it. Or we want God to instantly heal us. I make the point
that God could heal us, but we need to be very patient. It's time to
follow his timetable, not our own."

One of the first things we do is deny that our spouse has left for
good. It's the old "he'll come back as soon as he comes to his
senses" reaction. In most cases, weeks, months, maybe even years
pass, and he doesn't show. Meanwhile, we get mad—another stage
in the process—and express it by doing everything from refusing visitation with the children to launching more verbal barrages. Or we

try bargaining. "If you just leave Ms. X and come back, I won't ask any questions and I'll make your favorite dessert for the next decade."

Unfortunately, lots of folks get stuck at the anger or bargaining stages of the grieving process and spend several years using their children or financial concerns as weapons in an ongoing war.

It isn't until we quit our striving that the healing can really begin. Of course, this may not happen until depression sets in—a classic reaction to the loss of a spouse, and often the loss of the stuff that accompanies married life: mutual friends, standard of living, and even job or home.

"This is the point at which I want people to walk into my office for counseling," says Dr. Whiteman. "We make it seem like hitting bottom is so bad, but it isn't until someone hits bottom that the work begins. We struggle, struggle, struggle and try to avoid that pit. And yet we need to just let go and say, 'God, I give up.' That's the point at which God comes alongside of us and says, 'Are you done? Now let me take over.'"

If you're ready to heal from your separation or divorce, consider these tips.

**Put your heart in a cast.** One common way we try to mend our broken hearts and treat the inevitable loneliness caused by divorce is by diving into another romantic relationship. Wrong move, says Dr. Whiteman. Just as a broken arm or leg is immobilized by a cast so it has the time to heal, our hearts require the same kind of downtime, he says. And even after the emotional cast comes off, we need to be slow about getting deeply involved in a relationship again.

"If I try to use a broken arm, it's going to hurt, and it's liable to heal improperly," says Dr. Whiteman. "A broken heart can't trust or commit. Putting my heart in a 'cast' just means protecting myself and trying to not use it for a while."

**Take a step of faith.** Lying in bed praying that God will take away the pain is an experience with which most separated and divorced folks are all too familiar. But at some point, we have to kick off the blankets, shed the pajamas, and start living again—not rushing into another relationship, just getting on with life.

"It's true that God is the one who does the healing, but it's up to us to seek wholeness," says Dr. Whiteman. "If I don't like my life, I need to take steps to change it." In Dr. Whiteman's case, that meant quitting his job at a deli and applying to a school to get a master's degree in counseling. But even that took persistence: The first time he applied for school, he was rejected.

For Sorensen, it meant heeding a friend's advice to attend church—and that Bible study group where she met Peter.

# Healing Words
## Marital Conflict

Prince of Peace,
Your Word says that in marriage
the two become one flesh.
But today we feel
more two than one.
I'm tired of division,
of the clash of wills,
of combat.
Bring reconciliation to
our fractured relationship.
Plant seeds of healing in us
and nurture their growth.
Enable us to know a love that
is stronger than
We've ever known before.
Thank you for
marrying us to each other . . .
Thank you most of all
for loving us.

—*Norm Nelson, from* Thank You Most of All for Loving Me

**Look for life's lessons.** No matter how much it hurts, if we look hard enough, we can all learn something about ourselves from divorce. Some folks discover that they lack communication skills. Others find that they have been too demanding.

"One of the most important things that I learned was about compassion," says Dr. Whiteman, "and not just for divorced people. When anyone comes to me with any kind of hardship, I am filled with concern for that other person. I may not have been through exactly that same thing, but I've felt rejection, disgrace, and shame. It has also given me an extra measure of grace toward people who are struggling."

Sorensen says she learned that she placed unrealistic expectations on her ex-husband. "I was trying to make him my God and trying to get all my needs met by him, and I remember him saying to me, 'You know, if I were five men, it wouldn't be enough for you.' I was really looking for that void to be filled by a man. But I learned that only God can fill it."

**Learn to be content.** Are we still grumbling about who wronged whom in the marriage or how bad we have it now? Or are we developing an attitude of gratitude? "My paraphrase of what the Apostle Paul says about this is: Right where I am, I have learned to be content. I think it's best to say, 'This is not my first choice, but I'm going to be the best single mom I can be. Or, 'I'm going to be an every-other-week Dad and it really stinks, but I'm going to make the most of what I have.' Acceptance isn't saying, 'Oh well, that's it, I'm giving up.' That's depression. Acceptance is saying, 'You know, I would not have chosen this route, but it's okay. We'll be fine.'" Once we've accepted our situations, then we're able to set about changing what we can, like getting a new job or going back to school.

**Forgive.** It's one of the toughest things that we'll ever do. But our ability to forgive our ex-spouses lets us know that we've reached acceptance and are almost ready to move on in our lives. We just need to make sure our forgiveness isn't bitterness cloaked in acceptance.

For those who say, "Oh well, I'm going to let go of this," but secretly can't wait until calamity strikes their ex-spouses, Dr. Whiteman has words of warning. "We can't say that we've truly forgiven someone until we wish him well," he says. "We don't gain a fresh start until we truly forgive. That's why it takes so long to get there.

# The Road to Reconciliation

We've hired the attorneys, the paperwork is filed, and we're ready to head to court. Is our decision to seek a divorce final? Not unless we want it to be. Of course, we shouldn't excuse obvious, ongoing sin such as adultery or wait like an abused pup for a philandering ex-spouse to saunter back into our lives. But "when people are willing to admit that they have done certain specific wrongs that have contributed to a painful relationship, that is step number one toward true reconciliation," says Dr. Richardson.

If we sense an opportunity to travel the path to reconciliation with our spouse, whether we're just separated or already divorced, there are things that we can do to prepare ourselves. Here's how.

**Be prayerful.** Ask God to reveal his heart and will for us and our spouses, says Dr. Richardson. But we need to be sure that we're not allowing our judgment to be colored by bad habits of co-dependent behavior, like allowing our spouses' needs to override ours, or clinging to our spouses when things are clearly wrong. We need to be sure that we're not mistaking our will for God's.

**Be open to advice.** If we're stuck, sometimes a pastor, counselor, or even a friend will come through with some great insight into our situations. Sorensen says that she refused for years to finalize her divorce until a friend helped her see that it was time to move on.

**Be patient.** Just because we declare our intentions to reconcile doesn't mean that our spouses will readily admit the error of their ways and come running back. "Sometimes the spouse will say no and then see some hope in the other person and begin to say yes. But that can take time—a long time of waiting," says Dr. Richardson. "You're trying to demonstrate that you're genuine."

**Be proactive.** Waiting patiently doesn't mean sitting on our hands. In the meantime, we should be working with a pastor, a small support group, or a counselor to resolve the personal problems that we contributed to the relationship's demise. Not only that but we can also enlist our spouse in our reconciliation efforts. "We need one another," says Dr. Richardson. "If there are two parties who are willing to say, 'Yes I have done these things that have hurt my spouse and our relationship,' and if they are willing to say, 'I am willing to do things to contribute to the reconciliation and growth of this relationship,' relationships can be saved."

# Eating Disorders

## Solving the Food Puzzle

*J*ena Keller was a pigtailed 10-year-old when she simply stopped eating. Convinced that she was suffering from some mysterious medical problem, her parents took her to countless doctors, searching for a cure. But as the weeks passed, her weight continued to drop—from 70 to 48 pounds—and their desperation soared.

Finally, a doctor at one of the hospitals suggested that they make an appointment with a psychologist. But instead of trying to figure out a new way to make their daughter eat, the psychologist told Ward and Kay Keller that one of the best things that they could do for their daughter was to learn how to improve their troubled marriage.

The psychologist said that she was starving herself—a condition called anorexia nervosa—and her parents were at the center of the problem. Among other things, Ward was a demanding and controlling husband and father who drove his family relentlessly, while Kay's tendencies as a people-pleaser prevented her from objecting to her husband's behavior even though she knew that what he was doing was harmful.

"This counselor said to me, 'I believe that you're the kind of man who thinks that he doesn't need anybody in his life,'" says Ward Keller, "and my little daughter probably thought in her heart that I viewed her that way: completely dispensable. Understanding that was like a knife going into my heart."

Ward Keller cried out to God to ask forgiveness. And then he told Jena that he needed her, just as the counselor had suggested. The next morning, instead of rushing to school, Jena got up, popped a bagel into the toaster and promptly ate.

"We were so stunned, we didn't know what to say," says Kay Keller. Two years' worth of sometimes rocky family and individual counseling sessions later, Jena was on the road to recovery.

Since then, Ward Keller has left his businesses and, with Kay's help, opened Remuda Ranch, an inpatient eating-disorder clinic in Wickenberg, Arizona, that has helped more than 2,000 patients. Now, with a pre-med degree, 23-year-old Jena works full-time at the facility. "We got professional help, and that was important. But the main thing for us was the way things changed at home," says Ward Keller.

## The Root of the Problem

In the United States, at least eight million people have anorexia nervosa or the other major eating disorder, bulimia nervosa, defined as chronic binge eating and purging. Eighty-six percent of people with these conditions report that they began by the time they were 20 years old, and 77 percent say that the disorder lasted from 1 to 15 years.

What causes these disorders? Research shows that some people may be genetically predisposed to them, says Jacqueline Abbott, Dr.P.H., co-director of the Kartini Clinic for Disordered Eating in Portland, Oregon. But there are several other contributing factors, she says. "Feelings of low self-worth and sometimes trauma related to a history of sexual abuse may be involved."

Also, Dr. Abbott thinks that the current emphasis on low-fat foods and dieting is a major factor. Restricting the fat in our diets or the total amount of food that we eat starves our bodies, in effect. And when our bodies don't get adequate nutrition, they overreact, she says, sometimes leading to bingeing.

There's another factor, too: Some of us are obsessed with obtaining society's standard of the perfect body. "The average woman

# Answered Prayers

## Solid Ground

"Driving along in my car one day, I was feeling very discouraged about my life. I was disappointed in the progress I was making in recovery from a 20-year-old eating disorder. After all, I had been in two treatment centers, spent hours in counseling, and had heard lots of teaching from God's Word. I desired to live a life pleasing to God. Shouldn't my life be falling into place by now? I was in the grips of depression and anger. I felt defeated.

"Then a beautiful song came on the radio. The words were close to the words of Psalms 40 and 41. 'Oh Lord, have mercy on me and heal me. Place my feet upon a rock! Put a new song in my heart. Oh Lord have mercy on me.' The words and music flowed over me like a soothing oil. It was as if God were saying, 'You try so hard; you work so hard! Let me put your feet on the rock and put the song in your heart. Let me heal you!'

"Thank you, Lord, for having mercy on me. Please heal me!"

—*Anonymous, from* Beyond the Looking Glass: Daily Devotions for Overcoming Anorexia and Bulimia *by Ward Keller*

today is five feet four inches tall and weighs 140 pounds," says Ward Keller. "The 'ideal' woman portrayed by models and actresses is five feet seven inches tall and weighs about 100 pounds. And yet everybody is trying to focus on the idea that this is what success is all about—this look and this image."

When depressed women—and an increasing number of men—discover that they can find temporary solace in the comforts of their favorite foods, it's often the beginning of a vicious bulimic cycle. Several days of strict dieting gives way to binges. The only interruptions are trips to the bathroom to throw up, or purge.

It's nothing short of a minor miracle that family members even discover that a loved one is suffering from bulimia. While many people with anorexia are pencil-thin, most people with bulimia are close to normal weight or a little bit above, making it even more difficult to detect.

"We're talking about someone who eats, but before she throws up her food, her body might assimilate enough nutrition to keep her weight relatively normal," says Ward Keller. But if her weight isn't a clue to her behavior, there are other, not-so-pleasant physical symptoms to such binge-purge behavior. Vomiting several times a day eventually eats away at the sufferer's tooth enamel and damages the esophagus, intestines, and cardiac muscle. It can cause liver and kidney dysfunction as well. Frequent use of diuretics and laxatives to shed pounds also exacerbates many of these dangerous conditions.

Still, those with bulimia often manage to hide their behavior—for a while. "You wouldn't believe the number of cases that I've seen where a daughter or wife has been throwing up food for four to five years and no one ever knew it. They noticed that she went to the bathroom all the time right around dinner, but they never really put things together," says Ward Keller. This kind of behavior is why bulimia is called the hidden disease.

But this secretive behavior is also common among those who have anorexia. "The last patient I had with an eating disorder would exercise frequently—biking miles and miles—but wouldn't admit to exercising every day. I've even had patients put things in their pockets in an attempt to alter their weight before they stepped on the scale in my office," says Dickie Kay, M.D., medical director of the Rapha Treatment Unit, an inpatient psychiatric group that provides treatment with a Christian perspective at Forest Hospital in Des Plaines, Illinois.

# The Healing Effect

With all the deception and potentially serious health consequences involved, it may not seem that any good could ever come from having an eating disorder or having a daughter, spouse, or son with one. But some counselors say that properly treating this condition often has a healing effect not only on the one suffering from it but also on the entire family. "Somebody once said that the person with an eating disorder is the match, but the logs have already been set up for a fire. Often, the person who comes in is merely the catalyst for the rest of the family's problems being addressed," says Dr. Abbott.

If we or someone we love has an eating disorder, we should seek help immediately. "There is really no such thing as waiting until

## Prayer Pointers

### Pure and Clean

"As I faced myself in treatment (for an eating disorder), I became overwhelmed with guilt for all the rotten things I had done in my life. My guilt and shame paralyzed me and kept me from progressing. I knew that Christ had died for my sins, but I was unwilling to accept His forgiveness.

"One of the therapists put me through an exercise that helped me visualize being freed from my sins and guilt. She had spray-painted a rock white. I was instructed to write all of my sins on the rock with a marker.

"After I had done that, I was asked to walk around carrying the rock. It was so heavy and bulky; it was hard for me to make much progress with that huge burden. After I had lugged it around for a while, the therapist told me to put it in a box, cover it with a lid, and then carry the whole thing for some time.

"When I told her I was ready to let go and stop carrying my own burden of sin, we walked to a place where a cross stood. I buried all my sins at the foot of the cross and left them there.

"Father, when I start dwelling on the sins of my past, remind me that I left them at the foot of the cross."

—*Anonymous, from* Beyond the Looking Glass: Daily Devotions for Overcoming Anorexia and Bulimia *by Ward Keller*

someone with an eating disorder 'hits bottom,'" says Dr. Abbott. "People can die from the consequences of eating disorders, even in their early phases."

When we look for help, Dr. Abbott recommends that we seek a team that can address all the possible triggers for the disorder. First and foremost, a physician should provide treatment for any medical conditions. Then, a nutritionist trained in treating people with eating disorders can help us or our loved one learn to eat properly again. An individual psychotherapist and often a family therapist should also be part of the team. Most important, all team members should be encouraged to communicate among themselves and with us and our families.

Beyond this, there are plenty of practical things that we can do to try to prevent eating disorders in our families or end ones that exist. Here's what experts suggest.

**Eat dinner together.** This creates a regular eating pattern and lets the family provide care and support in a loving way, says Dr. Abbott. Also, it encourages the person with the eating disorder to be accountable.

**Fight the fix-it syndrome.** We may be tempted to try to "fix" a loved one who has anorexia or bulimia. Big mistake. "So often, moms take the burden on their own shoulders and try to force food or are constantly talking about food issues, and that only makes the situation worse. The family's main responsibility should be to provide a loving, nurturing environment in which to grow mentally, spiritually, and emotionally. It should be the treatment team's responsibility to tackle the eating disorder."

**Speak the truth in love.** Some may view this biblical admonition from Ephesians 4:15 as a license to harp, nag, or prod—with or without a smile. But "it means looking the person in the eye and saying, 'I'm very concerned for you. This is the behavior that I see. This is what it appears that you are doing to yourself. Here is what I see in your life, and we need to get help for you," says Ward Keller.

**Take a cue from the Apostle Paul.** When he found believers in Corinth giving in to the evils of that city, Paul reminded them that the Israelites did the same thing (the passage even refers to out-of-control eating and drinking), and it cost them their lives. To avoid the same consequences, he urged them to recognize God's power in their fleshly struggles, a concept that we'd do well to remember today. Said Paul, "No temptation has overtaken you except such as is common to man; but God is faithful, who will not allow you to be tempted beyond what you are able, but with the temptation will also make the way of escape, that you may be able to bear it." (1 Corinthians 10:13 NKJV)

## Eating-Disorder Symptoms

If we or a loved one exhibit several of the following symptoms, we should probably contact our family physician, says Jacqueline Abbott, Dr.P.H., co-director of the Kartini Clinic for Disordered Eating in Portland, Oregon.

- The desire to be thinner than others
- Spending an inordinate amount of time thinking about weight or physical shape
- Checking weight more than once a week
- Having a sense that gaining weight signifies failure
- Having a sense that losing weight signifies success
- Menstrual periods have ceased or become irregular
- Use of vomiting, laxatives, or diuretics as a means of weight control
- Eating all day whether hungry or not
- Having an extreme fear of gaining weight and looking fat
- Constantly starting new diets
- Getting angry when people ask what we've eaten
- Bingeing on large amounts of food to the point of sickness
- Eating during periods of stress

For more information about eating disorders, contact the National Association of Anorexia Nervosa and Associated Disorders at Box 7, Highland Park, IL 60035, or Eating Disorder Awareness and Prevention at 603 Stewart Street, Suite 803, Seattle, WA 98101.

"The underlying message is that through faith in Christ and what He has revealed to us in our relationships with Him, there is power to overcome and to change our situations," says Dr. Kay.

**Change those inner tapes.** Eating disorders can act like monsters that constantly play and replay shaming, self-defeating, and demoralizing tapes in the mind, says Dr. Abbott.

One of the best ways to rid ourselves of these negative messages is to meditate on Scripture that describes how God sees us. At the Remuda center, says Ward Keller, "Our foundational treatment philosophy is: 'All scripture is God-breathed and is useful for teaching, rebuking, correcting, and training in righteousness.'" (2 Timothy 3:16 NIV) Some other verses that Remuda encourages its patients to consider are Psalm 63:1, Isaiah 48:17, Lamentations 3:22, and Psalm 48.

**Stop dieting.** Instead of eating fat-free and other "diet" foods, we need to enjoy a variety of "real" foods at regular times each day, suggests Dr. Abbott. We should view food as the medicine that can nourish and heal an exhausted body, spirit, and self-worth. Also, we should throw away the bathroom scale. This is the most inaccurate way to measure self-worth. "Don't let weight be the gauge of a self-worth level," says Dr. Abbott.

**Build the body.** Although there's no question that exercise is important for good physical and mental health, we're talking about building the spiritual body. We can join Bible study groups or a church or simply get to know a new friend. This can help end the isolation and self-focus that anorexia and bulimia feed on. "Women with eating disorders like to be alone," says Ward Keller, but they need to be with others.

**Plan some prayer time.** At first glance, prayer might seem like yet another inner-directed activity that encourages self-focus. In fact, prayer allows us to take our heavy mental and physical burdens off our weary backs and place them in the powerful hands of a loving, compassionate God. "Even though people will say that they have tried prayer and it didn't work, I have a hard time believing it, because if we truly get the focus off ourselves and on a right relationship with God, that's when we begin to change," says Ward Keller.

# *Emotional Pain*

~~~~~✦~~~~~

## How to Tear Down the Walls

Who can forget President Ronald Reagan standing on West German soil in Berlin, pointing to the wall that separated the city and divided the Western world from the communist Union of Soviet Socialist Republics: "Mr. Gorbachev," Reagan said, "tear down this wall!"

How often do we sense twinges of emptiness, guilt, or pain when reality slams into one of our own emotional Berlin Walls? Perhaps these twinges are signals that God is pointing to a tall, thick emotional wall that we've erected to protect ourselves from hurt and saying to us, indignantly, "Tear down this wall!"

We all have a tendency to try to insulate ourselves from emotional pain and injuries by erecting invisible barriers that keep people and circumstances at bay and cut us off from the world. It could be that we're hiding from some horrible event in our past, like sexual abuse or the sudden, tragic death of a loved one. Or it could be something as simple as an innocuous event from childhood that we've long since consciously forgotten but misinterpreted to mean that we had done or experienced something awful.

We often do this instinctively and probably hide from hurt more often than we realize, say counselors. This is an unhealthy response.

Really, it is an act of fear, says the Reverend James E. Miller, doctor of ministry, United Methodist minister of Willowgreen

Productions in Fort Wayne, Indiana, a center that helps those experiencing grief and loss, and author of numerous books and videotapes used in hospices, hospitals, funeral homes, and counseling services.

Certainly, no one is asking us to beg for torture. But we do need to realize, as the Scripture says, ". . . God has not given us a spirit of fear, but of power. . . ." (2 Timothy 1:7 NKJV)

If we allow emotional wounds to send us into hiding, then we are adopting the role of victim. We are telling ourselves that we are hopeless and powerless and that our lives and futures are beyond our control. This is not a productive spiritual outlook. This is in direct opposition to faith, says the Reverend Mel Lawrenz, Ph.D., senior associate pastor at Elmbrook Church and director of the Elmbrook Christian Study Center in Brookfield, Wisconsin, and co-author of six books, including *Life after Grief* and *Overcoming Grief and Trauma*.

Fear is magnified by hiding. Faith is found by trusting God to protect us no matter what may come, says the Reverend Paul F. Everett of Pittsburgh, a Presbyterian minister at large with the Peale Center in Pawling, New York, and executive director emeritus of the Pittsburgh Experiment, a national and international ministry to the business and working communities. How do we learn to trust God? One way is to memorize verses like this one, which declares His intentions for us, says Reverend Everett:

For I know the plans I have for you," declares the Lord, "plans to prosper you and not to harm you, plans to give you hope and a future.
Then you will call upon Me and come and pray to Me, and I will listen to you."

—*Jeremiah 29:11–12 NIV*

## Handle Hurt Head-On

At times, emotional hurts, embarrassments, failures—in marriage, business, long-standing, valued relationships, or maybe even simply failing to impress a parent, teacher, sweetheart, or boss—can seem more than we can bear, more than we can handle. "But this is how we grow," says psychologist Michele Novotni, Ph.D., assistant professor of counseling at Eastern College, a Christian college of arts and sciences in St. Davids, Pennsylvania. "Often during deep, troubled emotional events, people really grow in their relationships with God in ways that they never would have imagined," she says.

These events do affect us, bend us, and stretch us, and they do change us. The goal, says Dr. Novotni, is to change for the better, to learn and grow. These are good times for quiet spiritual soul-searching, for in-depth Bible reading, and for prayer, she says.

Here are some great ways to handle emotional injuries.

**Seek support.** Don't try to go it completely alone, advise counselors. "Find someone to be with you as you go through it," recommends Dr. Miller. "Yes, there are some things that you have to do yourself, that no one can do for you. But counselors have found that the one variable that matters more than any other is the kind of support system people have. Those who have the better support systems, the more complete support systems, the healthier support systems, are the most likely to really heal."

Some of us will only need one person, one close confidante; others will need a dozen. For many, support groups help.

"For almost every kind of dilemma, there is a support group," says Dr. Novotni. To find one, call hospitals, look in newspaper listings of community services, check with your doctor and pastor, or call counseling centers. Most counseling centers will know about support groups in the area.

**Consult a counselor.** Some of us will want to seek professional counseling, and that can really help, says Dr. Novotni.

How will we know? Dr. Novotni suggests seeing a professional if we find ourselves unable to lift out of our sadness or despondency, if we are unable to function effectively in normal day-to-day duties, or if we find ourselves telling our same sad stories over and over to the same people. A professional can help us get unstuck, steer us away from increasingly destructive behaviors, and guide us into proper treatment for depression, should it be overtaking us.

(continued on page 264)

# How to Find the Right Counselor

When we hurt emotionally, we need to talk. Research studies show that even talking in an empty room is therapeutic, says psychologist Michele Novotni, Ph.D., assistant professor of counseling at Eastern College, a Christian college of arts and sciences in St. Davids, Pennsylvania.

But talking to a professional listener—a counselor or a psychologist—is even better, Dr. Novotni says, because of the way that these people have been trained to help.

Professional listeners do not dispense lots of advice. They don't offer to solve our problems. What they do is listen, empathetically. Sometimes they ask leading questions to help us sort through our thoughts and our feelings, says Dr. Novotni, who trains counselors with a Christian leaning. A good counselor may just encourage us to talk because that's what we need when we're down, perplexed, discouraged, and hurting.

"Most people can truly get to where they need to be as long as they're supported and have the opportunity to be heard," says Dr. Novotni. "They don't need to be 'Bible-whacked,' either. I instruct my counseling students to never do that. Bible-whacking is when, without taking the time to truly hear what a person is saying or to understand their feelings and their thoughts, the counselor says authoritatively or condescendingly, 'If only you were a good enough Christian, you would have faith.' Or they quote a Bible verse; that is, they whack the person with it, and leave. That's really detrimental."

Not that Bible verses can't help or aren't inspiring. It's just that when we're troubled, we need empathy first. We need a chance to spill out and sort through our thoughts and our feelings. Later, we may be ready to consider supportive or applicable Bible verses, she says.

That's one problem with some Christian counselors, says Dr. Novotni. All Christian counselors and psychologists are not created equal. Some preach to their clients and some hit them over the head with guilt and sin messages, and the clients leave ashamed and more hurt and mixed up than when they came. They practice a message that suggests that all emotional problems are the result of being out of alignment with God and God's will with little emphasis on a developmental healing process, she says.

Still, Christians should not shy away from therapy, Dr. Novotni says. "They should run to therapy." But it is important that we find a therapist with whom we feel comfortable, with whom we have rapport. One way to find a good counselor is to ask trusted friends if they have had any experience with one.

## Pose Some Questions

It's also okay to call therapists and interview them before setting up an appointment. In fact, Dr. Novotni recommends it. We should ask about their counseling approach and goals. That will give us a feel for whether or not we will be comfortable with the counselor. Then, after a few visits, we should assess whether or not the therapist is right for us. Most issues are not resolved in only a few sessions. "If we're not feeling good, if we're not feeling better, if we're not feeling hopeful that something is going to change, that this could work, then it might be time to move on. I've had people that have gone to 17 different therapists just looking for that right match."

Those with strong Christian beliefs may very well feel more comfortable with counselors who also are strong in the faith, says Dr. Novotni. "They're more likely to understand your perspective."

One way to get a referral to a trained counselor with a Christian perspective is to contact Focus on the Family, 8605 Explorer Drive, Colorado Springs, CO 80920.

Some other ideas from Dr. Novotni include visiting support groups and talking with people there about their counselors, asking a trusted minister or doctor for a referral, and checking employee benefits. Some companies contract with counseling services and make a limited number of confidential visits available to all employees and their families on a no-cost basis.

**Feel the pain.** We shouldn't avoid what is happening, but "go more deeply into it. We should immerse ourselves in it as we are able—as our support systems allow us to and as our health allows. We should move toward it rather than away from it," says Dr. Miller.

**Take responsibility.** Traditional Christian teaching says that we will be forgiven, no matter what we have done, and that we should forgive, no matter what someone else has done. Still, we must not rush forgiveness, says Dr. Lawrenz, particularly if we have somehow hurt another by our actions. First, we must acknowledge what we have done and take responsibility for our actions. Then, and only then, can and should we make amends, if possible, and forgive ourselves.

For instance, if we deeply hurt someone by saying harsh things, and we know that it's not the first time we've acted this way, we need to analyze our actions, understand what we did to cause the situation, and accept where we were at fault. Rushing forgiveness can be an effort to hide from hurt instead of using the hurt to grow.

Forgiveness is a gift that we need to give ourselves, says Pastor Dale Ryan, Ph.D., CEO and founder of Christian Recovery International, a ministry based in Brea, California. If we've hurt someone, we're rather out of order to run to them and say, in effect, "I've hurt you terribly. So give me something valuable." Our job is to make amends with others and make peace with ourselves, he says. The others can forgive us when they are ready and able.

**Seek strength in faith.** We should know that God will never abandon us, says Dr. Lawrenz. As it says the Bible, "The Lord Himself goes before you and will be with you; He will never leave you nor forsake you. Do not be afraid; do not be discouraged." (Deuteronomy 31:8 NIV) Focus on encouraging, faith-building Scriptures like, "I can do all things through Christ which strengthen me" (Philippians 4:13 KJV) or "We are hard pressed on every side, but not crushed; perplexed, but not in despair; persecuted, but not abandoned; struck down, but not destroyed." (2 Corinthians 4:8–9 NIV)

**Set goals.** We should imagine where we want to be a year or two from now, emotionally and otherwise, and hold on to that vision, suggests Dr. Novotni. We should work toward it. That's an essential part of the process of rebuilding hope.

For more information on emotional pain, see Forgiveness (page 284), Grief (page 290), and Loss (page 365).

# Enemies

## BREAKING DOWN THE WALLS OF HATE

*T*he trouble seemed to start over their father's health. Both brother and sister had different ideas about the kind of care that Dad should receive. But when he finally died, leaving them each with an equal share of the family homestead, the conflict grew more intense: Brother wanted to keep his half, sister wanted to sell. By the time they reached the counselor's office, they hadn't spoken anything but angry words to each other in four years.

"There was a lot of animosity," says Anne Bachle Fifer, an attorney, Christian mediator, and conflict resolution consultant based in Grand Rapids, Michigan. "The estate was standing open. Taxes were overdue because they couldn't agree on who was going to pay them. It was a mess."

But during the first few sessions with the mediator, something amazing happened. With some coaching, the sister revealed that she had always resented that her brother got to work with their father while she had to hang around the house doing "women's work." Then her brother recalled that he would have rather stayed at the house anyway because the father made him feel like he never could do anything right. Finally, they both agreed that Dad had been pretty cantankerous and that maybe some of their more recent conflict had more to do with him than with each other.

On the fourth visit, the sister tearfully dropped a bombshell: She wanted to settle immediately and she wanted to do it exactly the way her brother had suggested. Today, the two siblings share the farm equally and amicably. "Ultimately, they realized that their sibling wasn't the enemy," says Fifer. "They discovered that they really had a common bond, much stronger than what divided them."

## How Hate Hurts Us

If the common bond with someone we know feels more like a noose around our necks, there's a good chance that we've developed an enemy. And whether it's a neighbor, business associate, friend, or even spouse—it's likely that anger and bitterness didn't develop overnight.

Like bricks added to a wall, things like unforgiven insults, insensitivity, or outright betrayal build until there's so great an emotional barrier that we can't bear to look at, let alone speak to, the other person.

This attitude poisons our lives, our relationships with friends, even our relationships with Christ, says Cupid Poe, M.D., a pastor and medical director of the Community Christian Counseling Center in Nashville, Tennessee. "The Scripture says that before you bring your gift to the altar, make peace with your brother. I cannot have peace and joy and fulfillment in my life if I'm choosing not to forgive."

There's also reason to believe that long-standing disputes harm our mental and physical health. "Unresolved hate toward other people can manifest itself in many ways. Some of those ways are stress, unnecessary fears, anxiety, or even clinical depression. In addition, physical ailments, such as gastric ulcers and headaches, may be manifestations of unresolved hate," says Dr. Poe.

## The Scriptural Solution

When it comes to dealing with others, especially our so-called enemies, there's little room for debate on where the Bible stands. As Jesus hung beaten and humiliated on a cross erected on the town garbage heap, He uttered these amazing, healing words: "Father, forgive them; for they know not what they do." (Luke 23:34) And they weren't just words: He expects us to follow His example.

"No doubt about it, it's challenging to return good for evil. But

# When to Jump In

If we're like most people, latent hostility between, say, our two favorite neighbors makes us feel uneasy. The problem is that it's hard to know whether or not we should do something about it. But there is a way to decide. According to Anne Bachle Fifer, an attorney, Christian mediator, and conflict resolution consultant based in Grand Rapids, Michigan, we should urge some kind of reconciliation if we notice that the conflict is interfering with:

- Our relationships with the people involved
- Other people
- People's relationships with God
- People's relationships with their families
- People's attitudes

Finally, we need to pray about whether or not we should be the ones to bring the problem to light. "If we're looking forward to confronting somebody, if we think that it's going to be fun, then we're probably not the right ones to do it, or else we're not ready to do it yet. We don't have the right attitude." says Fifer. "It should be something that we do because it's our responsibility as Christians in community. But not because it's pleasurable."

that's what God did through Jesus—Jesus died for the forgiveness of our sins. To be the servants of God that He has created us to be, we have to learn to forgive," says Dr. Poe.

But the Bible doesn't just tell us that we should be reconciled with our enemies; it tells us how to do it. Here's a step-by-step guide to letting the healing begin.

**Get the heart ready.** One of the best ways to prepare for reconciliation is to make sure that we're not harboring resentment, unforgiveness, or similar sins in our lives. After all, they're what that wall of hate is made of in the first place. "If I were in this situation, I'd simply say, 'Dear God, please show me how I have wronged my neighbor. Please help me forgive him for the hurt that he has caused me. Please remove my anger toward him. Please help me reach out to him in appropriate ways," says Dr. Poe.

**Go alone.** There's probably no lonelier walk than the one to the front door of someone with whom we're angry. But there are good reasons why we should take these steps alone. Among them, the Bible says: "Moreover if your brother sins against you, go and tell him his fault between you and him alone. If he hears you, you have gained your brother." (Matthew 18:15 NKJV)

"Going in private is to our benefit," says Fifer. "We may not have the facts right or we might have misunderstood something, and that could be very embarrassing if we brought it up in front of a group of people and then found out that we're in error."

**Go for it.** We're face-to-face with someone we haven't seen eye-to-eye with for a long time. If appropriate, and as hard as it may be, we should probably start the conversation by owning up to our share of the problem. "Confess your trespasses to one another, and pray for one another, that you may be healed." (James 5:16 NKJV)

Here's one possible introduction: "I just want to tell you that I'm troubled by the condition of our relationship and want to take responsibility for my part of the problem." From there, we need to apologize and ask forgiveness for specifics: "I'm sorry that I gossiped about your personal problems. Will you forgive me?" Or "I never should have taken your idea without giving you credit for it. I was greedy and I'm sorry."

"The goal isn't to rebuke them, make them feel like a worm, or make yourself look like a saint. The goal is to restore that person to fellowship. And by confessing our mistakes, it opens the door for them to do that, too," says Fifer.

**Be patient.** "It's difficult when people feel passionate about how they have been wronged," explains the Reverend Terry Wise, Ph.D., director of the Trinity Center for Conflict Management at Trinity Theological Seminary in Newburgh, Indiana, and author of *Conflict Scenarios*. "You can't say, 'Okay, Mary, you have to forgive me—and do it right now.' Sometimes you have to let people vent. But in the end, when they feel like there's been some movement and they open up and begin to see that they've been viewing the conflict from their own perspective, and that you have some legitimate issues, too, then you're going to get restoration."

What if the other person doesn't respond? That's all right, says Dr. Poe. You just have to think, "I have started a process in my spirit of forgiving and praying for my neighbor and will continue to reach out in one way or another no matter what they do," he says.

**Take a friend along.** What if we get the door slammed in our faces or are asked to leave? Don't lose hope. The Bible says to go back again and bring a friend. (Matthew 18:16) "In this type of situation, we want a peacemaker, someone whom other people would look at and say, 'This individual is out for our best interests—not for himself, not for his agenda—he really can be trusted,'" says Dr. Wise. "We need someone who is mutually respected and has a lot of wisdom and tact, someone who brings calm to the situation."

**Go to the church.** If the person with whom we're having trouble is a member of our church or a local congregation, we can pursue the next step: "And if he refuses to hear them, tell it to the church." (Matthew 18:17 NKJV) "Different churches implement this differently, but the goal is still restoration of the relationship," says Fifer.

**Call in a mediator.** Like the brother and sister divided over the family farm, our wall may be so hard and tall that it's time to call in a professional mediator. "Skilled mediators can be of tremendous help because they're able to identify the key issues," says Dr. Wise. "One of the first things that I do with certain conflicts is let each side state its position and allow them to be antagonistic. We keep it in check so that they aren't trying to kill each other, but at the same time, it gets kind of ugly. Once they get a taste of the futility and know that they aren't going anywhere, they can begin to work on common interests and a mutually agreeable solution. It's not just communicating, it's directed communication."

**Take communion together.** When a nasty, long-standing dispute has finally been laid to rest, why not celebrate? And what better way than eating a meal or taking communion together? Highly symbolic and often deeply moving, celebrating communion may just bury the problem forever. "Depending on the situation, this can really bring some closure to it," says Dr. Wise. "It's a powerful and vivid illustration of what the Christian life is all about."

And that's a great way to break down a wall, once and for all.

# Fear

## FEELING SAFE IN A DANGEROUS WORLD

*W*atch out for the Under Toad!" Garp yelled to his son, as the boy entered the surf.

At least that's what the boy thought he heard. Actually, Garp, the main character in John Irving's 1976 bestseller, *The World According to Garp*, was urging his son to look out for the undertow, but the child misheard and imagined some beast lurking beneath the waves, ready to grab an ankle and drag him out to sea.

The fear of the Under Toad, of catastrophe, or of danger in general permeates many of our lives, much as it permeated Irving's novel. And we wish for the same thing that Garp did: a world safe "for children and for grownups."

But is that realistic?

To be alive is to be vulnerable. This is as true for Christians as for anyone else. As much as we would like to think that God will protect us from the misfortunes of the world—He may, in fact, have done so a thousand times already—an honest assessment tells us that at some point, He might not. "Christians fell on the beach at Normandy, and we die of cancer, just like everyone else," says the Reverend Neil Plantinga Jr., Ph.D., dean of the chapel at Calvin College in Grand Rapids, Michigan. "That's simply so, and we have to face that fact."

Still, even though fear may be a reality in our lives, we don't have to let it defeat us. We can triumph over the Under Toad and feel safe.

# Building a Sense of Confidence

The first step in dealing with our fears is understanding that they may be groundless. This is especially true when it comes to our fear of violent crime. "The chances of any one particular American being the victim of a violent crime is very tiny," says Stephen Klineberg, Ph.D., professor of sociology at Rice University in Houston. The chances of actually being a victim of crime are about 1 in 20,000.

The next thing we should realize about our fears is the role that faith can play in overcoming them. Dr. Plantinga believes that while it's true we can't expect God to protect us from every evil of the world during this life, we can have utter confidence that we are, indeed, loved by God, and that, ultimately, we will be redeemed.

"The most important thing for me is to believe that we are fiercely, finally, redemptively loved by God," says Dr. Plantinga. "If we step out of our houses or apartments each day and know that we have been fiercely loved to the point of death, to me, that is a reassurance about as profound and securing as anything that is granted to us as human beings."

The promise of the Christian life is the prospect of resurrection. But it is not only at the end of our lives that we are lifted up from death, Dr. Plantinga says. Resurrection can occur on a daily basis. We can be lifted up out of the smaller "deaths" that our fears cause by becoming attentive stewards of our thoughts. "Fear is a form of suffering, and we sometimes have to accept that," he says, "but we should not indulge it. We should try to muscle it gently aside with our trust, thinking less of what may come to us and our loved ones and more of who God is and what God wants. Then we turn ourselves over to the love and the care of God."

Here are some specific steps to take toward turning ourselves and our fears over to God.

**Use reasonable precautions.** Taking practical steps to improve home security not only helps prevent crime but it also makes us feel better. So says Wilford Wooten, a licensed marriage, family, and child counselor, a licensed clinical social worker, and director of the counseling department for Focus on the Family in Colorado Springs, Colorado. During a long career in the military, Wooten spent some time running a rape crisis program, and he saw how small steps, such as leaving the light on at night, often helped soothe women's fears considerably following traumatic experiences.

**Know when to get help.** Fears can develop into debilitating phobias if left unchecked. It's important to realize this and seek professional help if we feel that we're having a hard time handling our fears. How can we know? When a fear becomes immobilizing or interferes with our normal functions, says Wooten, it's time for us to seek counseling.

**Acknowledge fear, then take it on.** A fear faced is often a fear defeated, Wooten says. He quotes a saying that he used to have on his office wall: "Boats are safe anchored in the harbor, but that's not what boats are made for." People of faith have lots of things to do for the Lord, he says. Sitting at home afraid isn't among them.

He recalls an assistant of his who was frightened of speaking in front of groups. He asked her to make a presentation at a staff meeting. When she stood up, she realized that she was nervous, and said so. Her throat was dry, and she took a drink of water. Then she began. Acknowledging her fears and focusing momentarily on something else—getting a drink of water—helped her through the moment, Wooten says. The next time she spoke, she wasn't quite so nervous.

One more thing, Wooten adds. The young woman had prayed to Jesus before the meeting, asking directly for His help in dealing with her fear.

**Accentuate the positive.** The Apostle Paul in his letters wrote frequently of the need to focus our minds on the good things in life, not the bad. "Whatever is true," he wrote to the Phillipians, "whatever is honorable, whatever is commendable, if there is anything worthy of praise, think about these things."

To turn our minds away from our fears, Wooten recommends making a list of pleasant thoughts and memories and adding to it regularly. "When we're tempted to start dwelling on something negative," he says, "we'll have something that's good and true to put in our minds to replace it with."

## Do Not Be Afraid

Immediately He made the disciples get into the boat and go
on ahead to the other side, while He dismissed the
crowds.

And He went up the mountain by Himself to pray. When
evening came, He was there alone,

But by this time the boat, battered by the waves, was far
from the land, for the wind was against them.

And early in the morning He came walking toward them on
the sea.

But when the disciples saw Him walking on the sea, they
were terrified, saying, "It is a ghost!" And they cried out
in fear.

But immediately Jesus spoke to them and said, "Take heart,
it is I; do not be afraid."

Peter answered Him, "Lord, if it is You, command me to
come to You on the water."

He said, "Come."

—Matthew 14:22–29 NRSV

**Tune out bad news.** The media's obsession with crime and other horrors doesn't do our peace of mind any good. "All the studies of television viewers show that people who watch more television perceive a more violent world," says Dr. Klineberg.

To Wooten, the solution is simple: "Turn it off!"

**Practice the fundamentals.** Just as we feel better when we're eating right and exercising, so, too, are we likely to feel better when we're paying attention to the basics of spiritual life, Dr.

Plantinga believes. That means keeping up regularly on our prayer, worship, fellowship, and service. "I think that a lot of our insecurities come from an unspoken awareness that we've veered off the path someplace, that we're not living as we're called to live," he says. "If we stay on His path, we're going to feel as if we were walking where we were meant to walk, and there's security in that."

**Seek strength in numbers.** Dr. Plantinga adds that Paul's letters were constant reminders to his followers to promote the strength of their Christian communities through cooperation and mutual support. Community is an especially important element of our spiritual security blanket. We can do much to allay our fears if we wrap ourselves tightly in a network of believers by attending services regularly, participating in church social activities, and doing volunteer service.

For more information on fear, see Anxiety on page 168.

# *Financial Difficulties*

## MORE MONEY ISN'T THE CURE

*F*unny thing about money. "Whoever loves money never has money enough; whoever loves wealth is never satisfied with his income." (Ecclesiastes 5:10 NIV) These thoughts are attributed to wise old King Solomon, the man credited with writing the book of Proverbs and who reigned about 2,200 years before The Shopping Channel debuted.

Even today, how often we say, "If I just had more money" or "If I just had this or that item, then everything would be all right. Then I would be happy."

More money is not the answer, says Mary Hunt, founder, editor, and publisher of the *Cheapskate Monthly* newsletter, author of the *Cheapskate Monthly Money Makeover* and other books, and a regular financial advisor on Dr. James Dobson's *Focus on the Family* radio broadcasts. "It doesn't take much contemplation to realize that more money can't be the answer," she says. "Because who among us doesn't make more money than we made 10 years ago? Or even one year ago?" Has that increase solved all our problems? Are we now completely satisfied? Are we now debt-free? Are we living happily ever after?

The problem, says Hunt, is not a lack of money but what we do with our money, how we view our money, and how we care for our money. The answer is getting out of debt and staying out of debt. The answer is enjoying the money we are blessed with—sharing it, saving it, investing it, and spending it wisely and thoughtfully. There just isn't enough "more money" in this world to make us happy.

Hunt knows. Her family teetered on the brink of financial ruination before she asked God for forgiveness and spent the next 13 years digging out. Now, she helps others avoid messes like the one she made or clean them up much more quickly than she did. She advises *Focus on the Family* listeners on money matters and thrifty living. She has thousands of letters attesting that her advice has turned lives around. "There is always hope," she says.

The Bible offers many lessons about money. We are to recognize that money, even wealth, is a gift from God and we are to honor God with it. We are to be good stewards. We are to enjoy it. We are to invest wisely. We really are not supposed to run up unsecured debt, says Jerry McTaggart, founder of Christian Credit Counselors, a free, nondenominational service in Del Mar, California, that helps people in money trouble get control of their finances. Lend to many, but borrow from none, advises Deuteronomy 15:6.

But this is the real world. This is America. This is the land of TV commercials, magazine ads, billboards, new models of cars every year, and new-and-improved just about everything. Good people do get into bad debt for many reasons. They need good, sound advice and help.

# Pitch the Plastic

The numbers embossed on credit cards might as well be 6-6-6—the signature of Satan—for all the damage that they cause in people's lives, says McTaggart.

The first key to effective money management is to quit using the credit cards, unless we truly are going to pay the bills in full each month when they come due, says McTaggart. Give up instant gratification—the buy-now, pay-later syndrome. And give up the pocketful of cards. Most people don't need multiple credit cards, he says. Just keep one for emergencies or for purchases that we must order by phone or online.

# Answered Prayers

## One Money Junkie's Story

"I used to be such a credit-card junkie," says Mary Hunt, founder, editor, and publisher of the *Cheapskate Monthly* newsletter, author of the *Cheapskate Monthly Money Makeover* and other books, and a regular financial advisor on Dr. James Dobson's *Focus on the Family* radio broadcasts.

"I grew up in a pastor's home. I could preach every sermon. I could quote the entire Bible. All of that stuff got into my head but it never invaded my heart, never got into my life, until 1982, when I had a real turning-point experience and I'd come to the end of my rope.

"I'd gotten my husband, my family, and myself into so much financial trouble, it was more than just not having enough money to have the things I wanted. We were at the point of losing everything. We were $100,000 in nonmortgage debt.

"I was in my in-laws' kitchen, and I fell to my knees on the kitchen floor and begged God to forgive me for the horrible mess I had made. I vowed that I would stop spending irrationally and running up debt. I vowed to do whatever was necessary to pay back everything we owed. I asked God to forgive me because I had not trusted Him to take care of me, had not allowed the things I knew about Him and His way to direct my life, to become the center of my life.

"And it was at that point when I said, 'God, we're going to do it your way.'"

Some things turned around immediately for Hunt and her family. Within days, she was offered a job that helped her family chisel away at its debt. It took 13 years before they were debt-free, but in the process, she learned tremendous lessons that she now shares with others through the *Cheapskate Monthly* newsletter, her books, Christian TV and radio appearances, and speaking engagements.

Let's say the problem isn't a bad case of the I-want-it-right-nows. Rather, a job loss or car accident sends our finances flailing, and we see no short-term solution in sight. We should never borrow from credit cards to tide us over when money gets tight, no matter how great the temptation, says McTaggart. This is the quickest way to run up uncontrollable debt.

# God's Plan

How should we handle money?

"It's an easy formula," says Hunt. "And if you look back in time, you'll see that anybody who has been successful with money has followed this: They were givers, number one. They were savers, number two. And then, with what's left, they never spent more money than they had."

How can we apply this formula in our lives? Here are some tips.

**Give.** "I think that God blesses us, and it's like exposing your life to God's supernatural intervention if you will just obey Him. What He says is, 'I want the best and the first of whatever you have,'" says Hunt. "That applies to our talents, to our money, and to our time."

The Bible talks of giving 10 percent back to God to good, holy works, causes, and efforts, but you need not start there if that seems too daunting, says Hunt. "If you can't do 10 percent today, that's fine. Start with 1 percent. And I don't care where you give it. Just give it with no strings attached. Give it out of a heart of gratitude. Say, 'This is what I am doing because I am so thankful for the air that I breathe, for the place that I live, and for the wonderful abundance that I am enjoying right now, this is the most wonderful time in all of creation to have lived as far as I am concerned. I'm so grateful for that.'"

If you start with 1 percent, watch what happens, she says. "Then, as God blesses you with more, give more."

**Save.** "It's very clear in God's word that He wants us to prepare for the future, and I don't mean in an unbalanced way," says Hunt. "I know that in Matthew, it says not to lay up treasures on Earth because they're going to get rusty and they're going to rot out, so you need to lay up treasures in Heaven. But I think that the person who says, 'I'm not going to save money, I'm not going to think about to-morrow in any way' is missing the boat.

"Look at the parable of the talents, where the master gave money to three different servants and just checked to see what they are going to do with it. One servant just buried his money in the back-yard because he was so fearful of losing it. The master said that was horrible. He said, 'At least you could have earned interest if you'd put it in the bank.' I think that's the principle that we need to grasp."

So the second thing is, save 10 percent. It's a pretty good formula. Give away 10, save 10.

**Live joyfully.** "Live the best life, the most wonderful, fabulous, exotic life that you can on 80 percent of what you make," says Hunt. "And I have to tell you, I have drawers full of testimonials that this works. All I have to do is look into my own life and see where I am today as opposed to where I was 15 years ago, when I fell on my face on that kitchen floor and had to beg God for His forgiveness. Yes, I can tell you that it works."

**Spend wisely.** Think of it like this: This isn't really our money. We are simply entrusted with it; we are stewards, says McTaggart. He suggests that we ask ourselves before we spend money whether, in this situation and under the same circumstances, this is the decision that God would make.

# Banish Budgets

It's not that you don't have to set aside money for expenses. It's just that the B-word, *budget*, sounds so intimidating. "I don't like that word," says Hunt. "You know, to me, *budget, diet, straitjacket*—each is such a mean label. So I call it a spending plan."

So we should give 10 percent and save 10 percent. Then what percentage should we spend on various expenses like housing, food, and clothing?

She recommends that we come up with our own formulas by doing the following:

**Gather records.** Get together the credit-card statements, check-book registers, and other receipts going back as far as a year, if possible.

**Tally up.** Add up typical spending. Divide everything into ac-counts like mortgage, car payment, car repairs, gasoline, Christmas gifts, dining out, groceries, utilities, clothing, taxes, prescriptions, doctor visits, savings, life insurance, entertainment, kids' schoolbooks and supplies, and so forth. Total what is spent in each expense category.

**Divide and conquer.** We need to divide the total amount for each category by the number of paychecks that we get each year. That's about how much we need to set aside each paycheck in each category to cover our predictable expenses. Nearly all expenses should be predictable, says Hunt. If we create a spending plan like this, a property-tax bill won't be an emergency when it shows up in the mail. Nearly every conceivable expense will be covered. That's our spending plan.

**Keep simple, basic books.** Give each account a page in a notebook, and once each week, record deposits into that account and record any expenditures made during the previous week.

**Plan ahead.** We need a second checking account, Hunt says. This one is for expenses not paid on a monthly basis or for unpredictable items. She calls it our freedom account.

Our freedom account gets a notebook of its own, and we create a page for each item. The pages might include auto repair, retirement plan, new bedroom set, life insurance, kids' college, and property taxes, for instance. Figure out how much each of these costs on a yearly basis and divide by 12 to get a monthly figure. Put the pages in order of importance or priority.

Set up an automatic monthly deposit from your regular checking into your freedom account to cover the monthly totals of your irregular expenses. Enter the monthly amount deposited on each separate page.

What if we find that we spend more than we take in? Then we need to run through all the categories and see where we might trim, says Hunt. To get our accounts started, we might wish to have a garage sale and sell off some stuff so that we have a little extra money in reserve in each account.

# What If the Wolf Is at the Door?

Too late? The phone rings a dozen times a day and we dread answering because it's probably another bill collector hounding us. We can't fund a spending plan. We can't even predict whether we'll be able to buy groceries, pay the rent, and keep the electricity on. What to do?

The credit-card companies figure that it's better to help people stay solvent and repay their bills than to hound them, force them into bankruptcy, and lose them as customers, says McTaggart. So they will waive a portion or all of the interest payments and allow a delinquent customer, through the credit counseling service, to pay off the principal. That speeds things up tremendously. You can write to Christian Credit Counselors at 445 Marine View Avenue, Suite 260E, Del Mar, California 92014.

While not a specifically Christian company, the National Foundation for Consumer Credit is the nation's largest nonprofit organization of credit counselors. Contact them at 8611 Second Avenue, Suite 100, Silver Spring, MD 20910.

"When you're paying 18 percent interest, it will take you 10 years to get out of debt if you just pay the minimum payment," explains McTaggart. "If the companies will waive their interest and we can put the payment money all on just principal, we've found that it drops to around 27 months—2 to 3 years versus 10 years. What happens otherwise is that people get so frustrated along the period of 10 years that they just say, 'You know what? I'm not getting ahead at all. I send in $100 and I only get $20 knocked off the principal. This is killing me.' So they go and file for Chapter 7 bankruptcy. For biblical reasons, we're not supposed to do that. 'The wicked borrow and do not repay. . . .'" (Psalm 37:21 NIV)

A credit counseling agency will help us determine exactly the minimum amount of money required for our basic needs, including entertainment, and then, hopefully, find enough left over to pay our creditors under new terms that the agency negotiates. The agency will collect that amount of money from us each month, usually through direct deposit of a portion of our paychecks, and then pay our bills for us and send us a monthly statement, explains McTaggart.

**Stop hemorrhaging.** A credit counseling agency will insist that we turn in our credit cards until we are out of debt. Occasionally, they will let us keep one credit card with a low limit for true emergencies,

# Rapid Debt Repayment

Want to get out of the debt trap without paying any more toward your bills than you are now? Provided that you are making at least the minimum payment on every account, then you can, just by following these simple instructions, says Mary Hunt, founder, editor, and publisher of the *Cheapskate Monthly* newsletter, author of the *Cheapskate Monthly Money Makeover* and other books, and a regular financial advisor on Dr. James Dobson's *Focus on the Family* radio broadcasts.

1. Stop incurring new debts. Get rid of all credit cards except for a basic no-fee one.
2. Add up the monthly minimum payments on all debt. Be committed to paying that total amount toward debts each month until they're all gone.
3. Line the debts up in the order they will pay off rather than by the interest rates. That probably means that the one with the lowest balance will be first in line, then the next lowest, and so on.

says McTaggart. Whether we go to a credit counseling agency or not, if we find ourselves in over our heads, we must stop charging and debting, says Hunt.

**Enter a rapid-repayment plan.** The nonprofit credit counseling services can set one up for us. Or we can do one on our own, following Hunt's instructions above.

**Make room for joy.** "I want to help people see that paying back debt—that stopping that frantic I've-got-to-have-more-more-more-me-me-me-I-never-have-enough stuff—is a great relief," says Hunt. "If we can put the brakes on that sort of thing, that's when the joy starts coming back into our lives."

4. Pay the minimum payment on each one of these every single month—more, if you can, on the first one.

5. When the first one gets paid off, "instead of pocketing that extra money every month, add that to the second debt's monthly payment so that payment gets a real boost and that creditor gets paid off much more quickly," explains Hunt. "This is where the rapid part comes in. By doing this, we begin prepaying the principal, which pays the debt off much quicker. The second one is going to get paid off in maybe half the time because we've increased the payment. Then when it's paid off, take the money from the first two debts and add it to the debt that is third in line, and so on, until the debts are all paid.

6. Don't stop when you're out of debt. Take all or a sizable hunk of the money that was applied to the debts and begin saving and investing it wisely—for a down payment on a home, for the kids' college education, for your retirement, and so on.

The Bible tells us that we aren't supposed to love money. It also says, however, that we are supposed to enjoy it—that which we are given. King Solomon speaks to this: ". . . it is good and proper for a man to eat and drink, and to find satisfaction in his toilsome labor under the sun during the few days of life God has given him—for this is his lot. Moreover, when God gives any man wealth and possessions, and enables him to enjoy them, to accept his lot and be happy in his work—this is a gift of God." (Ecclesiastes 5:18–19 NIV)

A key, says Hunt, is accepting our lot, learning to enjoy it, and not envying others.

# *Forgiveness*

## A GIFT THAT FREES OUR SOULS

We have a choice.

- Forever bristle and brood under a burden of rage and hurt that we feel as the result of something that someone has done.
- Forgive the person.

Forgiveness is healing, though it may not be either easy or quick.

Failing to forgive clearly damages us emotionally and hampers our own growth, progress, and happiness. And, some say, it can make us sick or keep us from getting well. Yet frequently, it seems to be the path that we choose, says Pastor Dale Ryan, Ph.D., CEO and founder of Christian Recovery International, a ministry based in Brea, California.

Why?

Often, says Dr. Ryan, we become addicted to our rage. We are so indignant that a certain person violated us that we adopt indignation and the violation as part of our personality, as part of our being.

We should do that, but only for a while, Dr. Ryan says. If we stop at this stage, we don't heal. We don't grow. And, in fact, we stifle and limit ourselves.

Another reason why we often fail to forgive is that we have misconceptions about forgiveness, says Dr. Ryan. Forgiveness is not:

- Sanctioning or condoning abusive behavior
- Conditional ("I'll forgive you if you change")
- Reconciliation (though reconciliation can be a step in forgiveness)
- Denial
- Forgetting
- Saying, "Everything is okay now" or "I'm completely okay now"

Denying, forgetting, or glossing over are ways of burying hurts. None of them are good for us. When we bury our hurts or when we nurse them, we hurt ourselves emotionally and even physically, says prayer teacher Vernon M. Sylvest, M.D., a physician with a prayer-based holistic medical practice in Richmond, Virginia, and author of *The Formula: Who Gets Sick, Who Gets Well.* Forgetting is part of forgiveness, but it is not all there is to forgiveness, he adds.

So just what is forgiveness?

Forgiveness is acquitting the other person of whatever they've done to us, says Dr. Sylvest. He says that he has seen cancers go into remission once people process long-held resentments and forgive. Forgiveness is a process.

The process of forgiveness usually means changing a relationship, establishing new expectations and boundaries. It does not mean returning to business as usual, says Dr. Ryan. Forgiveness is discovering what hurt us—exactly how and why we were hurt—healing those hurts as best as possible, and growing from them and beyond them.

Forgiveness is something that we do for *us*, says Dr. Ryan, to heal *our* lives, not to help the person we feel has wronged us. And it is something that we do because we want to and need to, not because we are told that we must.

# Pray for Our "Enemies"

How do we forgive people who have inflicted injury upon us?

First, we should speak up and condemn the behavior, says Juanita Ryan, R.N, a counselor at Christian Recovery International who specializes in mental health nursing at Brea Family Counseling Center in California. Then, we can and should pray for them, she says. We need to remember that they, too, are fallible humans, just

*(continued on page 288)*

## Shame: The Hidden Tormentor

When we fail to forgive, often we are shaming ourselves.

We are taking on a role of victim, says Juanita Ryan, R.N., a counselor at Christian Recovery International who specializes in mental health nursing at Brea Family Counseling Center in California. This is not a healthy role.

We should never let shame fester, no matter what has happened to hurt us or what we may have done to hurt others, says Vicki Underland-Rosow, Ph.D., of Minneapolis, an international speaker and group facilitator on addictions and shame and author of *Shame*. True healing cannot occur until a person transforms shame.

Shame is a poor state of being. It causes emotional paralysis, confusion, and untold misery to people, says Dr. Underland-Rosow. It can lead to rage, violence, withdrawal, and other antisocial behaviors. And, amazingly, shame is a taught behavior, she says. Anthropologists have discovered cultures that don't experience it, but here in the United States, we're pretty practiced at it. We use it as a means of controlling people. We withdraw or threaten to withdraw love and affection when our children do not behave the way we want them to. We shame them into conformity.

How do we transform shame as adults? Here's Dr. Underland-Rosow's formula.

1. **Identify it.** We need to search our minds and hearts and the past for things that we may be feeling ashamed about. Often, a counselor or friend can help us find the source of our shame.

2. **Quit denying or hiding it.** Next, we should bring it out into the open and explore it in all of its facets. How does it feel,

sound, look? We should follow those feelings and images and see where they take us.

3. **Talk to the shame.** In private or with a counselor, say, "I know there is something underneath you that I am really scared of. My fear is forcing me to hold on to you and keep you hidden. Come on out and show me what you are," Dr. Underland-Rosow advises. When we discover the underlying feelings, we can choose to honor them and then finally let go of them.

   "These feelings will be different for different people, but if we give ourselves permission to stay with the feeling and go into the feeling, it will present itself, and we will no longer be paralyzed by it," Dr. Underland-Rosow says.

4. **Reconnect.** First, we connect with our inner selves. That happens in steps 1 through 3. Then, we reconnect with our sense of Higher Power. "People who feel a lot of shame can't feel connected to Christ, God, whoever they see as a Higher Power," she says. But calling out shame, identifying it, and meeting it head-on allow us to reconnect and feel something other than shame. "Shame will not exist in the sunlight," she says. Shame does not allow for spirituality, and true spirituality does not involve shame.

Participation in a 12-Step program, such as Alcoholics Anonymous, is the single best means of learning to reconnect, says Dr. Underland-Rosow. The purpose of a 12-Step program is to lead us through the process of reconnection with God, with self, with another person, and finally, with the universe.

like us; that they, too, are children of God. They may be running from God and from goodness, but we can pray that God will open their hearts so that they can remember who they are at the core.

We can pray that they, too, can release the anger, rage, shame, and fear that steer and cripple them, Juanita Ryan says. Maybe they can come to see themselves as God sees them: as loved and loving children.

And, adds Dr. Ryan, maybe they won't. Their response should not be a condition of our forgiveness.

But if we can hope and ask for blessings for someone who has hurt us, we will know that we have forgiven them, or are in the process of forgiving, says Dr. Sylvest. The feeling of forgiveness may not come instantly, but if we persist in our praying, thinking, and acting, it will occur.

How we will respond to the other person who has hurt us is all that we have control over, says Dr. Ryan. We can't control how that person will respond to us. "We can forgive an abusive person, and they still may be an abusive person," he says. "We can't recover for other people or from their problems; we can only recover from our own."

## Four Steps to Forgiving

How do we process the hurt and anger so that we can forgive? Dr. Ryan recommends four steps.

1. Recognize the hurt. This may require therapy if we've long buried a major trauma such as childhood sexual abuse, he says.

2. Own the hurt. We need to accept that we hurt, accept that this is *our* hurt. We should feel the anger, the shame, and the pain and watch where those feelings take us.

3. Explore the ways the original offense has been compounded by our denial and subsequent hurts. This one big hurt may have caused dozens of other hurts that cause us to cower, cry, or boil up in certain situations.

4. Work, one at a time, on each hurt and behavior or attitude that handicaps us. "We need to recognize that some of this is not 'our stuff,'" says Dr. Ryan. Instead, it is stuff that we can give back (in our minds and hearts) to the person from whom we got it. We can let go of it. Then we can see what changes we can make in our lives and attitudes that will be healing and set about making them.

"Set reasonable expectations about how to move on from here," advises Dr. Ryan. Forgiving does not mean that we have to reconcile with the people who hurt us, but we do need to discover how we will prevent that person's past (and perhaps even current) behavior from negatively affecting us and our behavior, both when we deal with that person and when we don't.

The process is sort of like cancer surgery. "The issue," says Dr. Ryan, "is not speed, but thoroughness. The question is, 'Did we get it all?'"

If we find it difficult to identify and resolve our hurts, we should seek help. If we've suffered severe trauma, we may wish to seek private counseling. Or we can turn to 12-step groups, which exist for nearly every hurt imaginable, and all of them can help us sort through and move beyond our hurt, says Dr. Ryan. (To find an appropriate group, we can call hospitals, look in newspaper listings of community services and meetings, check with our doctors or pastors, and call counseling centers.) Even if we only visit a group one or two times, we will benefit from being able to talk about our hurt with people who are constructively working through the same sorts of things, he says.

## Finding Release

What if we're the ones who need to be forgiven? The process is much the same, says Dr. Ryan. We need to accept that we have hurt someone. We need to explore all the ways that our hurtful behavior impacted them. We need to explore the hurt and shame that this causes us. We need to do what we can to make restitution or contrition to the person we hurt. We need to demonstrate in our current lives that we have changed. And then we need to forgive ourselves and move on in a constructive way.

We should not necessarily ask the people we hurt to forgive us, says Dr. Ryan. It's always appropriate to apologize, make amends, and stay in the relationship to help the recovery process. But by simply asking another for forgiveness, we run the risk of being perceived as demanding. We need to make a genuine effort to change our hearts and understand what we've done and then let the other person forgive us—if they choose to—in their own way and in their own time. That is their choice. Ours is to change and to keep our shame and guilt from forever crippling us.

# Grief

## A NATURAL
## AND NORMAL PROCESS

*J*ésus wept." (John 11:35 KJV)
This is the shortest verse in the Bible. "Jesus wept" because His friend Lazarus had died.

God wants us to know that grief is universal; grief is real; grief is okay. We need not hide grief, and yes, Jesus grieved; yes, "Jesus wept." Exhibiting signs of grief, even long after a loss, is not a sign of weak faith, says grief educator John W. James, co-founder of the Grief Recovery Institute in Beverly Hills, California, and co-author of *The Grief Recovery Handbook*. It is evidence of a feeling, caring person.

Grief is a natural and painful but healthy emotional response to profound loss of any kind, not just death. We grieve the loss of health, wealth, mobility, reputation, possessions, pride, youth, and so on. We grieve all losses, and we grieve each loss uniquely. Sometimes, the process of grieving for a new loss dredges up past ones and the pain associated with them, multiplying the effect and deepening the depths of our despair and angst.

Grief is a tough tiger to tame, and current thinking is that perhaps it is better not to tame it at all. Instead, grieve.

## Don't Give This Advice

Here are some no-no's, the sorts of things that we should not say when talking with a grieving person, even if we think they are true. They simply are not kind, considerate, compassionate, or encouraging words to a griever's ears, says the Reverend Mel Lawrenz, Ph.D., senior associate pastor at Elmbrook Church and director of the Elmbrook Christian Study Center, both in Brookfield, Wisconsin, and co-author of six books, including *Life after Grief* and *Overcoming Grief and Trauma*.

Don't say:

- I know exactly how you feel.
- You must be as strong as you can be now.
- God never gives us more than we can handle.
- You should count your blessings.
- It must be God's will.

Avoid saying anything designed to diminish the person's grief. Nearly every such statement backfires in the griever's heart.

## Dive In

Well-meaning folks will try to distract us from our grief and encourage us to suppress it, ignore it, and move beyond it. "We have a lot of what I call grief police, who say, 'Here is what you should and shouldn't do,'" says lecturer and ordained Episcopalian priest Harold Ivan Smith, doctor of ministry, who leads grief gatherings at St. Luke's Medical Center in Kansas City, Missouri, and is the author of many Christian self-help books. Grieving people don't need to be told what to do; they need to grieve.

Grievers don't need clichés and pat answers, either, says James. In fact, he has identified 141 clichés that people offer to grievers. Near the top of the list are things like, "It just takes time," "Just give it time," "Your faith will see you through," and "Keep a stiff upper lip."

Grievers don't need a stiff upper lip but, rather, opportunities to fully explore their grief and how it affects them and their lives. They need to remember the meaningfulness and significance of that which they have lost, to memorialize it and celebrate it, to keep alive the memory of the treasured aspects of whomever or whatever it is they have lost, say experts.

# Recognize the Good in Grief

Charlie Brown was right when he said, "Good grief!"

Grief truly is a necessary, healthy process. People and cultures that recognize grief as a necessary passageway handle life much better than those that try to short-circuit the process, says the Reverend Mel Lawrenz, Ph.D., senior associate pastor at Elmbrook Church and director of the Elmbrook Christian Study Center, both in Brookfield, Wisconsin, and co-author of six books, including *Life after Grief* and *Overcoming Grief and Trauma*. Those who short-circuit grief actually just repress it. Then, it's likely to nag at them negatively for much longer and more fiercely than it would have otherwise.

Here are some suggestions that pastors and counselors offer to help us sort through and effectively experience our grief. Some of these deal specifically with grieving a death. Most are applicable to any form of grief.

**Visit the grave.** But we should do this only if we want to. "Spend whatever time feels right there," says the Reverend James E. Miller, doctor of ministry, United Methodist minister of Willowgreen Productions in Fort Wayne, Indiana, a center that helps those experiencing grief and loss, and author of numerous books and videotapes used in hospices, hospitals, funeral homes, and counseling services. "Stand or sit in the quietness and do what comes naturally: Be silent or talk, breathe deeply or cry, recollect or pray," he says. We may wish to bring flowers or otherwise add distinctive touches or beautify the grave site.

**Make a memory album.** Fill it with photos, diplomas, awards, invitations, and newspaper clippings. Arrange them in an order that tells a story about our loved one's life or the aspect or period of our lives that has now closed (if we are grieving something other than a death), suggests Dr. Miller. Keep it out so that others can look through it. When we feel the urge, we can look through it and reminisce.

**Honor the spiritual.** A time when our world seems to be falling apart can become a time of revelation, enlightenment, and new understanding if we turn to God or to that which we consider Divine, suggests Dr. Miller. In the Old Testament, God explains this to Jeremiah. Jeremiah is imprisoned and learns that many of his people have been slaughtered in battle and that their city has been overrun and seized by enemies. As Jeremiah grieves, God tells him: "Call to Me and I will answer you, and will tell you great and hidden things which you have not known." (Jeremiah 33:3 RSV)

**Cry freely.** If we feel like crying, we should cry. It's natural for people enduring a serious loss. Some people cry a lot, and some seldom or never cry. Whichever, we shouldn't restrain the urge.

**Vent anger.** Grieving people often feel anger. We need to let it out. We can yell at the walls, if necessary, or hit a pillow, clean the attic, chop a cord of wood. We can physically work off the angry energy. We shouldn't repress it, advises Dr. Miller.

# Get Help

Earlier in this chapter, John W. James talks about the pat answers and clichés that well-meaning people may offer us after we've suffered a loss: "Time heals all wounds" or "Your faith will see you through." The speakers' intentions may be good, but their statements turn us off, anger us, and drive us deeper into a sense of isolation.

Just give it time? Faith will see you through?

James asks, "If you went to your car right now and found that the left front tire was flat, would you sit down on the curb and wait for air to get back in the tire? Would you sit down and pray for air to get back in the tire? I don't think so," he says. You would take action. You would call the auto club. Time and faith will not heal grief any better than they will put air in the tire. But we can use both in the process of healing."

*(continued on page 296)*

# A Visit with a Grief Group

*Note: Kenneth Winston Caine, co-author of this book, had to deal with staggering grief in his own life when his brother committed suicide. Here is Caine's account of grief groups, including one that helped him.*

My brother shot himself in the head with a $900 revolver in an Arizona jojoba field on a full-moon Fourth of July night. A week-and-a-half later, I, my wife, and my brother's lover were still in shock and decided to attend a grief group, hoping that it would provide some answers and make some of the emptiness go away.

So we sat in a circle on folding chairs with our eyes closed, listening to soothing music while the leader led a quiet, prayerful meditation and deep-breathing exercise to help us focus and relax. Then she explained the ground rules. We weren't to interrupt a speaker. We weren't to criticize a speaker. We weren't to give advice. We were to talk about our experiences. Talk about how we felt and what troubled us. We were to give only first names. Everything said was to remain confidential and was not to be shared with anyone outside the group. There were a few more rules along the same line.

The leader, a trained volunteer, asked us to each take about five minutes and introduce ourselves to the rest of the circle and explain why we were there and what was most troubling us or what we were feeling that evening. Nobody was required to talk. As it turned out, all of us did. The leader offered to go first to break the ice.

As we worked around the circle, we heard many of the same things: "Every day, somewhere, I think I catch a fleeting glimpse of him—in the grocery store, at the flea market, in line at the movie theater, in the lunch crowd downtown. And for a moment, I freeze and choke up and start to sob." Another said, "I didn't get to tell her how much I really loved her." Another said, "I hadn't said it in days (or weeks, or months, or years). I never told him I forgave him for the time he (did this or that)." Another said, "I forget to eat. Food, even my favorite dish, has no flavor. Nothing seems to matter."

We breathed sighs of relief because, yes, we'd been experiencing some of the exact same things.

Then the leader asked us to go around the circle again and tell, if we could, something that we'd learned in the past week or so about ourselves, or life, or how to cope.

As we heard others talk, there were "Eureka moments," a term coined by lecturer and ordained Episcopalian priest Harold Ivan Smith, doctor of ministry, who leads grief gatherings at St. Luke's Medical Center in Kansas City, Missouri, and is the author of many Christian self-help books. We realized that we really were not suffering alone. We were fascinated with each person's experiences and emotions. We really felt them, and also felt a sense of protectedness and community within the room. Sitting in that meeting, we felt comfortable in our grief for perhaps the first time since the tragedy struck.

## Letting It Out

Dr. Smith holds similar grief gatherings that meet weekly for six weeks. During his sessions, group members color pictures of their grief and share and explain them. He asks members to develop collages by cutting out pictures from magazines. He encourages them to bring items to add to their collages each week. He practices a process that he calls storytelling. The exercises are designed to help all of the group members find and tell their stories.

These are storytelling groups, Dr. Smith says. They are therapeutic, but they're not therapy. People sit in a circle and tell their stories. And the counselors promise that they will listen to them. That's the only promise that is made.

Some people repeat their stories week after week, says Dr. Smith. That's all right. Each time they tell their stories, they move a little closer to being able to understand them, he says. Simply finding the words for their losses and then saying the words out loud and knowing that they've been heard makes an incredible change in people's lives.

How? We can have faith that we will be comforted if we seek the comfort that we need, James says. We can take the time that we need to grieve and work through our grief effectively. But neither time nor faith alone will do the trick.

"Blessed are they that mourn: for they shall be comforted," says Jesus. (Matthew 5:4 KJV) It is okay to seek comfort. It is okay to be comforted. Jesus says so. Here are two ways to get the help that we need at a time of grief.

**Speak up.** We need to tell people what we need and want. Most don't know and are wary of saying or doing the wrong thing. We can tell them if we'd like them to go ahead and talk around us about our loss or the deceased person. If we need time alone or help with tasks, we should express that too.

**Find a support group.** While not for everyone, many people find support groups helpful. Quickly, we learn that we are not alone and that our feelings are natural. We also learn coping skills from others. In most large communities, some churches sponsor support groups, says James.

# The Regimen of Sorrow

Grieving, quite simply, is consuming and exhausting work, notes Dr. Miller. Not only do we tire ourselves out but we may also neglect essentials for our health and well-being, like nutrition, sleep, exercise, bill-paying, and medical care, to name a few. We do need to watch out for ourselves a bit. The following can go on our to-do lists.

**Take it easy.** Grieving is depleting. So it helps to give ourselves permission to rest and replenish our energy by taking naps, relaxing, and re-energizing.

**Plan and complete one thing each day.** Even if our grief is excruciating and our energy nil, we should plan to do something and then do it every day, says Dr. Miller. We don't need to convince ourselves to stay busy all day long; we just need to accomplish one little significant something to prove to ourselves that we are not totally at the mercy of seemingly all-engulfing grief, that we are capable of doing at least some things.

**Care for ourselves.** Eat regularly. Eat healthfully. Get proper sleep. Missing sleep and eating poorly, excessively, or not at all af-

# Faithbuilders

## Comforting Verses

At a time of profound loss, so much seems uncertain to us. But God's presence is unchanging, says the Reverend Mel Lawrenz, Ph.D., senior associate pastor at Elmbrook Church and director of the Elmbrook Christian Study Center, both in Brookfield, Wisconsin, and co-author of six books, including *Life after Grief* and *Overcoming Grief and Trauma*. Reading the Bible, in particular, these verses, can help us grasp that.

> Though He brings grief, He will show compassion, so great is His unfailing love.
> For He does not willingly bring affliction or grief to the children of men.
>
> —*Lamentations 3:32-33 NIV*

> Blessed are those who mourn, for they will be comforted.
>
> —*Matthew 5:4 NIV*

> Because I have said these things, you are filled with grief.
> I tell you the truth, you will weep and mourn while the world rejoices. You will grieve, but your grief will turn to joy.
>
> —*John 16:6, 20 NIV*

> Your sun will never set again, and your moon will wane no more; the Lord will be your everlasting light, and your days of sorrow will end.
>
> —*Isaiah 60:20 NIV*

fect how we think and feel both physically and emotionally, says Dr. Miller.

**Expect ups and downs.** We don't suddenly get over it. We may feel much better one day and then much worse the next, or even later the same day. Recovery from grief is the result of sustained effort over time, says James.

**Avoid major decisions.** Postpone them if at all possible. We are vulnerable when in the midst of mourning, warns Dr. Lawrenz.

**Remember to breathe.** "Most grievers do not breathe well," says Dr. Smith. "Practicing several minutes of deep, gentle belly breathing actually helps us release emotions and get in touch with ourselves and God."

**Try to laugh.** Yes, it is good to laugh later in the process of grieving. It's healthy. It's healing. It's needed, says Dr. Smith. We can rent funny videos, read funny books and comics, or watch favorite comedians. No one is suggesting that a griever should become Mr. or Mrs. Mirthful Happyface, but we do sense greater hope and wider perspective when we're able to squeeze in at least one good belly laugh every day. If we have to start with just one a week, it still helps.

# Let It Be

How long does grief last? "As long as it takes," says Dr. Miller.

Other experts agree. It varies from person to person and with the nature of the relationship, from a few weeks to five or more years in some cases. Experts warn, though, that if we find ourselves not just sad but careening out of control into destructive behaviors, we should see a qualified counselor.

Dr. Lawrenz explains: "In a normal grieving experience, a person is very sad about the loss. But there is such a thing as complicated grief, where a person moves into depression and despair. You recognize it if there is long-term isolation from other people or a general downward decline of the person's ability to function in life. What that basically means is that mourning is turning into significant depression. When that occurs, they should seek out medical or counseling help."

For more help, advice, and perspective, see Death of a Loved One (page 200), Heartache (page 311), and Loss (page 365).

# *Happiness*

## JOY GROWS FROM THE INSIDE OUT

*W*e hold these truths to be self-evident, that all men are created equal, that they are endowed by their Creator with certain unalienable rights, that among these are life, liberty, and the pursuit of happiness."

Ever since these immortal words were first published in the Declaration of Independence, the pursuit of happiness has been something of an all-American national obsession. Funny thing is, our pursuits always seem to take us in radically different directions. Some of us look for it in the mall, some of us look in the woods, some look on the job, and some look in the grocery store. Some of us even look in church.

How many of us are actually succeeding in the happiness quest depends on who you talk to. A 1998 poll in *USA Today* painted a rosy picture. Two-thirds of Americans say that they're very happy, the poll found. On a happiness scale of 1 to 10, one-fifth gave themselves a perfect 10. The average rating was 7.8.

Are we really that happy? Earlier studies—not to mention the national rates of alcoholism, drug addiction, divorce, and crime—have suggested that we're not. And even if *USA Today*'s overall percentages are reasonably accurate, they overlook the fact that during any one-year period, 17.6 million American adults experience some form of depression, says Christian psychiatrist and theologian Paul Meier, M.D., co-founder of New-Life Clinics, the largest provider of Christian-based counseling in the United States, and author of more than 60 best-selling Christian self-help books, including *Happiness Is a Choice*.

Happiness, then, eludes virtually all of us at one time or another. Which is not to say that we have to be satisfied with an ongoing state of struggle and sorrow.

## Connecting with God

God wants us to be happy, and the people who know God are happy because of it.

That's the conclusion of Father John Powell, a Jesuit priest at Loyola University in Chicago and author of several bestsellers, including *Happiness Is an Inside Job*. Father Powell believes that the serenity of those who are deeply in touch with God can be seen on their faces. "I think that's what God does. He achieves in us true happiness."

Happiness stems from a genuine relationship with God, Father Powell says. Like any relationship, our connection to God can grow and flourish or it can weaken and die, depending on how actively we cultivate it. Here are some suggestions for ways to keep that holy connection alive and well.

**Follow the plan.** Being happy is largely a question of eliminating the things that make us unhappy, according to Dr. Meier. That means, above all, avoiding sin. "Sin creates unhappiness in ourselves and in others," he says.

The best way to avoid sin is to follow the fundamentals: Love God, love ourselves, love our neighbors. Pray, worship, serve. That's the standard recipe for contentment, and still the best.

**Read Scripture.** Another basic ingredient in building our connection to God is reading the Bible. If we're struggling, the Reverend Alison Boden, master of divinity, dean of Rockefeller Chapel at the University of Chicago, suggests that we meditate on Psalm 63. "O God," it reads, "You are my God, I seek You, my soul thirsts for You . . . Because Your steadfast love is better than life." (Psalm 63:1, 3 NRSV) Leaning on that steadfastness can help us get past our struggles until we're happy again, she says.

**Study the beatitudes.** Think of each beatitude (Matthew 5:3–11) as a verb, not a noun, and consider how we can enact blessedness in our own lives, suggests the Reverend Harry Adams, professor of pastoral theology at Yale Divinity School. What can we do, for instance, as peacemakers in our own families or among feuding friends? How about organizing a demonstration against illegal sweatshops as a way of demonstrating our hunger for righteousness? Or tearing up a friend's IOU to show our mercifulness?

**Love the loveless.** Think of the curmudgeon in church or the grouchy neighbor down the block. Drop them a note asking how they're doing. Give them a phone call. Share a joke or a story with them. Be patient, and see if their ice-encrusted visage begins to melt just a little. As Doris Donnelly, professor of spirituality at John Carroll University in Ohio, says, "Maybe we need to redress the balance of somberness by gladdening others with support, kind words, encouragement, laughter, hope, time, and the simple gift of self. It wouldn't hurt. It could heal."

**Nurture joy.** God has instilled in all of us certain ways that we can easily find refuge and access our innate capacity for joy. We should find what those places or practices are and use them. "When I'm feeling bad, I'll often go out to my garden to work and meditate," says the Reverend Burrell Dinkins, Ph.D., professor of pastoral care and counseling at Asbury Theological Seminary in Wilmore, Kentucky. "It's my sacred space, the place I feel closest to God. For someone else, it might be a walk in the woods or an entry in their journal."

# A Happiness Tool Kit

Abraham Lincoln once said that most people are about as happy as they make up their minds to be, says Dr. Meier, and modern psychology basically agrees with him. Up to a point.

Attitude counts for a lot, but it's not everything, says Dr. Meier. We now know that genetics plays a role, for example, and that physical and mental illnesses can keep us from being happy no matter how hard we work at it. That doesn't mean that we can't make up our minds to be happy; it just means that there may be a few extra steps involved in getting there.

Attitude needs to be coupled with knowledge, Dr. Meier says. If we're going to successfully complete the happiness hunt, we need to know where to look, and we need some tools. Here are a few key things that we need to do on the journey.

**Get a check up.** If we're experiencing chronic depression for no observable reason, Dr. Meier says, it's important to see a doctor or

## Be a Balloon

What's the difference between happiness and joy? According to Father John Powell, a Jesuit priest at Loyola University in Chicago and author of several bestsellers, including *Happiness Is an Inside Job*, joy is a state of ebullience, lightness, and grace that is beyond day-to-day happiness. Joy is a state in which we are fully and totally filled with the Holy Spirit, regardless of the particular circumstances in which we may find ourselves at a given moment.

Practically, of course, we may not have the capacity to withstand all of life's blows with a blissful grin like the ones that martyred saints show in medieval paintings. Nevertheless, if we can remind ourselves of Jesus' promise of eternal life and believe in it, then joyfulness is the logical response, says Father Powell.

Happiness is the foundation from which joy can ultimately grow, says Father Powell. It needs to be thought about and worked at consciously. There are two major routes toward that goal. One is working to increase our relationship with God, to reach out toward the hand that He extends. The other is to work at eliminating the tethers that bind us to the source of our unhappiness. These tethers are our sins, in the form of psychological or emotional problems that distort our perceptions and interfere with our ability to love one another.

The more we cut away those tethers, the higher we can allow ourselves to ascend, Father Powell says. Unbound, we float naturally toward joy. Toward God.

psychiatrist who is trained to detect any physical problems that might be responsible.

**Keep fit.** Reams of scientific research have affirmed what most of us know intuitively: Mind, body, and spirit are interconnected. If we keep ourselves together physically by eating right, exercising regularly, and getting plenty of sleep, says Father Powell, we'll also feel better spiritually and emotionally.

**Stifle stress.** One of the major blocks to happiness in today's world is stress, according to Dr. Meier. Jesus says, "For my yoke is easy, and my burden is light," he points out. (Matthew 11:30 KJV) There's no reason to believe that He didn't mean it.

If we're burned out, we need to change, Dr. Meier says. We must make room in our busy schedules for rest and relaxation, time with the family, prayer, and meditation. If we're going to hear the voice of God—the voice of joy—we have to find the time to stop and listen.

**Be a "goodfinder."** Our attitudes are far more within our control than we often acknowledge. We can choose to wallow in negative thoughts, or we can make a conscious decision to focus on the positive. Father Powell calls those who have a talent for constructive thinking "goodfinders," and he says that it may be one of the most important single attributes of a happy person.

How can we change our attitudes from negative to positive? Father Powell recommends an exercise that can help move us in the right direction: Write several paragraphs describing our three best qualities, he says, and several paragraphs describing the three best qualities of someone we don't like. This focuses our intention on what's good.

**Learn from pain.** It's a maxim of the spiritual life that we often gain our deepest insights as we're going through our most painful moments, Father Powell says. We will be happier in the long run if we can learn to use life's inevitable difficulties as opportunities for growth. As practice, Father Powell suggests that we describe to a friend some disappointment that we've experienced recently, trying in the process to see what we've learned from the experience and how we've benefited from that learning.

**Feel the feelings.** Although teaching ourselves not to dwell on the negatives is vital, we should be careful that we don't keep our-

# Healing Words

## Prayers for Renewal and Joy

. . . is your life full of difficulties and temptations? Then be happy,
For when the way is rough, your patience has a chance to grow.
So let it grow, and don't try to squirm out of your problems. For when your patience is finally in full bloom, then you will be ready for anything, strong in character, full and complete.

—*James 1:2–4 TLB*

Very truly, I tell you, you will weep and mourn, but the world will rejoice; you will have pain, but your pain will turn into joy.
When a woman is in labor, she has pain, because her hour has come. But when her child is born, she no longer remembers the anguish because of the joy of having brought a human being into the world.
So you have pain now; but I will see you again, and your hearts will rejoice, and no one will take your joy from you.

—*John 16:20–22 NRSV*

So be truly glad! There is wonderful joy ahead, even though the going is rough for a while down here.
These trials are only to test your faith, to see whether or not it is strong and pure.

—*1 Peter 1:6–7 TLB*

selves from feeling legitimate pain, says Dr. Meier. Experiencing our emotions honestly is not self-indulgent. To the contrary, covering up grief, anger, or depression can create other, more long-lasting emotional problems, he says. The healthier way to happiness is to allow ourselves to experience painful emotions honestly, then return to our focus on the positive.

**Share what hurts.** Where do we take our grief, anger, and other negative feelings when we need to get them out? That's what friends are for. Dr. Meier recommends that we find a prayer partner of the same sex, someone with whom we can be totally honest. A small prayer group that meets on a regular basis can supplement that two-person partnership. "We all need to have one or more humans that we can let inside our skin," he says, citing the letter from James in the new Testament: ". . . confess your sins to one another, so that you may be healed." (James 5:16 NRSV)

If we feel that our problems warrant professional help, we need to seek out a qualified counselor. To find a Christian counselor, write the counseling department of Focus on the Family, 8605 Explorer Drive, Colorado Springs, Colorado 80995.

**Forgive.** Dr. Meier calls learning to forgive "the single most important thing we do" in learning to be happy. Nurtured resentments against others and against God can create a poisonous spirit that is the very antithesis of happiness. Peace of mind and spirit requires that we let things go, that we learn to forgive and forget.

How do we learn to forgive? By working at it relentlessly, Dr. Meier says. "Forgiving is an act of will," he says. "You have to re-forgive and re-forgive. It's not a one-time thing. Say to yourself, 'I choose to forgive.' And ask God for help in forgiving. We need to constantly remind ourselves that vengeance is not ours, but the Lord's."

**Avoid judgment.** Forgiveness is fine, but beware judgment, adds Father Powell. We need to keep in mind that people almost always have reasons for what they do, reasons even they may not understand. Ideally, we should let resentments go by loving people despite their behaviors. That's what Jesus would have us do.

For related information, see Anxiety (page 168), Depression (page 215), Fear (page 270), and Forgiveness (page 284).

# *Healing*

## THE REMEDY BEGINS IN THE MIND

*W*hen we're feeling sick or dealing with a chronic illness, how we think can greatly affect our attitudes and energy levels.

No, conjuring up a beautiful thought and holding on to it may not force remission of every disease or affliction. But certain attitudes and simple behaviors do seem to promote a healthy outlook. And a healthy outlook is a nice thing to have, particularly when we must face an unhealthy diagnosis or prognosis. A healthy outlook is spiritually rewarding.

And there is no reason why we should feel guilty or inferior or blame ourselves for being "infirm," as the Bible puts it, if we are unable to heal ourselves.

Statistically, studies suggest that those of us who constructively tend to the spiritual components of our nature tend to live longer, lead healthier lives, and cope better with disease and other setbacks, says psychiatrist and prayer researcher Dale A. Matthews, M.D., associate professor of medicine at Georgetown University School of Medicine in Washington, D.C., and author of *The Faith Factor.*

When faced with disease or disability, we have a choice that we can make, notes Christian psychiatrist and theologian Paul Meier,

M.D., co-founder of New Life Clinics, the largest provider of Christian-based counseling clinics in the United States, and author of more than 60 best-selling Christian self-help books. We can choose to become discouraged and invite defeat and depression. Or, as God tells us in the Bible, we can choose life. ". . . I have set before you life and death, blessings and curses. Choose life. . . ." (Deuteronomy 30:19 NRSV)

## Bringing Healing into Focus

Choosing life is a matter of choosing a healing state of mind, say counselors. How do we do that?

**Focus on the wonderful.** Look at all of the mighty, beautiful things that God does. This is worship, says the Reverend Eugene Harder of the New Hope Community Church in North Vancouver, British Columbia. Worship keeps us from falling into the pit of self-pity that is always beckoning when sickness has its black grip on us. How can we tell when we have crossed the line from normal, healthy grieving to unhealthy self-pity? Pastor Harder explains that we will find the answer if we ask ourselves this question: In spite of all of our suffering, are we still able to worship God as we see His power and beauty, or are we able to only see the swift kick that life delivered us?

**Focus on purpose.** "God has a role for each one of us to fulfill in life," says Pastor Harder. The healing mind, he continues, finds joy in exploring and positively pursuing all of the unique tasks, talents, and challenges that God lays before it. The healing mind is able to perceive how to grow through, beyond, and from hurts and suffering.

**Focus on sharing peace and joy.** The healing mind "promotes happiness in others," says Pastor Harder. The healing mind "hums when there is harmony."

**Focus on positive action.** The healing mind makes things happen. It "doesn't spend all of its time contemplating its navel. It says, 'The time has come for this dream, this vision that the Lord gave me to become a reality. I must initiate steps of action. I must begin to move," says Pastor Harder.

**Focus on forgiving.** The healing mind knows that it can't harbor resentment or bury hurt, but must give it away to God, says Vernon M. Sylvest, M.D., a physician with a prayer-based holistic medical practice in Richmond, Virginia, and author of *The Formula: Who Gets Sick, Who Gets Well*. He has witnessed remarkable medical turn-arounds at times when patients have uncovered hidden hurts and re-leased them—forgiven them.

# Answered Prayers

### Faith Helped My Premature Baby

"In 1985, I experienced a troublesome pregnancy. I found myself in the hospital at 28 weeks with leaking amniotic fluid. After five days at this stage, I woke up with a blood infection, and the periodic labor pains were more constant.

"I wanted this child removed from my body before I passed the infection on, but all the medical professionals were worried about the premature birth. I was told to prepare for my child's death.

"I saw no bright shining light, heard no thunderous voice speaking to me, saw no apparitions in my hospital room. Instead, I had the strongest feeling of assurance that my baby would do well, be born healthy, and have no complications. I truly believed that God was with me and that He held my unborn child safely in His hands.

"Benjamin Tyler Booker was born into this world pink and crying. He was tiny, but he needed no oxygen and no special care except a feeding tube until he was strong enough to suck. He amazed everyone in the hospital. God has been with me since that day, and I know that He is walking by Ben's side daily.

"This is not a flashy story, but deep-seated convictions are strong like steel, not flashy like tinsel."

—*Ginger L. Booker, Fort Wayne, Indiana*

**Focus on acceptance.** The world is not perfect, and we are not perfect in it. But God's love for us is unconditional, and so should our love for ourselves and for each other be, recommends Dr. Sylvest.

Perfectionists—those of us who cannot accept our errors, misjudgments, and shortfalls and the somewhat messy nature of our lives—are far too stressed-out, says Dr. Sylvest. And stress clearly has been shown to muck with our internal chemistries and interfere with wellness and healing.

Those of us who tend to be the healthiest, in Dr. Sylvest's observation, are those who accept that sometimes we win, sometimes we lose, and, at least until our tickets are finally punched, we always have tomorrow to tackle (or forget) those things that we haven't gotten quite right yet.

**Focus on others.** Numerous medical and sociological studies show that regular, positive social interaction—the greater number of different types of contacts, the better—tends to enhance our overall well-being and limit depressive episodes in our lives, says Dean Ornish, M.D., president and director of the Preventive Medicine Research Institute in Sausalito, California, clinical professor of medicine at the University of California at San Francisco, and founder of a mind-body-spirit-oriented program for treating heart attack patients that is used in hospitals world-wide.

Those of us who have the most diverse types of social contacts and networks are least susceptible to developing colds when exposed to cold viruses, according to Sheldon Cohen, Ph.D., professor of psychology at Carnegie Mellon University in Pittsburgh. What is important is the range of social contacts, not just the quantity. The wider the range, the healthier, he says. It may simply be that those of us with a wide range of contacts are more distracted from our problems. "Someone whose only social role is as 'worker' will find problems at home more distressing than someone who works, has a family, and belongs to social groups," he says.

Contact with others may contribute to our sense of meaning and sense of purpose, which are fundamental to our spiritual makeup, says Dr. Ornish, who is also a best-selling author of five books, including *Love and Survival: The Scientific Basis for the Healing Power of Intimacy.*

Dr. Cohen agrees. He says that people who have diverse social outlets generally feel better about themselves, have more positive approaches, feel more in control of their lives, and have a higher sense of self-esteem, and that those factors somehow translate into better health.

**Focus on fellowship.** Studies have shown that people who attend church regularly tend to get sick less often, heal quicker, and live longer, on average, than people who fail to fill the pews most Sabbaths, says Dr. Matthews.

# *Heartache*

———✦———

## TRAVELING THE ROAD
## TO RECOVERY

*L*ove is a towering building, often furnished one floor at a time.
But rarely is love as sturdy as it appears.

Abuse the intimacy or violate the trust, and the tower may im-
plode as if dynamited. And heartache—searing heartache—rises in
the clouds of dust and permeates the shifting rubble. Heartache, or
heartbreak, is the ugly underbelly of love. We all experience it now
and then. And when we do, we feel as though the world has ended.

We may feel outraged, angry, violated, cheated, hurt, humiliated,
hopeless, betrayed, empty, afraid, vengeful, drained, desperate, and
more. And we wonder if we can ever trust love again.

But the truth is, we must, says the Reverend Mel Lawrenz, Ph.D.,
senior associate pastor at Elmbrook Church and director of the Elmbrook Christian Study Center, both in Brookfield, Wisconsin, and co-
author of six books, including *Life after Grief* and *Overcoming Grief
and Trauma*. We must love again.

The Bible tells us that we retain our ability to love and our need
to love even when someone we love breaks our hearts, says Dr.
Lawrenz. We are supposed to love again.

# Healing Words

## Living through the Season of Pain

We are weeping now. We will not weep forever. Someday soon, we will enjoy laughter and find joy in life again, says author, lecturer, and ordained Episcopalian priest Harold Ivan Smith, doctor of ministry, who leads grief gatherings at St. Luke's Medical Center in Kansas City, Missouri. Remember, he says, what the Bible advises.

> To every thing there is a season, and a time to every purpose under the Heaven . . .
> A time to weep, and a time to laugh; a time to mourn, and a time to dance.

> —*Ecclesiastes 3:1, 4 KJV*

# The Kinds of Heartache

Heartache comes in many forms. We can be heartbroken over the actions or words of our children, our spouses, our close friends, our parents, even the company we work for. Anybody or anything in which we have deep heartfelt emotional involvement and investment can be the impetus for heartache.

Let's deal primarily with heartache as it occurs in romantic love.

In romantic love, we are vulnerable. We open our hearts and bare our souls. We trust and expect the one we love to reciprocate; to respect and honor the trust, the intimacy, the welcome dependency, and the deep level of private sharing that develops and builds between us. In love, we lose some of our separateness. We become not solely "you" and "I," but also "us."

How we value that. How comforting that is. And oh, how it hurts when it breaks down. Any way we slice it, experts say, when our hearts split in two, we will grieve. We will despair. We will need to call upon our sources of spiritual strength to pull us through.

# Healing the Hurt

The scenario at its simplest: Someone tells us they love us. We love them. We accept and give love fully. Then somehow, for some reason, we suddenly find that they do not love us anymore. We reel in pain. Now what?

The way out is the way to work through the pain, says the Reverend Paul F. Everett of Pittsburgh, a Presbyterian minister at large with the Peale Center in Pawling, New York, and executive director emeritus of the Pittsburgh Experiment, a national and international ministry to the business and working communities. We can't run from heartache, and we mustn't bury it, he says. Instead, we eventually must face it head-on, issue by issue, and work our way through all the pain and confusion.

It helps if we have relationships with God, says Reverend Everett. If not, we should develop them because the first place to take a broken heart is to God. We can always turn to God for strength, comfort, and support.

The change may not take place in an instant, but God tells us, ". . . I will turn their mourning into joy, and will comfort them, and make them rejoice from their sorrow." (Jeremiah 31:13 KJV)

Beyond God, we can look to others and within ourselves for support.

**Seek unconditional love.** We can join a Bible study or support group where people will unconditionally love us, pray with us, and support us as we heal, and we can use and count on that love and support, suggests Christian psychiatrist and theologian Paul Meier, M.D., co-founder of New Life Clinics, the largest provider of Christian-based counseling clinics in the United States, and author of more than 60 best-selling Christian self-help books.

**Identify the feelings and issues.** So much seems to be crashing down and pressing in on us. We need to figure out exactly what we are feeling and thinking, says Reverend Everett. What thoughts keep popping up and why? "Possibly, there might be a lot of anger," he says, "or there may be a tremendous sense of loss. We need to get in touch with these feelings and thoughts and work them out." Seeking people whom we can trust or qualified counselors is important to both identifying the problems and working through them.

"We experienced this situation with our friends last year," Reverend Everett says. "Their son's wedding was canceled three weeks before it was to take place. We all felt it. We loved him—the groom-to-be. We loved the family. So it was a death to us. We went through the grief process."

The first thing that he and his family did was talk to one another, says Reverend Everett. They talked about how and what they were feeling. And that's the first thing we should do, too: Find someone we can talk to, and talk to again, so that we can sort out our emotions. Then we can identify the practical matters and get on with them, as in his case. "They had to contact the wedding coordinators and undo the whole wedding. They had to send back all the presents. They had to get in touch with people and explain to them what was happening."

**Tend to the nitty-gritty.** Certain practical everyday matters must be taken care of. Bills must be paid so that the lights and phone don't get turned off. Beyond that, notes Reverend Everett, in some kinds of breakup, there are division of property matters to be settled, plans to be canceled, and so on. It helps to write these down as they come to mind each day and transfer them to to-do lists.

"You're in such terrible pain that it's very difficult to be practical. A lot of people just can't function," says Reverend Everett. If that's the case, we can ask friends to help us stay on track with the basics, to help us make lists, open mail, and write checks and mail them.

**Recall earlier strengths.** If we think back, before we met this person, we did somehow manage to get along, and sometimes we did so rather well, thank you.

The idea of counting our blessings sounds so glib, says Dr. Lawrenz, but "it is genuinely true that our lives have a broader context and that, over the years, the blessings have been the larger reality. Yes, we've lost someone whom we love, or we've lost jobs, or our kids are spinning out of control and have been arrested for drug possession, and we are just heartbroken. Of course we are. As heartbreaking as these things are, there is a larger context to our lives." Life is not all disappointment and sadness, no matter how bleak it may seem right now.

**Face reality.** The person is gone. Their love is withdrawn. "We need to come to terms with the way things really are," says Dr.

# Prayer Pointers

## Spew It Out

A wonderful and surprisingly effective way to get in touch with the feelings that underlie our heartache is to spew them out, says author, lecturer, and ordained Episcopalian priest Harold Ivan Smith, doctor of ministry, who leads grief gatherings at St. Luke's Medical Center in Kansas City, Missouri, and is the author of many Christian self-help books. All it takes is a couple of minutes, a notepad, and a commitment to do it first thing upon awakening every morning.

"The very first thing that you do when you get up, before anything else, is go to your notepad and write three pages. Write as fast as you can. Don't worry about punctuation and spelling. Don't think about what you're writing. Just write down the thoughts that are going through your mind about your loss," he says.

"In these early waking moments, when you're not quite awake and not quite asleep, all kinds of thoughts try to get your attention," says Dr. Smith. Many of them are threatening and try to doom our whole day. "Once they're in black and white, they're not nearly as threatening." And they give us a peek at the inner workings of our subconscious, which can help us begin to understand and heal.

We can destroy the pages each day or keep them to see which thoughts recur and which ideas we are struggling with, says Dr. Smith. It's amazing what can pour forth. "I had a lady come in after doing the exercise. She had 128 pages." Most of us won't come up with nearly that many pages.

"Another woman said, 'I never knew that I was angry until I did this exercise.' People told her that she was angry and she had denied it. But, she said, 'When I went back and read what I had written, I realized that I'm incredibly angry.' It was healthy that she had come to a point where she could admit the anger."

Lawrenz, and admit that some things are beyond our control. "Our heartbreak will be more severe if we don't, if we keep asking in bewilderment, 'Why can't I change this? Why can't I make this person love me?' There are all kinds of instances of people chasing after other people, figuring, 'If I just do this, I will cause them to love me.' Well, we can't. The spiritual principle is that we are part of a bigger picture. There are things in this life that we cannot control."

**Pray and forgive.** We can pray for the people who are no longer in our lives. The prayer is not for reconciliation but for their successful recovery and future. Sure, the temptation may be to trash them, tell their secrets, and expose their weaknesses. But that's not the advice that we find in the Bible. Consider these verses, says Reverend Everett: "Stop being mean, bad-tempered and angry. Quarreling, harsh words, and dislike of others should have no place in your lives. Instead, be kind to each other, tenderhearted, forgiving one another, just as God has forgiven you. . . ." (Ephesians 4:31–32 TLB)

Jesus paints a worst-case scenario in his command, "Love your enemies, do good to those who hate you, bless those who curse you, pray for those who abuse you." (Luke 6:27–28 RSV) Surely, we can eventually do that for someone we've loved.

**Love ourselves.** We must quit beating ourselves up. We must quit blaming ourselves. We need to commit to love ourselves and forgive ourselves, says Dr. Meier. "Practice seeing ourselves as God sees us, forgiving ourselves as God forgives us, loving ourselves as God loves us."

## Love Remains

Sure, we hurt. Sure, we are angry and doubtful and mistrustful. All that means is that we're normal, says Dr. Lawrenz. It means that we're going through normal changes. It means that we're alive and experiencing life.

The Bible "talks about all the things that change in life, and then it says, 'So faith, hope, love abide, these three; but the greatest of these is love.'" (1 Corinthians 13:13 RSV) says Dr. Lawrenz. The Bible is telling us that "even if we lose someone we love, someone we thought we loved, it is not the same as losing the ability to love and the ability to be loved. And, most important, we haven't lost God's love," he says. That is spiritual truth. Hold on to that as a spiritual foundation, and the momentary circumstances in life cannot rob you of faith, hope, and love.

At the moment, it may feel as though we'll never get over this hurt. But we will, with time. Yes, says Dr. Lawrenz, we will love again. "We will be able to love other people again in the future. We will love again if we are to live a genuinely human life. Love is an essential part of life. Love remains."

As we heal, there comes a time when we will want to pray for love, says Reverend Everett, and ask God to change the problem beginning with us first. Attitudes, relationships, and difficulties can be changed, healed, and resolved in some way.

For more help with others types of heartache, see Death of a Loved One (page 200), Defeat (page 211), Emotional Pain (page 259), Grief (page 290), and Loss (page 365).

# Honesty

## FABRICATE IT

*H*onesty is something that we all say we want. But the truth is, it's in short supply. It's hard to find in day-to-day life, in our culture, even in our churches. That's sad, and damaging, says Brad Blanton, Ph.D., a psychologist and former Methodist minister in Stanley, Virginia, and author of *Radical Honesty*.

Without honesty, we live in a world of pretense, unreality, and deception. Neither we nor anyone else is ever truly encouraged to deal forthrightly with our real needs, hurts, and feelings or the actual purposes and consequences of our actions. Everything is a spin on the truth, and we're left spinning and anchorless, says Dr. Blanton.

Being honest in all aspects of our lives does go against the grain. It violates the Gestalt of glitz—the "law" that says "image is everything." But image—pretense and hiding and glossing over our hurts, shortcomings, and differences—does not free us from these hurts, shortcomings, and differences. Freedom only comes from facing them, viewing them, and dealing with them directly under the bright spotlight of reality, says Dr. Blanton. Jesus says, ". . . the truth shall make you free." (John 8:32 KJV) With these words, Jesus offers the simplest success formula ever.

Life is oh-so-much easier, healthier, cleaner, more joyful, and more real when we tell the truth, says Dr. Blanton.

The method is almost magical. The Apostle Paul explains it like this: ". . . lovingly follow the truth at all times—speaking truly, dealing truly, living truly. . . ." (Ephesians 4:16 TLB)

Just how does this make life simpler and easier? Mark Twain explains it well. "Always tell the truth," he writes in *Vice and Virtue*. "That way, you don't have to remember what you said."

## So Simple, Yet So Hard

We aren't taught to tell the truth. "To be perfectly honest," as the phrase goes, we are taught to *say* that we're telling the truth, observes Pastor Dale Ryan, Ph.D., CEO and founder of Christian Recovery International, a ministry based in Brea, California. But, honestly, the truth is not expected or encouraged in many interactions. From the television advertisements we view to our personal appearances and actions, we expect to mislead and be misled; we expect that reality is colored; and we expect that nothing is really exactly the way it seems, says Dr. Ryan.

That is injurious to our health and well-being, says Dr. Blanton. Twenty-five years of practice as a psychotherapist has convinced him that "the primary cause of most anxiety, most depression, and most human stress is lying, and we lie all the time. We're taught systematically by the school systems, by parents, by the church, and everyone else to lie, to play like we are good little boys and girls regardless of how big a lie that is. We are taught to keep secret what is really going on in our lives and taught instead to play the right role."

## Confess and Testify

How can we move out of our role-playing and into reality?

Old-time religion had the right idea, and the 12-Step Recovery programs, like Alcoholics Anonymous, borrowed it, says Dr. Ryan. What they incorporated, and what modern Christian churches tend to shy away from, are what he calls the traditional Christian spiritual disciplines of confession and testimony.

Traditionally, notes Dr. Ryan, the church would rally around anyone who confessed shortcomings and who testified about their feelings, questions, and experiences with God as they wrestled with everyday problems. Now, he says, the church tends only to encourage "salvation" confessions and "good" testimonies—tales of total turnaround as a result of knowing Christ.

The church, Dr. Ryan says, doesn't encourage people to confess and testify week after week about their sadness, rage, disappointment, setbacks, and ongoing crises of faith. But those kinds of confessions and testimonies "actually help people get some traction in life so that they can grow and move past their problems," he says. And that's how people are helped in 12-step groups where participants go around a circle and tell—without interruption or comment from others—what's going on in their lives at the moment.

We need to encourage our churches to recover that old-style testimony, says Dr. Ryan. "If the only 'words' that someone has are tears, then tears are a wonderful testimony." We need to allow people to be honest and express their true feelings.

When true confession is encouraged, we learn not only that it is safe to tell the truth but also that we are supported by the community for doing it, says Dr. Ryan. It allows us to say, "I'm just a fallible human. I belong here because we all recognize our fallibility and all recognize our essential equality. We're all working on the same stuff." Encouraging (and learning to give) "bad," or honest, confessions and testimonies is essential to developing an honest, healing community, he says.

For testimony to be helpful and healing, it must be encouraged and given at each stage of processing any difficult situation that we encounter in life, says Dr. Ryan. The truth—the tears, anger, rage, and confusion—all need to be worked through and processed. Each of us can help by practicing, encouraging, and welcoming honest confession and testimony.

How?

**Just start.** Tell the truth. We don't have to tell the truth about much, just "what we've done, what we think, and what we feel," says Dr. Blanton.

**Make a pact with a friend.** We should agree with this person that we will only tell the complete truth and that it's okay and even expected for us to admit what we haven't previously told the truth about. Once we get a little practice at this and notice how good it feels and how great the relationship becomes, we'll want to expand the practice to other relationships, says Dr. Blanton.

## Healing Words

### The Truth Sets You Free

But whoever lives by the truth comes into the light, so that it may be seen plainly that what he has done has been done through God.

*—John 3:21 NIV*

. . . do not swear, either by Heaven or by Earth or by any other oath, but let your "Yes" be yes and your "No" be no, so that you may not fall under condemnation.

*—James 5:12 NRSV*

**Seek support.** We need help as we embrace honesty, even if it's from a community of one, such as a counselor. An easy way to get practice with truth-telling in a community setting is to join a 12-step group. Most metropolitan areas have groups for just about every imaginable behavior. For more information on support-group meetings, check your newspaper, the Yellow Pages, or the Internet.

These groups teach the skills of honesty, says Dr. Ryan. It's good to practice and develop these skills in a supportive environment because if we just start practicing total honesty before really learning the skills, we may just sound like we're dumping on people. "It can come out very messy, undifferentiated, and unfiltered, and it can be hurtful. The message here is not to moderate your honesty but to develop the skills."

It takes practice in expressing ourselves honestly and spontaneously to learn what things we need to sort through and consider in-depth and what things we should just blurt out, Dr. Ryan says. It takes practice to develop a tactful and loving approach. It takes practice to develop humility and realize that we're at least as fallible as the person with whom we are conversing.

**Observe one day at a time.** We shouldn't expect to replace habits overnight that took a lifetime to build, advises Dr. Ryan. We should consider each day a new opportunity to practice what we're learning.

**Shun secrets.** We should put everyone on notice "that we aren't going to keep their secrets for them or indulge in gossip anymore and that, basically, when they tell us something, they can plan on reading it in the paper the next day," says Dr. Blanton. That injects an amazing dose of truth serum and respect into relationships.

**Quit aggrandizing others.** We realize that we often lie or color the truth to paint what we think is a more impressive picture of ourselves. But do we realize that we do this with others, too? When we put others on pedestals, we create mythical superhumans and hurt them and us in the process, says Dr. Blanton. He jokes that Mark Twain had it right when he said, "All I have to know about anyone is that they are a human being. It doesn't get any worse than that." When we see each other simply as humans and not superiors or inferiors, we're making the most room for truthful, loving communication.

# *Hopelessness*

✦

## WITH FAITH COMES HEALING

*I*t's a rare saint who has the strength to keep on marching when all hope seems lost. But even if we can only manage to meet the day with a groan, we're on familiar ground; the giants of our faith have been there, too.

"That in and of itself should bring hope," says the Reverend Scotty Smith, senior pastor of Christ Community Church in Franklin, Tennessee, and co-author of *Unveiled Hope.* "It's comforting to know that the God who wrote the Bible would not just create this Pollyanna book that says once you become a Christian, there is always an extra check left over at the end of your month, your complexion clears up, and you run a sub-six-minute mile on your fortieth birthday," he says. "The Bible is real."

The Bible is packed with people whose hope had failed—along with just about everything else in their lives, says Reverend Smith.

- Moses wondered how an inarticulate old coot like himself was going to lead such a stubborn bunch across the street, let alone to the Promised Land.
- Jeremiah is known as the weeping prophet because of his grief over the destruction of Israel.

- On the run from King Saul, and again after his adulterous relationship with Bathsheba, David expressed his very real fears and pain at length in the Psalms.
- And, of course, there's Job, who for a time, was Satan's preferred punching bag. In a matter of only days, this guy lost everything: his family, his wealth, and even his health. "Job went through such chronic pain and trouble that at one point, he cried out, 'Cursed be the day that they brought news into the city that my mother had given birth to a son,'" says Reverend Smith.

The New Testament also details the lives of folks with more than their fair share of woes. The disciple John, for example, wrote the book of Revelation while exiled on the isle of Patmos—by all accounts, no tropical paradise. And his fellow believers weren't doing much better.

"The people John was writing to felt like the world was crashing down all around them," says the Reverend John Buckel, Ph.D., associate professor of Scripture at St. Meinrad School of Theology in St. Meinrad, Indiana, a Roman Catholic priest of the Archdoicese of Indianapolis, and author of *Free to Love.* "There were famines, volcanoes, earthquakes, and all kinds of natural disasters going on around the world. The Romans had lost a lot of battles, and there were revolts in the Roman Empire. In addition to that, Christians were being persecuted because they professed that Jesus is Lord."

Even Jesus wrestled with hopelessness in the Garden of Gethsemane, says Dan B. Allender, Ph.D., founder of Wounded Heart Ministries based in Kirkland, Washington, and author of *The Wounded Heart* and *The Cry of the Soul.* In that moving passage just before His arrest, Jesus tells Peter, James, and John that His "soul is overwhelmed with sorrow to the point of death. . . ." (Mark 14:34 NIV) Leaving them to pray, Jesus falls to the ground and says, 'Abba, Father . . . everything is possible for You. Take this cup from Me. Yet not what I will, but what You will." (Mark 14:36 NIV)

"What does that tell us? Hope isn't the absence of despair, but knowing it and leaning into the future. And the future is built on those past burdens," says Dr. Allender.

# The Purpose of Pain: Hope?

Because of the ache inside our own breast—caused by cancer, divorce, a rebellious teen, or just plain loneliness—we're better able to identify with the hopelessness of others.

But how can we respond the way John or Jesus did? With prayer and faith. "John was an optimist in pessimistic times," says Dr. Buckel. "He said, not in so many words, 'God knows exactly what's going on in your life and is in control no matter how it might seem. And in the end, the good will be rewarded and the bad will be punished. Hang in there.'"

Paul's answer is that ". . . we also rejoice in our sufferings, because we know that suffering produces perseverance; perseverance, character; and character, hope. And hope does not disappoint us, because God has poured out His love into our hearts by the Holy Spirit, whom He has given us." (Romans 5:3–5 NIV) Frankly, we may be at the point where we're saying to ourselves, or to anyone else who will listen, for that matter, "I have enough character, thank you very much! What I need is some hope!"

Then take hope from this: God is in control. Moses, with a lot of help from you-know-who, led his people out of Egypt and to the Promised Land. David eluded Saul, became King, and was called a man after God's own heart. Job's prosperity and health were restored. John died for his faith but was instrumental in establishing the early church. Jesus died on the cross but rose again three days later.

Even tear-stained Jeremiah couldn't remain hopeless after hearing God's promise to restore Israel: "'For I know the plans I have for you,' declares the Lord, 'plans to prosper you and not to harm you, plans to give you hope and a future. Then will you call upon me and come and pray to me, and I will listen to you. You will seek Me and find Me when you seek Me with all your heart. I will be found by you,' declares the Lord, 'and will bring you back from captivity.'" (Jeremiah 29:11–14 NIV)

Yet the purpose of our hope is not simply to develop our characters, keep our spirits high, and then hide them away in our own spiritual Swiss bank accounts. As the Apostle Paul points out in

1 Corinthians 13:13, the hope is that we express our faith in love for others, says Reverend Smith. After all, who can understand better the depth of someone's pain than those who have felt hopeless themselves?

## Bad Days

It's unreasonable to expect God to spare us from life's pain and problems, especially since He might be using them to tell us something. But over and over again in the Bible, He has told us to come to Him when times are tough. Here's a prayer designed for just that kind of a day.

> Creator God,
> I see a bad day taking shape
> like storm clouds
> on the distant horizon.
> There are thoughts in me
> of impending pain;
> I'm poised to absorb defeat.
> Remind me that You're
> the Creator of this day;
> the Lord of history;
> the Master of circumstances;
> that You will not fail me.
> Help me walk tall into uncertainty
> knowing that You can turn
> Bad days into the
> Best days.
> Thank you for being my Creator . . .
> Thank You most of all
> for loving me.

—*Norm Nelson, from* Thank You Most of All for Loving Me

# Nurturing the Seeds of Hope

If we're ready to bring some hope back into our lives, we should consider these tips.

**Look ahead.** We're tempted to measure God's love by our own circumstances. But that's never a good idea, says Dr. Allender. Circumstances are always in the process of changing, even if we aren't able to see any change on the horizon. Remember, hope is leaning into the future based on God's faithfulness in the past. Since He has carried us through before, we can know that He'll be there to do it again.

**Look to a familiar face.** Connecting with even just one good friend who has stood by us in tough times past can help us keep hope alive, says Dr. Allender. "These faces are the places where you have seen God's handiwork—His love lived out in a way that helps make Him real."

**Look for someone to help.** Helping someone who is in a worse way than we are not only helps restore their hope but also goes a long way in making us feel more alive, according to Dr. Allender. From literacy programs to prison outreach, there are literally hundreds of ways to help out in our own backyards.

**Look inside.** Since cynicism and negativism—opposites of hope—are learned behaviors that we may have picked up at home, we may simply have to develop new behaviors, like viewing problems as opportunities to grow, strengthen our characters, or make deep-seated change.

"Do you know anybody whom you really look up to as having tremendous character, not with just a public front but someone who is really high in integrity and strength of character?" asks William Backus, Ph.D., a Christian-licensed psychologist in Roseville, Minnesota, founder and director of the Center for Christian Psychological Services in St. Paul, and author of *Telling Yourself the Truth* and *The Healing Power of a Healthy Mind*. "And if you do, does that person have a life history of everything being easy? I'd guess that it's marked with various kinds of suffering. We don't like to think about it, but as Paul said, suffering produces positive traits."

**Look at the facts.** As it turns out, many depressed people don't have lives worse than the other guy; it's their interpretation that's flawed, says Dr. Backus.

"If you say that your future is hopeless, what is your evidence for that? What makes you think so? How can you say that if you don't know? Has the idea of a hopeless future made you feel better? Does it make you happy? Is it fun to wake up in the morning, look at the day, and say that the day is going to be terrible? And if it isn't, why don't you try talking yourself out of that and telling yourself the truth, Dr. Backus says. Finally, approaching a problem rationally is very effective for many.

**Look out.** When we feel hopeless, one of our first instincts is to run and hide from the world. Bad choice.

"Not in any way, shape, or form am I saying that we can earn our hope, but if a Christian has been out of fellowship—hasn't been spending time with other Christians for encouragement and accountability—I would want to redirect them back to that as one place to start," says Reverend Smith.

Just remember that people aren't perfect and can say some pretty dumb things when trying to comfort us. And for those of us who are inclined to give advice to those in despair, some words of caution: "We have our formulas and quick answers, and we can suppose that somebody has lost their hope because they did something wrong," says Reverend Smith. "Maybe, but not necessarily. Before I open my mouth, I would want to start where I thought the Gospel and the love of Jesus would start—which would be really listening."

**Look carefully.** We may not have any overtly destructive behaviors—like blowing an entire paycheck on cases of beer—that are destroying our hope. But what about those bad habits or secret sins that we're able to hide? Even something as fundamental as ignoring our health can take its toll on our attitude. There's little sense in praying to lose 50 pounds while we continue to overeat and refuse to exercise, says Reverend Smith.

**Look for some stained glass.** Worshipping every week at a solid church does three things simultaneously: It gets our focus off ourselves, it puts our focus onto God, and it ties us to a body of believers who can pray and help provide emotional support, says Reverend Smith, all of which build hope.

**Look to the Book.** Tucked in the Bible's wonderful passages of triumph and tragedy is a short but compelling piece that Reverend Smith turns to again and again to restore his hope: Psalm 73.

The author, named Asaph, apparently worked under King David and was one of the worship leaders in the temple. As it turns out, the story is a classic case of someone who is surrounded by religious activity yet loses hope because he loses focus. "Asaph talks about this time in his life where he took his eyes off the love of God and started looking at the culture, and he was miserable," says Reverend Smith. "In fact, he describes himself as becoming a brute beast before God. And then he talks about entering into the sanctuary of the Lord and regaining perspective.

"The Psalm ends giving this beautiful picture of hope when it says in the last few verses, 'Lord, whom have we in Heaven but You? And being with You I desire nothing on the Earth.' Asaph is a good example of how even believers can lose their sense of joy and focus just by living in the culture that tempts us to think that life can be found somewhere else other than in a vital relationship with God and the Gospel," says Reverend Smith.

**Look to hope.** Feeling like a lamb being led to slaughter? Revelation 5 shows that might not be such a bad situation after all, says Dr. Buckel. "Most people know that the personification of evil is the Beast—which has tremendous size and tremendous power. Interestingly enough, the symbol for good is not just a sheep, it's something even more vulnerable: a little lamb. And yet the lamb is triumphant. So often, we feel like sheep being led to the slaughter in life. John says that we may feel vulnerable like lambs, but good will ultimately triumph over evil," says Dr. Buckel, even if that evil manifests itself as health problems, emotional difficulties, or one of a dozen other problems. "In many cases, it seems like the beast is so big that it can't be conquered," he says, "but the blessing of Revelation is that it not only can be conquered, but it will be conquered. And that, ultimately, is the source of our hope."

# *Infidelity*

## SURVIVING AN AFFAIR

*A*nother marriage seminar behind him, counselor Rob Parsons was standing at the front of the empty auditorium when a young man, wife in tow, walked to the front.

"Not long ago, I had an affair," the man confided. "So I took my wedding band off and gave it back to my wife. And then I told her, 'Darlin', I'm sorry I hurt you. Don't put this on my finger till you can trust me again.'"

The man held up his left hand and broke into a smile. Light danced across a small band of gold on his ring finger. "Rob," he said with obvious joy, "the other day, she put it back on."

Parsons looked at the man's wife. Her head was bowed.

"Forgive me if I'm wrong," Parsons said, "but I think when she put that ring back on your finger, she wasn't saying, 'I trust you again.' She was saying, 'With all my heart I *want* to trust you again.'"

The woman slowly raised her head. "That's how I feel," she said.

Though the husband hadn't realized it, clearly, his voyage back to a loving, trusting relationship had just begun, says Parsons, executive director of Care for the Family in Cardiff, Wales, an organization created to preserve marriage and the family, and author of *The Sixty Minute Marriage Builder*.

# Good Love Gone Bad

Of all the damage caused by marital infidelity, it's no surprise that among the most painful is the loss of trust. It may also be the hardest to repair. But the hard work of restoring a marriage must begin with a careful and honest examination of what went wrong. And often, the problems and issues go beyond simple sexual attraction.

Frequent, angry fighting, for example, can destroy intimacy between a couple, forcing a spouse to first withdraw and then search elsewhere, says William Richardson, Ph.D., clinical director and professor in the department of marriage and family therapy at Reformed Theological Seminary in Jackson, Mississippi. Also, sexual addiction and lust put us at risk for one-night stands.

As we get older, major life and career changes are more likely to damage our marital foundations and open the door to affairs, according to Leslie Parrott, Ph.D., and Les Parrott, Ph.D., authors of *Saving Your Marriage before It Starts* and co-directors of the Center for Relationship Development at Seattle Pacific University.

For example, a woman who joins the work world after years of devoted—and often unrecognized—care for her family might find the admiration of a male colleague seductive. And a man in midlife who may not get many pats on the back at home might feel ripe for an indiscretion if the office secretary laughs at his jokes and generally makes him feel attractive.

In fact, the deficits created in a marriage by familiarity and neglect are hard to overstate. "When counseling, we'll often ask a couple, 'If you could change something about your marriage, what would it be?' In most cases, the man will say, 'I wish my wife were more concerned about sex,'" says Parsons. "When we turn to the woman, she will often say, 'Affection. I want him to listen to me when I talk to him. I wish sometimes he would touch me in a nonsexual way. I wish when we're shopping he would sometimes hold my hand rather than walking a mile ahead of me.'"

When a couple is committed to their marriage with a special kind of dedication called agape love—the highest form of love described in the Bible—research shows that two amazing things happen: They spend less time seriously thinking about what it would be like to be with

*(continued on page 334)*

# How to Avoid an Affair

How do we build a protective wall around our marriages to guard them from affairs? Here are some suggestions.

**Follow the 10-second rule.** The battle for keeping the marriage bed pure can be won long before anyone sets foot in the bedroom. In fact, the final outcome may be determined in those 10 seconds after we notice someone other than our spouse.

"When did David's affair begin? When he climbed into bed with Bathsheba?" asks Rob Parsons, executive director of Care for the Family in Cardiff, Wales, an organization created to preserve marriage and the family and author of *The Sixty Minute Marriage Builder*. "No. I reckon that affair was all sorted out the 10 seconds after he saw this incredibly beautiful woman naked and bathing, kept looking, and said, 'What's her name?' By the time he had said that, it was really a forgone conclusion," he says.

"When is the battle for the office affair won or lost? Not at the bedroom door. It's normally won at the office party where someone smiles at us across the room and we have 10 seconds to decide whether we're going to walk those 20 feet or keep talking to the boring person next to us. Incredible pain can be saved in those 10 seconds," says Parsons.

**Set some boundaries.** If we're starting to have feelings toward someone other than our spouses, we need to be swift and sure in our responses. "That can mean cutting down certain kinds of contact or certain kinds of communication. For example, we might decide, 'I'm okay if I just talk about this, but when we start to talk about this, that is a danger sign,'" says Scott Stanley, Ph.D., co-director of the Center for Marital and Family Studies at the University of Denver and co-author of *A Lasting Promise* and *The Heart of Commitment*.

**Think body, mind, and spirit.** At its simplest, sexual immorality is the triumph of the body over the mind and the spirit, "but it's when we remember that we're more than flesh that we're able to overcome sexual temptation," says Mark Ginter, Ph.D., assistant professor of moral theology at Saint Meinrad School of Theology in St. Meinrad, Indiana.

"One of my favorite passages that speaks to this is 1 Thessalonians 5:23: ' . . . may your spirit and soul and body be kept sound and blameless at the coming of our Lord Jesus Christ.' (NRSV) That passage is a prayer for integration for these three levels of human experience: body, mind (the words for mind and soul are interchangeable in Greek), and spirit. We have to try to reduce the focus on the one sphere—mainly, the physical sphere—and balance it with the other two," Dr. Ginter says.

**Pay attention.** "There's an incredible poem that was written about 100 years ago by a woman explaining why she had an affair," says Parsons. "A line in it says: 'I spoke little and he listened much.' And I think that sums it up, really: Women say, 'I had an affair because I found someone who gave me dignity and made me feel like a woman again.'" The bottom line is that marriage partners need not only to pay close attention to their spouse's needs but also to strive to know them intimately—mind, body, and soul.

**Plan some sex.** It sounds about as romantic as a trip to the dry cleaners. But in our stressed-out, not-enough-time-or-energy culture, planning a date night each week that includes the sexual intimacy of marital self-giving can be a great way to maintain our marriages, experts say.

**Get real.** We may think that affairs will re-energize our lives, and they actually may do that for a time. But, says Parsons, the reality is that even this new relationship will become ordinary after a while.

"And then, you will begin to wonder what your kids look like when they wake up first thing in the morning," Parsons says, "and why you made such a big deal out of the things that you hated about your spouse." Suddenly, you'll regret that you gave up all that for the temporary excitement that the affair provided.

somebody else. And when they're attracted to someone else, they perceive it as a threat to their marriage, says Scott Stanley, Ph.D., co-director of the Center for Marital and Family Studies at the University of Denver and co-author of *A Lasting Promise* and *The Heart of Commitment.* "Agape love doesn't mean that they're always happy, but they are dedicated to Christ-like unconditional love that keeps on giving, even when it's not too easy."

When confronted with even the possibility of an affair, a person with this type of commitment starts looking more at the negatives than the positives in the new person, to protect the commitment to his spouse. What's more, folks with this type of commitment seem to be less likely to neglect their mates, says Dr. Stanley.

Dr. Stanley notes, "In the Bible, the often-quoted passage on divorce says, '. . . guard yourself in your spirit, and do not break faith with the wife of your youth.'" (Malachi 2:15 NIV) "The word *guard* in Hebrew literally means 'hedge.' And they're not talking about wimpy American hedges. They're talking about hedges that work like the walls of a fort. God is saying that part of guarding our commitment in marriage is tending that hedge. And that starts with having a forgiving spirit toward our spouses, while maintaining it means keeping our thought lives—that seemingly secret realm where we ponder, mull, consider, entertain, and fantasize—as pure as possible."

## The Hard Work of Rebuilding

Suppose your marital "hedge" is in shambles and your spouse has an affair. Is the marriage doomed? It won't ever be the same, but it doesn't have to end. And in some cases, it may even get better. "One of the things that we've discovered is that there is more hope for a marriage after an affair than people believe. And I think that is exciting," says Dr. Leslie Parrott.

To overcome the effects of an affair, a couple needs to "find out what the affair means," says Dr. Les Parrott. "They'll ask each other, 'What does this tell us about our marriage? What is going on between us right now?' For a lot of folks, that can really be a window into a lot of growth and personal development between the two of them."

Here's a plan to help rebuild marriages.

**Confess, but not for just confession's sake.** "A confession should be designed to care for the person receiving it, not to just un-burden the person giving it," says Dr. Les Parrott. "And it's really hard sometimes for the person to not just confess to unburden himself. More than the words, we should check the motivation of our hearts."

**Go to God.** After we've confessed to our spouses, we need to confess to the Lord, says Mark Ginter, Ph.D., assistant professor of moral theology at Saint Meinrad School of Theology in St. Meinrad, Indiana. Make no mistake, He knows what we've been up to. But at this point, we need to restore our relationship with Him with a humble prayer of confession and repentance. One verse that we can use after this or any other sin was prayed by King David after his af-fair with Bathsheba. Part of it reads: "Create in me a clean heart, O God, And renew a steadfast spirit in me." (Psalm 51:10 NKJV)

**Call in experienced counsel.** Coming clean with our spouses is important, but in some cases, it may not be wise to attempt it alone. "Often, in the heat of the exchange, the couple doesn't hear each other and a priest or pastor or counselor can act as a calming force, a diffusing force, to slow the conversation down, if need be, and to reiterate what has been said. It's my experience that this type of intervention can make things safer and can diffuse what could erupt into a bad situation," says Dr. Ginter.

No matter what counsel we choose, we need to make sure that the person has experience working with couples who are over-coming affairs. "You don't want someone who just says, 'You've done wrong; let's just pray about it,' and that's it. Praying is important, but there's other work that needs to be done," says Dr. Stanley.

**Set some ground rules.** Another benefit to having clergy or a counselor present or available when we confess to our spouses is the opportunity to develop some ground rules for discussion. Without ground rules, true healing and reconciliation may never take place. "It has to be really clear that this hurt, and that it's going to hurt for a while," says Dr. Ginter. Some of the best ways to communicate when under pressure include speaking with "I" statements, practicing active listening, and avoiding generalities. (See "Did You Hear What I Said?" on page 179 for more on these techniques.) If we sense that an emotional meltdown is about to occur, it's probably wise to meet with a pastor, priest, or counselor again.

**Begin with the end in mind.** Not the end of the relationship but, rather, the time that we'll stop talking about the affair. For many couples undergoing counseling, that can range from six weeks to two months. During this pre-agreed time period, the couple will discuss all aspects of the affair, including details, if necessary. "That's when we'll deal with the worst part of it," says Dr. Stanley. At the end of that period, the couple agrees not to talk about it ever again. "Couples won't make it if they have this sense that the process is unending."

**Limit the session.** It may not be enough to limit just the overall time spent talking about the affair. It's probably also a good idea to limit the amount of time spent each session talking about the indiscretion. "If they're going to be here for an hour, we agree that we will start talking about less volatile issues and calming down about 15 minutes before the hour," says Dr. Stanley.

**Develop an interim agreement.** As the couple who visited with Parsons reminds us, trust, especially when fractured by an affair, can take a long time to restore. An interim agreement, on the other hand, allows time for healing to take place. "In the best possible world, the offended spouse would say something like, 'Okay. I am forgiving you. I'm not saying that I *have* forgiven you, and I'm not saying that it's a done deal. It's in the process. I am committed to it, and I am working on it, but there is still a lot of resentment and anger here that I eventually need to release.' If we get to that point, that is a tremendous advancement already," says Dr. Ginter.

**Start small and deliver.** For those of us who cheated, it could take months or years of promise-keeping and persistent behavior before our spouses truly trust us again. In other words, flowers or cooking our spouses' favorite meals every week are nice, but coming home on time, calling when we say we will, and being truthful are probably more important. "It comes back to the issue of empathy—trying to understand what our partners need right now and gently letting our partners know that we value the relationship," says Dr. Les Parrott.

For more information on how to prevent the kind of fighting that can destroy a marriage, see Arguing (page 177).

# *Jealousy and Envy*

## GAINING A RIGHT VIEW
## OF OURSELVES AND OTHERS

*A*nger. Character assassination. Catty, cutting comments. Unkind jokes. Gossip. Lying. Even murder.

Jealousy shows up in many damaging ways. But where does such a toxic brew get its start? Like many deep-seated emotional problems, jealousy and its alter ego, envy, tend to develop in childhood when we come to believe that resources, including our parents' love, are in short supply, says Charles Zeiders, doctor of psychology, a Christian psychologist and clinical coordinator of Christian Counseling Associates with offices in West Chester and Havertown, Pennsylvania, and a consultant to the neuro-behavioral unit at Riddle Hospital in Springfield, Pennsylvania. "Jealousy is characterized by a position of lack," he says, "the belief that there is only so much beauty or talent or happiness or love to go around."

If a child wants his mother to make him feel loved, soothe a hurt, or reassure him, and Dad consistently distracts her from the task, "the child learns that in a relationship with a woman, there really isn't enough of her nurturing to go around," says Dr. Zeiders.

Or if Mom simply isn't there when the child needs her, the child may start to think, "I'm going to lose whomever I love. I'm going to be rejected," according to Everett L. Worthington, Ph.D., professor of psychology at Virginia Commonwealth University in Richmond and co-author of *To Forgive Is Human*. The same thing can happen if certain children in a family seem to get more attention than the others, he says.

Another common cause of jealousy: When parents push a child toward independence and then pull the child back because they can't bear the thought of the child not relying on them, says Dr. Worthington. That child learns that independence is a bad thing.

## "Gifts" That Keep On Giving

How might these childhood experiences affect our later relationships? In the case of people who feel that they have been rejected, "they're always afraid that they're going to lose the other person. So they're anxious and alert to any possible way this might happen, including when the other person even looks at someone else," says Dr. Worthington.

Someone who struggled with independence as a child will likely become jealous if "their romantic partner tries to make any moves toward independence," Dr. Worthington says. "This kicks in the need for a glomming-on type of dependency that's uncomfortable."

A man who is jealous over his wife's other relationships "will often be consumed by rage," says Dr. Zeiders. "He'll berate his mate and accuse her of not loving him. He's constantly on the verge of ruining the relationship by 'guilting' her for her imaginary infidelities." A jealous woman in the same situation may operate more deceptively. "She'll drop a few well-placed comments to discredit the people she thinks the husband is interested in," he says.

Even if jealousy or envy don't manifest themselves verbally, they can spark an unhealthy sense of competition, where we're constantly comparing ourselves with others to see if we're just as successful, intelligent, or desirable. Keeping score in this way ultimately "undermines the jealous person's ability to celebrate the good things that happen to other people or themselves," says Dr. Zeiders.

Jealous and envious people may not just blame themselves over their perceived misfortunes. They're often mad at God, too. "The envious person has basically decided that God has made a mistake," says Ray Pritchard, doctor of ministry, senior pastor of Calvary Memorial Church in Oak Park, Illinois, and author of *The ABC's of Wisdom* and *What a Christian Believes*. Basically, the jealous person is saying, "God didn't give me enough. He gave somebody else too much, and they don't appreciate it; they don't deserve it."

# Finding Peace

King Solomon, thought by some to be one of the wisest men who ever lived, summed it up this way: "A heart at peace gives life to the body, but envy rots the bones." (Proverbs 14:30 NIV) One possible goal, then, is to turn our envious, jealous hearts into hearts at peace.

How? There are three important steps, says Dr. Pritchard: developing a right view of God, of ourselves, and of others.

Here are some suggestions to help make it happen.

**Watch the self-talk.** The way we talk to ourselves can reinforce feelings of jealousy and envy, says William Backus, Ph.D., a Christian-licensed psychologist in Roseville, Minnesota, founder and director of the Center for Christian Psychological Services in St. Paul, and author of *Telling Yourself the Truth* and *The Healing Power of a Healthy Mind*. "If we think, 'I must get what I want in order to be happy,' it can trigger feelings that it's terrible if we don't get what we want or that doing without is intense suffering. We may even feel that if other people have what we want and we don't have it, it's unfair."

All of these attitudes are patently false. Instead, says Dr. Backus, we need to tell ourselves, "It's not terrible when my every whim isn't gratified" or "It may be uncomfortable or inconvenient to do without certain things, but I can do it."

**Give others their due.** The words may get caught in our throats the first few times, but praising others when they've done well can help break jealousy's power over us. "Genuine, heartfelt praise can't exist in the same heart as envy," says Dr. Pritchard.

**Follow the commandment.** In His infinite wisdom, God issued a commandment—not a suggestion—dealing with this specific problem that is worth following even today. "You shall not covet your

# Healing Words

## Overcoming Envy

Who is wise and understanding among you? Let him show
by good conduct that his works are done in the meekness
of wisdom.
But if you have bitter envy and self-seeking in your hearts,
do not boast and lie against the truth. This wisdom does
not descend from above, but is earthly, sensual, demonic.
For where envy and self-seeking exist, confusion and every
evil thing are there.

*—James 3:13–16 NKJV*

Do not envy the oppressor, and choose none of his ways;
For the perverse person is an abomination to the Lord . . .

*—Proverbs 3:31–32 NKJV*

Let us not become conceited, provoking and envying each
other.

*—Galatians 5:26 NIV*

Love is patient, love is kind. It does not envy, it does not
boast, it is not proud.
It is not rude, it is not self-seeking, it is not easily angered, it
keeps no record of wrongs.
Love does not delight in evil but rejoices with the truth.
It always protects, always trusts, always hopes, always
perseveres.

*—1 Corinthians 13:4–7 NIV*

neighbor's wife. You shall not set your desire on your neighbor's house or land, his manservant or maidservant, his ox or donkey, or anything that belongs to your neighbor." (Deuteronomy 5:21 NIV) Of course, yesterday's ox is probably today's Lexus, but the concept still applies. And the best way to avoid such jealousy is by simply being thankful for what we have, says Dr. Pritchard.

**Set a new standard.** If we truly believe in our faith, we know that we should set our sights a little higher than a newer car or a bigger house than the folks across the street. "Remember that as Christians, we've pledged to pattern our lives after Jesus," writes former President Jimmy Carter in *Sources of Strength*. "The real measures of success are the things that He said were important—in the words of Saint Paul, the things that we cannot see, like truth, compassion, justice, service, and love."

**Stop 'em in their tracks.** Even if we don't personally have problems with envy or jealousy, we may help bring it to life or perpetuate it in others with our words and deeds. For example, if we fawn over someone's children in the presence of a single woman who is desperate for children, obviously, it's going to arouse her feelings. Or if our spouses tend to be jealous of our relationships, we should avoid personal, private discussions with members of the opposite sex.

"My husband is a pastor, and he will never meet with a woman alone," says Mary Ellen Ashcroft, Ph.D., professor of English at Bethel College in St. Paul, Minnesota, and author of *Temptations Women Face*. "That's treating our marriage relationship with the honor that it deserves."

**Seek God's intervention.** More stubborn patterns of jealousy and envy may very well require specific prayer to overcome. If we feel the need for greater help, we should "invite the Holy Spirit to speak the truth," says Dr. Zeiders. "Sometimes the Spirit will show up and give us a sense in the heart and mind that even if a parent forgot or rejected us, God has not and will not forget us. By inviting God's truth in, we learn that we are, in fact, nurtured and loved on some real and universal level by God."

**Adopt God's view of gifting.** Not only has God created each of us with specific gifts and talents that are unique to us but he also gave them to others so that we could work together to build His

Kingdom. "It's the idea that the church is a body and each of us is a hand, an eye, a head, or a foot. Each of us has a place in the body," says Dr. Zeiders. "Jealousy divides the body, so we need to come together. We compliment one another."

**Get self-worth from God.** If we have proof that our spouse has been flirting, we need to get to marriage counseling—fast. But even if our jealousy is well-founded, ultimately, we can't allow our self-esteem to be defined by someone else's sin or neglect.

"Larry Crabb wrote an important book called *The Marriage Builder*," says Dr. Worthington. "And there he argues that one of the keys to getting rid of jealousy is not trying to find security in our mates. Our security, if we have any at all, is in a loving and faithful relationship with God through Jesus. And to the extent that people can really come to believe that deep down in their hearts, they'll be better off."

# Job Trouble

## FINDING PEACE
## IN AN UNCERTAIN WORLD

*M*ost of us spend more of our productive, waking hours on the job than anyplace else. So naturally, how we get along on the job—with our co-workers, our supervisors, our clients, our customers, and even with the actual work itself—has a lot to do with our moods, our mental outlook, and our health.

We need to feel that we are doing good work and that we are appreciated for it if we are to feel good about ourselves, our jobs, and our lives, notes Krista Kurth, Ph.D., co-founder of Renewal Resources, a consulting firm in Potomac, Maryland, that specializes in organizational teaching, and the recipient of one of the first doctorates that George Washington University ever issued for studies about spirituality in the workplace.

Since we do spend so much of our time at work, it is natural that we will at times experience emotional upsets and conflicts through our jobs. And since we are dependent upon our jobs for what they allow us to buy—the lifestyles that they allow us to live—when we lose our jobs or are in danger of losing them for whatever reason, our world turns topsy-turvy. We find ourselves spiritually challenged, notes the Reverend Tim P. Van Duivendyk, doctor of ministry, a chaplain and marriage and family therapist at the Memorial Hermann Healthcare System in Houston.

Our jobs and our spirituality are tightly intertwined. We need to recognize this. We can most effectively ride the ever-changing seascape of modern corporate America if our spiritual outlook and values along with our jobs and how we perform them are closely aligned, says Dr. Kurth. And yes, it is possible to integrate work and faith, work and spirituality, and life purpose and mission from a spiritual perspective. We can even draw on our spiritual centers in handling day-to-day conflicts, bad bosses, job burnout, and even job loss.

Sometimes getting our work, our attitudes about it, and our approaches to it to reflect our spiritual values and our faith is more easily said than done. But if our work goes against our spiritual values, our faith suffers.

The Apostle Paul said, "Faith that doesn't show itself by good works is no faith at all—it is dead and useless." (James 2:17 TLB) In the larger context, he suggests that we should demonstrate our faith by and through our actions. If we don't do that on the job—where we spend as much or more time as anyplace else—where, then, will we live our faith?

# Why Am I Here?

Sometimes our work environments are so unpleasant that we dread clocking in. Our bosses and co-workers nag and belittle us and seem to unfairly dump the most undesirable and difficult tasks on us, and then gripe and complain about our performance and threaten us. Sometimes we are just so overwhelmed that we think we'll never get caught up—and that leads to mental and nervous exhaustion.

So, yes, when we find our work environments overwhelmingly unpleasant, we are likely to ask, "How did I get here? Why am I here? Why me, Lord?"

This is not to suggest that we should punish ourselves and stay in an untenable work situation. But we shouldn't just throw up our hands and walk away, either, according to the Reverend Paul F. Everett of Pittsburgh, a Presbyterian minister at large with the Peale Center in Pawling, New York, and executive director emeritus of the Pittsburgh Experiment, a national and international ministry to the business and working communities. "We have to work things

# Faithbuilders

## The Purpose of Work

We may curse our jobs and wish for lives of lolling in the sun on Montego Bay, but such dreaming and cursing is not likely to make us feel better about our lives, nor is it likely to land us on the beach. Idle wishing is not healthy, according to the Bible: "Whoever watches the wind will not plant; whoever looks at the clouds will not reap." (Ecclesiastes 11:4 NIV)

Work is an end in itself, and we should not shirk it, suggests this proverb: "Lazy hands make a man poor, but diligent hands bring wealth." (Proverbs 10:4 NIV)

Nor is there great reward in scams and schemes that take unfair advantage of others. "Dishonest money dwindles away, but he who gathers money little by little makes it grow." (Proverbs 13:11 NIV)

The Bible even offers a success formula: work, work, work. "Sow your seed in the morning, and at evening let not your hands be idle, for you do not know which will succeed, whether this or that, or whether both will do equally well." (Ecclesiastes 11:6 NIV)

And while God may seem a tough taskmaster, in the end, He does offer some respite. "Six days do your work, but on the seventh day do not work, so that your ox and your donkey may rest and the slave born in your household, and the alien as well, may be refreshed." (Exodus 23:12 NIV)

through; we have to deal with challenges and process the experiences," he explains.

"Our growth comes through stress and challenges in one way, shape, or form. What God is allowing in our lives is for our growth and transformation," says Reverend Everett. "We may think that it is a big mistake that we are in this job or in this particular position, but isn't God a part of it all? If I have invited God into my life to be my

Lord and Savior, then He wants to be a part of every area of my life, and that includes my job. We need to seek His plan for where we are and what we're doing."

Yes, we may well need to move on to a new job that better uses the talents and skills that God gave us and where we are more appreciated and treated more respectfully. But "the way out is *through*," says Reverend Everett. The answer is not to run, but to face the problems and understand what they are teaching us about ourselves, about life, and about others. "Ask this question: 'Am I willing to walk with God in the circumstances and situations in which I find myself right now in this job?'" suggests Reverend Everett.

Sometimes it is when we feel the most pain, the most frustration, and the most stress that God reveals the most helpful life-changing lessons, suggests Reverend Everett. "He that overcometh," says God in Revelation 21:7 (KJV), "shall inherit all things; and I will be his God, and he shall be my son."

By facing the challenges and discerning the lessons, we clarify our needs and purposes and open the door to satisfying, spiritually correct work.

# Dealing with a Dysfunctional Boss

"As rotten as a boss can be, we have to realize that God didn't promise us that we'd have wonderful bosses and that everything would be lovely and free of work problems," notes Reverend Everett. At times, we have to suffer a bad boss, for example, a power and control freak, an antagonizer, or a completely self-centered supervisor—one who is more concerned about his own ambitious goals than his people.

In these situations, the best course, if we can manage it, is to escape, says Paul Meier, M.D., Christian psychiatrist and theologian, cofounder of New Life Clinics, the largest provider of Christian-based counseling in the United States, and author of more than 60 best-selling Christian self-help books. Transfer to another department or find a new job, he advises.

Ideally, in the case of sexual harassment, we would report it and it would end. But the fact is, says Dr. Meier, most whistle-blowers face reprisals, suspicion, lies, smears, and humiliation. Before making any report of sexual harassment, Dr. Meier advises gaining the assis-

## Spiritual Aspects of Work

Here are ways that people can and do view work from a spiritual perspective, says Krista Kurth, Ph.D., co-founder of Renewal Resources, a consulting firm in Potomac, Maryland, that specializes in organizational teaching, and the recipient of one of the first doctorates that George Washington University ever issued for studies about spirituality in the workplace.

- An opportunity to grow and to serve society
- An opportunity to practice love, care, and compassion with fellow workers and with customers
- A chance to practice integrity and live by the principles that we believe in

tance of an attorney experienced in such cases. And even if we do report the abuse, Dr. Meier's best advice is to transfer to another department or find another job. As long as we work for an abuser, we are suffering mental and emotional damage.

If the boss is only mildly dysfunctional, consider these survival tips suggested by Dr. Meier.

**Keep cool.** Stay calm when attacked, when the boss is bellowing, blaring, or berating. Respond briefly, respectfully, and pleasantly. Avoid sarcasm and debating at all costs. It will only invite an escalation of the confrontation.

**Don't flinch.** People with abusive personalities seek victims. Don't become one. Instead, face the abuser eye-to-eye and respond with self-esteem and courage, politely, carefully, and briefly. If the behavior continues and causes anguish and unhealthy stress, then it's time to look for another job.

## Avoiding Overwork

As companies downsize and jobs are eliminated and combined, many of us find ourselves under more and more pressure to work harder,

# Expressing Spirituality on the Job

Here are ways that we can develop, integrate, and express our spirituality on the job and in our workplaces, says Krista Kurth, Ph.D., co-founder of Renewal Resources, a consulting firm in Potomac, Maryland, that specializes in organizational teaching, and the recipient of one of the first doctorates that George Washington University ever issued for studies about spirituality in the workplace.

- Have objects and sayings in our personal office space that remind us of and inspire us to live by our spiritual values.
- Listen from the heart.
- Practice prayer, meditation, and contemplative silence.
- Develop spiritually motivated discussion groups, if company policies allow.
- Bring in spiritually oriented workshops and speakers, if company policies allow.
- Conduct a spiritual audit of workplace policies and practices. Do they meet our spiritual values and objectives?
- Encourage spiritual growth and thinking.

faster, smarter, and longer. Even if our managers aren't pushing us, we feel a need to prove our value so that we will survive potential cutbacks or layoffs. Soon, we're in overdrive all the time and our mental and physical health suffers.

We do better work when we are calm and relaxed than when we plow through in a nervous rush, say Dr. Meier and Dr. Van Duivendyk. The most valuable thing that we can do to avoid stress damage, illnesses, and burnout is learn to relax, they say. Both cite the work of cardiologist Herbert Benson, M.D., associate professor of medicine and president of the Mind/Body Medical Institute at Harvard Medical School. Dr. Benson discovered a beneficial physical and emotional state that he calls the relaxation response. It is achieved through a simple form of relaxation that Dr. Benson discovered by studying the physiological effects of meditation.

The practices involved in meditation help us manage stress so that we function more effectively without damaging our health. The steps to eliciting the relaxation response are:

1. Sit in a relaxed, comfortable position.

2. Quiet the mind and breathe slowly and naturally.

3. Gently focus thinking on a single word, phrase, prayer, or sound. Meditators sometimes refer to this object of focus as a mantra. Repeat it during exhalation.

4. Passively disregard other thoughts that intrude, returning the focus to the mantra, statement of affirmation, or prayer.

We benefit from this practice if we do it for as little as 3 to 5 minutes at a time, several times a day for a cumulative total of 10 to 20 minutes, says Larry Feldman, Ph.D., director of the Pain and Stress Rehabilitation Center in Newark, Delaware.

Practicing meditation daily over a period of months has been shown to have a number of beneficial effects on health and well-being and tends to make people more positive and calmer in general, says Dr. Feldman.

Dr. Meier points out that the concept of meditation need not be in conflict with anyone's Christian faith. Incorporate faith in the process, he suggests, by using a favorite faith concept or Bible verse as a mantra and pray for guidance of the Holy Spirit.

In fact, Dr. Benson found that a person's religious convictions or life philosophy actually enhanced the effects of the relaxation response.

In addition to daily meditative relaxation, we must remember and respect the Biblical teaching about all work and no play. It's not put in those exact terms, but repeatedly in the Old Testament, we are admonished to respect a day of rest each week. We are told that such a day of rest is holy and mandated by God. That is the fourth of the Ten Commandments. "Six days you shall labor and do all your work, but the seventh day is a Sabbath to the Lord your God. On it you shall not do any work, neither you, nor your son or daughter, nor your manservant or maidservant, nor your animals, nor the alien within your gates." (Exodus 20:9–10 NIV)

# Dealing with Job Loss

When Houston took a crash in the mid-1980s, Dr. Van Duivendyk helped the whole city cope with job loss. The bottom fell out of the oil industry, real estate plunged, and some savings and loans went belly-up. A wave of unemployment swept across the city. Even Dr. Van Duivendyk's hospital faced layoffs. To deal with the crisis, he turned to the city churches and helped train many of them to support and set up job-counseling networks. He guided congregations in setting up job-referral centers at churches all over Houston. He organized job-loss support groups. He often counseled and assessed people who were depressed and needed to be referred to physicians for treatment.

The community of churches made a difference. The support groups, in particular, helped the unemployed realize that they were not alone and that there were creative ways to deal with sudden, seemingly catastrophic change. "People were losing their homes," Dr. Van Duivendyk says. "We're talking pain, frustration, and desperation."

At church seminars, Dr. Van Duivendyk would divide large groups into smaller ones of no more than eight people, and he'd let them tell their stories. After helping them identify and share their problems and pain, he would then ask the same groups to begin talking about resolutions. He'd ask them, "Now what can we do about that? How do we deal with these problems? How do we face this and go on?" He continues, "This provided a healing dimension for those on the backside of corporate life. For me, this is what prayer, faith, and healing are all about."

The programs in which Dr. Van Duivendyk consulted were later widely recognized, and calls came from churches in other cities asking about Houston's methods.

Let's say our community isn't facing massive job cuts and layoffs, but we ourselves have just been given the pink slip. What do we do now? The following are some principles that Dr. Duivendyk used in helping individuals, families, and congregations.

**Accept what's happening.** "First, understand that the confusion, pain, fear, anger, and sense of impaired self-esteem—these feelings, these emotions—are all normal," says Dr. Van Duivendyk.

**Talk it through.** Find someone empathic and loving with whom to talk out the feelings, he advises. "Feel your way through the feelings. Identify them, talk about them, and get them out with someone who cares."

When we locate a caring, loving person or community of people, we have found the real church, says Dr. Van Duivendyk. "They are practicing the faith. They are practicing spirituality. They are the loving church community."

We may not always find these people in our churches, he warns. People, including church people, often feel uneasy when around the downtrodden, particularly if the downtrodden are people whom they have previously known as peers. Perhaps they fear that the misfortune may be contagious and they don't want to get too close. Also, he says, when times suddenly are economically hard in an area and the first wave of layoffs hits, other people, not grasping the full situation, often are suspicious that those laid off were perhaps somehow in the wrong or not good employees. Those still employed don't want to be associated with perceived failure or possible wrongdoing and may shun the laid-off workers.

We may find this attitude in even our closest circles, he says. If so, we should expand our search for loving, caring, helpful people to find the help that we need.

**Seek help.** Try to find a job-loss support group in the community. "Just realizing that, 'Here I am, a competent person without a job and I am sitting next to another competent person who doesn't have a job' has tremendous value. It helps us realize that we are not alone," says Dr. Van Duivendyk.

In addition, the group can point us to many resources that can help us quickly organize and implement an effective job search.

**Take the anger to God.** Accept that we may have a faith crisis. We are likely to question God at times like these. We may express anger because we can't feel God with us.

Go ahead, express it, says Dr. Van Duivendyk. Expressing anger is one form of dialogue with God. "The anger itself, the frustration itself, are expressions of faith in God. You don't express anger toward someone you don't believe exists." God is there, he says. "God doesn't take our jobs away from us, and we don't lose our jobs because God doesn't want to bless us. God is a covenant God who walks with us in the valleys as well as on the mountaintops."

**Move into a make-do mode.** We need to reframe our thinking, says Dr. Van Duivendyk. A cheaper pair of jeans will get us through if we don't have money for a special name brand. Homemade sandwiches and a picnic in the park can be a fun family get-together when we don't have money for McDonald's and the movies.

**Level with the family.** "Sitting down with your kids and speaking openly about the pain and fears and asking for help in renegotiating the budget can bring the family together in a new emotional and spiritual way that they might otherwise never experience," says Dr. Van Duivendyk. Families, even kids, can be resourceful with options when parents level openly and honestly with them.

**Know that we have a job.** Our present job is to find a job. There is a tendency for the unemployed to discount their daily efforts to find work.

**Expect to change.** The only way that we can become new and different is to let go of the old. It's painful to enter the struggle of job loss, but when we do, we begin the journey toward personal growth. "It's true: It is in dying to the old that we rise to the new," Dr. Van Duivendyk says.

**Never forget the experience.** Once we have new jobs, we should draw on our experiences to help heal others who lose their jobs. We can pass on to others the empathy and care that we have learned in this experience.

# *Kindness*

———✦———

## PLANTING THE SEED OF COMPASSION

*O*ne day, Jesus accepted an invitation to have lunch at the home of a Pharisee. As they ate, a prostitute came into the house and approached Jesus carrying a flask of expensive perfume. She knelt by Him and wept, her tears falling on His feet. Carefully, the woman wiped away the tears with her hair, then kissed His feet and washed them with the perfume.

The Pharisee watched and thought to himself, "This proves that Jesus is no prophet, for if God had really sent Him, He would know what kind of woman this one is!"

But Jesus, who knew what was in the Pharisee's mind, said that, though the woman's sins were many, with her acts, "she loved Me much." And He said to her, "Your sins are forgiven. . . . Your faith has saved you; go in peace." (Luke 7:36–50 TLB)

We may never be called upon to show the kindness of this woman or receive as immediate a reward for our good deeds, but kindness is still central to our lives. It's what defines us as Christians, as people who care about the others who inhabit our world.

"Kindness isn't some benign little gesture; it's something that we're invited to love, to yearn for, to be drawn to, and to desire with ardor," says Melanie Morrison, author of *The Grace of Coming Home*. Should we practice kindness? Of course. But more than that, in faith,

# 10 Acts of Pure Kindness

Sometimes the most rewarding acts of kindness are the ones that we offer purely, without forethought, or to people we barely know. Here are 10 suggestions from *Random Acts of Kindness*, co-edited by Dawna Markova, Ph.D.

1. **Praise good work.** When an employee at a business does something helpful for us, write the person's boss to thank the boss for having such a wonderful employee.
2. **Brighten a day.** Select someone's name at random from the phone book and send the person a card.
3. **Make a memory.** Carry an instant-photo camera, then photograph strangers and give them the pictures.
4. **Clean the street.** Make a habit of picking up the first piece of trash that we see each day.
5. **Feed the flock.** Keep birdseed in the car on winter days and scatter it for birds.
6. **Thank a teacher.** Write a letter to teachers we once had and tell them that they made a difference in our lives.
7. **Purchase a pick-me-up.** Buy a mail-order gift anonymously for a friend or someone at work whose spirits need a lift.
8. **Share the wealth.** When going through a tollbooth, pay for the next car in line.
9. **Donate a dolly.** Have our children sort through their toys and pick some that they'd like to donate to children in need.
10. **Teach the children.** Visit our children's schools, explain what random acts of kindness are, and ask the kids to create books listing all the kind acts that they've done and that were done for them.

we are invited to love it. "Loving kindness is what knits us to one another, creates community out of the disparate parts that are our individual humanity."

Put another way, "Kindness is a matter of doing not what life requires us to do but what our souls invite us to do," says Dawna Markova, Ph.D., co-editor of *Random Acts of Kindness* and author of *No Enemies Within*. "We give to another person not out of a sense of obligation but out of a sense of compassion and connection, of feeling a kinship with that person, such that we can't not do for them."

# Nurturing Compassion

So kindness is an important thing, a good thing. We know that. But how do we develop our capacity for kindness, especially if it's not something that comes naturally to us? Here are a few suggestions.

**Start small.** Small gestures are a great place to begin, says Dr. Markova in *Random Acts of Kindness*. Even something as simple as planting a tree for everyone in the neighborhood to enjoy or letting another driver have an available parking spot are worthy acts.

**Help kids.** It's easy for children to feel left out or disrespected in an overly adult world, says Dr. Markova. "So sometimes, I'll walk down the street in my town and stick comic books in kids' bike baskets or give out balloons to little ones. It doesn't really matter what you do for children; what's important is that you find a gesture that helps you keep them in your daily thoughts. I suspect that it lifts their days a little bit. I know it lifts mine."

**Practice at home.** In order to avoid taking a spouse for granted, we can spend a few minutes together each night, suggests Dr. Markova, and take turns telling each other at least one reason why we are glad we're married.

**Listen.** Simply listening can be an expression of kindness, particularly if the people to whom we're listening are in distress. We may not always be able to help people solve problems, but we can assure them that they're not riding out the problems alone.

Morrison recalls having read a story that clearly illustrates this suggestion. Once in the dead of night, noted Austrian psychologist Victor Frankl received a telephone call from a distraught stranger who

# Faithbuilders

## The Glory of Giving

"The Sea of Galilee and the Dead Sea are made of the same water. It flows down, clear and cool, from the heights of Hermon and the roots of the cedars of Lebanon. The Sea of Galilee makes beauty of it, for the Sea of Galilee has an outlet. It gets to give. It gathers in its riches that it may pour them out again to fertilize the Jordan plain. But the Dead Sea with the same water makes horror. For the Dead Sea has no outlet. It gets to keep."

*—The Reverend Harry Emerson Fosdick, founding minister of New York City's Riverside Church, talking about serving others*

was on the verge of killing herself. "Frankl, being a good clinician, kept the woman on the phone for as long as he could, tried to offer reassuring words, tried probing for the roots of her despair, and finally got her to agree to see him the next day. He hung up the phone not knowing if she would indeed make it through the night," says Morrison.

To Frankl's delight, she did, and when he asked her what it was he said on the phone that kept her from killing herself, she answered that nothing he said really made much of a difference to her. It was the mere fact that at one o'clock in the morning, he would spend two hours on the phone with her, a complete stranger, that assured her that all was not lost.

## Loving Those Who Are Difficult to Like

There's another level of kindness: the type that we extend to people who aren't so easy to love. It might be a disagreeable neighbor who never seems to have a pleasant thing to say, a homeless person that we see each day on our way to work, or someone at work who has done something cruel. They, too, deserve our kindness, as the Bible makes clear. In the Scriptures, there are many examples of people extending kindness to strangers and even enemies. Consider Pharaoh's daughter rescuing Moses, Nehemiah restoring the fortunes of exiled Jews, and Jesus healing the centurion's slave.

How can we follow the example of these biblical figures and extend kindness to those whom it's difficult to like? Here are some ideas.

**Write a simple note.** If someone like the cranky neighbor or mean co-worker is more or less unapproachable in person, we can sit down and write them a compassionate letter, Dr. Markova recommends, and make it anonymous if we wish. Just let them know that we're simply thinking of them.

**Adopt a stranger.** Contact a social-service provider and get the name of one person or family who could be helped by a few extra dollars each month and send it to them on a regular basis, suggests Norma Rolson, director of social services for New York City's Riverside Church. Establish a direct relationship or simply funnel the funds through the provider.

**Keep it short-term.** Don't feel that the kindness we extend to difficult people obligates us to a lifelong friendship, says Dr. Markova. Think of it as a gesture of compassion, not a statement of commitment.

**Carry a reminder.** If we're stepping into situations where kindness will not come easily, we can feel closer to God's love by carrying something tangible, perhaps a rosary, an amulet, or even a photograph of someone we love as a reminder that God is with us, says Helen Hunt, collaborator with her husband, Harry, on *On the Nature of Consciousness*.

Helen Hunt offers an example: "Our daughter had had some rough encounters with a neighborhood bully. We discussed the situation as a family, talking about how, by considering the pain in this bully's life, she could rethink her feelings toward him. The next day, she went to school with a small religious medal in her pocket, which she would reach for and rub between her fingers for reassurance that God was with her. When she got to school, she steered clear of that bully and did not allow herself to be the brunt of his anger. But more than that, by keeping her distance, she could contemplate the pain in his life and gradually turn her anger into compassion."

# Prayer Pointers

## A Prayer for Benevolence

Lord,
Make me an instrument of Your peace.
Where there is hatred let me sow love;
Where there is injury, pardon;
Where there is doubt, faith;
Where there is despair, hope;
Where there is darkness, light; and
Where there is sadness, joy.
O Divine Master,
grant that I may not so much
Seek to be consoled as to console;
To be understood as to understand;
To be loved as to love;
For it is in giving that we receive;
It is in pardoning that we are pardoned; and
It is in dying that we are born to eternal life.

—*Saint Francis of Assisi*

# Doing Well by Doing Good

The fruits of kindness are a blessing not only on the people who receive them. We, too, can enjoy our good works. They help us feel connected to others, which helps us feel like part of the family of God, says Dr. Markova, who remembers one particularly meaningful example. "While working with a street gang in Pittsburgh, my group got the gang to agree to do something kind for a stranger," she recalls. "They chose a woman who lived on the street. Every night, the woman would sneak down to an abandoned basement and eat whatever scraps of food that she had collected on the street. One night, the kids sneaked down before she did and laid out a complete banquet, a real feast, candles and all. She was so touched that she wept, and they said that they never felt so connected to another human being in their lives. It was so good for everyone."

As Rabbi Abraham Twerski, M.D., a psychiatrist in Pittsburgh and author of *Do Unto Others*, says, "When I eat bread, I have but a single pleasure . . . when I give of my bread to the hungry, my pleasure is doubled. Long after my appetite has been satiated, I can enjoy having provided relief to another person's distress."

# Loneliness

~ ✦ ~

## A DEMON THAT WON'T LET GO

*W*hat is loneliness?

"It's a sleepless night that never ends, spent in front of a telephone that never rings, waiting for a sun that never comes up."

"It's a numbing nothingness, neither warm nor cool, as though all my nerve endings have gone limp, and the only thing that reminds me I'm alive is the inconsolable ache that I feel in my heart."

"Loneliness is the rest of the choir singing 'Joyful, Joyful We Adore Thee' and me welling up inside, finding it absolutely impossible to connect to the words, let alone sing them."

There are few things more poignant, more wrenching than being caught in a web of loneliness, as these testimonies from three parishioners at New York City's Riverside Church attest. Loneliness can leave us drained, defeated, weary, and depressed. It can rob us of motivation. And, says Joan Kavanaugh, doctor of ministry and director of the Riverside Church pastoral counseling center, "in a culture such as ours that puts such a premium on relationships, we also feel ashamed, as though it is some kind of stigma, a sign of personal failure. The refrain that I hear so often from people I treat is, 'What's *wrong* with me?'"

There isn't necessarily anything wrong, says Dr. Kavanaugh. There is no reason to feel ashamed. Loneliness is a normal, even an expected part of a full life. And once we understand this, once we understand what causes loneliness, we can take steps to find our way out.

# The Root of the Problem

The first step in overcoming loneliness is realizing what it isn't, says the Reverend Alison Boden, master of divinity and dean of Rockefeller Chapel at the University of Chicago. "It isn't simply a state of being alone. In fact, we can find ourselves feeling terribly lonely even when we're surrounded by others just as easily as we can find ourselves quite content and fulfilled when we have only ourselves to keep us company," she says.

If loneliness can occur even in a crowd, then what triggers it? It could be some loss, like the death of a loved one, the breakup of a relationship, or a child leaving home. And it could be a chronic condition that stays with us, says Dr. Kavanaugh, "like gum stuck to the sole of a shoe. The unifying theme for both is that it is a profound sense of alienation, disconnection, not belonging, or not feeling a part of a loving community."

Regardless of how universal it is, loneliness is a condition that most of us would rather live without. So what do we do when we encounter it in our own lives, when, to play on Dr. Kavanaugh's words, loneliness sticks to our souls? Try some of these tips.

**Listen to loneliness.** Figure out why it's there. It's providing a warning that something's not right, and we need to heed that warning, says Dr. Kavanaugh. "When we're lonely, we no longer trust in the security and durability of loving relationships, including our relationships with God, so we don't let anyone get too close to us," she says. "By exploring where our loneliness originates, we can grow beyond our suspicions and dare to trust again."

Dr. Kavanaugh says that we can begin examining our loneliness by writing up a list of the important people in our lives and then next to each name writing one word that characterizes the current state of the relationship, one word or phrase describing where we want that relationship to go, one word or phrase describing what we might be doing to prevent the relationship from getting there, and one word or phrase describing what we can do to move it along. For example, we might write the word *spouse* and use the word *distance* to characterize the relationship. Then, we might describe our goal with the word *intimacy* and use the phrase *afraid to talk* to describe what's preventing the intimacy. Finally, after analyzing this string, we might use the phrase *risk showing my real feelings* to describe one possible solution.

**Don't fight it, join it.** One of the great fears with loneliness is that it will grow and overwhelm us. It doesn't have to play out that way, says the Reverend Marc Mullinax, Ph.D., pastor of the Bedford Park Presbyterian Church in the Bronx and assistant professor of religious studies at Iona College in New Rochelle, New York, whose courses address the issue of religion and loneliness. "Our immediate impulse is to lash out, to resist it. But with loneliness, I think that we're better served when we permit ourselves to explore its roots and trust that it won't devour us," he says.

"One way to draw close to this idea is by meditating on the fourth verse of the twenty-third Psalm: 'Even though I walk through the valley of the shadow of death, I fear no evil, for Thou art with me.' Repeat this verse, over and over. Live with it for a while. Visualize it. Make a list of what we see strewn about in our shadowed valleys. And list evidence of God's presence there with us. It allows our hands to be open in prayerful supplication rather than clenched in angry defiance," says Dr. Mullinax.

**Find strength in God.** Even when things seem loneliest for us, we can take solace from knowing that God is always there as a friend and guide. Job learned that lesson, though he did go through a period of doubt along the way. "Here was a guy who believed that as long as he prospered God was close to him, but as soon as calamity befell him, he was sure that he'd been abandoned," says Dr. Kavanaugh. "Only when he suffered through his torment, presented himself to God, and heard God's answer did he learn that no matter what his lot, God was with him. He was never alone. That's strong testimony."

**Find God in good works.** We draw closer to God by drawing closer to one another, says Dr. Mullinax, by placing a phone call to a long-lost relative, by spending a day at a local drop-in center for troubled kids, or by shoveling snow for an elderly neighbor. These tasks are not only worthwhile in and of themselves but are also good for us because they connect us with people.

# Prayer Pointers

## Building Bonds through Prayer

If we're turning to prayer to alleviate loneliness, one of the best things we can do is pray in groups, says Joan Kavanaugh, doctor of ministry and director of the Riverside Church pastoral counseling center in New York City. When we pray out loud with others, we feel a bond with other group members, a sense of commonness of need and commonness of faith. That is often the first step toward overcoming the feelings of isolation and alienation that accompany loneliness, she says. Also, the prayers that are offered up by others often mirror our own concerns, and there's comfort in knowing that we're not the only ones who experience loneliness.

In addition, members of prayer circles can show enormous empathy for one another, as the concerns of one individual become the "common property" of the entire group. To find a prayer group, Dr. Kavanaugh advises asking at churches, pastoral counseling centers, or clergy associations.

In a similar vein, praying alone but out loud instead of in silence can help us articulate and clarify the amorphous feelings attendant to loneliness, says Dr. Kavanaugh. This aids the process of prayer as self-exploration.

**Find intimacy through prayer.** Prayer, says Dr. Kavanaugh, helps us "go deeper into ourselves. We can ask God for the power to discern how we might be unwittingly encouraging loneliness and what power we have to cope with it or see ourselves through it."

**Find intimacy through outreach.** Praying can be an effective treatment for loneliness, but it works best if we use it as a bridge to others, says Elizabeth Tener, a social worker and pastoral counselor at the Blanton-Peale Institute in New York City, a counseling and training center founded by the late Reverend Dr. Norman Vincent

Peale. God often works through others to answer our prayers, but we're usually the ones who have to take the steps to make it happen. So by all means, we should pray, she says, but then we should find someone to talk to, be it a friend or professional counselor. We need to share feelings with them and develop an intimacy. Even though we may not feel like it at first, we should make the effort to join a group, church, or club that has similar interests or problems as we do. We need to get out among people.

**Be open to change.** Lonely people are often fearful and quick to find fault with themselves and others. To help overcome these feelings, Tener recommends beginning each day with this simple prayer: "Lord, keep my heart gentle, open, and receptive to others."

# Letting Loneliness Weave Its Course

There's an old story about a young man whose frustrated prayer went like this: "God, give me patience, and give it to me right now!" We're sure to feel a sense of urgency when we're lonely. But we must accept that curing the problem will take time. And, says Tener, when we pray, "we need to know what not to expect. One of my patients was terribly lonely because she had a very difficult time getting close to people. She prayed, 'God, give me friends!' She was literally seeking divine intervention, a bolt from the blue. For her, learning to pray meant learning how to ask God's help in discovering what *she* had to do to relieve her loneliness."

"In the end, of course," as Dr. Mullinax observes, "none of us is immune to loneliness. This is a good thing, really, because it confirms that it is a necessary part of life, that it doesn't make us odd, it makes us human. And it teaches us that we can survive it, even grow from it. I think of Psalm 13, which begins, 'How long, O Lord? Wilt Thou forget me forever?' and ends with, 'I will sing to the Lord, because he has dealt bountifully with me.' (NIV) This is our journey, from the first verse to the last, through loneliness, in prayer, to God."

# Loss

## COPING WITH THE VOID INSIDE

We feel empty, incomplete, unsure, and sometimes utterly lonely when we suffer a loss. We may feel cheated, robbed, angry at ourselves, angry at others, and angry at God. We may be heartbroken. We may cry frequently and unexpectedly.

This is all perfectly okay, all perfectly natural, says the Reverend James E. Miller, doctor of ministry, United Methodist minister of Willowgreen Productions in Fort Wayne, Indiana, a center that helps those experiencing grief and loss, and author of numerous books and videotapes used in hospices, hospitals, funeral homes, and counseling services. These are the things that we feel when we lose.

Lose what? A loved one, a job, a home, a dream, honor and self-esteem, a best friend, our savings, a marriage, our health, our mobility, or anything that we deem vital and important to our existence. We lose it, we grieve. We sink into some form of despair. This is normal. And so is loss.

## Accepting the Inevitable

Feeling victimized when we suffer loss or believing that losses ought not happen in life is a trap, says the Reverend Mel Lawrenz, Ph.D., senior associate pastor at Elmbrook Church and director of the Elmbrook Christian Study Center, both in Brookfield, Wisconsin, and co-author of six books, including *Life after Grief* and *Overcoming Grief and Trauma*. "The Bible indicates pretty clearly that it's not a matter of ought and ought not." Yes, he says, we may feel slapped down and insulted when we suffer a loss. "But that is the way this world is."

Dr. Lawrenz continues: "Jesus says, 'In the world you will have tribulation; but be of good cheer, I have overcome the world.'" (John 16:33 NKJV) "I've seen people really benefit from grabbing hold of that. Jesus is saying, 'Trouble is inevitable in this world, but I am bigger than this world, and if you attach yourself to Me, I'll help you ride it out.' It's like you're out in the ocean and there's a severe storm that comes up. Don't deny the fact that there's a storm there, but if you're in a good, secure ship, you'll get through the storm."

Fortunately, says Dr. Lawrenz, trauma and loss, while inevitable, are rarely frequent visitors. They are not constants. They are not the norm. That's the big picture, and it's an important perspective to hold in mind when we are flailing in the depths of loss.

Yes, loss is inevitable. But, Dr. Lawrenz reminds, our culture tries to deny it. It encourages us to bury it as quickly as possible and to shield children from its reality. He's not sure that this is healthy for anyone. It's particularly unhealthy for children, he believes, especially when it comes to dealing with death. "We don't bring children to funerals. We wait until they're adolescents or older. So they never see people mourning, and they have unrealistic expectations. Our culture encourages unrealistic expectations in regard to loss. Somebody ends up sick in the hospital and if the doctor can't cure him, they are shocked because the expectation is that doctors are supposed to cure anything," he says.

"In many other cultures, and certainly in biblical culture, death is accepted as a part of the reality of life. And nobody tries to tell somebody else that we will hold on to every last breath that we can no matter what it takes," says Dr. Lawrenz. People have a tendency to take that approach if they have no hope of any positive existence beyond this life, beyond this body. But throughout the Bible, we find promises of life eternal. "God will redeem my life from the grave; He will surely take me to Himself." (Psalm 49:15 NIV)

## Does God Care?

At the time of loss, it is easy to cry out to God, as did Jesus while He was being crucified: "My God, My God, why has Thou forsaken Me?"

Did Jesus really believe that God had forsaken Him?

The Bible has many examples of saints and prophets—and in this case, even Jesus—who wondered if God had abandoned them, says the Reverend Mel Lawrenz, Ph.D., senior associate pastor at Elmbrook Church and director of the Elmbrook Christian Study Center, both in Brookfield, Wisconsin, and co-author of six books, including *Life after Grief* and *Overcoming Grief and Trauma*. He thinks that those examples are in the Bible to show us that God understands that at times we will feel that way. "But the flip side is that our losses are not going to be easier to bear if we come to believe that there is no God. Those questions come up, but becoming an atheist doesn't make the losses any easier to deal with."

Usually, when people are asking that question, they are really throwing themselves on God's mercy, says Dr. Lawrenz. They are saying, "God, just help me, whatever way you can. I am wiped out." Then, when they look back, maybe 10 years later, they realize that God did help them and offer some sustaining grace, says Dr. Lawrenz. It may have been "a friend who came along or someone who didn't have any answers but was there to support them. Or maybe it was something that they read. And they'll say, 'I just cannot believe what a blessing that person was who was there' or 'This little booklet/this book/this part of my Bible got me through.'"

Yes, says Dr. Lawrenz, we may question God's intentions, but we should never give up hope. Because even in the darkest moments, hope can pull us through a loss.

A faith perspective, a Christian perspective, accepts that death is inevitable, Dr. Lawrenz says. But death is not the end. The spiritual perception is that "death is a doorway. This is not to say that we should precipitate our own deaths or look for them prematurely, but we should live our lives with the acceptance of death's inevitability and the hope for eternal life," he says. "My health fails; my spirits droop, yet God remains! He is the strength of my heart; He is mine forever!" (Psalm 73:26 TLB)

# A Path to New Experiences

Loss is a doorway. It is an opportunity to discover what God has in store for us next, if we're willing to seek.

Loss could mean many things. It could be that someone we have trusted implicitly violates the trust. We will be hurt. We will grieve. We will be angry. It could be that a fire destroys all pictures and mementos of our deceased parents and grandparents. It could be a loss of honor or respect. It could be a material loss. It could be the loss of youth. It could be the loss associated with broken or unfulfilled dreams. It could be "a mother waving good-bye to her kid getting on the school bus for the first time, starting kindergarten," adds Dr. Lawrenz. "If you talk to almost any mother, she'll say that she cried at that moment because the little kid was growing up and there was a little bit of a loss there. It was good, but it was a loss."

"Loss is loss is loss is loss," says lecturer and ordained Episcopalian priest Harold Ivan Smith, doctor of ministry, who leads grief gatherings at St. Luke's Medical Center in Kansas City, Missouri, and is the author of many Christian self-help books. What may seem trivial to one person may be a profound loss to another. There is no official scale by which we can gauge how someone should experience loss, Dr. Smith says. We should never trivialize another person's loss. Instead, we should ask him to tell us about it. And we should try to feel it with him. Don't give advice; just listen and empathize. That's the best way to comfort someone who has suffered a loss, he says.

Remember, Jesus says, "Blessed are they that mourn: for they shall be comforted." (Matthew 5:4 KJV) Our job, when we see someone who is mourning a loss, is to comfort him, suggest pastoral counselors.

# Growing beyond Our Pain

We should turn to our faith at the time of a loss if for no other reason than to find the courage to seek out the help that we need to cope with it effectively, says John W. James, grief educator, co-founder of the Grief Recovery Institute in Beverly Hills, California, and co-author of *The Grief Recovery Handbook*. Here are some ways to get a handle on the volcano of emotions that erupt and overtake us when we experience loss.

**Dive in.** Immersing ourselves in the swirling emotions and confusion and facing what we are feeling are musts if we are to heal. Farther down the road, we can look for meaning and value, recommends Dr. Miller.

**Talk to God.** "Pray in whatever way you're able to at that time," says Dr. Lawrenz. "If it is personal, open, spontaneous prayer in solitude, great. If you're really at a low point and don't even know what to say to God, then pick up somebody else's prayer and read it to God. Read the Psalms out of the Old Testament. Or read hymns or find one of the many devotional prayer books that are available and let somebody else put the words in your mouth." It may be, he says, that no single verse or passage will soothe the sting of the loss, but in the process of reading and meditating on the words, we may well begin to sense God's presence.

"Keeping a conversation with God ongoing keeps that channel open for you to receive faith, hope, and love from Him," says Dr. Lawrenz.

**Reach out.** Find someone to talk to, advise counselors. Not someone who wants to sermonize or save us from grief or fix us, just someone who will listen with love and caring.

**Enjoy a treat.** From time to time, we should indulge in little things that bring us pleasure, advises Dr. Miller. What sorts of things? Maybe a vase of fresh flowers. Maybe an evening out. A new shirt or blouse. A book we've been wanting to read. Get the idea?

**Seek vibrance.** Mingle with people who refresh and recharge us, those people we enjoy. Avoid those who bring us down or drain us.

**Take a chance.** Go ahead and learn new things; try something different. "That's a sign that rebirth is working its way into our lives," says Dr. Miller.

**Help out.** Do little things for others. Our lives feel more meaningful when we can have a positive effect on someone else's, notes Dr. Miller.

**Look for humor.** No matter how heavy our predicaments, our hearts, or our days, we are, after all, just silly humans. Surely, we do some things that we can laugh at and that others will laugh about, too, when we tell them. We need to lighten up when we can. Smile at ourselves. Forgive ourselves. Lightening our load this way is truly healing, says Dr. Miller.

**Write it down.** Record feelings in a private journal. Keep track

# Across the Aisles

## Comforting Words

In Jewish tradition, when a person grieves a loss, they recite a group of 10 Psalms: Psalms 16, 32, 41, 42, 59, 77, 90, 105, 137, and 150. They repeat them over and over, says lecturer and ordained Episcopalian priest Harold Ivan Smith, doctor of ministry, who leads grief gatherings at St. Luke's Medical Center in Kansas City, Missouri, and is the author of many Christian self-help books. The 10 Psalms are beautiful prayers and offer much consolation and perspective. Here is one of them, Psalm 41, from the New King James Version, as an example.

> Blessed is he who considers the poor; The Lord will deliver him in time of trouble.
> The Lord will preserve him and keep him alive, And he will be blessed on the Earth; You will not deliver him to the will of his enemies.
> The Lord will strengthen him on his bed of illness; You will sustain him on his sickbed.
> I said, "Lord, be merciful to me; Heal my soul, for I have sinned against You."

of the thinking that's going on, the internal dialogue. And after a few weeks, go back over it and notice how it is changing and evolving. This is evidence that we are growing and learning, and it's reassuring, says Dr. Miller.

**Own it.** Accept the pain. If we deny it, chances are that we won't move beyond it, says Dr. Miller.

**Keep an open mind.** Maybe we can learn something or gain something from this terrible experience, even if we have no clue what that might be. The converse is to decide that this is nothing but a nega-

My enemies speak evil of me: "When will he die, and his name perish?"

And if he comes to see me, he speaks lies; His heart gathers iniquity to itself; When he goes out, he tells it.

All who hate me whisper together against me; Against me they devise my hurt.

"An evil disease," they say, "clings to him. And now that he lies down, he will rise up no more."

Even my own familiar friend in whom I trusted, who ate my bread, has lifted up his heel against me.

But You, O Lord, be merciful to me, and raise me up, that I may repay them.

By this I know that You are well pleased with me, because my enemy does not triumph over me.

As for me, You uphold me in my integrity, And set me before Your face forever.

Blessed be the Lord God of Israel from everlasting to everlasting! Amen and Amen.

# Answered Prayers

## The Holy Spirit Helped Me Accept Death

My husband and I had been happily married for 34 years and had just built a new home when he died suddenly. My whole world was turned upside down.

I have been a Christian all my life. I believe that the Holy Spirit came to me, and I felt this supernatural faith and comfort. God reached down, took my hand, and assured me that eventually, everything would be okay.

I've learned to trust God, minute by minute, hour by hour, day by day.

I think that we have two choices: We can pitch our tents in grief, or we can choose life. I have chosen life and with my faith and with God by my side, life is going to be beautiful.

—*Linda Keyser, Eugene, Oregon*

tive influence in our lives. The latter attitude is crippling, notes Dr. Miller.

**Endure and grow stronger.** If we choose to grow stronger, chances are that we will, says Dr. Miller. The key is to make the positive choice. So often when feeling down, we are tempted to believe that we'll never get better. Such a prophecy can be self-fulfilling.

**Allow others to help.** Let them offer support and come closer. The other option is to keep people away, which can increase loneliness and isolation and feelings of mistrust and sadness. Dr. Miller thinks that recognizing and appreciating the strength of companionship and community is the better choice.

**Keep an eye on attitude and approach.** How we go through an experience of profound loss—whether a disgrace, a heartbreak, a death, a physical loss, a material loss, loss of love, loss of a loved one, loss of reputation, loss of security, loss of home and hearth, loss of money, loss of trust, or a profound loss of any type—the attitude that we take as we experience the loss determines to a great extent how well we will heal, how fully we will bounce back, and how well we will move on, says Dr. Miller. We need to be aware that we are making those choices.

**Develop spiritual aspects.** We need to do this even if we feel uncomfortable doing it. We all have our own ways and needs. And some of us refuse to admit, even to ourselves, that we do have spiritual aspects; a part of us that questions and considers the bigger, more transcendent picture—the mysteries of life. But getting in touch with that aspect of self really seems to help us grow through a loss experience, says Dr. Miller.

How can we do that? We might set aside time for daily periods of prayer or meditation. We might make time to read inspirational or spiritual writings. We might record our journeys in a journal—our faith and our doubts and how they've evolved through the years, suggests Dr. Miller. We might go on a spiritual retreat for an hour, a day, or a week and spend time in solitude and contemplation. Sort of *Thoreau* ourselves upon God and the universe and see how they respond. See what we notice. See what we learn.

While going through and recovering from loss, we may find ourselves in a period of questioning, anger, hurt, confusion, and lots of conflicting, alternating emotions and thoughts, according to James. That's why it may be a time to explore and learn about our spiritual cores, to seek what's really important to us and important in this life.

# The Sun Also Rises

It is important to realize, while in the midst of the dark night of loss, that we still have some control, that we do choose how we will experience this terrible and terrifying experience, says James. And those of us who choose to accept it, feel it, and experience it as fully as possible and believe that we will grow, learn, and become stronger from that process are the most likely to move forward productively and grow from the experience spiritually. "Part of this growth comes from taking action to help ourselves complete the pain. We can't expect pain of loss to go away by itself or expect God to take the pain away. Sadness is normal. We must look to our spirituality and ask God to give us the strength to take the actions to work through it," says James.

Yes, we do have some control. And one of the lessons that we learn as we experience loss and exercise control is that life is bigger than us. It's mysterious, full of surprise, full of change, won't fit in a box, won't be confined and, ultimately, is beyond our control in many ways. When we come to accept that, we learn to appreciate the bit of control that we do have and the utter hugeness, the mind-boggling magnitude of this gift of life that God has given us.

For related advice, see Death of a Loved One (page 200), Defeat (page 211) and Grief (page 290).

# *Love*

## More Than Emotion, It's an Action

They're everywhere—on TV, in advertisements, the movies, the romance novels—couples locked in all manner of passionate embrace. In fact, watching 50 hours of television a week (the national average) exposes us to more than 14,000 or more images of sexual behavior and innuendo a year.

But who would confuse what these couples on TV are doing with real love?

Romance and attraction are important parts of developing relationships and maintaining loving marriages. But "the tingles" are just that: part of a much larger package that makes marital love last, says Gary Chapman, Ph.D, director of adult education at Calvary Baptist Church in Winston-Salem, North Carolina, and author of *The Five Love Languages* and *Loving Solutions*.

In fact, whether we're trying to develop or maintain a loving relationship with our spouse, our children, or even a friend, the real key is learning that love is an attitude and a behavior rather than just a feeling whipped by the ever-changing winds of our emotions, says Dr. Chapman.

In other words, love is something that we need to choose to *do*—even when events may make it difficult to love the other person.

# News from the Love Lab

Several studies conducted at the University of Washington in Seattle help underscore the power of being loving—especially when we disagree. Researchers found that when couples discussed issues that were clearly sources of conflict, the couples with the strongest love relationships were affectionate, appreciative, and accepting. Not only that, they joked, shared their joy, and demonstrated concern. And if they said something that hurt, they tried to repair the damage, according to John Gottman, Ph.D., professor of psychology at the University of Washington, co-director of the Seattle Marital and Family Institute, and author of *Why Marriages Succeed or Fail*. On the other hand, those couples headed for divorce were sarcastic, emotionally uninvolved, and defensive.

Although designed to investigate why some marriages work and others fail, the research seems to confirm what we already know: People are drawn to relationships in which people act lovingly and are poised to bolt from those where they don't.

But running isn't an option from our friends, kids, even spouses. We're supposed to model what's known as agape love, a selfless love in which we'll go the extra mile or two or three or whatever it takes for the other person. It's Christ-like love, probably best reflected in this passage, often read at weddings as a sort of marching order for both bride and groom: "Love is patient, love is kind. It does not envy, it does not boast, it is not proud. It is not rude, it is not self-seeking, it is not easily angered, it keeps no record of wrongs. Love does not delight in evil but rejoices with the truth. It always protects, always trusts, always hopes, always perseveres. Love never fails. . . . " (1 Corinthians 13:4–8 NIV)

Loving people when they treat us well isn't much of a challenge. But loving them always? What about when someone has hurt us or let us down? "To start with, Christ-like love treats small offenses as just that: small," says the Reverend Steven Estes, senior pastor of Community Evangelical Free Church in Elverson, Pennsylvania, and co-author of *When God Weeps*.

"Christ-like love gives people the benefit of the doubt. It says, 'Hmmm, she certainly was curt with me in the elevator this morning, but maybe she has a headache, or got some scary results from a medical test last night, or her marriage isn't going well, so I'll assume the best about her,'" says Reverend Estes.

"This is what the Bible means when it says that 'love covers over a multitude of sins,'" says Reverend Estes. (1 Peter 4:8) "As we go through life, we jostle each other with our elbows all the time and thus, shouldn't take everything so personally."

What if our spouses or friends are caught in abuse, addiction, or adultery or have abandoned us? Probably the most loving things that we can do are draw some firm boundaries to try to influence their behavior and demand that they seek professional help. But, again, that's just part of the answer.

"When we're in difficult marriages, there is always something that we can do," says Dr. Chapman. "The question is, what can we do for the benefit of our spouses in difficult situations? If we can find what is best for our spouses and do it, it's going to help our marriages. Love always helps. It's the most powerful weapon for good that there is in the world." .

Here are some suggestions to help our love flow more freely.

**Tap God's love.** The biblical answer is simple but toweringly profound, says Pastor Estes: "Be kind and compassionate to one another, forgiving each other, just as in Christ God forgave you." (Ephesians 4:32 NIV)

"God loved us enough to bleed on a cross for us, even though our sins were a slap in His face," Pastor Estes says. "So how can we hold grudges against anyone?"

**Ask Him to change us.** Often, we want God to change the other person and their annoying habits and insensitivity. "But we're better off if we ask God to change us," says Dr. Gottman. "When we come to a problem and we both say, 'I see my part in this and I own up to it,' we can solve that problem much more easily."

**Practice reality living.** Reality living means taking responsibility for our own thoughts, feelings, and actions rather than believing that they are somehow dictated by our circumstances, says Dr. Chapman. From Helen Keller to Franklin Delano Roosevelt, people have chosen to overcome their disabilities. And if we have bad marriages or friendships on the rocks, we need to take responsibility for our share of the problem. Another tenant of reality living, he says, is recognizing that we can't change others, but we can influence them positively.

**Go to the other guy.** "Who is more likely to point out the dandruff on your shoulders, an enemy or a friend?" asks Pastor Estes. "A friend, of course, because he loves you. The Bible says, 'Do not hate your brother in your heart. Rebuke your neighbor frankly. . . .' (Leviticus 19:17 NIV) If you truly love somebody, you'll do this privately, gently, and humbly, but you will do it."

# The Four Horsemen of the Apocalypse

What can predict the demise of a marriage with 90 percent accuracy?

The persistent presence of four faulty communication habits ominously nicknamed "the four horsemen of the apocalypse."

To prevent marital disaster—or, for that matter, problems with any relationship—we need to avoid the following habits when we argue and replace them with healthier communication, says John Gottman, Ph.D., professor of psychology at the University of Washington in Seattle, co-director of the Seattle Marital and Family Institute, and author of *Why Marriages Succeed or Fail*.

*The first horseman: criticism.* "This is a global statement that there is something wrong with the partner's personality," says Dr. Gottman.

*Example:* "What is wrong with you? You are just emotionally unavailable to me."

A *better approach:* "I feel like I'm last on your list of people, and I'm getting kind of lonely."

*The second horseman: defensiveness.* "This is often a response to criticism. And although it appears quite innocent, denying responsibility puts the blame on the other partner," says Dr. Gottman.

*Example:* "I'm not emotionally unavailable. You are the one who never listens to me. I tried to talk to you about some problems that I was having at work and you weren't even there."

A *better approach:* "I'm sorry you feel that way. I've been so busy, maybe I have been neglecting you. What can we do to solve the problem?"

*The third horseman: contempt.* "This is your standard, direct insult," says Dr. Gottman.

**Tear down the wall.** Left untreated, even minor grievances can harden into walls between us and our loved ones, says Dr. Chapman. We begin knocking them down and restoring our relationships when we choose to forgive or ask forgiveness. If we're the ones being

*Example:* "You're a blockhead and your mother is a blockhead!"

Also damaging are facial expressions of contempt, says Dr. Gottman. They may seem harmless to us but, like insults, they are demeaning. In fact, he says, research shows that attitudes of contempt can damage a person's health. "A contemptuous husband can wind up having a sick wife. And a contemptuous wife can have a physically sick husband if he gets lonely in the marriage."

*A better approach:* We should never insult our mates. Instead, our goal should be to build them up by praising the qualities in them that we like. And when the urge to insult comes to mind, we should stop short and refocus on a specific concern as outlined in the discussion of criticism.

**The fourth horseman: stonewalling/withdrawal.** "This is often a male response to heightened conflict, and it's kind of an emotional withdrawal from the marriage," says Dr. Gottman.

*Example:* Silence.

"Stonewallers don't gives cues that they're listening—there's no eye contact, they won't move their faces, and there aren't any vocalizations," he says.

*A better approach:* Instead of clamming up, we need to express our feelings without blaming or criticizing the other person.

For example, we can say, "I really get frustrated and concerned about our future when we don't stick to our spending plan. How would you like to go over it together and try to make some adjustments so that we can achieve our financial goals?"

asked to do the forgiving, we should recall what Jesus told Peter when Peter asked how many times we're supposed to forgive. Jesus answered, "I tell you, not seven times, but seventy-seven times." (Matthew 18:22 NIV)

**Ask some questions.** Instead of asking, "What have you done for me lately?" we need to ask, "How can I help you?" We have

# Answered Prayers

### Friends' Love and Prayers Saved My Life

"A sharp, sudden pain behind my right eye. Extreme nausea. A need to lie down. My friends and one of my roommates said, 'We need to get you to a hospital right away!' I kept saying that I only wanted to lie down.

"I lay in bed and prayed hard: "God, I'm scared. Help me. Let Thy will be done." Within minutes, I was unconscious. An ambulance took me to an emergency room and from there, I was flown to a hospital that specialized in head trauma. The doctors told my family and friends that I had arterial venous malformation (the brain and arteries meet in a malformed way), and it had ruptured suddenly. They said that 95 percent of the patients with this diagnosis die.

"My roommate called our Catholic priest. He told the choir, which was practicing, to pray for me. Three days later, I received the last sacraments. But hours later, to the shock of the medical staff, I woke up.

"The hospital was my home for the next month, and the recovery process continues to this day. But I am convinced that my prayers and the prayers from my good friends, loved ones, and my religious community were heard and granted."

—*Nancy McLaughlin, Phoenix*

to make the choice to look out for the other person's interests, says Dr. Chapman, no matter how the person may have angered or hurt us.

## Learning a New Language

Ever tried ordering food in a restaurant where no one speaks our language? Not only is it frustrating but it's rare that we get what we want. For some of the same reasons, we need to learn how to speak the "love language" of those we care about. Dr. Chapman says that there are five basic love languages.

*Words of affirmation.* Plain and simple, this is praise—for what someone has done, what they're wearing, whatever. "A good solid word of affirmation may carry someone for a week at a time. But others may want and need to hear one every day," Dr. Chapman says.

*Quality time.* The trick here, Dr. Chapman says, is making sure that we give our undivided attention. "We can be doing lots of things with the person: playing a game, taking a walk, or sitting down and just talking. The important thing isn't what we're doing, it's that they have our attention."

*Giving gifts.* No need to search the Neiman Marcus catalogue—even a flower from the garden may do, Dr. Chapman says. "The old saying is: It's the thought that counts. But it's not the thought that is left in your head. It's the gift that came out of the thought," he says.

*Acts of service.* From cooking a meal to hanging wallpaper, loving actions can score big points. We just need to make sure that we're doing the right act of service. "We may be expending a lot of time and energy painting the bedroom, but the person is not going to see that as very loving if they wanted us to paint the front door," says Dr. Chapman.

*Physical touch.* This means hugs, pats, hand holding, kisses, or any number of loving gestures. And it means offering them solely for their own sake, not as a quick buildup to lovemaking. "One of the most common problems is to make the mistake that physical touch means sex," say Dr. Chapman. "It may not."

## Take Action

After experimenting with the different love languages and finding the ones that work best, we need to use them often, even if others are resistant. "Not every spouse will respond," says Dr. Chapman, "but we are better for having loved."

In her book *A Gift for God*, the late Mother Teresa explained how people could lead better lives: "Smile at each other; smile at your wife, smile at your husband, smile at your children, smile at each other—it doesn't matter who it is—and that will help you grow up in greater love for each other. . . . I find it difficult sometimes to smile at Jesus. And it is true, Jesus can be very demanding also, and it is at those times when he is so demanding that to give him a big smile is very beautiful."

# *Lust*

———⟶———

## TAMING THE MAD
## DESIRE WITHIN

*D*avid and Bathsheba.

Yes, that was a classic case of wild lust, of libido run amok. But most experts say that lust isn't limited to just the illicit loves of our lives. It is broader than that, encompassing untamed desires of pretty much any ilk.

"Lustful behavior is behavior that is unhealthily fixed upon one particular form of personal gratification that is never satisfied, be it the desire we hold for food, clothing, sexual pleasures, the corner office, the neighbor's wife, or the friend's sports car," says the Reverend William Lenters, doctor of divinity and author of *The Freedom We Crave*.

Here's another surprise: We may be experiencing lust even if our desire isn't overwhelming us. "There are gradations implied in the word *lust*," says Vincent Wimbush, Ph.D., professor of New Testament at Union Theological Seminary in New York City. "I needn't drive myself into bankruptcy buying things before I admit that I have an excessive desire to accumulate material goods. I need only recognize that my desire is too heavily weighted to be healthy and that I find it difficult to satisfy it."

# Where It All Starts

What spurs this wide-ranging and sneaky desire? What's at the root of this maddening want for something, for someone, for whatever it is that we don't have? "Think of a garden," suggests Catherine Wallace, Ph.D., author of *For Fidelity*, "and think of one section of that garden becoming overgrown with aggressive weeds. The weeds take root, spread throughout the whole of the garden, and because of their insatiable appetite, in short order crowd out even the healthiest of plants and flowers," she says.

"Lust is that weed. But the real problem isn't the weed; the real problem is what allowed it to take root in the first place," explains Dr. Wallace. "Weeds grow well just about anywhere. If the soil is poor, the beneficial plants will die back. Queen Anne's lace blooms wonderfully even in a crack in the pavement. Roses don't. And so lust, like a thriving patch of weeds in the lawn, is a symptom of something gone wrong at a deep level."

In our lives, the weakness may start with a lack of love, discipline, self-worth, or meaning. Whatever the cause, it represents an imbalance. "Human beings have many different parts that must be integrated and function together in order for us to be healthy," says Dr. Wallace. "Our appetites for food, pleasure, company, or sex are one piece of who we are. They have to work in harmony with our judgment, our conscience, and our intelligence in such a way as to ensure that no one piece of who we are dwarfs the others." With lust, one of those appetites becomes divorced from the whole and devours us, she says.

What are the early warning signs of lust? Here are some that Dr. Lenters has identified.

***Nonspecific unhappiness.*** We're sad for reasons that are unclear and we can't seem to overcome it.

***Increasingly recurring fantasies.*** We obsess about a particular person or object.

***Unshakable resentment.*** We begrudge other people and their seemingly enviable lives.

***A feeling of emptiness.*** We feel caught in a void so profound that we are desperate to fill it but can't figure out how.

Tackling lust, then, involves "creating a new orientation, a new focal point that can foster a sense of wholeness and balance that

## Healing Words

**The Sin of Misplaced Love**

"It's not money that's the root of all evil, but the love of money that's the root of all evil," (1 Timothy 6:10), says William Backus, Ph.D., a Christian-licensed psychologist in Roseville, Minnesota, founder and director of the Center for Christian Psychological Services in St. Paul, and author of *Telling Yourself the Truth* and *The Healing Power of a Healthy Mind*.

"It's a wonderful instructive from Timothy, who then adds that it is through this craving that some have wandered away from the faith and pierced their hearts with many pangs," says Dr. Backus. "If you are pierced with many sorrows over your holdings, income, future security, the whole gamut, then maybe you ought to see if you are in love with money. And if so, perhaps you've wandered away from the faith and need to return."

eliminates the impulse for the destructive behavior," says Dr. Wallace.

God's continued presence in our lives can help us maintain that kind of balance, according to the Reverend Linda Mercadante, Ph.D., professor of theology at the Methodist Theological School in Ohio, near Columbus, and author of *Victims and Sinners*, because "as long as we have a vital awareness of the one true God, the God who calls us to be whole, integrated human beings, we are going to be less susceptible to bowing to the altars of false gods—gods of a material or sexual nature, gods that demand our undivided attention and bring us no peace."

## The First Step Is the Hardest

Just recognizing that we are subject to lustful thoughts, feelings, or actions is an important first step, says Dr. Lenters. Once we have ad-

# Prayer Pointers

## Drawing on the Strength of Others

"Theologically, all addiction can be considered lust, in the sense of inordinate desire. This can be harmful, because you desire something more than you desire God. When we're battling to overcome lust, groups and group prayer can be extremely helpful to us," says the Reverend Linda Mercadante, Ph.D., professor of theology at the Methodist Theological School in Ohio, near Columbus, and author of *Victims and Sinners*.

"As long as the group doesn't moralize, as long as its focus is on turning lives toward God, the energy and company provided by the group can help the lusting person feel supported rather than abandoned, encouraged rather than discouraged, and understood rather than outcast," she says.

mitted that and are ready to battle lust in our lives, here is what experts suggest we do.

**Find and treat the source.** Since lustful thoughts—whether about money, power, or sex—are rooted in deep, unfulfilled longings, we need to recognize them as such and discover how they developed. "Our fantasies, what we're lusting after, to me are windows to the soul," says Mark Laaser, Ph.D., author of *Faithful and True*. "We need to ask ourselves what we are lusting for and how it compares with some of the early traumas that we've had. If that's too painful to do on our own, a trained counselor can help us get to the bottom of these issues."

**Inventory what we do have.** We should make lists of everything that we have, including friends, funds, family, health, and the like. "Our lustful drives are often grounded in a desire to add to our lives because we lose sight of all the good that surrounds us," says Dr. Lenters. "Simply compiling and studying a list can help us regain perspective on just how rich our lives really are."

**Define the foundation.** "Think of your life as you would a home built on pylons," says Dr. Lenters. "Sketch two homes on one piece of paper. On the first one, give it only one pylon. Let it teeter on the shaky foundation of lust. On the second, give it four or more. Make it solid. Contemplate the pylons, the foundations of life, and label the ones in the second picture. Ask yourself what you want your foundations to be—love of family, of faith, of honest labor—and then consider what it will take to build that house."

**Remember God's promise.** In the Lord's Prayer, we ask in faith that God give us our daily bread. "When we lust to acquire things, we lose sight of the fact that in that prayer, God is promising to meet our daily needs, not our obsessive desires," says Dr. Lenters. "One way to bring our lives back into perspective is to simply pray each day, 'Lord, please allow me my daily bread; just enough for this day.'"

**Think of someone else.** The simple act of doing a good deed for another person can play a role in the fight against lust, says Rabbi Abraham Twerski, M.D., a psychiatrist in Pittsburgh and author of *Do Unto Others.* "The body and spirit are in a tug of war, with the body pulling toward instant fixes and the spirit fighting for devotion to matters outside the self," he says. "Thus, if someone is afraid of giving up his or her dependency, they need only "to take one little step toward another person, offer one selfless act of kindness, and the rest will follow."

**Retrain the brain.** It may sound gimmicky, but Doug Weiss, Ph.D., director of Heart to Heart Counseling center in Fort Worth, Texas, and author of several books, including *The Final Freedom: Pioneering Sexual Addiction Recovery*, says that he has had incredible success with this technique for banishing lustful thoughts: Place a rubber band around one wrist, and every time a lustful or sexually inappropriate thought comes to mind, snap the rubber band. "You begin to recondition your brain so that it starts to say, 'Wait a minute—lust equals pain,'" he says. "After 30 days of this treatment for sexual lust, about 80 percent of the people that Dr. Weiss works with say that their inappropriate thoughts end.

**Get personal.** Viewing other people as sex objects makes them easier to lust after. Instead, says Dr. Weiss, we need to start thinking about who these people really are: "They're someone's precious daughter, wife, sister, or son, not to mention a child of the living God.

And to just kind of scan them into your brain and use them as sexual entertainment is just plain wrong."

**Take out the trash.** If our lust is sexual, then immediately get rid of books, magazine, movies, television shows, or whatever it is that's feeding it. If a person is the object of our lust, we need to stop seeing them alone. If we need to speak with them, we should bring a friend along just to be safe, says Dr. Weiss

## It's Worth It

What does it feel like to kick addiction to lust and reclaim our lives? "We feel humble, because we finally accept the reality of our own limits. We feel grateful for the lessons we've learned. We feel acceptance, which is the freedom from the strain of inner conflicts. And we feel surrender, which is the emotional state of accepting reality," says Dr. Lenters.

"It's all the parts working together, a satisfied appetite, a capacity for spontaneity rather than impulsiveness," observes Dr. Wallace. "As Samuel Taylor Coleridge explains, we have spontaneity when the right choice or the right action arises within us naturally or easily. And that's God alive and ascendant in us."

# *Marital Problems*

———◆———

## RECOVERING THE MAGIC

*P*astors know what plagues and dooms marriages. They counsel couples all the time. The two biggest problems are lack of effective communication skills and lack of commitment to drive the relationship through the inevitable rough and tough terrain.

"Marriage breakdowns don't occur because of 'differences;' they happen because a couple can't seem to handle those differences. Relationships don't cause conflicts; they bring out whatever incompleteness we have in us anyway," explains the Reverend Rowland Croucher, doctor of ministry, marriage counselor, an evangelist in Healthmont, Victoria, Australia, and director of John Mark Ministries in Melbourne.

Anyone who has experienced marriage knows that living "happily ever after" requires work. It requires sensitive, dignified discussion of touchy issues. It requires a willingness to resolve conflict amicably. And it requires a solid commitment to do both by both partners.

If those things were easy and automatic, more than half of all marriages would not end in divorce, notes Michael J. McManus, president/founder of Marriage Savers in Potomac, Maryland, syndicated columnist, and author of *Marriage Savers*. Fortunately, many communities and churches offer programs teaching constructive communication for couples, ways to resolve conflicts amicably and fairly, says McManus, whose nonprofit organization has helped establish programs in more than 100 metropolitan areas in America.

## Marriage Insurance

Programs like Marriage Encounter and Retrouvaille have such great track records of improving and saving marriages that they can be called marriage insurance, says Michael J. McManus, president/founder of Marriage Savers in Potomac, Maryland, syndicated columnist, and author of *Marriage Savers*.

Marriage Encounter, started by the people of the Catholic church in the 1950s, is a weekend-long experience. Couples who have good marriages and want to make them better meet in a retreat setting and listen to a series of talks by two or more presenting couples. The experience is designed to enrich a marriage. Couples are given time to be alone together without the normal everyday distractions, and they learn a technique of communication that will build intimacy and understanding of each other.

Marriage Encounter is inexpensive and is offered by 12 denominations. To locate the program locally, write to Worldwide Marriage Encounter, 2210 East Highland Avenue, #106, San Bernardino, CA 92404.

Unlike Marriage Encounter, Retrouvaille is for couples whose marriages are troubled. The mentoring couples have actually been separated or to the brink of divorce and have successfully rebuilt their marriages. Write to Retrouvaille, P.O. Box 25, Kelton, PA 19346 for a brochure and information on how to contact mentors in your area.

Marriage Savers tracks all programs designed to strengthen marriage and helps churches and ecumenical councils establish marriage ministries and community marriage policies. Write to Marriage Savers, 9311 Harrington Drive, Potomac, MD 20859.

# We Have to Talk

Good communication is crucial for a healthy marriage. So, regularly, we should assess how we talk to our spouses—what we look like when we speak, how we act, the tone we use, and more, says the Reverend Steve Carr, minister of Calvary Chapel and founder of Covenant Keepers, both in Arroyo Grande, California, and author of *Married and How to Stay That Way*. Here is some of Pastor Carr's advice.

**Check the attitude.** Consider not what we say so much as how we say it. Are we being sarcastic, arrogant, superior, or indignant? Are we resentful, bitter, or unforgiving? Are we indifferent or apathetic? Are we harsh? Are we deceitful? If the answer to any of these is yes, an attitude adjustment may be in order.

**Watch the words:** King Solomon said, "A soft answer turns away wrath, but a harsh word stirs up anger." (Proverbs 15:1 NRSV) "Harsh, condemning words are incredibly destructive," says Pastor Carr. We need to think of how we feel when someone condemns or belittles us and then remember Apostle Paul's instruction to husbands (though it applies to both spouses): ". . . love your wives and never treat them harshly." (Colossians 3:19 NRSV)

Also, we must avoid using exaggeration, particularly the kind of exaggeration found in accusations like "You always do this" or "You never do what I ask." Pastor Carr says, *"Always, never,* or *every time* are like gasoline on the fire of an argument."

**Stick to the present.** Don't bring up past failures or grievances. "That kind of ammunition should never be used to win an argument," says Pastor Carr. "If you have forgiven your spouse for a past failure, then it should be off-limits."

**Hold the tongue.** Interrupting and finishing our spouses' sentences suggests that we are not listening. It's impolite and fuels anger. ". . . be swift to hear, slow to speak, slow to wrath." (James 1:19 KJV)

**Curb the anger.** Some people learn to use anger to manipulate their spouses and control conversations. "They know that the spouse will cower and retreat once the rage appears," says Pastor Carr. This tends to discourage and destroy intimate, direct, and honest communication and, thus, relationships.

Uncontrolled anger is equally noxious and needs to be curbed. "No one wants to communicate the deepest things of the heart with

# Should We See a Counselor?

Marriage counseling can work wonders when a couple reaches an emotional impasse. However, we must pick our counselors carefully, warns the Reverend Rowland Croucher, doctor of ministry, marriage counselor, an evangelist in Healthmont, Victoria, Australia, and director of John Mark Ministries in Melbourne.

Talk to counselors by phone before making an appointment. Insist on this. Ask them if they are committed to saving marriages or if they often recommend that couples part. Ask about their approach to counseling and how they help couples resolve problems and get back together.

Choose a counselor committed to making marriages work, says Dr. Croucher. Many feel that it is their job to help people get out of painful situations, and they see ending the relationship as the most expedient route. Most pastors trained in marriage counseling are dedicated to saving marriages, he says.

someone who rages out of control in an angry fit," says Pastor Carr. If we cannot control our anger, we should seek counseling, he urges.

## Communicating Love

If we commit with our spouses to keep our marriages alive and healthy, not just during the easy times but also during the tense and tough times, then we have taken giant steps, says McManus.

Marriage, says Dr. Croucher, "is a commitment of one imperfect person to another imperfect person. The person to whom we are relating is made in God's image. He or she is like God, so we should treat our spouse with courtesy and dignity even when we don't feel like it."

We have to love our partners even when they are mad, when they frown at us, and when they hold us in contempt. Love requires a spiritual commitment, says McManus. In fact, he says, 1 Corinthians defines love as requiring an act of will in 15 different ways: "Love is patient, love is kind. It does not envy, it does not boast, it is not proud. It is not rude, it is not self-seeking, it is not easily angered, it keeps no record of wrongs. Love does not delight in evil but rejoices with the truth. It always protects, always trusts, always hopes, always perseveres." (1 Corinthians 13:4–7 NIV)

For healthy marriages, couples must assure each other that divorce is not an option, says McManus.

"Too many times, partners do the opposite and in arguments threaten to leave or to divorce," says Pastor Carr. "When people are threatening to destroy the marriage, they can never build it because the other partner doesn't have any security. "In the Bible, God says, 'I will never leave you or forsake you.' (Hebrews 13:5 NRSV) How much more we need to make that commitment to each other."

We must communicate commitment, love, and respect every day to strengthen and build our marriages, recommends McManus.

**Pray together.** This doesn't have to be a long, dreaded ritual. Five minutes is a good place to begin, says Pastor Carr. Just do it. Daily. How do we get started? See Marriage on page 395.

**Offer loving acceptance and forgiveness.** Acceptance is not something that our spouses should have to earn from us. "I love my wife before she changes or whether she changes or not," explains Dr. Croucher. "Nothing is unforgivable. Nothing will ever stop me from loving her. She can utterly count on that. A good marriage is the union of two good forgivers. It is three parts love and seven parts forgiveness."

**Expect and encourage growth and change.** A healthy marriage, says Dr. Croucher, includes "a commitment to grow, to become the persons that God intends us to be. Growing couples set growth goals: to read a good book and discuss it, to go away every year on a retreat, to pray together, or to take a course together." Besides doing things together, spouses should help each other grow and develop in their own unique ways.

**Be brutally honest.** But only about ourselves. We need to acknowledge our faults, mistakes, and failures with our partners. We should apologize for hurtful behaviors and actions. We should tell our mates that we "truly want to change in these areas," says Pastor Carr. Communication will leap forward.

**Lose control.** We shouldn't tell our spouses what to wear, how to wear their hair, or what to do. Discuss things, yes. Offer opinions, sure. But our partners must be allowed free choice and personal freedom, says Pastor Carr.

**Put spouses first.** We should keep our spouses as the priority in the marriage in every action that we take. In everything we say and in everything we do, we must demonstrate that the person to whom we are committed is really the priority," says Pastor Carr.

Our spouses and their needs, concerns, and plans must always come first, ahead of our parents, children, in-laws, neighbors, and jobs. "The marriage and the time with one another must always be top priority, and that must be clear," says Pastor Carr. Communicating that communicates love, and a loving, caring commitment.

For tips on ways to fight fairly or to avoid fights but still get down to the nitty gritty, see "Our Arrows in the Battle" (page 162).

# Marriage

---

## The Prayer Path to Intimacy

*H*e says, "Dear God, gimme, gimme, gimme."

While she says, "Dear God, in this situation, Your will be done."

Or, she says, "Let's pray."

While he says, "Gulp," because this is not something he is familiar or comfortable with.

Or, he says, "Heavenly Father."

While she says, "Mother/Father God."

No wonder it can be so awkward learning to pray with someone with whom we share intimacy on every other level. Our relationship with God is personal, private, and unique. To share it out loud, particularly with someone with whom we feel quite vulnerable, can be challenging. This is especially so if we and our spouses do not share a religious upbringing that gives us common rituals and a common spiritual vocabulary, and if we have been married for years and have not previously prayed together.

Still, do we want to have marriages without prayer? Without God at the helm? We do not, says Michael J. McManus, president/founder of Marriage Savers in Potomac, Maryland, syndicated columnist, and author of *Marriage Savers*. Regular shared prayer in a marriage, he says, "is divorce insurance." Numerous studies confirm his point, showing that couples who share spiritual practices, including prayer,

## Healing Words

### Partners in Prayer

... if two of you agree on Earth about anything you ask,
it will be done for you by My Father in Heaven.
For where two or three are gathered in My name, I am there
among them.

—*Matthew 18:19–20 NRSV*

Confess your faults one to another, and pray for one
another, that ye may be healed.

—*James 5:16 KJV*

are much less likely to divorce than those who do not. Why is this so?

**Prayer unites couples.** "It naturally brings us into agreement with each other as we place our needs before God," says the Reverend Steve Carr, minister of Calvary Chapel and founder of Covenant Keepers, both in Arroyo Grande, California, and author of *Married and How to Stay That Way.* "By coming before God together, we are naturally uniting our hearts for one common end."

**Prayer encourages honesty and humility.** "If we want to grow in our prayer lives together, it is necessary to bare our souls before our mates as well as before God," says Pastor Carr. "As we admit our weaknesses and confess our needs openly, we are communicating to our mates that we are open, vulnerable, and sincere. And we can't help but be drawn closer as a result."

## If Our Marriage Doesn't Have a Prayer

Yes, introducing prayer to a prayerless marriage can seem daunting and awkward, but there are some simple steps that you can take, says

McManus. Daily prayer is the key to a successful marital prayer life. If we are praying with our partners any less than that, then we should examine why.

The first step, says Pastor Carr, is to talk about it with our spouses. We need to talk about why we haven't prayed together or aren't praying together regularly. We should discuss it and commit to a routine. A routine can seem intimidating, but it doesn't have to be. Here's Pastor Carr's advice for couples just starting to pray together.

**Keep it short.** When beginning prayer together, we need to keep the entire daily sessions to no more than five minutes. This will help the less-enthusiastic spouse to be more inclined to give it a try. We can select a daily agreed-upon time, whatever best fits the schedule. "One couple I am counseling right now are night owls," says Pastor Carr. "They are musicians accustomed to staying up late playing different gigs. So their best time to pray is in the evenings. With another couple, he's in the floor-covering business and gets up very early every morning. His wife is a morning person. So they have breakfast together and then have prayer together before the kids even get up for school."

**Pray back and forth.** "Each spouse should pray a short prayer concerning an issue of special importance. By keeping the prayer short, this allows the other spouse to add postscripts." For instance, he might say, "Lord, help us to love each other more," and she could add, "Yes, and help us find ways to show each other our love, even when we're both tired and overwhelmed after a hard day at work."

**Keep it personal.** We should pray for our own needs and admit our own failings but never, ever use prayer as a weapon. None of that "Dear Lord, help my spouse get over those mean, selfish tendencies and nagging ways" stuff. "Jesus gives us some really clear direction on how to keep ourselves from condemning others," says Pastor Carr. "He says, ' . . . first take the plank out of your own eye, and then you will see clearly to remove the speck from your brother's eye.'" (Matthew 7:5 NIV)

**Pray for the marriage.** After praying for our personal needs, we need to thank God for our mates and for the strengths they have that we admire. We can pray for tender hearts, forgiveness, and growth

# Faithbuilders

## The Key to Lasting Relationships

"Try to worship together regularly and pray with and for each other." says the Reverend Rowland Croucher, doctor of ministry, marriage counselor, an evangelist in Healthmont, Victoria, Australia, and director of John Mark Ministries in Melbourne. "Yes, those who pray together are much more likely to stay together. Having a Christian commitment that is both real and similar to each other's is a healthy indicator of future marital harmony. That ought not preclude each partner relating to God uniquely.

"Remember God in the marriage. God was the first marriage celebrant. He invented marriage."

in the relationship. Then we can pray for others we know who are in need.

Another approach for those just starting out or for those wishing to strengthen their prayer lives as a couple is to start with daily Bible reading, suggests McManus. He recommends the book of Proverbs.

"There just happen to be 31 chapters in the book of Proverbs, so there's one for every day of the month," McManus says. The wisdom found all through Proverbs helps strengthen and build marriages. "Couples can use the book of Proverbs to bring the mind of the Lord into their relationships, then close with a prayer for each other's days, the problems that they may be having, or whatever the issues are."

"What we have found," says McManus, "is that prayers that are in the will of the Lord are answered, and that answering of prayers builds faith. The faith builds trust, and the trust makes the marriage a rock."

# Pain

## FINDING RELIEF AND ACCEPTANCE

Tim Doyle is a thirty-something accountant in Indianapolis who has created his own Web site on the Internet entitled "Hope for Those Who Suffer." It's devoted to the meaning and experience of suffering from a Christian perspective. This is a topic that he knows quite a bit about, not through academic study but from firsthand experience. As Tim explains on his Web site:

- His family consists of seven children, now all adults, and his parents.
- Growing up, they were a very athletic and loving Catholic family. However, during their high school years, Tim and three of the other children developed weaknesses that they now know are caused by muscular dystrophy.
- One of the children who has muscular dystrophy and another one who doesn't have been diagnosed with multiple sclerosis.
- Today, four of the seven kids, including Tim, use wheelchairs.

All this agony has left the Doyle family wondering, "Why us?" "Why this?" "Why now?" When it comes to pain, "Why?" is definitely the burning question. The experience of physical suffering seems so cruel and so unfairly distributed that it can turn even the most literal-minded among us into skeptical theologians. Does God wish us ill?

If He doesn't wish us ill, why does He allow so much pain? If He does wish us ill, why?

Tim Doyle has struggled over these questions, too. And though he has found comfort in reading the Bible, the question of "Why, Lord?" still exists.

But as Tim notes, "The Bible is clear: We're never going to understand all of our suffering on this side of eternity. But it really helps me to see that in His sovereignty, God chose suffering for His own Son. I feel that God is honoring me by saying, 'Tim, the path of pain that I chose for My Son is the same path that I'm using to bring you to Me.'"

# Soothing the Wounded Spirit

Pastoral counselors who work day in and day out with people in pain will tell you that Tim Doyle's story is neither unique nor universal. Certainly, there are many people who, at least initially, find their beliefs more a stumbling block than a blessing in coping with pain. "I see a lot of anger," says the Reverend Kent Richmond, doctor of sacred theology, chaplain at the Lutheran General Hospital in Park Ridge, Illinois, and author of *Preaching to Sufferers*. "A lot of people feel that their faith should have protected them, should have made them special, if you will. The discovery that that doesn't happen is often difficult."

So difficult, Dr. Richmond adds, that many of them decide that they want nothing to do with God anymore. That's a tragedy, because as difficult as it may be to reconcile suffering with belief, an overwhelming amount of evidence documents that faith and prayer can help people learn how to live with pain, if they have to, and in some cases, overcome it. Here are some suggestions for getting in touch with God when we're in pain.

**Have faith in God's presence.** Maybe we can't understand why God allows pain. Nonetheless, says Dr. Richmond, we can be certain that He stands with us in our suffering. Far from being aloof and unmoved, God suffers with us. He actively participates in our pain. This shared suffering, Richmond adds, is central to the meaning of Christ's journey to the cross, as prophesied in the Bible: "Surely He has borne our infirmities and carried our diseases. . . ." (Isaiah 53:4 NRSV)

**Find your own understanding.** Believers throughout the ages have found different ways to view the problem of pain, and we need to search for answers that make sense in our own hearts. Dr. Richmond, for example, doesn't necessarily share Tim Doyle's view that God wills suffering as a means of drawing sinners closer to Him. "I think that we live in an unfinished creation," he says. "God seeks our willingness to participate in the completion of that creation and the humanizing of it. Pain is part of that. God is not responsible for it, but God will give us strength to help us cope."

If our particular view of God is adding to our suffering rather than easing it, we may want to re-examine those beliefs, Dr. Richmond suggests.

**Share sorrow.** It's not surprising that pastoral counselors believe that sharing our pain with someone can help lighten the load. That view is supported by research scientists who have found that communicating the experience of illness has definite therapeutic advantages. "Telling our stories is a way of processing what's happening," says Frank Baker, Ph.D., director of the Behavioral Research Center at the American Cancer Society. "It helps put life in order and gives meaning to suffering."

Many people have found tremendous comfort in attending support groups where they can share what they're going through with others undergoing the same experience. Thousands of such groups exist, meeting in person and on the Internet, and they address an amazing variety of conditions and situations, from cancer and miscarriage to Lyme disease and arthritis. Doctors, pastors, and social workers at hospitals and local health departments often have lists of such groups. For free information, write to the American Self-Help Clearinghouse, Saint Clare's Hospital, 25 Pocono Road, Denville, NJ 07834-2995. To find groups on the Internet, connect to one of the major search engines and enter search terms such as *pain, support group*, and/or the name of the particular condition.

The Reverend Justin Tull, doctor of ministry, senior pastor at the Oak Lawn United Methodist Church in Dallas, and author of *Why God, Why? Sermons on the Problem of Pain*, recommends approaching these groups with some caution, initially. "Many support groups are tremendously helpful," he says. "But some groups tend to dwell on the problem rather than moving forward. Also, support

# To Fight or Submit?

Is it more appropriate to pray that our afflictions be healed or to accept them as God's will? Do both, says psychiatrist and prayer researcher Dale A. Matthews, M.D., associate professor of medicine at Georgetown University School of Medicine in Washington, D.C., and author of *The Faith Factor*.

Jesus demonstrated how to do this when He prayed desperately in the Garden of Gethsemane just before His betrayal and arrest. "Abba, Father, all things are possible to Thee; remove this cup from Me; yet not what I will, but what Thou wilt." (Mark 14:36 RSV) For Dr. Matthews, two points stand out in this prayer. First, Jesus showed that there is no sin in praying for relief from our trials.

The second point is even more important, in Dr. Matthews' view. Jesus' prayers weren't answered, yet He was fully prepared to accept the possibility that they wouldn't be. "That's the key," Dr. Matthews says. "We pray for what we want, but we lay all that at the foot of the cross. It's an error to believe that if we pray for healing, it must happen. There's no scriptural evidence for that belief."

The Apostle Paul's prayers for relief weren't answered, either, as shown in this passage from his second letter to the Corinthians.

> . . . a thorn was given me in the flesh, a messenger of Satan to torment me, to keep me from being too elated.
> Three times I appealed to the Lord about this, that it would leave me.
> But He said to me, "My grace is sufficient for you, for power is made perfect in weakness."
> So I will boast all the more gladly of my weaknesses, so that the power of Christ may dwell in me.

—*2 Corinthians 12:7–9 NRSV*

groups may not be the right solution for every person at a particular time." Be prepared to attend several meetings before making up your mind.

**Serve others.** Research has shown that it's possible to ameliorate pain by distracting yourself from it, Dr. Baker says, and one of the most effective ways of doing that is to think about helping others.

Dr. Tull cites the case of two members of his church: one, a woman who had just lost her husband, and the other, a young man with a chronic illness. He sent her flowers and cards to let her know that he was thinking of her in her time of grief, and she did the same when he was in the hospital. "Here were two people in pain for different reasons," Pastor Tull says, "and the fact that they would take the time to think of each other had tremendous power."

For Tim Doyle, testifying to God's power in his life, both in person and through his Web site, has been a major factor in his coming to terms with his disease. "I've been a much more powerful witness for Him in this wheelchair than I ever could have been without it," he says. "I just thank God for choosing me to be in His service."

**Cope with one day at a time.** Suffering is easier to handle in small doses, says Dr. Tull. "Don't ask how you're going to endure this for the next 20 years," he says. "Just concentrate on how you're going to get through today."

**Take the long view.** Paradoxically, Tim Doyle finds that he can get through difficult days by focusing on what he calls God's eternal perspective.

He cites the Bible passage in which Paul writes, "I consider that the sufferings of this present time are not worth comparing with the glory about to be revealed to us." (Romans 8:18 NRSV) Another key passage for Doyle: "For this slight momentary affliction is preparing us for an eternal weight of glory beyond all measure." (2 Corinthians 4:17 NRSV)

"I receive tremendous comfort in God's eternal promises, as they provide an endless source of strength to help me through the toughest days. As my body weakens, His strength, through His promises, increases," says Doyle.

**Pray with others.** Praying to God while being supported by others who care for you is a potent combination. "I can hardly think of anything more helpful than that," says the Reverend Steven Estes, senior pastor of Community Evangelical Free Church in Elverson, Pennsylvania, and co-author of *When God Weeps*. Reverend Estes's church holds regular Sunday night prayer sessions where people in various types of need are prayed for by the congregation.

# Spiritual Healing

A lot of people think of prayer and faith as basically passive activities: We ask God for help and sit back and let it happen. Not so. As it says in the New Testament, faith without works is dead (James 2:17), and nowhere is that more true than with pain.

Some pain experts say that attitude has everything to do with how well, or how poorly, people deal with pain. Happily, attitude is something that prayer and faith can rectify dramatically. Pastoral counselors see the evidence of that in their rounds at hospitals every day, and research studies on the health benefits of religion confirm it.

Often, the influence that our attitudes have on our health is described in terms of the mind-body connection, which refers to the growing body of research demonstrating that what goes on between our ears has a dramatic impact on the entire body. That's fine, as far as it goes, but experts such as psychiatrist and prayer researcher Dale A. Matthews, M.D., associate professor of medicine at Georgetown University School of Medicine in Washington, D.C., and author of *The Faith Factor*, and Kenneth A. Larsen, doctor of ministry who is board certified in psychopharmacology and director of pastoral services and clinical psychology at the New England Baptist Hospital in Boston, have been busily demonstrating in their own practices that what's really involved is a "mind-body-spirit" connection. Each element of the triad influences the other.

The effects of the mind-body-spirit connection are especially clear when it comes to the relationship between pain and stress, according to Dr. Larsen. Pain causes stress, and stress unleashes a cascade of physiological responses, from the release of toxic hormones to the suppression of the immune system. All can exacerbate and prolong pain. Prayer and a faithful attitude of calm acceptance can help keep all those processes from setting in. "The body has its own internal wisdom, which we can learn to facilitate," Dr. Larsen says. "By finding a place of peace and tranquillity, we can touch our connection to God, and that can have a direct effect on interrupting the pain process."

Here are some specific ways that we can use the mind-body-spirit connection to relieve pain.

**Breathe.** Breathing peacefully is the starting point in learning how to relax, in Dr. Larsen's view. The key is a technique that he calls diaphragmatic breathing. Most of us focus our breathing on inhaling, using the muscles of the chest to pull air into our lungs. Diaphragmatic breathing reverses that. We use our abdominal muscles as a pump to push all the air *out* of our lungs.

To practice diaphragmatic breathing, we need to pull our abdominal muscles in sharply as we exhale. That forces our diaphragms upward, which in turn forces air out of our lungs. The lungs are emptied far more efficiently, so we exchange more stale air with fresh air with every breath. That increased efficiency helps fight pain by enhancing the body's healing processes, and by helping us become more relaxed, says Dr. Matthews.

Deep breathing is an important element in almost any form of meditation. Dr. Larsen describes it as a form of body prayer.

**Relax.** Progressive muscle relaxation takes us to the next level of serenity, says Dr. Larson. The idea is to systematically guide ourselves mentally through each part of our bodies, concentrating on relaxing the muscles in each area. Some teachers recommend using what is called the clench-and-release approach to this exercise, meaning that we clench each group of muscles tightly for a few seconds before releasing them. This has the advantage of reminding our muscles what the difference is between tension and relaxation.

Here's how it's done, according to Dr. Larsen, step-by-step.

- We begin by closing our eyes and relaxing them.
  Focus on relaxing the eyelids as well.
- Focus on relaxing the face and the crown of the head.
- Focus on relaxing the neck and shoulders. We need to
  concentrate our efforts here, Dr. Larsen says. This is the
  most critical area as far as stress is concerned.
- Focus on relaxing the arms and hands.
- Focus on relaxing the lower back.
- Focus on relaxing the buttocks.

- Focus on relaxing the pelvic area.
- Focus on relaxing the thighs and the calves.
- Focus on relaxing the feet.

If we're in pain, Dr. Larsen recommends practicing progressive muscle relaxation for 20 minutes, two or three times a day. By coupling progressive muscle relaxation with diaphragmatic breathing, he says, eventually, we'll be able to initiate a state of physical, psychological, and spiritual repose almost automatically, any time we wish, with a single cleansing breath.

**Meditate.** Both the breathing and muscle relaxation exercises set the stage for meditation. Research has shown that meditating has myriad physical and psychological benefits, from lowering blood pressure to lowering anxiety and depression. More to the point, patients with chronic pain who meditate can lessen the severity of their pain, according to Dr. Larsen.

One of the leaders in meditation research is Herbert Benson, M.D., associate professor of medicine and president of the Mind/Body Medical Institute at Harvard Medical School, who first described the relaxation response. The relaxation response could be brought forth by a secularized form of meditation, since most of us tend to associate meditation with various forms of Eastern mysticism. Nonetheless, over the years, Dr. Benson has observed that 80 percent of his patients use a religious focus for their meditations, and that faith enhances meditation's healing effects. Ultimately, he came to believe that there is an inherent, genetic connection between prayer and health. Human beings, Dr. Benson writes, are "wired for God."

**Visualize.** Another common pain-fighting tool is visualization. The idea is to mentally picture a peaceful, relaxing scene or some other image that helps distract us from our pain. Dr. Larsen says that he has had patients who visualize Jesus walking or sitting beside them when they're in pain. One woman, a Catholic, pictured Jesus on the cross, so Dr. Larsen suggested that she try to place some of the pain she was suffering on Him so that He could help her carry it. "I believe that these sorts of images have authority in the psyche and help remove patients' anxiety by triggering specific chemical responses in the body," Dr. Larsen says.

## Answered Prayers

### Laying On of Hands Removed My Pain

"To fix bone spurs and hammer toes on each foot, surgeons had to make incisions on the inside and outside of both feet and break and reset my great toes. I had 147 stitches in my feet. Needless to say, I could only sit with my feet elevated. One day, I was just at the end of my endurance. My husband's best friend from childhood came to visit and asked about the surgery and the pain. After I answered, he asked if I had asked for God's help. I said no because I just asked for help with big things and I said I would try to handle this myself. He reminded me that God knows and cares for everything no matter how small. He put his hands on my feet and prayed a simple prayer for the pain to go away and for a rapid healing. My feet never hurt again. The recovery was quick.

"I hope that this story will help others realize that nothing is insignificant to pray about."

—*Carole L. Stephenson, Charlotte, North Carolina*

**Think positively.** It's easy to get depressed and discouraged when we're in pain. We need to fight those negative feelings. Keeping a constructive mental attitude literally enhances the body's healing process, according to Dr. Larsen. "Motivation changes chemistry," he says.

One way to promote constructive mental attitudes is to set goals for ourselves, Dr. Larsen says. These should be simple, specific, achievable goals that we can accomplish without having to depend on others. If pain is keeping us away from our jobs, for example, we might set a specific date to return to work. Or if we've been bedridden for awhile, we might resolve to get back into shape by walking once around the block today and twice tomorrow.

**Exercise.** Physical exercise releases endorphins, those wonderful hormones that act like natural opiates in the body, says James G. Garrick, M.D., director of the Center for Sports Medicine at Saint Francis Memorial Hospital in San Francisco. Endorphins are thought to directly improve our tolerance for pain. By promoting a sense of calm and well-being, endorphins may also enhance the body's self-healing process, he says.

**Listen.** Music is a delightful way to relax and distract yourself from pain. It can also heal. Research suggests that music can lower respiration, heart rate, and blood pressure and reduce muscle tension. Choose soothing music, though, because our heartbeats respond to rhythm. An aggressive, driving beat can make you more tense and less relaxed, says Stephen Halpern, Ph.D., a composer of more than 50 albums, recording artist, sound healer, and researcher in San Anselmo, California, who has studied the relationship between music and healing for more than 20 years. Dr. Halpern also recommends choosing music with simple melodies rather than scores that swell to giant crescendos.

For more information on these techniques, see Mindfulness and Meditation (page 80) and Visualization (page 123).

# *Pride*

## THE CURE: LEARNING TO BE HUMBLE

*I*s it wrong to be proud that we've maintained our sleek figure after our friends have lost theirs? Is it wrong to be proud of the job and power that we've attained or the good works that we do? It is, if we feel like we've done it all on our own, say theologians. Such an attitude demonstrates a sense of vanity, arrogance, haughtiness, or whatever you want to call it, suggesting a dangerous independence from God.

*St. Augustine's Prayer Book* defines pride this way: "It is the refusal to recognize our status as creatures, dependent on God for our existence, and placed by Him in a specific relationship to the rest of His creation."

In fact, this kind of attitude puts us in direct opposition to God and in worse shape spiritually than someone whom we may view as wretched and sinful, but who is contrite. "As the Bible says, 'God opposes the proud but gives grace to the humble. Humble yourselves, therefore, under God's mighty hand, that He may lift you up in due time.'" (1 Peter 5:5b–6 NIV)

Maybe that's what Solomon meant when he wrote these famous words: "Pride goes before destruction, and a haughty spirit before a fall." (Proverbs 16:18 NIV)

## Choosing Our Own Way

But of all the truly nasty sins around, such as murder or adultery, how could God think that pride is so bad? For one thing, folks who do things that are really wrong often are repentant, deeply sorry that it ever happened, willing to make amends and then change their ways. Proud people, on the other hand, simply don't think that they have done anything wrong, and therefore have no need for God, let alone His love or forgiveness. And, as the Bible says, God has no tolerance whatsoever for that kind of attitude.

Consider the fate of Nebuchadnezzar, perhaps one of the best examples of pride run amok in holy writ. At one time the ruler of the known world, Nebuchadnezzar thought that he was such hot stuff that people should worship him. For his arrogance, he earned a special comeuppance: He lost his sanity and ended up living in the wilderness, grazing like a cow in a field for several years. (Daniel 4:33 NIV)

This seemed to change his highness's tune. When released from his punishment, he said, "Now I, Nebuchadnezzar, praise and exalt and glorify the King of Heaven, because everything He does is right and all His ways are just. And those who walk in pride He is able to humble." (Daniel 4:37 NIV)

## Live the Humble Life

Pride is clearly evil, bad, and wrong—number one with a bullet among the seven deadly sins. So how do we defeat it? Maybe by not trying to, says Everett L. Worthington, Ph.D., professor of psychology at Virginia Commonwealth University in Richmond and co-author of *To Forgive Is Human*. "I used to think that you should try to defeat pride. But I have come to the conclusion that that's not the way to go about it. That is just another form of a pride trip." The trick, he explains, is to forget about pride and concentrate on living humbly. "Nineteenth-century Christian author and pastor Andrew Murray wrote: 'Humility is not thinking of one's self to be less than one is. Humility is not thinking of oneself at all.'"

Such humility is exactly what Jesus demonstrates with His teaching, His attitude, His very life. Remember when He washed the disciples' feet? Jesus wasn't demonstrating the importance of good hygiene. He was making a powerful point: The greatest of all isn't the most prideful; he's servant of all.

The Lord therefore set us an example and teaches that the greatest in the Kingdom is the one who is the least.

Not only that, but when we take off our masks of pride and perfection and are open and humble about our own problems, others become more willing to admit their failings, says David Stoop, Ph.D, an addictions counselor in Newport Beach, California, author of *Forgiving Our Parents, Forgiving Ourselves*, and executive editor of *The Life Recovery Bible*. That, in turn, means there's even less pressure for us to act perfect, which helps everyone be more humble in the long run.

Make no mistake, trading pride for humility is tricky stuff. After all, some of us are already prideful over how humble we are. But here are some suggestions to get us on the right track.

**Serve somebody.** Nothing cures a case of pride quicker than humbling ourselves with simple tasks of serving, like cleaning the bathrooms of a church, washing dishes in a soup kitchen, or assisting a disabled person, says Dr. Stoop. Not only is it exactly what Jesus would do but it's also a reminder to be thankful for all that God has given us. After Jesus washed the disciples' feet, He said, "I have set you an example that you should do as I have done for you. . . . Now that you know these things, you will be blessed if you do them." (John 13:15, 17 NIV)

**Make amends.** Have a friendship that's on the rocks because of someone's prideful refusal to admit a mistake or wrongdoing? The biblical prescription is simple: "Go and humble yourself; press your plea with your neighbor! Allow no sleep to your eyes, no slumber to your eyelids." (Proverbs 6:3–4 NIV) Even if they're too proud to respond, at least we'll have done the right thing, says Ray Pritchard, doctor of ministry, senior pastor of Calvary Memorial Church in Oak Park, Illinois, and author of *The ABC's of Wisdom* and *What a Christian Believes*.

**Take a cue from the tax collector.** If we're proud of our religiosity, the story that Jesus tells about the tax collector and the Pharisee is guaranteed to set us straight: "Two men went up to the temple to pray, one a Pharisee, and the other a tax collector. The Pharisee stood up and prayed about himself: 'God, I thank you that I am not like other men—robbers, evildoers, adulterers—or even like this tax collector. I fast twice a week and give a tenth of all I get.'" (Luke 18:10–12 NIV)

"But the tax collector stood at a distance. He would not even look up to Heaven, but beat his breast and said, 'God, have mercy on me, a sinner.'" (Luke 18:13)

The tax collector, not the Pharisee, went home "justified before God," says Jesus. "For everyone who exalts himself will be humbled, and he who humbles himself will be exalted." (Luke 18:14 NIV)

**Do some comparing.** Sometimes, when our lives seem to be going better than those around us, we can start to feel pretty important. The quickest way to shut that down is to compare ourselves with the king of humility, Jesus. In *Sources of Strength*, former president Jimmy Carter suggests that we ask ourselves, "Have I lived in a way that is truly compatible with the teaching of the humble, human, yet all-loving and all-knowing God I have pledged to follow?" The answer, he says, "can be troubling, even humiliating—though *humbling* may be a better word."

**Be thankful.** Do we really love our spouses? Our dogs? Where we live? Instead of patting ourselves on the back, we need to be thankful. The Bible tells us: "And whatever you do, whether in word or in deed, do it all in the name of the Lord Jesus giving thanks to God the Father through Him." (Colossians 3:17 NIV) It also advises: ". . . give thanks in all circumstances, for this is God's will for you in Christ Jesus." (1 Thessalonians 5:18 NIV) Giving thanks to God or being thankful helps us keep humble because it reminds us that God has given us all that we have, says the Reverend Siang-Yang Tan, Ph.D., professor of psychology in the graduate school of psychology at Fuller Theological Seminary in Pasadena, California, and senior pastor of the First Evangelical Church in Glendale, California. One simple way to develop a more thankful spirit in ourselves and our loved ones is to say grace when we gather for meals.

**Get closer to God.** "No matter how great our achievements or success, getting closer to God can help us see more clearly how great He is and how small we really are," says Dr. Tan. The story of Job in the Old Testament is a good example. He had this to say after encountering the might of God: "My ears had heard of You but now my eyes have seen You. Therefore I despise myself and repent in dust and ashes." (Job 42:5–6 NIV)

# *Relationships*

~❈~

## BUILDING THE TIES THAT BIND

Husband to wife.
Mother to child.
Sister to sister.
Friend to friend.

We exist in a world that depends on relationships, closeness, and camaraderie. Yet sometimes the structure breaks down. Sometimes we feel incapable of nurturing the kinds of friendships that offer us support, understanding, pleasure, and companionship. And when that occurs, our lives are a bit emptier, our souls less fulfilled. Even our health can be affected.

In fact, in a five-year-long study of heart disease patients, those who had neither a friend nor a spouse were three times more likely to die than people involved in strong relationships, according to Redford B. Williams, M.D., professor of psychiatry and director of the Behavioral Medicine Research Center at Duke University Medical Center in Durham, North Carolina.

"The capacity to form relationships is critical to our survival as human beings," says Carole Bohn, doctor of education and executive director of the Danielsen Institute, a pastoral counseling center and mental health clinic at Boston University.

Even the Bible agrees: "It is not good that man should be alone." (Genesis 2:18 RSV)

# The Root of the Problem

So relationships are essential. We can accept that. Then why do some of us have such a hard time fostering them? One possibility is the way we were raised. "When we are born, we must form a relationship of trust with our mothers and then with the rest of the family members," says Dr. Bohn. "We need these people to care for us and sustain us and very often, the texture of these first relationships will go far in determining how well we will be able to form the other relationships that we will need later in life."

In other words, trust begets trust. "When a child is cared for in a loving, nurturing, and supportive environment, that child is likely to have an easier time developing intimate relationships than one who is brought up in an atmosphere of indifference or neglect," says Dr. Bohn. "Just as relationships are vital to our existence, the quality of our earliest relationships are vital in shaping the quality of our later ones."

But our relationships with our parents don't provide the only reason why we may find it difficult to form connections. "Other experiences work to our advantage or disadvantage," says Amy Miller, doctor of psychology, a psychologist with a private and hospital practice in New York City. "Perhaps we grew up in relative isolation on, say, a farm or an Air Force base, or our families moved a lot from city to city when we were young. Perhaps we attended schools where we weren't the prettiest, or brightest, or most athletic kids, and as a result, we were ostracized by others," she says.

"Maybe an unscrupulous lover took advantage of us at a vulnerable time in our lives, Dr. Miller continues. "Any number of environmental factors earlier in life, often beyond our control, can influence our ability to make and keep friends later."

We shouldn't rule out what Dr. Miller calls genetic predisposition. "It's entirely possible that a person is just naturally shy or cautious, and so might be more reluctant than others to go out and strike up new friendships." When this is the case, she says, it's helpful to ac-

# Prayer Pointers

## The Essense of Friendship: Love

This, then, is what the love of God consists in: the love of our neighbor. It is also written: "This is My commandment, that you love one another as I have loved you." (John 15:12) What more desirable, what more delightful than these commandments of the Lord, on which all the law and all prophets depend! And how did the Lord love us? "Greater love than this no man has, that a man lay down his life for his friends." (John 15:13) And how will you lay down your life for me, if you will not lend me a needle and thread when I need it? How will you shed your blood for me, if you think it beneath you to give me a cup of cold water, if you cannot be bothered to take your hand out of your pocket for me? If you refuse to say a good word of or for me, when will you die for me. . . . Let us, therefore, obey each other, love each other, for love is the fulfilling of the law."

—*From the twelfth-century abbot, Aelred of Rievaulx*

knowledge two things: first, that our predisposition can be an obstacle, and second, that it can be overcome.

Whatever the cause, we shouldn't feel embarrassed or ashamed if relationships don't come easily, says Dr. Bohn. Nor should we try to fix blame. Instead, we should fix the problem through steps like these.

**Look inside.** If we tend to avoid intimacy, we should explore what makes us uncomfortable by talking with a therapist or pastoral counselor or asking ourselves tough questions, such as, "What am I afraid will happen if I allow myself to draw close to this particular person?" or conversely, "What part of me am I protecting by steering clear of this person and why do I think I need to protect myself?" Says Dr. Bohn,

"By facing fears in this way, we may actually reduce their power over us." (To find a pastoral counselor, write to the American Association of Pastoral Counselors, 9504A Lee Highway, Fairfax, Virginia, 22031-2303. Include a self-addressed envelope with first-class postage.)

**Look for safe terrain.** It may seem obvious, but when we seek relationships, we should start with settings in which we feel secure, such as groups and organizations that reflect our values, beliefs, and interests. "We're far more likely to be open to the possibility of intimate relationships in such contexts," says Dr. Bohn. What type of places might be good? "Church fellowships, volunteer organizations, hiking clubs, and cultural societies. Even 12-step meetings have proven a wonderful place for people to meet one another."

**Take a first step.** When we're ready to seek friends, we should start simply. "Even just saying hi to a co-worker with whom you don't normally speak is a good exercise in encouraging friendship," says Dr. Miller. "Beyond that, we may want to think about inviting someone to do something of limited duration, say a half-hour coffee break or lunch at a local diner. Or, if we're new in town, we can introduce ourselves to our neighbors and ask them what they think of the neighborhood and where they recommend we shop. They'll be flattered, and sincere flattery is a foolproof icebreaker."

**Accept rejection.** We need to remember that not everyone is going to want a friendship. "Chances are that if someone rejects our overtures, the friendship wouldn't have worked out anyway. They're probably doing us a favor," says Dr. Miller. "But it's important to not personalize rejection and not blame ourselves. I'm reminded of the story of the sower (Matthew 13:3–9) who threw a lot of seeds on the ground. Some of them took root and others didn't. Likewise with friendships, we need to accept that what happens is simply a part of nature, not a defect or shortcoming in ourselves."

# Nourishing Relationships

Once we enter the realm of relationships, we'll want to know how best to thrive in it, which, according to experts, means understanding that a relationship is a two-way street. If all we seek is our own gratification, what we're likely to end up with is our own frustration. To develop healthy relationships, we can try some of these tips.

## Finding Friendship with God

What's true of our sense of kinship with one another is equally true of our sense of kinship with God. "An added dimension of the quality of human relationships is the fact that they can often help shape our faith, our relationship to God," observes Carole Bohn, doctor of education and executive director of the Danielsen Institute, a pastoral counseling center and mental health clinic at Boston University.

Put another way, our understanding of God reflects our experiences of life. "If, for instance, we've raised our kids in a home in which punishment was doled out liberally and love intermittently, chances are that they're not only going to find it hard to open themselves to other human beings but they're probably going to develop an image of God as punitive and dictatorial," says Dr. Bohn. "If, however, they're raised in an atmosphere of love, acceptance, and protection, they're more likely to believe in a God who will care for them unconditionally."

**Love ourselves.** Good relationships start with solid foundations based on our own happiness and security. If we come to relationships in misery, then "we'll view our friends with jealousy, which breeds resentment and anger, which in turn destroys friendships," says Sharon Scott, licensed marriage and family therapist in Dallas and author of *How to Say No and Keep Your Friends.* How can we be happy? By treating ourselves well, says Scott. "Take yourself out to dinner, or to horseback riding lessons, or to a movie. Treat yourself to what you enjoy. Be good to yourself. And write a journal entry each evening describing one thing you are pleased with about yourself that day," she suggests.

**Love our neighbors.** How much? As much as we love ourselves, says Father Kurt Stasiak, a Benedictine priest and associate professor of sacramental and liturgical theology at St. Meinrad School of Theology in St. Meinrad, Indiana. "The goal for Christians is not to give to others so that we receive something in return but to give as much as we possibly can because that is the right and good thing to do."

**Use solitude.** Time spent alone can prepare us for more enriching time with others. Solitude can be thought of as an extended form of prayer, says Dr. Bohn, because it offers us an opportunity to pause, reflect, give thanks, and understand our current needs so that we can be a better friend when we then re-engage with the people we care about.

Adds Dr. Miller, "In solitude, we want consciously *not* to do things—not watch television, not clean house, not do things that distract us. Simply think about what our lives look like at this very moment and why our friends are important to us."

## Feeding Friendships

In addition to a healthy attitude, relationships require a healthy dose of human effort. "They're a little like a house plant," says Scott, "They don't just jump up and tell us they need attention. But if we ignore them for too long, they wither, atrophy, and maybe even die."

Unfortunately, for many of us, there are many activities and concerns competing for the time that we would otherwise give to our relationships. There are jobs to be done, kids to be raised, groceries to be purchased, and mortgages to be paid. "We're pulled in any number of directions, with any number of what we perceive as urgent issues that deserve our immediate attention," notes Scott, "and inevitably, relationships suffer." How can we correct it? Experts have some suggestions.

**Work out a schedule.** We can formally schedule time each month for people who are important to us but who we otherwise wouldn't see, suggests Dr. Bohn. "My husband and I have been part of a dinner group that has met monthly for 20 years. All the people in that group mean a great deal to us, but without the scheduled meeting, we'd probably never see half of them," she notes.

**Make resolutions.** "Resolve to limit both your own activities and those of your children," advises Scott, "so that you have time for friends. Don't overbook, or you'll spend all your time driving yourself and your children from one event to the next. For example, I limit myself to two volunteer activities that last one year. Most recently, that involved nursing-home visitations and volunteer work with homeless animals. I politely say no to other commitments."

**Anticipate change.** When one member of a relationship undergoes a life transition, like marriage, divorce, or a new career, both members need to talk it through. "I remained single many years beyond my friends. When they began having babies, it really put us in different worlds," Scott recalls. "We didn't know what to talk about at first because our interests were now so different. We talked about it and agreed to maintain our friendships with visits, perhaps less frequent, yet filled with our old selves."

**Pray with friends.** We don't set out to pray solely to build relationships. But lifting our worries and concerns to Heaven with another forges a powerful bond, says Father Stasiak. "Prayer can hold people together," he says. Not only that, but praying with and for others is an act of service commanded by Scripture: "Carry each other's burdens, and in this way you will fulfill the law of Christ." (Galatians 6:2 NIV)

As Aristotle put it, "What is a friend? A single soul dwelling in two bodies."

For more advice on relationships, see Loneliness (page 360).

# Salvation

━━◆━━

## GATEWAY TO HEALING—
## AND ETERNITY

*H*e was an inquisitive eight-year-old, as kids that age usually are. So the house on the big Texas property with the woods and the bushes was the ideal place to explore. There was only one problem: Unknown to the boy and his parents, someone had set some steel animal traps in the backyard.

As one pastor tells it, the boy's father was in his study when he heard his son's cry for help. "Daddy, Daddy, Daddy!" the child wailed over and over again. Sure enough, the child had taken a wrong step, and the jaws of a trap had slammed shut on his foot.

When the father heard the crying, he didn't stop and think, "Has my son been good lately? Has he done the dishes? Did he do his chores?" No, the pastor explains. When a father hears that cry, he responds. In an instant, the man rushed out the back door to save his child.

In the same way, the Bible tells us, God will always respond to our cries. And that is where salvation starts—with a cry to God for help.

# Many Cries, One Motivation

We cry out for many different reasons. Sometimes we're angry, as after the tragic death of a loved one, after a divorce, or in the midst of a long illness. Other times, disappointment is the trigger, like when we discover that the things that we believed would make us happy—money, power, prestige, success, even family—leave us feeling empty. Also, desperation can lead to cries for help from those who have tried to medicate their emotional pain with alcohol, drugs, sex, or food.

And sometimes, it's not tragedy at all that makes us seek God and salvation. We simply feel an emptiness inside and long for the sense of peace and confidence that we see in others who have deep faith.

They're different cries, but they all have the same fundamental motivation: trying to fill an empty space or void inside. "There is a vacuum in all of us that only God can fill, through Jesus Christ," says the Reverend Siang-Yang Tan, Ph.D., professor of psychology in the graduate school of psychology at Fuller Theological Seminary in Pasadena, California, and senior pastor of First Evangelical Church in Glendale, California. "We all, deep down inside, long to come home to what we were created for—loving, intimate fellowship and communion with God."

The problem that we all wrestle with is how to develop that closeness and, through it, find salvation.

# How We're Saved

Though the finer points of salvation are a matter of debate among the major branches of Christianity, there are many things on which they agree.

**Belief in the divinity of Christ.** "The teaching on the person of Jesus Christ from the Scripture is very clear. He was fully God and at the same time fully man. Any deviation from this position is not only unscriptural, it is also heretical," says Josh McDowell, international speaker and author of *Evidence That Demands a Verdict* and *More Than a Carpenter.*

**Belief in the Bible.** Although Roman Catholic and Eastern Orthodox churches go beyond the Bible as their source of authority, they agree with Protestant denominations that the Old and New Testaments are divinely inspired.

**_Belief that true faith involves more than attending church._** As C. S. Lewis wrote in _Mere Christianity_, "Sitting in a church doesn't make someone a Christian any more than sitting in a garage makes someone an automobile."

# Healing Words
## True Faith Defined

One thing that we owe Our Lord is to never be afraid. To be afraid is doubly an injury to Him. Firstly, it means that we forget Him; we forget He is with us and is all powerful; secondly, it means that we are not conformed to His will; for since all that happens is willed or permitted by Him, we ought to rejoice in all that happens to us and feel neither anxiety nor fear. Let us then have the faith that banishes fear. Our Lord is at our side, with us, upholding us.

—_From_ Meditations of a Hermit _by Charles de Foucauld_

But I can imagine someone say, "If that is to have a new birth, what am I to do? I can't create life. I certainly can't save myself." You certainly can't, and we don't preach that you can. We tell you it is utterly impossible to make a man better without Christ, and that is what men are trying to do. They are trying to patch up this old Adam's nature. There must be new creation. Regeneration is a new creation, and if it is a new creation it must be the work of God."

—_D. L. Moody, nineteenth-century evangelist_

***Belief in the concept of salvation.*** "The doctrine of salvation," says McDowell, "is linked with the atoning death of Christ on the cross" as God's perfect sacrifice for the sins of the world.

But just how we "appropriate" salvation is another matter, according to McDowell. Many Catholic denominations, for example, believe that we must work for it. Jesus' life, His death on the cross, and His resurrection planted the seeds of our salvation, and that salvation is a gift.

But that gift is given to us so that we may unwrap it and use it, says Father Kurt Stasiak, a Benedictine priest and associate professor of sacramental and liturgical theology at St. Meinrad School of Theology in St. Meinrad, Indiana. "Christians should be living their lives in such a way that the eternal life that we speak of should not come as too much of a shock. There should be a relationship with God already strongly established, and there should be an attitude of forgiveness that is already a habit," he says.

Nearly all Protestant denominations believe that we cannot earn salvation. Good deeds alone will never make us good enough in God's sight to be saved, according to Dr. Tan.

Instead, salvation—the deliverance from sin and God's punishment for sin—is by grace, a free gift from God to all who believe in Christ. "This view simply says, 'I realize that Jesus died for me. I repent from my sins and I receive Him into my heart as my Savior and Lord,'" says Dr. Tan.

Where Protestant denominations seem to differ with regard to salvation is their level of commitment to Christ. Evangelical Christian churches believe that it is not enough to simply know that Jesus died on the cross for our sins; we need to make a personal commitment to accept Jesus into our hearts and make Him Lord of our lives. In other words, that commitment must guide how we live from that point forward.

"Saving faith begins with the truth about who God is, who we are, and who Jesus is, but it doesn't end there," says Ray Pritchard, doctor of ministry, senior pastor of Calvary Memorial Church in Oak Park, Illinois, and author of *The ABC's of Wisdom* and *What a Christian Believes.* "True saving faith is complete trust in the person of Jesus Christ."

# Common Ground

How we ultimately decide to take the final steps toward salvation will depend largely on the teachings of our own individual churches and our own personal beliefs. But regardless, there are several things that we ourselves can do to get closer to God and closer to the salvation that He offers.

**Ask God for direction.** Who would we rather get directions from, someone who studied a map, or the guy who built the road? If we're having doubts about our faith, salvation, or God, we should simply talk to God, says Dr. Tan. "Pray a simple prayer like this: 'Dear God, if you're really there and you can show me what life is all about, and if Jesus is really the answer, please make this clearer to me. I really want to know. I am really seeking after you. Help me to find you.' This is opening our hearts up to the God who is there, who will then reveal Himself eventually. It's a real, heartfelt sincere cry for God to reveal Himself. And God always answers that prayer."

**Study God's Word.** Between its covers, the Bible contains literally thousands of promises and truths on everything from taming our tongues to having better marriages. If we're faithful in our studies, God will show us these and other insights that will help us grow in our faith and find salvation.

**Give Mark a try.** Lots of folks say that they've tried to read the Bible but stopped in frustration when they encountered Old Testament names that they couldn't pronounce or ancient battles that seemed irrelevant. Instead of trying to read from beginning to end, says Dr. Tan, it may be more helpful for seekers to explore the New Testament Gospels, especially Mark. "For the modern mind, Mark may be the best. It's the shortest of the Gospels and provides fast-paced snapshots of Jesus' life and words," he says. And for those who believe that the Bible is just a collection of boring stories written from a human point of view, Dr. Tan suggests another prayer before reading: "If this is really Your Word, God, please speak to me through it."

**Seek an inspiring service or small group.** We have a flavorless meal at a restaurant. Or the waitress is surly. Does that mean

## Healing Words

### Hymn: "O for a Faith That Will Not Shrink"

O for a faith that will not shrink,
Though pressed by every foe,
That will not tremble on the brink of any earthly woe!

That will not murmur or complain
Beneath the chastening rod,
But, in the hour of grief or pain,
Will lean upon its God;

A faith that shines more bright and clear
When tempest rage without;
That when in danger knows no fear,
In darkness feels no doubt:

Lord, give me a faith such as this;
And then, whate'er may come,
I'll taste, e'en now, the hallowed bliss
Of an eternal home. Amen.

—*William H. Bathurst*

we'll never eat out again? Of course not. In the same way, if we have a bad taste in our mouths from boring or irrelevant sermons or unfriendly church members, we simply need to find another church or group. "Some churches have what are called seeker-sensitive services that are offered on Saturday night or Sunday morning with bands or music and a relevant message that isn't preachy," says Dr. Tan. Small-group Bible studies are often an informal and surprisingly fun way to explore the big questions such as salvation, he says.

**Accept God's grace—and share it.** "In her book, *Stripping Down*, Donna Schaper says that God spreads grace around like five-year-olds spread peanut butter. He gets it everywhere. And if I had to tell you my theology in a nutshell, that is it," says lecturer and ordained Episcopalian priest Harold Ivan Smith, doctor of ministry, who leads grief gatherings at St. Luke's Medical Center in Kansas City, Missouri, and is the author of many Christian self-help books. "There has been great emphasis on salvation from sin, but to me, it's salvation into inclusion in the Kingdom and the family of God. It's an invitation to participate in the great purposes of God for humankind."

# *Stress*

———✦———

## FINDING RELIEF THROUGH FAITH

*A* lighter load. Renewed strength. Rest for our weary minds and souls.

Yes, these ideas sound good, too good to be true if we're caught in the jittery, irritable, dispirited, and overwhelming world of stress. But it is possible to bring our lives under control, to better cope with the anxiety and tension that stress causes. How? By using prayer, our faith, and biblical principles written thousands of years ago to manage and even reduce the stressors in our lives.

In fact, studies show that those people who pray regularly and have a deep commitment to religion may be uniquely equipped to handle pressure, according to David B. Larson, M.D., president of the National Institute of Healthcare Research in Rockville, Maryland, an organization that has systematically explored and, with its fellows, published many of the studies linking faith and health. Strong faith, he continues, can help people cope with stress because it can help us slow down our automatic responses to stressful events and make us less likely to rush to judgment.

Everett L. Worthington, Ph.D., professor of psychology at Virginia Commonwealth University in Richmond and co-author of *To Forgive Is Human,* agrees. "When we recognize that God is ultimately in control, that's going to change how we react to most situations."

# Where It All Starts

Although stress is triggered by a variety of factors, it's no surprise that some of its most damaging sources are traumatic events beyond our control, such as the death of a loved one, divorce, separation, or chronic illness. And when we experience two or more of these events at the same time, we may feel so physically and mentally devastated that we literally have trouble getting out of bed, according to Charles Zeiders, doctor of psychology, a Christian psychologist and clinical coordinator of Christian Counseling Associates with offices in West Chester and Havertown, Pennsylvania, and a consultant to the neuro-behavioral unit at Riddle Hospital in Springfield, Pennsylvania.

More insidiously, we can bring on stress by our own desires—our demands for more money, better jobs, more recognition, bigger houses, or more of whatever, says Dr. Zeiders. Other causes include career and financial problems, the tension that comes from raising teens, trouble with neighbors, bitterness, and weight gain.

Whatever the trigger, stress takes a heavy toll, and not just because we toss and turn and can't sleep at night. During a crisis, our bodies produce adrenaline, epinephrine, and other chemicals that heighten our senses and quicken our reactions, essentially putting us on red alert.

This can come in handy if we need to pull a grandchild out of the way of a speeding car or confront other sudden dangers. But people under constant stress never stop producing the stuff, setting themselves up for serious health problems. These include headaches, high blood pressure, irritable bowel syndrome, ulcers, panic attacks, muscular tension, insomnia, chest pains, and heart problems, says Grat Correll, M.D., a family practitioner in Bristol, Tennessee, and a member of the Christian Medical and Dental Society.

"Whether stress is the primary diagnosis or whether it's masked by another one of these medical problems, a very large percentage of people I see have stress-related problems," says Dr. Correll.

So how do we turn off energy-sapping levels of stress? Try these prescriptions.

**Don't sweat the small stuff.** It's the title of a best-selling book. But it has always been solid biblical advice. "Consider how the lilies grow," Jesus says. "They do not labor or spin. Yet I tell you, not even Solomon in all his splendor was dressed like one of these. If that is how God clothes the grass of the field, which is here today, and

# Stress's First Cousin, Fatigue

By some estimates, it's the reason for one-quarter of all doctor visits.

"Typically, the patient will say, 'Doc, I get eight to nine hours of sleep and when I wake up in the morning, I still feel wiped out,'" says Grat Correll, M.D., a family practitioner in Bristol, Tennessee, and a member of the Christian Medical and Dental Society.

The trouble? Fatigue.

But more often than not, a battery of medical tests won't show a physical problem. Instead, the cause of their fatigue is spiritual. Either they're depressed about something or not coping with the stress in their lives very well, says Dr. Correll. "I check their thyroid and their kidneys, and I make sure that they're not anemic, but when everything comes back normal, then I tell them that we need to explore something that isn't going to show up in those kinds of tests." Such as:

- How's their home life? What's the status of their relationship with their wife, husband, or kids?
- How are things going at work?
- Do they attend church on a regular basis? And if so, what kinds of things have they been wrestling with spiritually?

All of these issues can cause the type of high stress that leads to fatigue, says Dr. Correll. Often, when his patients hear this diagnosis, they ask for some kind of pill to put some pep in their step. But he says that isn't the answer.

"I think that handing out pills is a very poor way of dealing with fatigue and stress. That teaches people to rely on medication for life's problems," Dr. Correll says. "But it doesn't change what causes stress: problems at home, problems at our jobs, whatever. So I try to focus in and say, 'Let's find the root cause,'" and then address it.

# Healing Words
## Transcending Pressure

Heavenly King,
The world squeezes me into its own mold.
It's easy for me to let that happen.
I'm attracted to the tangible, seduced by the temporary, and
tempted to journey up dead-end roads.
Give me discernment, strength, and courage,
to live for Your Kingdom,
to conform to Your Kingly rule.
Guide me in Your steps.
Enable me to resist the
pressures of those who are set against You.
Thank You for being my King.
Thank You most of all for loving me.

*—Norm Nelson, from* Thank You Most of All for Loving Me

tomorrow is thrown into the fire, how much more will He clothe you, O you of little faith!" (Luke 12:27–28 NIV) In the light of eternity, it's *all* small stuff.

**Make like a monk.** The monks who first employed Christian meditation in the Egyptian desert had no concept of stress. They were interested in becoming still and finding Jesus, says Dr. Zeiders. But as it turns out, these monks, known as Desert Fathers, discovered a pretty solid stress buster. Studies show that by getting quiet, disregarding passive thoughts, and repeating a word or phrase, we can actually decrease our heart rates, lower our metabolic rates, and slow our breathing and brain waves. What might we repeat? Dr. Zeiders prefers "Lord Jesus, behold me a sinner" or "Lord Jesus, behold me." Such a manner of prayer triggers the relaxation response, in which tension eases and heart rate and blood pressure drop, the opposite of the stress response, says Dr. Zeiders.

**Get out—and stay out—of debt.** Money in and of itself isn't bad, as the Bible points out. (1 Timothy 6:10) It's the love of money and the junk that it buys that hurts us, causes financial hardship, and, you guessed it, brings on stress. "We can't even enjoy what we bought because we practically have to work ourselves to death to pay for it," says Dr. Zeiders. If we want less-stressed lives, we need to control our desires to spend and pay off the debts that we've already accumulated.

**Take Sunday off.** Some may consider it old-fashioned, but the wisdom of carving one day a week from our overbooked schedules for worship and rest is beginning to look more attractive all the time. Not to mention scientifically sound.

"Look at the biology," says Dr. Worthington. "A Sabbath allows us to relax and focus on entirely different things, to think and feel and act differently. That has to reduce the flow of stress chemicals through our bodies, at least for that day." How do we do it? Cook a roast or casserole on Saturday so that we don't have to fuss making meals. Postpone all but the most basic of chores. Attend church and ponder what the pastor says. And then take a nice, long nap. Studies show that we're getting less sleep than ever.

**Learn when to say no.** We never should ignore someone's need, but in our sincere desire to help, sometimes we overdo or overcommit. This not only causes untold physical and emotional stress but it can also frustrate others who are counting on us. "Jesus speaks directly to people with this kind of problem in Mark 6:31," says Dr. Zeiders. "He and the Apostles had been working hard healing a lot of people. But instead of digging deeper and ministering even more to the crowd, he said to his disciples, 'Come with me by yourselves to a quiet place and get some rest.' He wanted them and us to know that we need to take time to get away with Him by ourselves."

**Make prayer a life preserver.** One of the many unmistakable benefits of prayer is reduced stress. "This has been researched a lot," says Dr. Worthington. "Most Christians believe that God is active in intervening in people's lives and if that is true—and I believe that it is—then prayer can bring a different force to act in a stressful situation. Prayer is a relationship with God, first. But it has calming effects, no question about it."

**Meditate on God's Word.** Whether reading the Psalms or memorizing passages that highlight God's faithfulness, we can use Bible study to not only help relieve stress but also to lead to a solution to our problems. "Focusing our minds on Christian truths in a situation where danger or threat is all around reminds us of what is really true: that God loves us and He is never going to leave us or forsake us," says Dr. Zeiders.

Or as Jesus puts it: "I have told you these things, so that in Me you may have peace. In this world you will have trouble. But take heart! I have overcome the world." (John 16:33 NIV)

# Suicidal Tendencies

## FAITH OFFERS A BETTER CHOICE

*H*e had throat cancer—a disease that, unless a miracle occurred, would surely take his life. The doctors gave him only four months, six at best. Soon, the increasing pain prevented the monk from even helping out around the monastery. But he refused to concede to the pain or to seek a quick way out through suicide with "help" from some Kevorkian clone.

As the months turned into years, the monk's suffering became a source of inspiration for his friends and colleagues at the St. Meinrad Archabbey in St. Meinrad, Indiana. Slowly, the brave and human way that he faced his mortality took on greater meaning than all his work at the monastery combined. In a very real way, it became his work. "It was a witness to us that he wasn't giving up," says Father Kurt Stasiak, a Benedictine priest and associate professor of sacra-mental/liturgical theology at St. Meinrad School of Theology. "And it was a witness to him that we weren't giving up on him. There's a lot more to life than what chores you can perform."

Two years after his diagnosis, the monk completed his journey in this life, "in a great deal of pain, but not alone and not despairing," says Father Stasiak. "Nobody likes to suffer, but there are things that can happen to us and to others when we are called to suffer that I don't think can happen any other way."

# Purpose in the Pain?

In a world where some talk about suicide as a quick answer to life's problems, the monk's willingness to endure might seem just plain crazy. But it fits perfectly with the Bible's teachings. A careful reading of Scripture reveals that although heartache, disease, pain, and even depression were as common as unleavened bread in biblical times, it's never suggested that anyone should take his own life. And in the best known example of someone who did—Judas Iscariot—it's clear that he didn't understand the true Gospel of grace.

The overriding principle in the Bible is that God gives life, and only He knows what He has planned for us, says Wilford Wooten, a licensed marriage, family, and child counselor, a licensed clinical social worker, and director of the counseling department for Focus on the Family in Colorado Springs, Colorado. Even if we're in the depths of despair or pain, we need to leave the future to Him. "As Christians, we need to recognize that pain can be managed and that there is hope," he says.

The problems that can tempt us to question whether life is worth living are maddening and, unfortunately, all too real. Disease, depression, loneliness, low self-esteem, abuse, addictions, parental problems, mental illness, marital difficulties, job loss, and crushing financial burdens all can help push us to the brink. Or we may contemplate suicide to gain attention, to punish, to manipulate, or even to join a loved one who has died.

Experts say that it's often a combination of traumatic situations and a growing anger at God or at friends and relatives who don't seem to be able to help that can then lead us to consider taking our own lives. "We all can feel pretty beat up sometimes," says Father Stasiak.

But, obviously, suicide is a drastic and permanent conclusion to what may be temporary problems. And the irony, say experts, is that our problems may be a sign that God is reaching out to us. "God may allow things to reach desperate and crisis proportions to get our attention. If we continue to ignore our need to turn to Him, the results can be severe," says Cupid Poe, M.D., a pastor and medical director of the Community Christian Counseling Center in Nashville, Tennessee.

## Suicide Watch

If we're worried that someone is on the verge of committing suicide, we should consider these symptoms, compiled by Gary Collins, Ph.D., president of the American Association of Christian Counselors, in his textbook for counselors called *Christian Counseling*.

- Talk of suicide
- Evidence of a plan of action for committing suicide
- Feelings of hopelessness or meaninglessness
- Indications of guilt and worthlessness
- Recent environmental stresses, such as job loss, divorce, or death in the family
- Inability to cope with stress
- Excessive concern about physical illness
- Preoccupation with insomnia
- Evidence of depression, disorientation, and/or defiance
- Tendency to be dependent and dissatisfied at the same time
- Sudden and unexplained shift to a happy, cheerful mood, which often means that the decision to attempt suicide has been made
- Knowledge regarding the most effective means of suicide
- History of prior suicide attempts

## Judas' Story

One tragic story is found in Matthew's account of Judas. After betraying Jesus for 30 pieces of silver, Judas is seized with guilt and tries to return the blood money. "I have sinned by betraying innocent blood," he said. (Matthew 27:4 NKJV) "Then he threw down the pieces of silver in the temple and departed, and went and hanged himself." (Matthew 27:5 NKJV)

Judas' reaction speaks volumes about how not to handle our failures and problems. And, yes, even our pain. "I like to compare Judas with Peter," says the Reverend John Buckel, Ph.D., associate professor of Scripture and priest at Saint Meinrad School of Theology, a Roman Catholic Priest of the Archdiocese of Indianapolis, and author of *Free to Love*. "Both of them sinned and maybe their sin was equal. Peter denied our Lord. But Judas seemed to think that he was beyond forgiveness. And Peter recognized that God's forgiveness is bigger than his sin."

Peter became the chief Apostle. What might the future have held for Judas if he had recognized that he, too, could be forgiven? "There are two ways to approach big-time failure: Peter's way and Judas' way. And Peter's way is the way to do it," says Father Buckel. It appears that Judas took the rope into his own hands and said, "I'm going to end it because this is the way that I think it should be, because this is the punishment that I think I deserve," still kind of independent, stubborn, and dominant. Whereas Peter is the perfect picture of helplessness, says Father Buckel. He breaks down and cries, which symbolically is a picture of dependence on God and helplessness. In his tears, he's saying, "I can't do this, so God, you have to."

"Often, people who are suicidal have decided that they are worthless, hopeless, unloved, and unlovable," says Dr. Poe. "Such a negative self-assessment is never true. The Scripture says, 'trust in the Lord with all your heart and lean not on your own understanding,' which includes our negative opinions about ourselves. God is always aware of what we're going through."

# A Fresh Start

So it comes down to this: We can either use the pain of our situations to accelerate our demise or to make a new start, something that all of us have to do every single day when the alarm clock rings. Of course, if we're feeling suicidal, we should immediately seek help from a medical doctor or trained counselor, says Wooten. But if we feel that we can confront the problems ourselves, here are some other suggestions for healing.

**Talk to somebody.** The last thing that we should do when we think we might be on the brink of suicide is to isolate ourselves. Instead, we need to talk to friends or relatives. If that's not possible, we should call a suicide prevention hotline, often listed with directory assistance or in the phone book under "crisis intervention" in the human services section, says Wooten. Or we could try a Christian counselor or other health professional. The bottom line is that we need help. And we shouldn't stop talking after the worst is over; we

## A Friend in Need

Clinical depression, often a key factor in suicide, can be triggered by sudden and severe emotional trauma, like the death of a loved one, divorce, or loss of a job. But we don't have to guess whether someone is truly depressed or simply down in the dumps. More severe cases have fairly distinct symptoms, including "not eating enough or eating too much, not sleeping or sleeping too much, an inability to concentrate and focus, lack of energy, or lack of interest in jobs or other people. Things like that," says Wilford Wooten, a licensed marriage, family, and child counselor, a licensed clinical social worker, and director of the department of counseling for Focus on the Family in Colorado Springs, Colorado. "Often, with teens, again, it's a loss of a key relationship—a boyfriend or girlfriend. But serious clinical depression is much more than just being sad."

Anyone who expresses the desire or makes plans to harm himself should be taken seriously, especially those who have a family history of suicide. No one knows why, but those families that have been victimized by this tragic loss in the past seem more likely to be scarred by it again. "The statistics show it, but whether it's genetic or something that's learned is a flip of the coin. We still just don't know," says Wooten.

If we encounter someone whom we suspect is having suicidal thoughts, we need to do two things: Tell a pastor or counselor, and then stand by that person as best we can. "We need to come alongside and say, 'We're not here to make judgments, but we want you to know that God loves you, we care about you, and we are here to be helpful,'" says Wooten.

need to have others in our lives. "If we tend to give up quickly or withdraw, we tend to be more at risk when bad things happen because we're not relying on a support system," says Father Stasiak.

Even those of us who are unwilling or ashamed to admit that we need help can find it in the anonymity of the confession booth. "No one needs to know who we are, and there's no follow-up. What the priest hears he can never, ever, divulge, report, or tell. This sacrament offers that kind of safety and freedom for someone to come out and say, 'I'm not only just upset or afraid but I'm also thinking of killing myself.' And it's not going to be thrown back in anyone's face in any way," says Father Stasiak. Suicide hotlines also offer the same kind of anonymity.

**Pray.** "People who are depressed to the point that they're having suicidal urges should go to God in prayer and ask God for help, says Dr. Poe.

"Jesus says, 'Come unto me all who are weary and heavy laden and I will give you rest,'" says Wooten. "If we don't come, it doesn't happen."

**Give credit where it's due.** Just the fact that we're thinking about asking for forgiveness, help, or treatment demonstrates that there's hope, says Father Stasiak. "That's clearly an indication of strength that we might not realize we have. It's also an indication of God's grace and that we're not alone. God is there, and this is a good first step to make."

**Fix the focus.** Even the most optimistic among us are bound to get depressed when focusing on failures, problems, and difficulties. "When someone runs off the road, it's because they're looking at something else," says Wooten. "Part of the danger of depression is that once we get in that mental state, we tend to lock in and focus on our problems. If we're trying to deal with addictions and other problems, we can't keep thinking about them. We have to retrain ourselves to think about something else." What should we think about instead? Consider this Bible verse, recommends Wooten: "Finally, brethren, whatever things are true, whatever things are noble, whatever things are just, whatever things are pure, whatever things are lovely, whatever things are of good report, if there is any virtue and if there is anything praiseworthy—meditate on these things." (Philippians 4:8 NKJV)

**Accept the pain.** Like the monk with throat cancer, or anyone experiencing nearly any other form of human suffering, our lives can have an impact far beyond what we think or imagine if we're willing, with prayer, to endure. "There are all kinds of ways that we hide from one another, ourselves, and God," says Father Stasiak. "But the suffering that we are sometimes called to do here on Earth is a stripping away of the layers that separate us from each other and God and even from ourselves."

**Stop running.** There are many causes of suicidal tendencies, including those that have been linked to chemical changes in the brain. But some cases may be rooted in the "determination to have one's own way," says Dr. Poe. This is a scenario suspiciously similar to the one found in the book of Jonah. As recounted in the Bible, God told Jonah to go to Nineveh to preach. Instead, Jonah took the first boat out of town, which quickly became caught in a storm that threatened to sink the boat. Scripture tells us that he was thrown overboard and then was swallowed by a great fish. After three days and nights in the belly of the fish, Jonah vowed to do what God had asked him to do, which was the beginning of his deliverance. "When we are willing to repent and are willing to try to live the way that God wants us to live, God begins to deliver us, as he delivered Jonah from the belly of the great fish," says Dr. Poe.

"Many people are overwhelmed by grief and depression because they're running from God, because they're living in rebellion against what God wants them to do. Seeking our own way and pursuing our own goals place us in opposition to God." If this is true for us, Dr. Poe says, then he suggests that we go to God in prayer, asking Him to forgive us and help us put Him first in our lives.

**Join a church.** Several studies have found that those with regular church attendance are less likely to commit suicide. For example, among 91,900 residents surveyed in Washington County, Maryland, those who attend church once or more a week have a 53 percent lower suicide rate than those who don't attend, as well as fewer health problems overall.

A National Institute of Aging study of 4,000 people found that those who attend church at least once a week are half as likely to experience depression as those who attend church less frequently. A study of 1,855 New York City residents found that "failure to attend

## Seasonal Risks

While it's true that more people are depressed around holidays than any another time of the year, suicide rates are heavier in spring, according to Wilford Wooten, a licensed marriage, family, and child counselor, a licensed clinical social worker, and director of the counseling department for Focus on the Family in Colorado Springs, Colorado.

It seems that many of those who are depressed around Christmas are also hopeful that their lives are going to change. Then, if their lives don't change, they get even more depressed. "And when the weather gets a little warmer and they get a little more energy in March, April, and May, that's when they're able to carry out their plans," Wooten says.

The message here is that we need to continue to watch out for those who talk about suicide and not assume that they're cured simply because they've gotten through one difficult time. "Everybody wants to help out the first week or two, but then we just kind of back off and get on with our normal lives. Then the depressed person is left alone. The numbness wears off and they're more at risk," says Wooten.

church services at least weekly was associated with an almost 40 percent increase in the risk of depression," a risk factor for suicide.

**Find a small group.** Joining a small group at church or agreeing to meet once a week with another friend or two, even if it's just for coffee, can help provide someone with whom to share our struggles. "We're going to find some hope and strength in that," says Father Stasiak. "One of the values of confession for people who are contemplating suicide is sharing, revealing, and opening up the heart, even the dark part of the heart that you would think would be so hideous that nobody would understand. And when we can do that with a caring friend or two, that can be healing."

**Build self-esteem.** We can't build our self-esteem by building our bank accounts, our empires, or our egos. Instead, it's as simple as just doing the right thing. "Self-esteem is really a spiritual phenomenon, a gift and by-product of essentially loving others as Christ loves us, says Dr. Poe. And if that sounds a little too esoteric to be of any practical good, consider this: In one study, researchers at the University of Michigan found that the people who had the highest levels of self-esteem were those who relied on religion to help them deal with problems. Those with little religious connection had the lowest feelings of self-worth.

**Meditate on Scripture.** The Bible is loaded with verses that can provide comfort and encouragement in times of distress. "I would suggest Psalm 23," says Dr. Poe, or the first six verses of John 14: "Let not your heart be troubled; you believe in God, believe also in Me. . . ." Also Proverbs 3:5: "Trust in the Lord with all your heart and lean not on your own understanding."

"Isaiah chapter 55," suggests Father Stasiak, "has a beautiful image: Just as the rain comes down from the Heavens and doesn't return to the sky until it does what it is supposed to do, namely water the Earth, so God's Word is not going to come down and return to God frustrated—if we take time, it will take root and make a difference." (Isaiah 55:10–11) And finally, Jeremiah 29:11: "This passage reminds us that we just need to trust God that He has a purpose and plan—and He has the power."

For related information, see Depression (page 215).

# *Surgery*

## LET GO, LET GOD

*A*s a staff chaplain at Memorial Sloan-Kettering Cancer Center in New York City, Sister Elaine Goodell offers to pray with virtually every patient who goes into surgery there—some 35 or 40 patients a day. Whatever their religious affiliations or beliefs, very few of them refuse the offer, not even one seemingly tough guy named Bill.

He was in his late twenties or thereabouts, and when Sister Elaine came to his room, he was gulping down a beer. This was the afternoon prior to his surgery, and beer is definitely not on the hospital's approved pre-surgery menu. His wife, his brother, and his sister were waiting with him.

"I was shocked," Sister Elaine recalls, "but I acted as if we give beer to everybody and I gave my usual introduction: 'Bill, I don't know if you have any belief system, but if you like, I could say a little prayer for you and your surgeon.'"

Bill's three family members were audibly thrilled. "Oh, yes!" they cried in unison. But Bill lay silently, sipping his beer.

"What about you, Bill?" Sister Elaine asked.

Bill paused and looked at his family. "I suppose it wouldn't hurt," he finally said.

While Sister Elaine prayed, Bill drank his beer and fidgeted. It wasn't until she began praying for God to guide the hands of his surgeon that he bowed his head and listened.

"When I finished, no one said a word," Sister Elaine recalls. "All at once, Bill jumped off the bed, grabbed hold of me tightly—he wouldn't let me go—and he said, 'Oh, thank you! Thank you! That was *exactly* what I needed!'"

# How Prayer Can Help

Not every surgery is as dramatic as the ones that take place at Memorial Sloan-Kettering, but when we undergo operations, they are often significant enough to count among the more memorable events in our lives. Prayer and faith can help us get through them. In fact, research has regularly shown that religious people survive major surgery more often, with fewer problems, than people who are not religious. Why would that be so? Many reasons.

For one, believers who pray before surgery often have a sense of calm acceptance that helps prepare them psychologically and physiologically for the operation.

"Statistics show that surgery has a better outcome if the person goes in with a sense of tranquillity," says Kenneth A. Larsen, doctor of ministry who is board certified in psychopharmacology and director of pastoral services and clinical psychology at the New England Baptist Hospital in Boston. Calm also helps the body heal itself effectively after surgery, he adds.

Another important advantage that religious people often enjoy is social support—the loving presence of friends and family—which numerous studies have shown to be a major factor in recovering health after illness.

Cumulatively, these benefits add up to a good foundation for successful surgery, says psychiatrist and prayer researcher Dale A. Matthews, M.D., associate professor of medicine at Georgetown University School of Medicine in Washington, D.C., and author of *The Faith Factor.*

Dr. Matthews adds that there is one other benefit that he believes may be the most fundamental of all: the training that religious people have in letting go. "In a sense, faith is like anesthesia," he says.

# Answered Prayers

## Prayer Made a Difference

"On August 15, 1984, my husband, Bob, found a lump in my breast. I was only 36 years old and had never had a mammogram.

"When I went in for a biopsy, I had been praying with my husband and our prayer group from church. I was scared but I knew that God was with me and would protect me. The surgeon told me that if the tumor was benign, I would go home. If not, they would admit me. When I came out of the anesthesia, the nurse said, 'We're going to take you to your room.' Later, our surgeon came and explained that this tumor probably had roots but he wouldn't know for sure until he started operating.

"I was crushed and scared. I tried to be calm for my family, but the doctor was sure that the cancer had spread further than my breast. That evening, my prayer group came and prayed with Bob and me for some time.

"Next, the anesthesiologist came in to tell me about the surgery. He asked me about my faith and then began to pray with me. I felt a peace come over me. I was no longer scared and helped my family get through the night.

"When I had my surgery, the doctor changed the procedure from a radical mastectomy to a modified mastectomy. My surgeon came up to my room and told me that he could not find the malignant tumor that he had seen originally. He was in tears and totally shocked.

"My husband and I were also very thankful, but we knew what had happened."

—*Yvonne Killon, Florissant, Missouri*

"You're saying, 'I don't know what's going to happen, but I trust that everything is going to work out fine.' That's an important attitude to have when we're going into surgery. It's like getting on a plane; there's nothing you can do. It's all up to the pilot."

## Preparing for the Best

We don't have to have a lifetime of spiritual discipline behind us to get help from prayer and faith when we're preparing for surgery. To the contrary, doctors who spend lots of time in hospital wards say that surgery is one of those events that can summon a strong sense of spiritual connection for almost anyone, as the tough guy at Memorial Sloan-Kettering found out.

"A lot of times, our spiritual lives remain mostly on an intellectual level," says Dr. Larsen. "It's only in times of suffering that we have this great opportunity to bring our intellectual understanding together with the reality of our physical and emotional lives."

Indeed, preachers and doctors agree that surgery can be one of the greatest spiritual opportunities that many of us will ever have. Here's how to weather surgery—whether it be to remove tonsils or a tumor—as peacefully and productively as possible.

**Summon support.** In addition to the prayers that our friends and families may offer on our behalf, we have a long list of prayer resources that we can draw on, says the Reverend Siang-Yang Tan, Ph.D., professor of psychology in the graduate school of psychology at Fuller Theological Seminary in Pasadena, California, and senior pastor of First Evangelical Church in Glendale, California. We can ask our pastors to visit us at home and in the hospital. We can ask members of our churches to conduct small group prayer sessions, perhaps including praying for us while laying hands on us, as has been done since biblical times. We can take part in special healing services and prayer chains that can extend to a whole network of believers.

At some point in their Sunday services, many churches also offer individual prayer requests up before the entire congregation, Dr. Tan adds. If we're not concerned about privacy, we can have literally hundreds of people in our immediate community praying on our behalf.

With all these resources at our disposal, we shouldn't let shyness prevent us from taking advantage of them. "So many patients feel that they don't deserve this kind of attention," says the Reverend George Handzo, master of divinity and director of chaplaincy services at Memorial Sloan-Kettering, "but they do."

**Call on the elders.** The New Testament describes a healing ceremony that Dr. Tan particularly recommends. It's in the letter from James: "Are any among you sick? They should call for the elders of the church and have them pray over them, anointing them with oil in the name of the Lord. The prayer of faith will save the sick, and the Lord will raise them up; and anyone who has committed sins will be forgiven." (James 5:14–15 NRSV) The "elders of the church" usually refers to church pastors and leaders who are spiritually mature Christians, says Dr. Tan, who feels that the ceremony can appropriately take place either at a home or at church.

**Call a counselor.** We should also have no shyness about taking advantage of the pastoral counseling services that are offered by the hospital when we get there, says Reverend Handzo. "It helps that someone cares enough to come pray with us," he says.

The experience of Sister Elaine shows that we don't have to know the person praying for us personally to get a tremendous boost from such services. Nor is it necessary for the prayers to be lengthy ones. Sister Elaine has many letters from people who tell her that she had a profound impact on their lives, all in the course of a hurried minute or two before the escorts wheeled them off to the operating room.

**Pray for the surgeon.** We should feel perfectly comfortable praying for our surgeons, for the attending doctors, the nurses, or anyone and everyone on the hospital staff. Asking others to pray for them is a good idea, too. Sister Elaine makes a habit of doing this for the patients she prays with, and they seem to appreciate those prayers as much as, if not more than, the prayers that she says for the patients themselves. That's only logical, she says. Our primary need when we go in for surgery is that the person performing the procedure do the job well.

**Pray with your surgeon.** Many patients want to go a step further and actually pray *with* their doctors. This is a bit more delicate, because not all doctors are comfortable with such requests. Many are, however. The growing body of research showing that prayer

## Healing Words

### A Guiding Hand

Where can I go from Your spirit? or where can I flee from
Your presence?

If I ascend to Heaven, You are there; if I make my bed in
Sheol, You are there.

If I take the wings of the morning and settle at the farthest
limits of the sea,

Even there Your hand shall lead me, and Your right hand
shall hold me fast.

If I say, "Surely the darkness shall cover me, and the light
around me become night,"

Even the darkness is not dark to You; the night is as bright
as the day, for darkness is as light to You."

*—Psalm 139:7–12 NRSV*

. . . The Lord is near.

Do not worry about anything, but in everything by prayer
and supplication with thanksgiving let your requests be
made known to God.

*—Philippians 4:5–6 NRSV*

and faith can contribute to the success of surgery has made some doctors receptive to prayer, according to Dr. Tan. At the same time, we need to appreciate that our doctors may be hesitant to offer prayers because they don't want to force their beliefs on others. What to do? We can use our instincts to judge how our doctors are likely to respond, Dr. Tan says. Ultimately, it doesn't hurt to ask, and it could help—a lot.

**Relax.** We can enhance the sense of inner peace with which we enter the operating room by practicing deep breathing, meditation, and muscle-relaxation exercises, says Dr. Larsen. All will help speed recovery, as well.

Dr. Larsen has a regimen of relaxation exercises that he teaches to his patients who are experiencing chronic pain, These exercises, which are detailed on page 405, are just as useful in preparing for surgery.

**Clean house.** Unburdening ourselves of resentments toward others is a key element of preparing ourselves for surgery, Dr. Larsen believes. He also suggests trying to let go of regrets for losses that we've suffered in the past.

The reason? The body remembers these losses and grudges as wounds, Dr. Larsen believes, and therefore is clenched defensively against new wounds, which can interfere with surgical healing.

We can't expect to solve years' worth of emotional problems in a few weeks or days, but we can take steps to temporarily put some of our baggage aside, Dr. Larsen says. He suggests that we off-load our problems onto someone we trust. This can consist of sharing burdens verbally or simply "assigning" the load symbolically and mentally to another person. "We need to let our hurts and resentments breathe by talking about them," he says. "It doesn't have to be in detail; just let off some of the steam." In this way, we can practice the forgiveness that the Bible encourages.

**Pray for acceptance.** It's important that we not fall into the trap of believing that prayer is some form of magic that will make all our anxiety disappear. There's nothing wrong with our faith if we still feel somewhat nervous as the big day nears, Dr. Tan says. Some nervousness in the face of surgery is perfectly normal and appropriate.

We can still pray for a sense of peace. "We can be tense but, at the same time, have certain peace and hope and faith that will help us go through the surgery," Dr. Tan says.

For related information, see Science Finds God (page 3) and Pain (page 399).

# Temptation

---

## Taming the Savage Self

*M*uch has been said about the courage of lions. But when hunting, they almost always prey on animals that are weak, weary, sick, or wounded.

Temptation is like that—crouched at the door of our lives, ready to pounce "when we let our guard down or get too tired, too hungry, or too needy," says David Stoop, Ph.D., an addictions counselor in Newport Beach, California, and executive editor of *The Life Recovery Bible.*

Think of it. We've been running errands all day and we're hungry from lack of food. But instead of driving home and having a lean, sensible dinner, we answer the call of the drive-up window and chow down on fatty burgers and fries. Or rather than making the rounds at the office Christmas party, we spend time alone with that friendly, attractive *married* co-worker, who we like just a little too much.

When we act in these ways, we're giving in to something that appeals to "our lower nature, our physical, glandular, carnal self," says Dr. Stoop. In other words, the animal in us.

Obviously, things that look good or taste good or puff us up are tempting to us all. But there's some evidence that a woman's temptations are slightly different than a man's, says Mary Ellen Ashcroft, Ph.D., professor of English at Bethel College in St. Paul, Minnesota, author of *Temptations Women Face,* and the wife of an Episcopal

Church pastor in Minneapolis. "If you asked a number of women, 'Why did you commit that sin?' the answer would have more to do with lack of self-esteem, a lack within that drives them to become compulsive spenders or overeaters or get involved in extramarital affairs." For men, pride is more typically at the root of sin.

## How It Harms Us

Male or female, if we indulge, we may gain a measure of satisfaction for a short time. But then comes that sickening feeling, the one that gnaws at us when we realize that what has lured us away was built on a false promise and that it will never fully satisfy. In the words of Jeremiah the prophet, "My people have committed two sins: They have forsaken me, the spring of living water, and have dug their own cisterns, broken cisterns that cannot hold water." (Jeremiah 2:13 NIV)

The trouble doesn't stop there. Repeatedly yielding to temptation can lead to addiction. "Regardless of what the temptation is, if we get a high from it—a temporary emotional lift—it can be very addictive, says Dr. Stoop.

A few words on what temptation is not. For one thing, it's not a sin to be tempted. If it were, Jesus would be in big trouble, since He was tempted at least three times by Satan himself. And temptation isn't going away. Even if we get to the root of something that is tempting us and master it, we will always face another temptation, says Dr. Ashcroft.

The good news is that our temptations can be tremendous points of growth for us. But we need to develop strategies for dealing with them, says Dr. Ashcroft. Here are the 13 "Rs" for resisting temptation.

**Run!** While some temptations may legitimately require time to ponder, others should simply make us turn tail and run. "These are the ones that can really do us in, like sexual situations," says Dr. Ashcroft, "or times when we would say something out of rage that we'd later regret."

**Resist.** Standing our ground against one temptation can prepare us for the next, a spiritual truth best illustrated by the old hymn, "Yield Not to Temptation," says the Reverend David Wigley, pastor of the First Congregational Church in Kennebunkport, Maine. "The first few lines go like this: 'Yield not to temptation, for yielding is sin.

Each victory will help you, some other to win,'" he says. "One victory over temptation makes us stronger to face the next. Because then we can say to ourselves, 'I know that I can say no.'"

"Some people look at prayer as kind of a magical incantation," says Dr. Stoop. "But it's the relational aspect of my praying that gives me strength. The fact that I believe that I'm talking to God and that God hears me and cares about me is where that strength is going to come from."

**Re-collect the ultimate reward.** If temptation's pull seems too strong, we need to remind ourselves that a few minutes or hours of pleasure aren't worth sacrificing our marriages, our health, or God's blessing, says Dr. Stoop. "Blessed is the man who perseveres under trial, because when he has stood the test, he will receive the crown of life that God has promised to those who love Him." (James 1:12 NIV)

**Respect escape routes.** Ever had the phone ring just when you were about to get into a major fight with your spouse? Or has your child ever called out with a question from another room when your face was buried in the refrigerator? Don't ignore them; the Bible promises that heavenly exit signs will appear as temptation draws near. "And God is faithful; He will not let you be tempted beyond what you can bear. But when you are tempted, He will also provide a way out so that you can stand up under it." (1 Corinthians 10:13 NIV) "Look at the story of Joseph and his temptation by Potiphar's wife. Often, when a man gets into that type of situation, his glands take over and he doesn't run. And then he gets mad because he was seduced. Well, he didn't use the escape route," says Dr. Stoop.

**Reduce stress.** Since we're more likely to give in to temptation when we're stressed out, hungry, or at wit's end, we also need to take better care of ourselves, says Dr. Stoop. Regular exercise, eating right, and getting enough sleep should all help keep our physical cravings in check and our spiritual defenses intact.

**Re-evaluate.** If we know that we're liable to go crazy with our credit cards when we go shopping in an attempt to soothe a serious emotional hurt, our best defense may be to leave them at home, says Dr. Stoop. The same approach works for nearly all tempting situations. If we have problems with sexual lust, we need to re-evaluate whether it's wise to view or read magazines or books that may inflame us.

**Recall the Garden.** The next time a smooth-talking someone tries to tempt us, we need to remember Adam and Eve. Sure, they succumbed to fruit that was ". . . pleasing to the eye, and also desirable for gaining wisdom . . ." (Genesis 3:6 NIV), something that looked good and promised much, says Dr. Stoop. But they may not have messed up at all if they hadn't listened to that lying reptile in the first place.

**Rely on healthy relationships.** This is the best guard against temptation, says Dr. Stoop, especially if the healthy relationships are with people to whom we wish to be accountable. "Not because we have been forced to be accountable, but because we have chosen to be mutually accountable," says Dr. Stoop. One way to build these into our lives is to ask a friend to meet with us once a month or more and invite them to ask some tough questions about how we're spending our time and money and what we're thinking about.

**Read the writing on the wall.** If we're honest, our temptations can tell us a lot about ourselves. Dr. Ashcroft offers an example: "Anytime I'm doing a talk somewhere, I have this feeling that I need to go out and spend money on a new outfit," she says. "What I've figured out is that sometimes I'm not feeling very confident and somehow this outfit will be a solution to my lack of confidence." Talking to a pastor, counselor, or trusted friend will often help clarify the source of our temptation.

**Research new directions.** If our temptations are rooted in a lack of self-esteem or fulfillment, we may never gain the upper hand until we get in touch with the true calling that God has for us. How can we possibly figure that out? "Look back at the times when you really felt tremendous satisfaction in your life," says Dr.Ashcroft. "Times when you really felt like you did something good that was meaningful or you felt strongly about. Or that someone said you were really good at. That's probably your calling."

**Reconnect.** Even if every wish we make is being granted, ultimately, we're not going to be satisfied until we get and stay in touch with our Creator, says Dr. Ashcroft. Three of the best ways to deepen our relationships with God are to attend church regularly, spend time in Bible study, and pray.

**Replicate God's love.** If we're married and struggling with sexual temptation, we need to love our spouses the way that God loves us, says Reverend Wigley. "God loves each of us as if we're the only one He has to love, and we need to carry that into our own relationships. We're to love them as if they're the only ones among humanity."

**Rejoice!** That's right, temptation can be good for us. "Consider it pure joy, my brothers, whenever you face trials of many kinds, because you know that the testing of your faith develops perseverance. Perseverance must finish its work so that you may be mature and complete, not lacking anything." (James 1:2–4 NIV)

"You know that old saying, 'No pain, no gain?' There's no growth without having to struggle with something, whether it's temptation or tribulation," says Dr. Stoop.

For related information on temptation, see Addictions (page 148).

# Terminal Illness

## FULFILLMENT ON THE FINAL JOURNEY

*I*f we're handed a death sentence, or told that a serious illness could lead to one, our psyches are going to twist and torque. Our outlooks will change dramatically, possibly many times, possibly from minute to minute.

Suddenly, life and all that it offers and entails will take on a different hue, an urgency, and possibly despair.

The disheartening diagnosis can come at any time. As Jesus' brother James wrote: ". . . you do not know what will happen tomorrow. For what is your life? It is even a vapor that appears for a little time and then vanishes away." (James 4:14 NKJV)

No, we do not know what will happen tomorrow. Neither do the doctors. Despite their best guesses, however, we are allowed to hope.

## Hold On to Hope

We are allowed to hope that somehow, miraculously, we will get better. Such miracles do happen. Try to hold on to hope. And try to hold on to an appreciation for all that is beautiful and good in life, says the Reverend James E. Miller, doctor of ministry, United Methodist minister of Willowgreen Productions in Fort Wayne, Indiana, a center that helps those experiencing grief and loss, and au-

# Answered Prayers

## Prayer Wiped Away My Cancer

"In 1982, I was rushed to the Troy Beaumont Hospital emergency room and was in surgery 20 minutes after my arrival. Doctors discovered that a large tumor on my ovary had burst, causing serious infection.

"Three days later, my doctor came to my room. My prognosis, he said, was 6 to 12 months at best. The tumor was cancerous. He told me to put my affairs in order. He said that when the tumor burst, it sent cancer cells all over, spreading the cancer and causing new cancers to appear. He likened it to scattering seeds on the ground.

"I called my pastor right away. He laid hands on me, anointed my head with oil, and we prayed. Many people from the church prayed for me. My family prayed.

"I have just celebrated my sixteenth year of being cancer-free. I'm living proof that with prayer, patience, and a positive attitude, anything is possible. Miracles happen."

—*Dorothy Bergen, Roseville, Michigan*

thor of numerous books and videotapes used in hospices, hospitals, funeral homes, and counseling services.

We need to try hard because life-threatening illness and terminal disease may twist our perspectives and change our outlooks. If we have only a limited time—or there's a possibility we have only a limited time—should we spend it feeling sorry for ourselves, feeling miserable, concentrating on and cursing the disabling elements of our illnesses? "A better approach is to do what we can to appreciate and find meaning in whatever time we have left," says Dr. Miller. ". . . I have set before you life and death," God says. ". . . therefore choose life." (Deuteronomy 30:19 KJV)

That's not to say we won't feel sorry for ourselves. That's not to say we won't feel angry at times and curse our fate. That's not to say we won't feel excruciating pain or incredible waves of illness at times. But they need not be all that we feel, says Dr. Miller.

We may also feel grateful that God gave us this day; gave us another day. We may realize this could be our last chance in this life to experience the majesty of a sunrise or sunset; or to experience the sensations of love, joy, awe, pleasure, and laughter; or to make a difference in someone else's life; or to let someone know how much they've meant to us. This may be the day we write the poem that will light up lives 100 years from now. This may be a day in which we simply appreciate beauty in the world around us or hold a loved one's hand. This day is, to a great extent, what we make it.

Want to make a day better? Consider this Bible verse.

... **Whatsoever things are true, whatsoever things are honest, whatsoever things are just, whatsoever things are pure, whatsoever things are lovely, whatsoever things are of good report: if there be any virtue , and if there be any praise, think on these things.**

—*Philippians 4:8 KJV*

We can do that despite our pain, despite our illnesses. We can do things that we enjoy despite even disabling pain, says Margaret Caudill, M.D., Ph.D., a doctor who specializes in pain management, former co-director of the Arnold Pain Center at Beth Israel Deaconess Medical Center in Boston, and author of *Managing Pain Before It Manages You.*

Yes, we should respect the stress of pain, says Dr. Caudill. But it's important to engage in pleasurable activities that can balance the stress, like watching sunsets and sunrises, eating ice cream, fishing, and feeding the birds, she says.

"Move as much as possible," Dr. Caudill says, "because that keeps the body from becoming weaker, which can increase dysfunction and increase the pain." Gentle stretching, yoga exercises, and isometrics might be just what the doctor ordered. And if we can't get out of bed, we can get a massage, listen to books on tape, ask somebody to rent us some great funny videos, and continue to live in the time that we have.

# Find Strength in Faith

Science can prove that people with and without illnesses who attend church regularly live longer and fare better than those who do not, says psychiatrist and prayer researcher Dale A. Matthews, M.D., associate professor of medicine at Georgetown University School of Medicine in Washington, D.C., and author of *The Faith Factor*. He says that well-researched studies show that seriously ill religious people require less pain medication and experience less death anxiety and depression than do the nonreligious.

The power of prayer itself seems evident in an unusual study in San Francisco, where approximately 400 patients were divided into two groups. Roughly half the patients were prayed for by Christian prayer groups and half were not. Neither doctors nor patients knew which patients were being prayed for. Those praying only knew the patients' first names, diagnosis, and general condition. They were asked to pray daily specifically for rapid recovery and prevention of complications and death. The prayer group required less medication, had fewer incidences of pneumonia, fewer cardiac arrests, and needed intravenous fluids or mechanical ventilation less frequently than those in the group that was not prayed for.

Of course, there was no way to control which patients also were prayed for by friends and family. That is considered one of the inherent problems with the study. The results of the study have not been replicated to date; thus, its findings are not considered conclusively proven. But, says Dr. Matthews, how can it hurt to ask our churches and friends to pray for us?

Need further proof that faith is good for us in times of trouble? Dr. Matthews says we can look at other studies that show that regular churchgoers and highly religious people are less likely to die following major surgeries, are less likely to develop debilitating diseases, and tend to live longer, in general.

Why do people with spiritual orientation tend to face death with less fear and anxiety? "Most cultures, at most times, in most places in the world, believe and have believed that there is a life beyond this physical life," says the Reverend Mel Lawrenz, Ph.D., senior associate pastor at Elmbrook Church and director of the Elmbrook Christian Study Center, both in Brookfield, Wisconsin, and co-author of six books, including *Life after Grief* and *Overcoming Grief and Trauma.* That belief, he says, gives believers hope. It tells them that "the end" is not "THE END," but rather a passage from this life to what various world religions teach is a more divine form of existence.

"If we believe that the only lives we have are the physical lives of our own bodies, then we will desperately cling to that," explains Dr. Lawrenz. The tip here is to explore our faith and what it teaches us and what we believe about life on "the other side." We will find comfort in that.

## Healthy Ways to Die

So we're told we are dying, or that we may be. We can do it poorly or we can do it well. To do it as well as we can, consider these suggestions from Dr. Miller, author of *When You Know You're Dying.*

**Demand dignity.** We are more than our illnesses. But maybe it's all our doctors talk about. Sometimes, even friends and relatives seem to want to discuss nothing else. "With some people, we feel completely depersonified," Dr. Miller says. We become simply a case, a disease, a patient, another experiment, or a walking death certificate. It's as though they have completely written off all the rest of us. They see us only as sick bodies.

They're wrong, and they may need to be told so. After all, we have minds, hearts, and souls, besides bodies. Remember, we are and always have been someone. We do have personalities and interests and a uniqueness that has always set us apart from the rest of the world. This was true before we got sick. This is true now. We mustn't let anyone rob us of that.

**Go ahead and feel.** Our feelings will be many, unpredictable, and intense. We should feel whatever we feel. It's okay, says Dr. Miller. We have permission.

Expect sadness, pain, fear, confusion, shock, panic, anger, envy,

## Where to Find Comfort

When serious or terminal illness strikes, good advice and compassion can help us work through the concerns and fears that we may have. Here are some places to turn for help.

- Regional cancer treatment centers can direct you to local hospices, support groups, and other resources in your immediate area. Find them under hospitals or medical centers in the Yellow Pages or call any large nearby hospital.
- Willowgreen Productions publishes a number of inspiring videos and small, inexpensive books filled with comforting tips and advice for the seriously and terminally ill, for their caregivers, and for grievers. For a catalog, write to them at P.O. Box 25180, Fort Wayne, IN 46825.

emptiness, pressure, and more. And besides the downers, we may also feel love, joy, and pride at times. We may feel a jumble of feelings. They may arrive exactly when we wish they wouldn't. That's the way it is with feelings. Only they know for sure when they are going to show up, how, and for how long. So invite them in and let them be what they are. Don't pass judgment on them. They are neither good nor bad; they just are. They are proof that we are feeling people, that we care. We shouldn't let anyone tell us to subdue them or hide them, advises Dr. Miller.

**Find a friend.** We should look for someone we can really talk to, who won't judge us, correct us, or cut us off. Tell them of our confusion, of our emotions, of our fears and doubts, and so on. Or seek out support groups or several friends with whom we feel comfortable venting. "There is not a firm rule of thumb as to who those people should be or how many there should be," says Dr. Miller. "We're all different; we all seem to have different needs in that way. For some people, just having one other person is all it takes. And

(continued on page 462)

# How to Help

Someone we love is dying, suddenly disabled, or confronted with a life-threatening illness. We feel empathy, certainly, but we may also feel awkward with them because we don't know what to say or do. Do we talk about the situation or do we ignore it? Do we continue to talk about things happening in the outside world and with our greater circle of friends and in our work environments? Or do we avoid those kinds of subjects because they remind the stricken one of their limits and confinement—of what they are missing?

"There is a tendency to treat dying people differently. Voices are often lowered," says the Reverend James E. Miller, doctor of ministry, United Methodist minister of Willowgreen Productions in Fort Wayne, Indiana, a center that helps those experiencing grief and loss, and author of numerous books and videotapes used in hospices, hospitals, funeral homes, and counseling services. Faces turn somber or falsely cheerful, he says.

Don't do that, says Dr. Miller, author of *One You Love Is Dying*. Don't treat them differently. This loved one or friend is the same person they have always been. "They are as full of life as we are," he says. Treat them as equals. They don't want pity; they want compassion. They want to be treated as very much alive. They want to live as fully as they are able.

Here are some other rules of thumb from Dr. Miller.

**Don't go it alone.** We shouldn't try to be the sole caregiver and do everything ourselves. We won't be able to. We'll get frazzled and upset. We need to encourage others to help and, when they offer, take them up on it. There are meals to be cooked, household chores to be done, medical supplies and prescriptions to be picked up, shopping to do, trips to the doctor to be made, bills to be paid, phone calls to be made, and on and on. Atop all that is the sick one's need for companionship. It's too much for one person to do. "If others do not offer help, we should ask for it," says Dr. Miller.

Setting boundaries and limits—how much time we can give, what we can do—early in the caregiving phase will help ensure that our needs are respected, as well, so that we don't burn out or feel abused.

**Let the loved one lead.** They have needs, so we should let them make basic decisions about their care and their environment: which room they would like, where to put the bed and the lighting. Will there be music? Reading material? They should decide when visitors are welcome and how many and for how long.

Likewise, the loved one "should play the central role on their medical team," says Dr. Miller. The patient, if possible, should decide which doctors, which hospitals, and what treatments they want. Those are not our decisions; they are theirs. They have every right to be fully informed of their medical options and choose how they will exercise them.

We do need to guide them away from self-destructive behaviors. But beyond these parameters, it's their life. We need to let them choose how to live it.

**Draw them out.** We've heard it before: Sometimes the most valuable thing we can do is listen. When someone is dying or on the verge of dying, they usually need to talk to others, but they may not know where to start, says Dr. Miller. We can talk about how they're feeling, encourage them to relay memories, and let them know that we're there for them if they need to talk. And when they do need to talk, we should let them, he says. And at times when they do not feel like talking, it's okay to just be there. This can be beneficial to the caregivers, too. Often, a gentle touch is also appreciated. It, too, is a form of communication.

**Get advanced directives.** That's the proper term for a living will. While the loved one is still able, we or a hospice representative should help them draw up instructions for their care should they become so physically disabled that they are unable to communicate or make such decisions. In addition, they should visit a lawyer and make sure that their will and other important documents are in order and as they would like them to be.

others value having complete networks of people."

**Let the tears flow.** It's our party, we can cry if we want to—as loud and long as we like. And if we feel like it, we might explore on paper what we are crying about, what we are feeling, and what we are remembering that is important to us, suggests Dr. Miller.

**Make history.** We could consider keeping a journal. Or, "have someone help us write a journal," says Dr. Miller. "Sometimes, people are just too ill to do it themselves and it's a great help if someone else will write down what they tell them to." What do we put in a journal? Record thoughts about life and death. Tell about things we've learned. Share our wisdom and wit. We can record stories about our families and their accomplishments that others may have forgotten or may not know. We can talk about how our perspectives have changed now that we know our time is at hand. This can be a wonderful gift and memory for the family and friends we leave behind as well as a great spiritual exercise to experience.

**Talk to God.** Praying has always been considered an appropriate way to unburden and pour out our souls. If we feel so inclined, we should do it. Or we can meditate or worship in whatever way we are comfortable. "As a mother comforts her child, so shall I comfort you," promises God. (Isaiah 66:13 NIV)

**Create a list of wants and needs.** Our lists can be ever-developing because our needs and desires can change from day to day. But this way, when anyone says, "If you need anything, just let me know," we are prepared to respond with things that we really need. People feel better when they know that their efforts are really helping and are needed and appreciated. No one else knows for sure everything we want and need until we tell them. Keeping a list is a great way to do this, says Dr. Miller.

**Take care.** We need to eat healthfully. We should take an active role in treatment decisions; that is, study, understand, and choose life-enhancing medications and therapies. We should get plenty of rest and do everything we reasonably can that gives us a fighting chance at survival and/or enjoying our final days, says Dr. Miller. We should pamper ourselves. Now. Because that's where we live.

# *Thankfulness*

## An Attitude for Good Times and Bad

*R*emember how easy it was to thank your mom and dad for the shiny new bike that you got for your 10th birthday, but how hard it was to say thank you when Aunt Martha gave you that ill-fitting monogrammed underwear?

Thankfulness can be a breeze when it's a response to something that brings us obvious pleasure, but a real struggle when we have to dig a little deeper in order to find out what, exactly, there is to be thankful for. Yet it is possible to maintain a sense of thankfulness, as the Bible describes it, even when things aren't perfect, even when the world seems bleak and it doesn't seem that an end to our misery is in sight.

Think of Jesus, who on the night when He was to be given over to the Roman authorities, still managed to give thanks for the food and drink that He received. Think of Daniel, who offered thanks and praise to God even though the Jews were locked in pitched struggle against pagan intruders. Think of the Psalmist who gave thanks to God despite suffering unjust accusations. Their secret? Thankfulness for them, this true biblical sense of thanksgiving, was not just tied to the offering of earthly rewards. That's a lesson that's still valid today. "Thanksgiving needn't be bound to the immediate pleasures or pains

# Faithbuilders

## Thankful for the Little Things

In *Sleeping with Bread: Holding What Gives You Life*, authors Dennis Linn, Sheila Fabricant Linn, and Matthew Linn tell a story of thankfulness in a thankless time.

In England, during World War II, guardians of groups of children who were separated from their parents noticed that the children were having a particularly difficult time sleeping through the night, their fears and uncertainties being so pitched. To rectify the problem, they gave each child a piece of bread to hold on to as they drifted off to sleep. The message of the bread was simply, 'I've eaten today, and I'll eat tomorrow,' and this was enough to comfort them, as thereafter they all slept through the night. Daily bread is really enough to be thankful for.

of life," says the Reverend Eleanor Morrison, co-director of Leaven, a nonprofit agency dedicated to social justice in Lansing, Michigan. "It can be rooted instead in the abiding sense that no matter what happens on Earth, we put our trust in a God who, in the words of Psalm 121, 'keeps me, and will not slumber.'"

Or, as Paul put it ". . . give thanks in all circumstances, for this is God's will for you in Christ Jesus." (1 Thessalonians 5:18 NIV)

## Getting by the Barriers

It's not always easy to receive God's love with a demeanor of thanksgiving. "Any number of things can get in the way of thankfulness," says the Reverend Dennis Knight, senior minister at Pakachoag Church, UCC, in Auburn, Massachusetts, and co-founder of Keeping Company, an AIDS ministry in Worcester. For one thing, the trials of life sometimes can be so overwhelming that we lose sight of God. He cites an example: "Not long ago, our parish suffered the death of a wonderful young woman to breast cancer. She left behind a husband and two small children, and the best that we could do at her funeral service was confess that 'life stinks and praise God.' I suspect that it was a whole lot easier for us to grasp the first part of that statement than the second."

Another obstacle to thanksgiving is simply our inability to appreciate the little pleasures of everyday life. "I remember some years ago when an ice storm knocked out our town's electricity," Reverend Knight says. "After a few days, a lot of our congregants started grousing about the situation, so I preached a sermon about thankfulness, about small daily pleasures for which we give little thanks but without which we'd be so much the poorer. I think that it's difficult for any of us to feel thankful for things or services—food, water, electricity, good health, considerate neighbors—that are right at our disposal every time we wake up."

And there's a third obstacle to thankfulness, says the Reverend Brian H. Childs, Ph.D., a Presbyterian minister, director of health and human values for Shore Health System in Easton, Maryland, and author of several books on pastoral theology and pastoral care. It's our "compulsive need to treat gifts as things that are traded rather than given."

"It's hard to receive a gift and not want to repay it, whether that gift comes from God or from your Uncle Louie," Dr. Childs says. "Recently, when a friend invited me over for dinner, I asked what I could bring. A bottle of wine? A salad? Some flowers? But I was told only to bring myself, nothing more. It was an odd feeling, to receive the gift of this person's meal and not somehow compensate them for it. Initially, I felt indebted.

"Finally, our own egos can interfere with our ability to be thankful, says Dr. Childs. "I remember counseling a family in which the son had been abused by his father. We reached a point where the boy was extending forgiveness to his dad, but in order to receive this extraordinary gift, the man had to completely humble himself, accept it despite his unworthiness, know that he couldn't repay it, and admit his need for it. But the hardest part was, as it often is, accepting one's acceptability, that God embraces us no matter how heinous our sins might be. This acceptance required of the man a posture of utter thanksgiving," he says.

# Prayer Pointers

## God Is in the Details

"When I was a child, my friends and I would come inside from playing and my mom would have sandwiches and bowls of soup waiting for us," recalls the Reverend Dennis Knight, senior minister at Pakachoag Church, UCC, in Auburn, Massachussetts, and co-founder of Keeping Company, an AIDS ministry in Worcester. "I didn't appreciate it, I expected it, because it was there every day for me, without fail. To me, as a kid, the meal 'just appeared.' I had no sense of the labors of my mother.

"Had I been truly grateful, though, I think I might have behaved differently, might have thanked her more honestly, maybe done a little more to help her out around the house, or found ways to show her that I appreciated her.

"It's not much different with God, is it? God is so steady in our lives that we come to expect that steadiness rather than give thanks for it. Maybe if we took a moment to appreciate God's labors, we'd do a little more to help out, find ways to show our appreciation."

"As a counselor, I realized that the worst thing I could do at that moment was to get in the way, so I sat back and let the two of them play it out themselves," says Dr. Childs. The boy was wonderfully relentless—very much like Jesus—in his willingness to forgive. And the dad was terrified. But the boy just stood at the 'door' and knocked. And knocked and knocked. And finally, in a heap of tears, the father answered. In subsequent sessions, we spent long hours helping the father come to terms with two striking realities of pain and promise: First, that like all of us, he was a sinner who had to take account of his sins, and second, that like all of us, he had this enormous capacity to beg and receive forgiveness, and that being able to do so is something for which we must all be profoundly thankful."

# Growing a Grateful Attitude

If we look carefully at our lives, we'll see that they are rich with things both profound and small for which we can feel thankful. And rich, too, with opportunities to build the sense of thankfulness that Dr. Childs suggests "we feel in the face of the limitless outpouring of God's love for us." Here are some suggestions.

**Give thanks for everyday things.** We can offer prayers of thanks to God for the simple things that we normally take for granted, such as health, friendships, or the support of a church fellowship, suggests Reverend Morrison. We should choose one such item each day and give thanks for the ways in which it brings some sliver of happiness to our lives.

**Thank God for small surprises.** We can thank God in prayer for the old friends we ran into, for example. In Dr. Childs' view, things like this are small symbols of the serendipity of God's love.

**Study the Psalms.** In particular, we can use Psalm 100 as a prayer and meditate on what kind of "joyful noise" we might make to God, says Reverend Morrison. Perhaps it's singing an impromptu hymn, thanking a neighbor for being a neighbor, or complimenting the grocery clerk for being a conscientious worker. The thing to do is make sure that our thanks are conveyed so that the recipient knows that we really mean it.

**Do without.** We're not ascetics, but spending just one day without products, services, or activities that we take for granted—television, telephone, our daily walk in the park—will deepen our thanksgiving for them, says Reverend Knight.

**Accept the thanks of others.** If we're in a situation like the one that Dr. Childs described, in which a friend or relative wants to offer us a meal or a gift, we need to quell any feelings of indebtedness. "Thankfulness is a dance that requires two partners," says Dr. Childs, "one giving and the other receiving freely. It is the same with God. He offers us His grace, His mercy, and His love, but if we refuse to receive it, it falls dead at our feet."

# Showing That Lovin' Feeling

When we are feeling thankful for our lives, for God's love, or for the world in which we live, we can do specific things to sustain that feeling.

**Make a thankful gesture anonymously.** We can try doing a few good deeds for others, with no expectation of compensation. Hand out free balloons on a street corner. Cut a neighbor's lawn. Offer to carry someone's luggage to a bus stop.

# Answered Prayers

## God Saved My Husband

"Rushing home to take me to the hospital for the birth of our daughter, my husband, Bob, lost control of his car and went down a mountain three hundred feet. Somehow, his car landed in a tree with its headlights shining up toward the sky. He was thrown from the car and landed another hundred feet down on a ledge. A few minutes later, a woman and her husband who always went to visit relatives had a gut feeling and turned around and headed back home. They saw the lights from Bob's car and contacted a rescue team.

"Bob was badly injured and the crew thought he was dead. They were zipping him into a body bag when all of a sudden, he let out a gurgle. They immediately did a tracheotomy on him and rushed him to the hospital.

"Doctors said that Bob did not even have a 50-50 chance of surviving. As I lay in my hospital bed after the birth of our daughter, I prayed to God to let Bob live. With tears rushing down my face, I suddenly felt a rushing warmth run through my body. I immediately knew that it was God telling me that Bob was not going to die.

"Bob had a tough road ahead and was in intensive care for months. They had to amputate his right leg below the knee. But six months later, Bob came home. Now, more than 25 years after the accident, he is doing very well. I thank God every day for answering my prayer."

—*Penny Golding, Ridge Manor, Florida*

**Spend a day with a public servant.** We entrust ourselves to countless workers that we never see, from the postal worker to the town clerk. We can spend part of a work day visiting with one of them and let them know how much we appreciate the importance of their work, suggests Reverend Knight.

**Thank a family member.** We can write an unsolicited letter of thanks to one member of our family for one act of kindness that they showed us at one time in our lives. If it's an obscure memory, we can remind them of the details of the event.

**Collect food for the neighborhood pantry.** We could organize a semi-monthly food drive at a local grocery store, invite shoppers to purchase one food item, collect them, and donate them to the local pantry. It's a tangible way of giving thanks to God for our ability to feed our families, says Dr. Childs.

In a world for which we give constant thanks, no gesture is too small, nothing is meaningless, and everything is sacred. As Reverend Morrison puts it, "In thanksgiving, I know that I and all that is around me are grounded in God."

# *Tolerance*

## SEEING PAST OUR DIFFERENCES

*O*nce every quarter, Reconciliation Sunday is held at the Rock, an evangelical free church on the west side of Chicago. First, in what they call the "chocolate" meeting, Senior Pastor Raleigh Washington meets with African-American members of the congregation to discuss any issues from the Black perspective. Then, in the "vanilla" meeting, he meets with the White membership, and their views are aired.

Immediately afterward, there is "fudge ripple" meeting. Fudge ripple ice cream is served, as are Oreo cookies. But the main course is exposed feelings. As Pastor Washington puts it, "My job is to go in there and rat on both groups."

Airing issues before they turn into resentments is what Pastor Washington calls acting in a preventive mode. The idea is to promote tolerance by short-circuiting misunderstanding. "If you deal with an issue before it becomes a problem and talk about it," he says, "you can reach common ground. If you don't, never the twain shall meet."

Reconciliation Sunday is an example of a very basic fact about achieving true tolerance: It takes work. This applies to tolerance between spouses and between drivers racing along the highway as much as it does to tolerance between racial, religious, or political groups. "In any human relationship, there's one thing I can guarantee you," Pastor Washington says. "Conflict will come. That's inevitable. The question is, what are you going to do about it?"

## It's More Than Just Acceptance

Many spiritual leaders aren't particularly fond of the word *tolerance*. They feel that it doesn't adequately convey the degree of love and commitment that the Bible requires. Pastor Washington, who is also vice president of reconciliation for the Promise Keepers men's movement, shares that view. "The Bible says that we have to do more than tolerate one another," he says. "We have to actively love one another."

This is not to say that conflicts are to be ignored. To the contrary, the Bible spells out quite clearly that differences are to be actively confronted: "If another member of the church sins against you, go and point out the fault when the two of you are alone. If the member listens to you, you have regained that one. But if you are not listened to, take one or two others along with you, so that every word may be confirmed by the evidence of two or three witnesses." (Matthew 18:15–16 NRSV)

This passage demonstrates that tolerance is not a synonym for acquiescence. "Tolerance often has a very superficial meaning of simply putting up with people you don't like, pretending that your most important differences don't really make any difference," says Father Richard John Neuhaus, editor in chief of *First Things*, a monthly journal of ideas, and director of the Institute for Religion in Public Life in New York City. "It's not tolerance that you want to cultivate so much as respectful engagement and Christian love." The appropriate stance, he says, is to stand up for what we believe in but to do so without coercion or deception. Referring to the Apostle Paul's advice to the Ephesians (4:15), Father Neuhaus adds, "We 'speak the truth in love' and hope to persuade."

Often, it is the respectful part of engagement that we have trouble with, which is a large part of the reason why tolerance is such hard work, says Richard Mouw, Ph.D., president and professor of Christian ethics at Fuller Theological Seminary in Pasadena, California, and author of *Uncommon Decency*. Remaining civil in the company of people whose views we find repugnant—neo-Nazis, for example— requires a degree of patience that may be hard to muster.

Dr. Mouw believes that Christians are often guilty of intolerance—

# Home Work

Sometimes we can show more tolerance toward entire ethnic or religious groups than we can for the individual across the breakfast table, says Wilford Wooten, a licensed marriage, family, and child counselor, a licensed clinical social worker, and director of the counseling department for Focus on the Family in Colorado Springs, Colorado. Here are two of his most important recommendations for achieving a more tolerant marriage.

**Lower your expectations.** Often, we expect more of our spouses than they can deliver. That's our problem as much as theirs, according to Wooten. "We enter relationships with very high expectations," he says, "some of which we're not even aware of. They're based on movies, on our families of origin, on lots of things. Often, they aren't a source of conflict until after we're married. Then we start to come up against them."

True tolerance, Wooten says, requires us to step back and examine the preconceived notions that we're bringing to the relationship. The goal is to accept our partners as they are rather than forcing them to meet our expectations.

**Accentuate the positive.** Many of us have a tendency to focus on what's wrong in our relationships, Wooten says, rather than on what's right. We also have a tendency to chew over old resentments rather than letting them go. Both of these habits can be changed and, for the sake of tolerance, need to be. "We can make a choice of what we want to dwell on," he says. "That doesn't mean that we won't have temptations, that Satan isn't going to bring things to us. Christ was tempted, too. But we can make a choice to move on."

Wooten advocates what he calls the replacement principle, which means consciously replacing negative, destructive thoughts with positive, constructive ones, as suggested by the Apostle Paul: "Fix your thoughts on what is true and good and right. Think about things that are pure and lovely, and dwell on the fine, good things in others."(Philippians 4:8 TLB)

a weakness with which they are frequently charged—because they tend to focus more on declaring their own moral convictions than on listening carefully to the convictions of others. "I don't want to make tolerance the ultimate virtue," he says. "Faithfulness to God is what we're ultimately all about. But I think that we Christians often rush to judgment without thinking of how we relate to other people." He explains that preachers often quote the first part of 1 Peter 3:15–16 (NRSV): "Always be ready to make your defense to anyone who demands from you an accounting for the hope that is in you . . ." but forget the second part: ". . . yet do it with gentleness and reverence."

It is a Christian duty, Dr. Mouw says, to strive for compassionate understanding, both for the sake of tolerance and for constructive dialogue. "If the goal is really to bring the truth to people, then listening, patience, empathy, and civility can be an important part of that."

In the end, of course, Christians should be tolerant simply because it is God, not us, who ultimately judges. "It's not our job to make everything go right and to correct all the mistakes in the world," Dr. Mouw says. "Every human being has to stand someday before God. That's when things will really be straightened out."

## While We're Waiting

Given that the task of Christian love is difficult to achieve, at least showing tolerance can be a big step in the right direction. Here are some steps that can help bring it closer.

**Make a commitment.** Pastor Washington remembers one of his African-American parishioners saying, "My mother never taught me to hate White folks," to which he replied, "Yes, but did your mother teach you to go out of your way to actively love White folks?" The answer to that was no, Pastor Washington says. It should be yes, for all of us. We must actively dedicate ourselves toward the goal of increasing tolerance in the world and in our own hearts.

**Take the initiative.** The best way to work on actively loving our neighbors, Pastor Washington says, is to actively seek them out. "We must establish committed relationships with people of different races or colors," he says. "Virtually none of us lives in a vacuum where we don't come into proximity with people who are racially different from ourselves. Wherever we have that proximity, then we must capitalize on it by initiating a relationship."

The direct approach is often best, Pastor Washington says. He offers as an example a White person who might have a Hispanic mailman. "You can go up to that person and say, 'You know what? You're my mailman. I don't know you, and you don't know me, but this world would be a better place if we could learn more about each other. Could we get together and have lunch? I'll buy!'"

Another route toward developing relationships with people of different ethnic groups, Pastor Washington says, is to regularly attend a church with a different racial makeup than the one we usually attend. Similarly, there are community service organizations such as Habitat for Humanity that do volunteer work in neighborhoods that we might not ordinarily frequent. We should pick one that will bring us into regular, loving contact with people who are different from us.

**Keep practicing.** True tolerance takes practice, just as golfing or playing the piano takes practice. "Practicing tolerance is not a one-time thing," says Jim Carnes, editor of *Teaching Tolerance*, a magazine published by the Southern Poverty Law Center in Montgomery, Alabama. "It's continuous. You make it a priority on a regular basis to consider and evaluate your own attitudes and your own behavior."

One way to do that, Carnes says, is to take a regular inventory of the restaurants we patronize, the clubs we belong to, and the voluntary organizations we support. "See if there's a pattern there that may be limiting your interaction with people who are really different," he says. "Seek out organizations that have more diverse makeups. These things sound self-conscious, and they are, but that's the point. It's the unconscious patterns that trap so many of us into narrow habits."

**Tell the truth.** Sitting down with people whose opinions may differ from our own is only half the task. The next step is telling them the truth about ourselves, especially about our perceptions and differences. "Sincerity is when you're willing to be vulnerable," says Pastor Washington. "If you're not willing to do that, you'll never establish an atmosphere of trust."

**Listen.** Few things are less tolerant than refusing to listen. If we need help understanding someone, there's no better way to get it than by asking. "Three of the most critical words that you can use in any situation are 'help me understand,'" says Pastor Washington.

## Healing Words

## Bearing Fruit That Will Last

This is my commandment, that you love one another as I
have loved you.

No one has greater love than this, to lay down one's life for
one's friends.

You are My friends if you do what I command you.

I do not call you servants any longer, because the servant
does not know what the master is doing; but I have called
you friends, because I have made known to you
everything that I have heard from My Father.

You did not choose Me but I chose you. And I appointed
you to go and bear fruit, fruit that will last, so that the
Father will give you whatever you ask Him in My name.

I am giving you these commands so that you may love one
another.

—*Jesus addressing the Apostles (John 15:12–17 NRSV)*

"When you say that in a loving fashion, people are glad to oblige."

**Watch our reactions.** Intolerance tends to emerge in moments
of frustration, says Carnes. We need to pay attention to our thoughts
when we get stuck in traffic or in line at the store. Do we blame certain ethnic, sexual, or economic groups when things don't go our
way? If so, we need to step back. "Try to accept and appreciate the
dimensions of the lives of the other people who are involved."

**Avoid generalizations.** Stereotypes take on a different dimension when we get to know individuals who supposedly fit them,
Carnes points out. The classic example is the homophobic mother
and father who discover that their own son is gay. Our negative generalizations will tend to disintegrate if we subject them to scrutiny.

# *Trust*

---

## REASONS TO BELIEVE

$W$e live today in a culture that's drenched in suspicion.

Conspiracy, betrayal, dishonor, and deceit are staples of our daily entertainment, not to mention our news reports. We habitually joke about the dishonesty of politicians and lawyers. We take it for granted that used car salesmen and advertising pitchmen will cheat us if they can. Doctors, bosses, even ministers come in for their share of derision. And sometimes we think twice about our spouses and our children. Ultimately, not even God is safe from the skepticism of this cynical age.

"Study upon study shows that people have low confidence in their leaders, the government, and the press, in addition to a lack of trust for one another," says Amitai Etzioni, Ph.D., professor at George Washington University in Washington, D.C., and author of *The Spirit of Community*. "It's not a sound foundation for a system of government or for anything else."

What's even more painful is the way mistrust isolates us personally. After all, if we can't trust the people around us, we're all alone. "Trust connects us to the world," says John Townsend, Ph.D., a licensed psychologist in Newport Beach, California, and co-author of *Safe People* and *Boundaries*." It's the link that brings us into a relationship—any kind of relationship. Without trust, we're lost in our own orbit."

# The Truth Hurts

How likely is it that somebody we meet will lie to us today? Very likely.

Deborah A. Kashy, Ph.D., is an associate professor of psychology at Texas A&M University in College Station, who has conducted extensive research on lying. Her studies show that people who claim to be thoroughly honest probably aren't. "Lying is a practice publicly condemned but privately practiced by almost everybody."

But, she hastens to add, "Most lies are small lies of very little consequence," she says. "Often, people lie in order to present themselves in a slightly better light or to protect someone else's feelings." Such lies fall into the category of "impression management," and they often represent people trying to be kind rather than manipulative. Dinner guests lying to the cook about an awful meal is a common example, or telling someone that they look great when they don't.

In Dr. Kashy's view, these sorts of lies actually make people more trustworthy rather than less. "People are smoothing over their social interactions," she says. "They're making their lives and other peoples' lives a little bit easier, rather than filling the world with deceit."

These sorts of "white" lies are more useful with strangers or acquaintances than with those who know us best, Dr. Kashy adds, and consequently, we tend to tell fewer lies at home.

"There's no point in telling your wife some stupid little untruth about yourself because she's going to know it's not true," Dr. Kashy says. On the other hand, more often we're more likely to tell big lies to the ones we love most. Hiding an affair is a classic example.

Probably the least surprising of Dr. Kashy's findings is that a lot of lies get told in dating situations, when people are romantically involved but not married. Impression management obviously counts most when love is at stake, which helps explain why for so many of us marriage constitutes a rude awakening.

Often, people who have trouble trusting learned to be that way in early childhood. "Psalm 22:9 tells how God teaches us to trust at the mother's breast," Dr. Townsend says. "That's backed up by a lot of clinical evidence and research. We don't come into the world trusting. We emerge from the womb in a state of alienation, and one of the first tests of the parenting process is to teach the child that reaching out into a relationship is a good thing."

Failing to learn that most basic of childhood lessons can lead to problems later in life with sustaining almost any type of relationship. Mistrustful people tend to withdraw at the first sign of difficulty. Since difficulties are inevitable in every relationship, that makes it hard for them to develop long-lasting connections. "That's why you see people having serial relationships, serial jobs, serial churches," Dr. Townsend says. "When they get let down, they tend to regress to the point of original injury; they become that terrified infant again. They feel that a relationship is a bad place to be, so they go into what the Bible calls darkness."

Dark as our hiding places are, venturing out of them into the light isn't always easy, but it's far from impossible. There's a lot that we can do to strengthen our own ability to trust others and a lot that we can do to become more trustworthy ourselves.

## It Starts with Small Steps

Developing our ability to trust is a lot like developing our muscles in a gym, Dr. Townsend says. We must practice, building up gradually from trusting a little to trusting a lot. Here's where to start.

**Have faith.** We will find it easier to trust ourselves and others if we first trust God. One step toward developing trust in God, says Dr. Townsend, is realizing that God will stand by us through thick and thin. Knowing that His love for us is secure—unshakable, in fact—allows us to relax, trusting Him. Jesus states explicitly that God will open the door if we knock on it (Matthew 7:8), and in the Beatitudes (Matthew 5:1–6), Jesus makes it clear that the love of God extends *especially* to the weak "He doesn't expect us to stand alone," Dr. Townsend says.

**Risk honesty.** An essential step in learning to trust is to open up and talk honestly about ourselves, our problems, and our needs, even

## Healing Words

### Taking the First Step

Ask, and it will be given you; search, and you will find;
knock, and the door will be opened for you.

For everyone who asks receives, and everyone who searches
finds, and for everyone who knocks, the door will be
opened.

Is there anyone among you who, if your child asks for bread,
will give a stone?

Or if the child asks for a fish, will give a snake? If you then,
who are evil, know how to give good gifts to your
children, how much more will your Father in Heaven give
good things to those who ask Him!

In everything do to others as you would have them do to
you; for this is the law and the prophets.

—*Matthew 7:7–12 NRSV*

when it feels uncomfortable to do so. "It's a very difficult but very important task to bring our needy, broken parts into the light," says Dr. Townsend.

When we take that risk, the people around us will tend to be more open and honest with us, and trust begins to build. "We need to have the experience of seeing that people can be warm, accepting, tender, encouraging, open, and honest," Dr. Townsend says. "Eventually, we learn to say to ourselves, 'The world is a better place than I thought.'"

**Be generous.** We can encourage people to behave in a trustworthy fashion by trusting them, says Maxie Dunnam, doctor of divinity and president of Asbury Theological Seminary in Wilmore, Kentucky. "The key is to give people the benefit of the doubt," says

Dr. Dunnam. "It's very easy for us to jump to judgment. We need to resist that temptation."

**Protect ourselves.** Despite the need to extend trust to others, we also need to be realistic in accepting the fact that some people aren't trustworthy. Identifying who fits that description and who doesn't is essential, says Dr. Townsend. Yet many people put their trust in untrustworthy people and situations over and over again. This scriptural reference applies, he says: "As a dog returneth to his vomit, so a fool returneth to his folly." (Proverbs 26:11 KJV)

To end this destructive pattern, we need to examine closely our reasons for choosing such relationships. Dr. Townsend suggests asking ourselves the following questions.

- Are we choosing to be involved with this person for purely emotional reasons, despite what an objective look at his character might tell us?
- Are we choosing to be involved with this person because we're afraid of being alone?
- Are we choosing to be involved with this person as a means of avoiding our own issues?
- Are we choosing to be involved with this person because we think that being associated with him will make use look good to others?
- Are we choosing to be involved with this person because we think that he will take care of us?
- Are we afraid of confronting this person?
- Are we trying to rescue this person?
- Do we enjoy playing the victim?
- Are we simply afraid to change?

"Yes" answers to most or all of these questions suggest that we're choosing a relationship for the wrong reasons, Dr. Townsend says. Untrustworthy relationships are the likely result.

**Look for friends in the right places.** Once we've sworn off untrustworthy people, we need to find alternatives. Dr. Townsend advises looking in places where people with whom we might have deeper relationships are most likely to gather, where sharing honest feelings is the specific goal. Where might we look? To Bible study groups or support groups sponsored by a church.

In the Methodist tradition followed by Dr. Dunnam, sharing with fellow believers is called Christian conferencing. The idea is for each person to testify to what God has done in his life, thereby strengthening the faith of the others in the group that God will move in their lives, as well. "When one person is down, another is up," Dr. Dunnam says. "I think that's the whole meaning of Christian community."

**Practice acceptance.** Recognizing that someone can't be trusted in certain ways doesn't mean that the entire relationship should be automatically discarded. "We need to acknowledge that there's only so far that some people are able to go," Dr. Townsend says. The task then is to work on forgiving and accepting, meanwhile searching out other relationships in church and in other safe places that can provide the emotional support we need.

## To Be Worthy

Finding role models of trustworthiness in this day and age isn't all that easy. There seem to be more crooks than heroes around. But we really need look no further than the New Testament. Who was more trustworthy than Christ?

The challenge is how best to follow His example. Here are some suggestions.

**Be reliable.** This is perhaps the most basic and simplest of all the rules of trustworthiness, according to Wilford Wooten, a licensed marriage, family, and child counselor, a licensed clinical social worker, and director of the counseling department for Focus on the Family in Colorado Springs, Colorado. "Trust is doing what we say we will do, whether or not it's convenient," he says. That means coming through on small as well as large commitments: calling when we say we will, showing up for appointments on time, or bringing what we say we'll bring to a picnic. Such details may not be as momentous as sticking to our wedding vows or meeting our responsibilities to take care of our kids, but they count.

**Be a steward of relationships.** Trustworthy people are those who can successfully nurture and preserve relationships with others, says David Schroeder, D.Ed., president of Nyack College in New York and author of the Christian discipleship book and manual *Follow Me!*.

That takes commitment and effort. "Relationships are among the most important assets we have," he says, "and we shouldn't be quick to compromise them or place other things above them."

For example, it's easy to place our careers above our relationships, Dr. Schroeder says. Being a steward of relationships means

# Answered Prayers

## Trust in God Led Me to Safety

"On my annual ski vacation in Europe, a couple invited me to ski from Cervina, Italy, to Switzerland. I'm not that proficient a skier, but they said that the runs were easy.

"The runs were steep, narrow, and quite difficult, but after five hours of skiing, exhausted and quite relieved, we were in Switzerland. We toured the village and ate, and the time got away from us. The last gondola ride to the top of mountain was packed, and I was separated from the couple. At the top, I couldn't find my friends, and soon I was left alone. It was getting dark and the snow was a complete blur to me. I was still exhausted and did not know if I could make the trip back down the other side of the mountain. I knew I could not stay, but I was frozen; I could not ski. I screamed, "God help me!" It was only a second before an incredible blue-white light appeared in front of me and said, 'Follow me.'

"Without question, I put on my skis and followed. It was pitch black, but in front of me was the light. Down, down, down I went until I reached the bottom and was safely in Cervina.

"I dropped down and thanked God, and when I was composed, I went to thank the light, but it was gone. To this day, I know that it was God or one of God's angels who guided me all the way down the mountain."

—B. J. Janis, Miami

leaving work early to show up for our sons' baseball games, doing our share of the housework to lighten the load on our spouses, and taking the time to check in with our friends periodically on the phone.

**Take the lead.** Trustworthy people are those who set an example by living lives of integrity and Christian purpose, says the Reverend Leo J. O'Donovan, a Jesuit priest who is president of Georgetown University in Washington, D.C. "We cannot alleviate the mistrust around us and inspire the caring and trusting leaders of the future if we wilt beneath challenges," he says. This might mean, for example, speaking out clearly on a difficult issue of public importance and working to solve the problem, rather than quietly wishing it would go away or letting others take care of it. Or it might mean being honest about the limits of what we might be able to do in a certain situation. The opportunities for demonstrating what Father O'Donovan calls "trust in action" appear daily in each of our lives.

**Pause to reflect.** Spiritual leadership is easier, Father O'Donovan says, if we know where we're going. Taking the time to pause and reflect on our sense of mission and direction can help solidify our sense of purpose.

For Father O'Donovan, reflecting on his mission means each morning repeating the Latin vows that he took when he was ordained as a priest more than 30 years ago. "Sometimes I need to hear the words so that I can translate their meaning in new ways," he says. "At other times, I am simply invigorated by knowing that they have become a part of me."

**Trust to get trust.** Beyond the example that He set with His actions, Jesus spells out a simple maxim for trustworthy behavior, says Wooten. "We call it the Golden Rule (Matthew 7:12). If we begin to treat other people as we'd like to be treated," he says, "more often than not, that will be mirrored back to us."

# *Violence*

## CONFRONTING CONFLICT

*I*f it's violence you're after, Dubboya Street in Hebron on the West Bank is as good a place as any to find it. Kathleen Kern did.

Kern works with a group called Christian Peacemaker Teams, headquartered in Chicago, which sends volunteers into areas of conflict around the world to serve as witnesses to what happens there. The hope is that their presence will help ameliorate the violence, and sometimes it does. But not always.

On a Saturday morning in 1995, Kern was on the lookout for trouble between Hebron's Palestinian residents and Israeli settlers. There was a disturbance brewing, and she went to investigate. Suddenly, Kern saw a group of between 20 and 40 Israeli men coming down the street toward her, walking quickly. She turned around and started walking in the other direction. She willed herself not to run.

The next thing Kern heard was a roar behind her. She felt herself being jerked backward. Someone had grabbed her backpack and was pulling her down from behind. She found herself staring upward as the Israeli men stood in a circle around her, spitting and yelling. After a terrifying moment, they moved on, smashing all the car windows on the street as Palestinians scattered.

"I jumped to my feet and started taking pictures," Kern says. "I don't think I was aiming my camera very much—it was just snap-

snap-snap-snap. Then the Israelis spotted me, and they came over and started hitting me and trying to get my camera."

The settlers did get her camera, but for Kern, there was a victory that they weren't able to take. "One of the things I felt good about afterward was that I never felt tempted to strike back."

## The Root of the Problem

You don't have to go to the Middle East to know that we live in a violent world. Any TV newscast tells the story. Violence surrounds us, drenches us, threatens to overwhelm us. Peace seems a distant and unattainable goal. The question that all of us have asked ourselves at one time or another is, why?

Fundamentally, as some theologians believe, it happens because we're all capable of it, even in the smallest things we do. When we shout at our spouses or edge ahead of the lady next to us in line at the grocery store, we're resorting to violent acts. Insignificant in comparison to assault and murder? Sure. But the source is the same: our fallen natures.

"Evil is at the core of every person," says Ron Sider, Ph.D., professor of theology and culture at the Eastern Baptist Theological Seminary and president of Evangelicals for Social Action, both in Philadelphia. "We put ourselves at the center of reality rather than letting God be the center. As a result, we selfishly grasp what belongs to others."

## The Solution Starts with Love

Given that violence is intrinsic to our culture, what can we do to lessen its destructive impact on our lives?

The Bible gives some pretty clear answers to that question. Dr. Sider cites the Sermon on the Mount as being the decisive New Testament text on the subject. "Love your enemies and pray for those who persecute you," Jesus says. (Matthew 5:44 NRSV) And this: "Blessed are the peacemakers, for they will be called children of God." (Matthew 5:9 NRSV)

Kara Newell, executive director of the American Friends Service Committee in Philadelphia, cites in addition Matthew 22:37–39, in

## The Third Way

There are three basic ways of responding to institutional or political violence, according to Ched Myers, ecumenical theologian, fellow in urban theology at the Claremont School of Theology in California, and author of *Binding the Strong Man: A Political Reading of Mark's Story of Jesus*.

The first way, and by far the most common, is to return violence with more violence. The second way, associated most commonly with the civil disobedience of Henry David Thoreau, is passive resistance. The idea isn't so much to actively seek out confrontation as it is to refuse cooperation when asked to participate. In Thoreau's case, that meant going to jail rather than paying his taxes when the United States went to war with Mexico over Texas.

"The third way," which is the term that nonviolence activists use to describe this approach, is more confrontational. Myers describes it as "militant nonviolent resistance." Mahatma Gandhi and Martin Luther King Jr. are the best known practitioners of the third way. Both actively sought out nonviolent confrontations as a means of winning institutional reforms. Gandhi was best known for staging hunger strikes; King organized sit-ins and marches.

which Jesus says that the two greatest commandments are love of God and love of neighbor. "There's no way you can love your neighbor and still do violence to him," she says.

That doesn't mean that the proper course of action to take in the face of violence is necessarily clear or simple. In fact, the ethical debates present some of the most agonizing of all religious dilemmas: Was killing Nazis in World War II a sin? Is it okay to shoot a man who breaks into your home? Is it okay to ask the police to shoot the man who breaks into your home?

Each of us must search for answers to quandaries such as these, but there are some general guidelines that can be applied overall.

**Repent.** The violence that we can do the most about is that which originates in our own hearts. Dr. Sider says the best way to cleanse our sinfulness is to invite God to flush it out. Prayers of repentance are one means of doing that, as are other attributes of Christian life: regular worship, Bible study, service work, and fellowship with other Christians. "The promise is that there is a divine power that goes beyond anything we can manage with human willpower," he says, "a power that will slowly transform our very nature."

Is there a prayer that promotes nonviolence? Dr. Sider offers the following simple phrase: "Lord Jesus, teach me to share your heart of peace."

**Quiet a violent heart.** With practice, we can learn how to control our own violent impulses, according to Redford B. Williams, M.D., professor of psychiatry and director of the Behavioral Medicine Research Center at Duke University Medical Center in Durham, North Carolina, and author of two books on emotion and health, *Anger Kills* and *Lifeskills*. When confronted with a situation that provokes anger, Dr. Williams says that we can literally shout "Stop!" at the thoughts that torment us. Another useful strategy is distraction. Count to 10, say a prayer, or recite the Ten Commandments.

Once we've regained some composure, Dr. Williams recommends asking ourselves four questions.

1. Is it important?

2. Is the reaction that we're having appropriate to the facts of the actual situation?

3. Is there anything we can do about it?

4. If the answer to the first three questions is yes, Dr. Williams says, the final question to ask is whether the offense is worth the action it would take to change the situation. If the answer is yes, take an appropriate action (see "Working through Conflicts" on page 488).

**Practice peace.** Having a sense of peacefulness within us helps spread peace around us. "Most of us have a couple of dozen opportunities every day to humanize the world we live in," says Gil Bailie, president and founder of the Florilegia Institute, a nonprofit educational institute in Sonoma, California, and author of *Violence Unveiled*. "We do it in the tiniest ways, by being a little more generous in the way we treat others or by trying to do some little thing to help restore somebody's dignity."

## Working through Conflicts

We live in contentious times. On TV, on the street, and on the road, all too frequently we see people arguing and often fighting. It's not surprising, then, that a whole area of academic study has focused on various techniques for reducing and resolving conflicts. One expert in this burgeoning field is Heidi Burgess, Ph.D., co-director of the Conflict Research Consortium in Boulder, Colorado. Here's a list of steps that she recommends we take to actively work toward resolving problems with other people nonviolently.

1. *Don't get caught up in emotions.* We need to try to separate the person with whom we've disagreed from the problem. Try to look upon the problem as something that we and the other person can work together to resolve.
2. *Gather the relevant facts.* Many times, simply having the correct information can resolve a disagreement.
3. *Try to limit misunderstandings.* Conflict causes people to say things that they don't mean and hear things that weren't said,

**Confront violence.** As far as institutional or political violence is concerned, Newell believes that remaining silent is not an option. Jesus' confrontation with the moneychangers in the temple is evidence, she feels, that Christians are called upon to speak out and to resist. "That was clearly an act of civil disobedience," she says. "It was also fully consistent with the idea that we can love our opponents and still be actively engaged in opposing them."

One constructive method of active resistance that Newell recommends is asking questions. For example: "Can we talk about a different approach to this? How would you feel if someone were doing that to you?" Newell adds, "Asking questions is a way of engaging the other person while putting the power in their hands."

**Look for the underlying causes.** Often, there are deep-seated reasons for violence, and these need to be analyzed. Racism, for ex-

Dr. Burgess points out. Listen carefully and don't exaggerate statements in the heat of the moment.

4. *Back off.* The emotional heat of arguments causes their intensity to naturally escalate and frequently to spiral out of control. Such escalation is counterproductive. Try to defuse the momentum before it starts.

5. *Honor the other person.* We can hold our own ground but still acknowledge and try to respect the other person's point of view.

6. *Minimize backlash.* People don't like being forced to do things against their will, Dr. Burgess says. We need to give logical, legitimate reasons for what we're doing and for what we want the other person to do and also offer a concession, or trade, if possible. For example, we might say, "I can't do this for you, but I will do that."

7. *Hang in.* Keep trying to persuade and allow yourself to be persuaded. More talk usually means less conflict and less violence.

ample, has huge implications for American culture as a whole, but at its most fundamental level, it's about one person being emotionally wounded by another person and reacting. Ched Myers, ecumenical theologian, fellow of urban theology at the Claremont School of Theology in California, and author of *Binding the Strong Man: A Political Reading of Mark's Story of Jesus*, says that in order to truly understand the causes of violence, we must look at both specific individual actions and the broader social forces.

"Jesus demonstrated quite clearly that individual and social pathology are fundamentally interrelated," Myers says. "Every story of healing or exorcism in the Gospel tradition addresses a larger structural issue of injustice or violence."

For related information, see Anger (page 160) and Tolerance (page 470).

# Weight Loss

## ENDING OUR EMOTIONAL EATING

When she was 35, Carre Anderson of Westerville, Ohio, was trying a new diet nearly every week. Most of them tried to change what she ate. Yet none forced her to confront her growing love affair with food. "I was constantly organizing, planning, and scheming to make sure that I got enough to eat," says the stay-at-home mother of three.

Years of this behavior left Anderson frustrated and extremely overweight. Although she's only five feet five inches tall, Anderson tipped the scales at 217 pounds.

Finally, her failure to handle her eating drove her to her knees. "Lord," she prayed, "You know my needs, but I can't stand any more diets and I want to lose weight." Soon after, the wife of the pastor of her church invited her to preview a videotape for a faith-based weight-loss study program that the church was considering. The video said that weight loss was simply a matter of putting God first and using our internal controls over hunger and fullness to "rise above the magnetic pull of the refrigerator."

While watching the video, Anderson was transfixed. "The Bible verses convinced me that I was dealing with more than just an issue of controlling the food. I wanted the freedom that only God could give me."

Anderson joined the church study group and adopted its principles. The result? In one year, she lost 100 pounds. And not only has she kept the weight off for a year but she now leads the church weight-loss group as well.

# Eating for the Wrong Reasons

Can praying and reading Scripture really help someone lose weight? Gwen Shamblin, R.D., author of *The Weigh Down Diet* and founder of the Weigh Down Workshops, one of the most popular faith-based weight-loss programs, says yes, because it sets the right priorities.

"Diets make the food 'behave.' But it's not the food's fault," says Shamblin. Instead, she believes that overeating is caused by a deep-seated spiritual emptiness. "We have two empty needing-to-be-fed holes in our bodies," Shamblin says. "One is the stomach and the other is the heart."

And when we don't get the love, acceptance, and approval that we need to fill our hearts, some of us try to fill it up with food. "The term that I use for this is emotional eating," says C. Dwight Bain, a Christian counselor and regional communications director in Orlando for New Life Clinics, the largest provider of Christian-based counseling in the United States. "Say something happens at work that makes me mad. If I think that there's nothing I can do about it, I'll go home and eat and eat and eat. I'm not eating out of hunger or any physical desire. I'm eating because I'm upset."

In fact, "A high percentage of eating disorders like anorexia, bulimia, and overeating have a direct correlation to biochemical depression" says Jacqueline Abbott, Dr.P.H., co-director of the Kartini Clinic for Disordered Eating in Portland, Oregon. Biomechanical depression occurs when we have a deficiency in the naturally occurring chemicals in the brain.

One of the most common symptoms of depression is unhealthy eating habits, says Dr. Abbott. "It could be not wanting to eat or, more likely, eating all the time in an attempt to help soothe or calm yourself," she says.

Some of us get so fanatical about our love of food, it borders on worship. "We dress for it, putting on stretch clothes to make sure that there is nothing coming between us and that binge," says Shamblin.

# Healing Words

## Putting Food in Perspective

> Therefore I tell you, do not worry about your life, what you
> will eat or drink; or about your body, what you will wear.
> Is not life more important than food, and the body more
> important than clothes?

—*Matthew 6:25 NIV*

> Do not join those who drink too much wine or gorge
> themselves on meat,
> For drunkards and gluttons become poor, and drowsiness
> clothes them in rags.

—*Proverbs 23:20–21 NIV*

"We plan a secret rendezvous with food all day long. Thinking about it, anticipating it, buying it, cooking it, smelling it—all our senses are alive for it."

We soon discover, though, that overeating not only doesn't satisfy our emotional hunger but it leaves us worse off than when we started. "It robs us," says Shamblin. "It robs us financially. It robs us of our clothing. It robs us of our self-esteem. It robs us of relationships. It robs us of our freedom. And so we wake up and realize that our health is bad—mental health and spiritual health. Our souls are empty. We're longing. We're hurting."

## Getting It Right

Instead of turning food into a god, Shamblin says that we need to worship the one true God. "We need to quit making rituals of this stuff. Our 'food' is to do the will of the Father. Listen for His voice. Take the time and energy and love for food or anything else that is a strong hold and give it back to God," she recommends.

"We are talking about healthy eating and regular exercise as opposed to compulsive overeating," says Bain. "We are talking about freedom from food."

Here are some suggestions on how to put food in its rightful place in our lives.

**Study someone thin.** One quick way to get insight into how obsessed we are with food is to observe the role that it plays for someone who is lean and healthy and has been for most of their lives. Shamblin says that she did this when she had a weight problem, and she was shocked. In the time that it took her to gobble a full fat-laden meal at a fast-food restaurant, her thin friend had barely eaten half of a hamburger. And then, her friend had the nerve to start wrapping the rest up to bring home! "This was a real eye-opener," she says.

**Keep a food diary.** This will tell us when and why we're eating. "In other words, what was the motivation behind our eating?" says Bain. "Were we eating because we're hungry or because we're lonely? Because our bodies required fuel to go out and exercise or because we were bored, angry, or stressed out and just couldn't stop?"

**Respond to the signals.** Forget diet shakes, fat-loss pills, and fat-free products. Shamblin says that the best way to lose weight is by responding to our body's true signals of hunger and fullness. True hunger, she says, "is a rumbling, a growl that's felt at the top of the stomach under the sternum." And true fullness is "a polite feeling—we're simply no longer hungry."

When our bodies signal that we're truly hungry, we should eat, and we should stop when it says that we're full, suggests Shamblin. This may mean that we eat one large meal a day or small meals five or six times a day, depending on what's right for our bodies.

Often, people eating this way discover that their volume is reduced to about one-half to one-third of what they used to eat. "That automatically decreases fat intake by about 50 to 75 percent," says Shamblin.

**Slow down.** Eating more slowly allows the food time to hit our bloodstreams, which in turn allows our blood sugar levels to rise, triggering the brain's appetite center and producing a feeling of fullness so that we don't overeat, says Elizabeth Lee Vliet, M.D., founder and medical director of HER Place: Health Enhancement and Renewal for Women, in Tucson, Arizona, and Dallas/Fort Worth, Texas.

Breaking food into smaller pieces, taking smaller bites, getting involved in conversation while we eat, and stopping for a minute or two during our meals all can help, Shamblin says.

**Enjoy it.** God did not put chocolate or lasagna on this Earth to torture us, says Shamblin, so we should give thanks for each and every bite. And savor them, allowing them to melt in our mouths.

**Take emotional pain to God.** If we're having problems at work or in our relationships or if we're feeling emotional or spiritually barren, we shouldn't turn to snacks. We should turn to God. "I cry in His arms. I laugh. I share everything with Him," says Shamblin.

**Beat back binges with prayer.** And when a binge really hits? "We should cry out to God and say, 'God what I'd really like to do is finish off all the cheese dip and chips and the rest of the gallon of rocky road ice cream. Don't let me, God. Make me feel better than a binge,'" says Shamblin.

**Join a group.** Whether it's the Weigh Down Workshop or one like it, getting involved in a weight-loss group can help improve our chances of success during those first crucial months, says Bain. "A lot of people who have struggled for years with weight problems wonder, can I do this? That's where resources and people in a weight-loss group can step in the gap early on and help out."

# _Prayerphernalia_

## An Explanation of Religious Terms

Over the centuries, objects, places, and events have taken on specific, significant meaning for the many denominations of Christian faith. Here is a glossary of some of the most important ones that relate to prayer and prayer practices.

**_Altar:_** In Old Testament tradition, an altar was a structure established for the purpose of making offerings or as a memorial. Altars were used in Jewish holy rites for the offering of sacrifices and for burning incense. In Hebrew, the word means "place of slaughter." In the Catholic tradition, an altar is the table on which the communion is prepared. Altars are cited 433 times in the King James Bible, and they can be as simple as a single stone, a pile of stones, or ashes or as elaborate as carved tables of bronze, marble, wood, and more.

**_Angels:_** While found sparingly in the New Testament other than in the book of Revelation (where they are exceedingly numerous), angels are quite common throughout the Old Testament. They are a godly creation and come in numerous ranks and forms, such as archangels, cherubim, seraphim, and guardian angels. According to biblical writings, their primary purposes are to worship God and to serve as messengers of God. Lucifer, however, is described as a fallen angel and is said to have angels of his own.

The Greek word for angel means "messenger." They are depicted as spiritual beings with wings, though they can also appear as humans, apparently, according to the Apostle Paul's admonition: "Do not forget to entertain strangers, for by so doing some people have entertained angels without knowing it." (Hebrews 13:2 NIV) According to the writer of Revelation, the angel population is quite significant: ". . . the number of them was ten thousand times ten thousand, and thousands of thousands." (Revelation 5:11 KJV) Many people use figurines as well as pictures of angels as inspiring reminders of their faith.

***Ark:*** This word enjoys many meanings. In Genesis, chapters 6 to 9, it refers to the ship that Noah built to survive the great flood (and some churches and temples today are built in the shape of Noah's ark). In Exodus

25:10–22 and Deuteronomy 10:2–5, it is used as part of the term the "ark of the covenant." This was a chest that God instructed Moses to build and decorate to hold the laws that He was about to give, which included the Ten Commandments. The ark was carried by the Hebrews as they journeyed in search of the Promised Land. In present-day Jewish religion, the ark of the covenant is a holy chest in the temple that holds the Torah, the scrolls of the law as found in the books of Moses: Genesis, Exodus, Leviticus, Numbers, and Deuteronomy. Catholics refer to Mary, mother of Jesus, as the ark of God because she carried Jesus in her womb.

***Ashes:*** In biblical times, ashes were sprinkled on people, or people chose to sit among ashes, as a sign of mourning or in self-degradation because of offenses against God. Also, ashes were symbolic remains from burnt offerings. Today, in Catholic tradition, ashes from the previous year's Palm Sunday palms are smudged onto the foreheads of the faithful in the shape of the cross as a sign of intention to practice sacrifice and repentance during the 40 days of Lent.

***Beads:*** Beads have been used in various religious faiths since antiquity. Beads worked their way into Christianity with the rosary, whose origins seem to trace to the fifteenth century. A rosary consists of five sets of 10 beads. Catholic monks were expected to read or pray the 150 Psalms each day. Those who could not read, though, were allowed to recite a rote prayer for each Psalm, and the beads, which eventually became known as the rosary, helped them keep count. The rosary is used today by Catholics as a means of focusing on the life and love of Christ while reciting prayers to help quiet the mind.

# Prayerphernalia

**Candles:** Candles are used symbolically in personal and formal religious rites to indicate the presence of God—the light that destroys the darkness. In the Catholic tradition of burning prayer candles, a popular belief is that the prayer is heard the instant the candle burns out.

**Cross:** The cross is the Protestant symbol of Christianity and is symbolic of Christ's crucifixion. They may be rough-hewn or polished, made of any material—wood, metal, stone, plastic, and so on. They may be elaborately carved, decorated, and bejeweled or simply plain.

**Crucifix:** The crucifix, a cross on which Jesus is depicted as suffering and dying, is the Catholic symbol of Christianity. As with crosses, crucifixes may be simple or ornate.

**Holy places.** Certain places are deemed holy places because they seem to evoke spiritual awe or prayerful emotions or were the actual site of significant spiritual occurrences, such as the Blessed Mother's appearance at Lourdes. Sometimes churches or shrines are built on these spots. Other times, people simply come to these places for the spiritual experience to feel closer to God.

**Holy water:** Water is used to symbolically cleanse away the past and sin in many religions and spiritual rites. Holy water is water blessed by a priest and is used mainly in Catholic churches as a reminder of the spiritual cleansing of baptism. Priests and others may sprinkle it on believers. Holy water is found at the entrance of every Catholic church, and those who enter are expected to dip a finger in it and place it on their foreheads in the sign of the cross as a symbolic gesture of affirming baptism.

**Incense:** Incense is a dried gum resin that is perfumed. When burned, it emits a scented smoke. The smoke rising is symbolic of prayers rising to God. Incense was used in ancient biblical times as a blessing to God, and it is still used today in numerous spiritual rites.

**Lent:** The 40 days before Easter, observed as a time of reflection, repentance, and fasting in renewal of faith or to prepare for baptism.

**Lourdes:** An apparition of Mary, mother of Jesus, reportedly appeared to a girl at Lourdes, France, in 1858 and created a spring as a sign of her coming. Many people have reported miraculous cures when they touch the water from the spring.

**Medals:** Catholics carry medals of Jesus, Mary, and/or various saints in reverence and as a form of prayer of protection.

**Oils:** Oils are used to anoint the faithful. In Catholic tradition, the Bishop blesses three different oils, each of which is used for a different purpose. The most venerated of these is called Chrism, which is made of olive oil to which a balm or scent, usually balsam pine, is added. Chrism is used to anoint those being baptized, confirmed, or ordained. The English Episcopal Church—the Church of England—uses Chrism to anoint Kings and Queens upon their assumption of the throne. Another oil is the "oil of the sick," which is used to anoint the ill and the dying or deceased. While olive oil is preferred, this can be any vegetable oil, and it need not be scented. The Catholics also use the "oil of the Catechumens" to anoint those preparing to be baptized at Easter. It, too, is olive oil, with no scent added.

Oil may be placed any number of places on the body, including the feet, chest, mouth, eyes, ears, hands, and forehead.

**Pictures:** People of nearly all faiths revere depictions of certain objects or beings as symbolic of their faith. Catholics, in particular, are likely to carry small pictures of Jesus, Mary, and/or various saints in reverence, as a reminder of faith, as a focal point for prayer, and as a form of prayer of protection. The Orthodox churches use icons, non-life-like paintings created while the artist prays and fasts that depict biblical characters and scenes. Saints are often depicted with the symbol with which each traditionally has been associated, such as Saint Patrick holding the staff he used to drive the snakes out of Ireland. It is believed that icon paintings and other sacred artistic creations help create a worshipful atmosphere in which the presence or sense of God can come to us.

**Pilgrimage:** A prayerfully made journey, often involving some sort of sacrifice with physical suffering such as fasting, for the purpose of seeking divine guidance or help. In Catholic tradition, the journey is always made to a sacred place, and the person or people making the pilgrimage carry little with them and depend upon those they meet along the way to supply their food, shelter, and other needs. The whole process of a pilgrimage is considered a form of prayer.

**Prayer book:** A book of prayers designed to lift the heart to God. Recording and reading or reciting written prayers is a way to share in the spiritual insights of others.

**Prayer chain:** A form of group prayer in which a group of people agree to pray individually or together for listed needs. The list can be posted, passed from one prayer participant to the next, or read to the whole group during prayer. Prayer chains can also be done by phone and now over the Internet, where prayer lists are posted online for all who call them up to pray over and add to, if they desire.

**Prayer cloths:** Acts 19:11–12 tells how handkerchiefs and other cloths that the Apostle Paul touched had healing powers when taken to the sick and afflicted. Pentecostal and Catholic believers have continued the tradition using blessed cloths. In Catholic tradition, cloths sometimes are blessed in memory of the Lebanese Maronite monk, Saint Sharbel, with a liturgical prayer. The believer is instructed to place the blessed cloth on an afflicted area and to pray for Saint Sharbel's intercession.

**Prayer room:** People consecrate a special room or portion of a room as a prayer altar, a place of devotion, meditation, and prayer. They may designate the space by placing a cross, icon, prayer book, Bible, candle, or other religious objects there. The text of the Bible refers to "prayer closets," places in the home where people can pray in private.

**Rosary:** See Beads.

**Sacraments.** Things, symbols, and actions that indicate personal interaction with God and, in Catholicism and some Protestant sects, the actual living presence of God or Christ. The word was not used in the Greek New Testament, but near the end of the second century, it was added to the Old Latin Bible as a translation of the Greek word meaning "mystery." Thirty sacraments evolved as official church rites during the first 12 centuries of the church. Two sacraments are recognized by Protestants: baptism and the Lord's Supper, also known as communion or the Eucharist, which is the breaking and taking of bread and wine in remembrance of Jesus. Catholic and Orthodox churches have many more sacramental rites, including marriage.

**Stations of the Cross:** Saint Francis of Assisi formalized and popularized the grassroots tradition of the Stations of the Cross in the thirteenth century as a devotional prayer ritual for people who could not read. It involves the portrayal of 13 biblical and 1 apocryphal, or unauthenticated, scenes of Christ's suffering in His final hours. These scenes may be sculpted or presented as plaques, paintings, carvings, or just 14 crosses. The opening scene is Christ being condemned to death by Pilate, and the final scene is Christ lying in His tomb. A series of prayers and Scripture readings are prescribed for each station.

**Statuettes:** Little statues of holy figures designed to remind us of the divine presence and intercession of holy ones on our behalf.

**Tithing:** The practice of donating one-tenth of all gifts and income that we receive to the church, missions, ministries and/or humanitarian causes doing godly work. This comes from the Lord's commandment to Moses in Numbers 18:26–29 that we should give back to God one-tenth of all that He gives us, and that it should be the best and holiest portion.

*Unleavened bread:* A yeastless bread that the Jews eat on the Feast of Passover, which also is known as the Feast of Unleavened Bread. Since it is believed that this was what was being celebrated during the Last Supper, it is likely that Jesus picked up, broke, and gave unleavened bread to the disciples before saying, "Take, eat; this is my body." (Matthew 26:26 KJV) The tradition of Eucharist, or communion, using unleavened bread follows from that. The Orthodox churches contend that the bread at the Last Supper was not unleavened and therefore use risen bread in their communion services.

*Wailing Wall:* The west wall of the Temple Mount in Jerusalem is said to be what is left of King Solomon's original temple. It is called the West Wall or Wall of Prayer by the Jews and was named the Wailing Wall by European travelers who saw faithful Jews holding mourning vigils there. The Wailing Wall is considered an especially holy place. People stuff written prayers in the cracks between the bricks and mortar.

*Wine:* Fermented and unfermented grape juices are used in various churches during the communion observance as a sacramental symbol of the blood of Christ, which Jesus told the disciples at the Last Supper would be "shed for many for the remission of sins." (Matthew 26:28 KJV)

*Zither:* A stringed musical instrument and one of many musical instruments cited in the Bible. It's listed here as a reminder that the Bible encourages joyful music and song as a form of prayer and reverence and that even the Psalms are presented as "songs of David."

*The information in this glossary was provided by Father John Hanley, Oblates of St. Francis de Sales, chaplain at Allentown College of St. Francis de Sales in Center Valley, Pennsylvania; and the Reverend Steven Frock, pastor of the Brayton Evangelical Lutheran Church in Hamlin, Iowa.*

# Credits

"Suicide Watch" on page 435 was adapted from *Christian Counseling: A Comprehensive Guide* by Gary Collins, Ph.D., copyright © 1988. Reprinted by permission of Word Publishing, Nashville, Tennessee. All rights reserved.

"Answered Prayers: Solid Ground" on page 253 and "Prayer Pointers: Pure and Clean" on page 255 are from *Beyond the Looking Glass: Daily Devotions for Overcoming Anorexia and Bulimia* by Ward Keller. Reprinted by permission of Ward Keller, Remuda Ranch.

Scripture quotations marked (KJV) are taken from the King James Version of the Bible.

Scripture quotations marked (NLT) are taken from the *Holy Bible*, New Living Translation, copyright © 1996. Used by permission of Tyndale House Publishers, Inc., Wheaton, Illinois 60189. All rights reserved.

Scripture quotations marked (NIV) are taken from the Holy Bible, New International Version®, copyright © 1973, 1978, 1984 by International Bible Society. Used by permission of Zondervan Publishing House. All rights reserved.

Scripture quotations marked (NASB) are taken from the New American Standard Bible®, copyright © 1960, 1962, 1963, 1968, 1971, 1972, 1973, 1975, 1977, 1995 by The Lockman Foundation. Used by permission.

Scripture quotations marked (NKJV) are taken from the New King James Version, copyright © 1979, 1980, 1982 by Thomas Nelson, Inc. Used by permission. All rights reserved.

Scripture quotations marked (AMP) are taken from *The Amplified Bible, Old Testament*, copyright © 1965, 1987 by The Zondervan Corporation. *The Amplified New Testament*, copyright © 1954, 1958, 1987 by The Lockman Foundation. Used by permission.

Scripture quotations marked (NRSV) are from the New Revised Standard Version Bible, copyright © 1989, by the Division of Christian Education of the National Council of Churches of Christ in the U.S.A. Used by permission. All rights reserved.

Scripture quotations marked (TLB) are taken from The Living Bible, copyright © 1971. Used by permission of Tyndale House Publishers, Inc., Wheaton, Illinois 60189. All rights reserved.

# List of Contributors

**Jacqueline Abbott, Dr.P.H.**, co-director of the Kartini Clinic for Disordered Eating in Portland, Oregon

**The Reverend Harry Adams**, professor of pastoral theology at Yale Divinity School

**Dan B. Allender, Ph.D.**, founder of Wounded Heart Ministries based in Kirkland, Washington, and author of *The Wounded Heart* and *The Cry of the Soul*

**Sperry Andrews**, director of the Human Connection Institute in San Francisco

**Mary Ellen Ashcroft, Ph.D.**, professor of English at Bethel College in St. Paul, Minnesota, and author of *Temptations Women Face*

**William Backus, Ph.D.**, founder and director of the Center for Christian Psychological Services in St. Paul, Minnesota, and author of *The Healing Power of a Healthy Mind*

**Gil Bailie**, president and founder of the Florilegia Institute, a nonprofit educational institute in Sonoma, California, and author of *Violence Unveiled*

**Dwight Bain**, a Christian counselor and regional communications director in Orlando for New Life Clinics

**Frank Baker, Ph.D.**, director of the Behavioral Research Center at the American Cancer Society

**Herbert Benson, M.D.**, associate professor of medicine and president of the Mind/Body Medical Institute at Harvard Medical School

**Brad Blanton, Ph.D.**, a psychologist and former Methodist minister in Stanley, Virginia, and author of *Radical Honesty*

**The Reverend Alison Boden, master of divinity**, dean of Rockefeller Chapel at the University of Chicago

**Carole Bohn, doctor of education**, executive director of the Danielsen Institute, a pastoral counseling center and mental health clinic at Boston University

**The Reverend John Boyle, Ph.D.**, founder of the pastoral counseling center at Chicago's Fourth Presbyterian Church

**William Braud, Ph.D.**, professor and research director at the Institute of Transpersonal Psychology in Palo Alto, California

**Dr. Bill Bright**, founder and president of Campus Crusade for Christ in Orlando, Florida, and author of *The Coming Revival*

**Lois Brokering**, contributing writer for *Lutheran* magazine

**The Reverend Stephen Brown**, professor at Reformed Theological Seminary in Orlando, Florida, and author of *Approaching God*

**The Reverend John Buckel, Ph.D.**, associate professor of Scripture at St. Meinrad School of Theology in St. Meinrad, Indiana, and author of *Free to Love*

**Heidi Burgess, Ph.D.**, co-director of the Conflict Research Consortium in Boulder, Colorado

**Jim Carnes**, editor of *Teaching Tolerance*, a magazine published by the Southern Poverty Law Center in Montgomery, Alabama

**The Reverend Steve Carr**, minister of Calvary Chapel and founder of Covenant Keepers, both in Arroyo Grande, California, and author of *Married and How to Stay That Way*

**Margaret Caudill, M.D., Ph.D.**, former co-director of the Arnold Pain Center at Beth Israel Deaconess Medical Center in Boston and author of *Managing Pain before It Manages You*

**Gary Chapman, Ph.D.**, director of adult education at Calvary Baptist Church in Winston-Salem, North Carolina, and author of *The Five Love Languages* and *Loving Solutions*

**The Reverend Brian H. Childs, Ph.D.**, a Presbyterian minister, director of health and human values for Shore Health System in Easton, Maryland, and author of several books on pastoral theology and pastoral care

**Sheldon Cohen, Ph.D.**, professor of psychology at Carnegie Mellon University in Pittsburgh

**Grat Correll, M.D.**, a family practitioner in Bristol, Tennessee, and a member of the Christian Medical and Dental Society

**The Reverend Neva Coyle**, a conference speaker based in Ahnwahnee, California, and author of *A Woman of Strength* and *Loved on a Grander Scale*

**The Reverend Rowland Croucher, doctor of ministry**, an evangelist in Healthmont, Victoria, Australia, and director of John Mark Ministries in Melbourne

**Cheryl Cutrona**, executive director of the Good Shepherd Neighborhood Mediation Program in Philadelphia

**Norma Dearing**, director of prayer ministry at Christian Healing Ministries in Jacksonville, Florida

**The Reverend Burrell Dinkins, Ph.D.**, professor of pastoral care and counseling at Asbury Theological Seminary in Wilmore, Kentucky

**Brian J. Dodd, Ph.D.**, professor of philosophy at Asbury Seminary, director of the Share Jesus Ministry, both in Wilmore, Kentucky, and author of *Praying Jesus' Way*

**Doris Donnelly**, professor of spirituality at John Carroll University in Ohio

**Larry Dossey, M.D.**, prayer researcher and author of *Healing Words*

**Maxie Dunnam, doctor of divinity**, president of Asbury Theological Seminary in Wilmore, Kentucky

**Wayne Dyer, Ph.D.**, psychologist and best-selling author of *You'll See It When You Believe It*

**The Reverend Steven Estes**, senior pastor of Community Evangelical Free Church in Elverson, Pennsylvania, and co-author of *When God Weeps*

**Amitai Etzioni, Ph.D.**, professor at George Washington University in Washington, D.C., and author of *The Spirit of Community*

**The Reverend Paul F. Everett** of Pittsburgh, a Presbyterian minister at large with the Peale Center in Pawling, New York, and executive director emeritus of the Pittsburgh Experiment

**Larry Feldman, Ph.D.**, director of the Pain and Stress Rehabilitation Center in Newark, Delaware

**Anne Bachle Fifer**, an attorney, Christian mediator, and conflict resolution consultant based in Grand Rapids, Michigan

**Sharon Fish, R.N.**, a Ph.D. candidate in Rochester, New York, and author of *Alzheimer's: Caring for Your Loved One, Caring for Yourself*

**The Reverend Steven Frock**, pastor of the Brayton Evangelical Lutheran Church in Hamlin, Iowa

**Joel Fuhrman, M.D.**, director of the Amwell Health Center in Belle Mead, New Jersey, and author of *Fasting— And Eating—for Health*

**The Reverend Richard L. Ganz, master of divinity, Ph.D.**, pastor of the Ottawa Reformed Presbyterian Church, president of Ottawa Theological Hall, and author of *The Secret of Self Control*

**Ruthanne Garlock**, former missionary and co-author of *A Women's Guide to Getting through Tough Times in Life* and *Prayers Women Pray*

**James G. Garrick, M.D.**, director of the Center for Sports Medicine at St. Francis Memorial Hospital in San Francisco

**Mark Ginter, Ph.D.**, assistant professor of moral theology at St. Meinrad School of Theology in St. Meinrad, Indiana

**Sister Elaine Goodell**, staff chaplain at Memorial Sloan-Kettering Cancer Center in New York City

**John Gottman, Ph.D.**, professor of psychology at the University of Washington in Seattle, co-director of the Seattle Marital and Family Institute, and author of *Why Marriages Succeed or Fail*

**Kathleen Greider, Ph.D.**, associate professor of pastoral care and counseling at Claremont School of Theology in California

**Marilyn Gustin**, Catholic Scripture scholar and author of the treatise "What the Bible Says about Forgiveness

**Stephen Halpern, Ph.D.**, a composer of more than 50 albums, recording artist, sound healer, and researcher in San Anselmo, California, who studies the relationship between music and healing

**The Reverend Mac Hammond**, of Living Word Christian Center in Minneapolis

**The Reverend George Handzo, master of divinity**, director of chaplaincy services at Memorial Sloan-Kettering Cancer Center in New York City

**Father John Hanley**, Oblates of St. Francis de Sales, chaplain at Allentown College of St. Francis de Sales in Center Valley, Pennsylvania

**The Reverend Eugene Harder** of the New Hope Community Church in North Vancouver, British Columbia

**The Reverend Steve Harper, Ph.D.**, vice-president and dean of the Asbury Theological Seminary in Orlando, Florida

**The Reverend Norvel Hayes**, charismatic faith minister, director of the New Life Bible College in Cleveland, Tennessee, and author of *Divine Healing*

**Father Victor Hoagland**, a Passionist priest from Union City, New Jersey, and author of *Companion in Illness*

**The Reverend R. Kent Hughes, doctor of ministry**, senior pastor at the College Church in Wheaton, Illinois, and author of *Disciplines of a Godly Man*

**Helen Hunt**, collaborator with husband, Harry, on *On the Nature of Consciousness*

**Mary Hunt**, founder, editor, and publisher of the *Cheapskate Monthly* newsletter and a regular financial advisor on Dr. James Dobson's *Focus on the Family* radio broadcasts

**John W. James**, grief educator, co-founder of the Grief Recovery Institute in Beverly Hills, California, and co-author of *The Grief Recovery Handbook*

**Deborah A. Kashy, Ph.D.**, associate professor of psychology at Texas A&M University in College Station

**Joan Kavanaugh, doctor of ministry**, director of the Riverside Church pastoral counseling center in New York City

**Dickie Kay, M.D.**, medical director of the Rapha Treatment Unit, an inpatient Christian psychiatric group at Forest Hospital in Des Plaines, Illinois

**The Reverend Thomas Keating**, a Trappist monk at St. Benedict's Monastery in Snowmass, Colorado

**The Reverend David Kelsey, Ph.D.**, professor of theology at Yale Divinity School

**Kathleen Kern**, of Christian Peacemaker Teams, in Chicago, which sends volunteers into areas of conflict to serve as witnesses to what happens there

**Dana E. King, M.D.**, associate professor in the department of family medicine at East Carolina University School of Medicine in Greenville, North Carolina

**Stephen Klineberg, Ph.D.**, professor of sociology at Rice University in Houston

**The Reverend Dennis Knight**, senior minister at Pakachoag Church, UCC, in Auburn, Massachusetts, and co-founder of Keeping Company, an AIDS ministry in Worcester

**Harold G. Koenig, M.D.**, director of the Center for the Study of Religion, Spirituality, and Health at Duke University in Durham, North Carolina

**Krista Kurth, Ph.D.**, co-founder of Renewal Resources, in Potomac, Maryland, and recipient of a doctorate from George Washington University for studies about spirituality in the workplace

**Mark Laaser, Ph.D.**, author of *Faithful and True*

**Kenneth A. Larsen, doctor of ministry**, a board certified psychopharmacologist and director of pastoral services and clinical psychology at the New England Baptist Hospital in Boston

**David B. Larson, M.D.**, president of the National Institute of Healthcare Research in Rockville, Maryland

**The Reverend Mel Lawrenz, Ph.D.**, senior associate pastor at Elmbrook Church in Brookfield, Wisconsin, and co-author of six books, including *Life after Grief*

**James Gilchrist Lawson**, author of *Deeper Experiences of Famous Christians*

**The Reverend William Lenters, doctor of divinity**, author of *The Freedom We Crave*

**Francis S. MacNutt, Ph.D.**, co-founder of Christian Healing Ministries in Jacksonville, Florida, and author of *Healing* and *Deliverance from Evil Spirits*

**Reverend Ron Mahn**, licensed marriage and family therapist and a pastoral counselor with the Center for Counseling and Care of Oklahoma in Oklahoma City

**Dawna Markova, Ph.D.**, co-editor of *Random Acts of Kindness* and author of *No Enemies Within*

**Dale A. Matthews, M.D.**, associate professor of medicine at Georgetown University School of Medicine in Washington, D.C., and author of *The Faith Factor*

**Michael J. McManus**, president/founder of Marriage Savers in Potomac, Maryland, syndicated columnist, and author of *Marriage Savers*

**Jerry McTaggart**, founder of Christian Credit Counselors, a free service in Del Mar, California, that helps people in money trouble get control of their finances

**Paul Meier, M.D.**, Christian psychiatrist and theologian, co-founder of New Life Clinics, and author of more than 60 best-selling Christian self-help books

**The Reverend Linda Mercadante, Ph.D.**, professor of theology at the Methodist Theological School in Ohio and author of *Victims and Sinners*

**Amy Miller, doctor of psychology**, a psychologist with a private and hospital practice in New York City

**The Reverend James E. Miller, doctor of ministry**, United Methodist minister of Willowgreen Productions in Fort Wayne, Indiana, and author of numerous books and videotapes on grief and terminal illness

**The Reverend Eleanor Morrison**, co-director of Leaven, a nonprofit agency dedicated to social justice in Lansing, Michigan

**Melanie Morrison**, author of *The Grace of Coming Home*

**Richard Mouw, Ph.D.**, president and professor of Christian ethics at Fuller Theological Seminary in Pasadena, California, and author of *Uncommon Decency*

**The Reverend Marc Mullinax, Ph.D.**, pastor of the Bedford Park Presbyterian Church in the Bronx and assistant professor of religious studies at Iona College in New Rochelle, New York

**Ched Myers**, ecumenical theologian, fellow of urban theology at the Claremont School of Theology in California, and author of *Binding the Strong Man*

**Kara Newell**, executive director of the American Friends Service Committee in Philadelphia

**Michele Novotni, Ph.D.**, psychologist and assistant professor of counseling at Eastern College in St. Davids, Pennsylvania

**The Reverend Gary J. Oliver, Ph.D.**, executive director of the Center for Marriage and Family Studies at John Brown University in Siloam Springs, Arkansas, and co-author of *When Anger Hits Home*

**Dean Ornish, M.D.**, president and director of the Preventive Medicine Research Institute in Sausalito, California, and author of *Love and Survival*

**The Reverend John Osteen, doctor of divinity**, pastor of the 20,000-member Lakewood Church in Houston and author of numerous books and booklets on adopting a successful attitude spiritually

**Father Richard John Neuhaus**, editor in chief of *First Things*, a monthly journal of ideas, and director of the Institute for Religion in Public Life in New York City

**The Reverend Leo J. O'Donovan**, a Jesuit priest and president of Georgetown University in Washington, D.C.

**Les Parrott, Ph.D., and Leslie Parrott, Ph.D.**, authors of *Saving Your Marriage before It Starts* and co-directors of the Center for Relationship Development at Seattle Pacific University

**Rob Parsons**, executive director of Care for the Family in Cardiff, Wales, and author of *The Sixty Minute Marriage Builder*

**The Reverend Neil Plantinga Jr., Ph.D.**, dean of the chapel at Calvin College in Grand Rapids, Michigan

**Cupid Poe, M.D.**, a pastor and medical director of the Community Christian Counseling Center in Nashville, Tennessee

**Father John Powell**, a Jesuit priest at Loyola University in Chicago and author of *Happiness Is an Inside Job*

**Ray Pritchard, doctor of ministry**, senior pastor of Calvary Memorial Church in Oak Park, Illinois, and author of *What a Christian Believes*

**William Richardson, Ph.D.**, clinical director and professor in the department of marriage and family therapy at Reformed Theological Seminary in Jackson, Mississippi

**The Reverend Kent Richmond, doctor of sacred theology**, chaplain at the Lutheran General Hospital in Park Ridge, Illinois, and author of *Preaching to Sufferers*

**The Reverend Herman Riffel**, retired minister in Villanova, Pennsylvania, who conducts religious seminars

**Norma Rolson**, director of social services for Riverside Church in New York City

**Pastor David Roper**, co-founder with his wife, Carolyn, of Idaho Mountain Ministries in Boise and author of *A Man to Match the Mountain* and *Psalm 23: The Song of a Passionate Heart*

**Vicki Underland-Rosow, Ph.D.**, an international speaker and group facilitator on addictions and shame and author of *Shame*

**Pastor Dale Ryan, Ph.D.**, CEO and founder of Christian Recovery International, a ministry based in Brea, California

**Juanita Ryan, R.N.**, a counselor at Christian Recovery International who specializes in mental health nursing at Brea Family Counseling Center in California

**Marilyn Schlitz, Ph.D.**, director of research for the Institute for Noetic Sciences in Sausalito, California

**David Schroeder, D.Ed.**, president of Nyack College in Nyack, New York, and author of the Christian discipleship book *Follow Me!*

**The Reverend Dr. Robert Schuller**, Crystal Cathedral founder and author of *My Soul's Adventure with God*

**Sharon Scott**, licensed marriage and family therapist in Dallas and author of *How to Say No and Keep Your Friends*

**Gwen Shamblin, R.D.**, author of *The Weigh Down Diet* and founder of the Weigh Down Workshops

**Ron Sider, Ph.D.**, professor of theology and culture at the Eastern Baptist Theological Seminary and president of Evangelicals for Social Action, both in Philadelphia

**The Reverend Mahan Siler, master of divinity**, former pastor of Pullen Memorial Baptist Church in Raleigh, North Carolina

**Harold Ivan Smith, doctor of ministry**, leader of grief gatherings at St. Luke's Medical Center in Kansas City, Missouri, and author of many Christian self-help books

**The Reverend Scotty Smith**, senior pastor of Christ Community Church in Franklin, Tennessee, and co-author of *Unveiled Hope*

**Charles Stanley**, pastor of First Baptist Church in Atlanta and author of *How to Listen to God* and *The Reason for My Hope*

**Scott Stanley, Ph.D.**, co-director for the Center for Marital and Family Studies at the University of Denver and co-author of *A Lasting Promise*

**Father Kurt Stasiak**, a Benedictine priest and associate professor of sacramental and liturgical theology at St. Meinrad School of Theology in St. Meinrad, Indiana

**David Stoop, Ph.D.**, an addictions counselor in Newport Beach, California, and author of *Forgiving Our Parents, Forgiving Ourselves*

**The Reverend Gregory Sutterlin**, pastor of Ascension Lutheran Church of Franklin Square in New York City

**Vernon M. Sylvest, M.D.**, a physician with a prayer-based holistic medical practice in Richmond, Virginia, and author of *The Formula: Who Gets Sick, Who Gets Well*

**The Reverend Siang-Yang Tan, Ph.D.**, professor of psychology at Fuller Theological Seminary in Pasadena, California, senior pastor of First Evangelical Church in Glendale, California, co-author of *Disciplines of the Holy Spirit*, and author of *Managing Chronic Pain*

**Elizabeth Tener**, a social worker and pastoral counselor at the Blanton-Peale Institute in New York City

**John Townsend, Ph.D.**, a licensed psychologist in Newport Beach, California, and co-author of *Safe People* and *Boundaries*

**The Reverend Justin Tull, doctor of ministry**, senior pastor at the Oak Lawn United Methodist Church in Dallas and author of *Why God, Why? Sermons on the Problem of Pain*

**Rabbi Abraham Twerski, M.D.**, a psychiatrist in Pittsburgh and author of *Do Unto Others*

**The Reverend Tim P. Van Duivendyk, doctor of ministry**, a chaplain and marriage and family therapist for the Memorial Hermann Healthcare System in Houston

**Elizabeth Lee Vliet, M.D.**, founder and medical director of HER Place: Health Enhancement and Renewal for Women, in Tucson, Arizona, and Dallas/Fort Worth

**Catherine Wallace, Ph.D.**, author of *For Fidelity*

**Raleigh Washington**, senior pastor at the Rock in Chicago and vice president of reconciliation for the Promise Keepers men's movement

**Doug Weiss, Ph.D.**, director of Heart to Heart Counseling center in Fort Worth, Texas, and author of *The Final Freedom: Pioneering Sexual Addiction Recovery*

**Tom Whiteman, Ph.D.**, president of Life Counseling Services in Paoli, Pennsylvania, director of Fresh Start Seminars, and author of *Fresh Start*

**The Reverend David Wigley**, pastor of the First Congregational Church in Kennebunkport, Maine

**Redford B. Williams, M.D.**, professor of psychiatry and director of the Behavior Medicine Research Center at Duke University Medical Center in Durham, North Carolina, and author of *The Trusting Heart*

**The Reverend William Wilson**, a Trappist monk at the New Melleray Abbey in Peosta, Iowa

**Vincent Wimbush, Ph.D.**, professor of New Testament at Union Theological Seminary in New York City

**Joan Winfrey, Ph.D.**, professor of counseling at Denver Seminary and contributor to *Women, Abuse, and the Bible*

**The Reverend Terry Wisc, Ph.D.**, director of the Trinity Center for Conflict Management at Trinity Theological Seminary in Newburgh, Indiana, and author of *Conflict Scenarios*

**Daryle R. Woodward**, clinical director of Colorado MOVES (Men Overcoming Violence Effectively Services) in Denver

**Wilford Wooten**, licensed counselor and clinical social worker and director of the counseling department for Focus on the Family in Colorado Springs, Colorado

**Everett L. Worthington, Ph.D.**, professor of psychology at Virginia Commonwealth University in Richmond and co-author of *To Forgive Is Human*

**Iris Yob, doctor of education**, author of *Keys to Teaching Children about God*

**Charles Zeiders, doctor of psychology**, a Christian psychologist and clinical coordinator of Christian Counseling Associates in West Chester and Havertown, Pennsylvania

# Subject Index

Underscored page references indicate boxed text.

## A

Abandonment, as justification for divorce, 245

Abuse, 141–47
  boundary setting and, 197–98
  control and, 142–43, 145
  ending, 145–47
  as justification for divorce, 245–46

Abusers, characteristics of, 142–43, 144

Acceptance
  of death, 372
  healing and, 309
  in marriage, 393

Active listening, as communication technique, 179, 335

A.C.T.S. prayer model, 105

Acts of service, as expression of love, 381

Actualizing, in visualization, 126

Addictions, 148–52
  causes of, 149–50
  ending, 150–52

Adoration, in prayer, 105

Adultery, as justification for divorce, 245

Advanced directives, of terminally ill, 461

Affairs, extramarital. See Infidelity

Affirmations, 41–43

AIDS, effect of prayer on people with, 11–12

Alcoholism
  abuse and, 146
  prayer for recovery from, 151–52

Altar, 495

Alzheimer's disease, 153–59
  impact of, on caregiver, 154–55
    controlling, 155–59
  importance of faith and, 156–57

Angels, 495

Anger, 160–67. See also Arguing
  biblical references to, 160
  depression and, 222
  effects of, 161
  toward God, after
    death of a loved one, 201–2
    disaster, 228
    job loss, 351
  with grief, 293
  handling, 161–67
  as obstacle to communication, 391–92
  preventing violent response to, 487

Anorexia nervosa, 251, 252, 254, 256, 258, 491

Answered prayer, factors contributing to, 35–37

Answered Prayers, regarding
  acceptance of loss, 372
  anxiety, 174
  depression, 221
  eating disorders, 253
  financial difficulties, 277
  healing, 184, 194, 308, 380, 444, 455, 468
  pain relief, 407
  safety, 482

Antidepressants, 217–19

# G

# H

## N

## O

## P

# Bible Verse Index

Note: Underscored page references indicate boxed text.

## A

Abandonment, 245
Abundance, 186
Acceptance, 30, 34
Adultery, 245
Affirmations of faith, 42
Agreement, 44
Anger, 161, 165, 166, 181, 222, 228, 391
Anxiety, 170–71, 175
Arguing, 179, 181

## B

Beauty, appreciating, 19
Blessings, 238–39

## C

Care of family, 155
Change, 210
Christ as intercessor, 87
Comfort, 63–64, 172, 202, 205, 296, 297, 313, 368, 370–71, 441, 447, 462
Communication, 245
Condemnation, 397
Confession, 65, 268, 305
Confronting differences, 471
Connection with God, 300

Counsel, 129
Courage, 198, 199

## D

Defeat, 212, 214
Differences, confronting, 471
Difficulty, overcoming, 346
Disaster, 225
Discipline and self-control, 232–33
Discouragement, 236
Divorce, 245, 334

## E

Endurance, 236
Enemies, 316, 485
Enlightenment, 82
Envy, 339, 340, 341
Eternal life, 87, 366, 368
Evil, 136

## F

Faith, 22, 25, 42, 65, 89, 92, 124, 236, 264, 344
Family, care of, 155
Fasting, 56
Fear, 170, 171, 175, 273